JOURNAL FOR THE STUDY OF THE PSEUDEPIGRAPHA SUPPLEMENT SERIES

6

Editor
James H. Charlesworth

JSOT Press
Sheffield

REVEALED HISTORIES

Techniques for Ancient Jewish and Christian Historiography

Robert G. Hall

Journal for the Study of the Pseudepigrapha
Supplement Series 6

Copyright © 1991 Sheffield Academic Press

Published by JSOT Press
JSOT Press is an imprint of
Sheffield Academic Press Ltd
The University of Sheffield
343 Fulwood Road
Sheffield S10 3BP
England

Typeset by Sheffield Academic Press
and
Printed on acid-free paper in Great Britain
by
Billing & Sons Ltd
Worcester

British Library Cataloguing in Publication Data

Hall, R.G.
    Revealed Histories: techniques for ancient Jewish and
    Christian historiography.
    1. Bible. Interpretation, history
    I. Title   II. Series
    220.609

    ISBN 1-85075-249-4

CONTENTS

Acknowledgments 8
Abbreviations 9

Chapter 1
INTRODUCTION 11

PART I. JEWISH LITERATURE

Chapter 2
PROPHETIC HISTORY 22
　Interpretive Prophetic History: Josephus 24
　Inspired Prophetic History: *Jubilees* 31
　Jubilees and the *Jewish War* as Works of
　　Prophetic History 45

Chapter 3
INSPIRED HISTORICAL SERMONS 48
　Ezekiel 48
　Liber Antiquitatum Biblicarum 52
　Judith 56
　The *Jewish War* 57
　Inspired Historical Sermons and Revealed History 60

Chapter 4
APOCALYPTIC WORLD HISTORY 61
　1 Enoch 83–90 62
　2 Baruch 53–74 68
　Apocalypse of Abraham 21–32 75
　Apocalyptic World History 79

Chapter 5
LIMITED APOCALYPTIC HISTORY: DANIEL   82
     Daniel 2   83
     Daniel 7   83
     Daniel 8   86
     Daniel 10–12   89
     Daniel 9   91
     A Judicial Historical Sermon: Daniel 5.17-28   92
     Daniel as Limited Apocalyptic History   93

Chapter 6
REVEALED HISTORY: A FLEXIBLE TECHNIQUE
   FOR PERSUASION   97
     4 Ezra   97
     Sibylline Oracles   107

Chapter 7
TECHNIQUES OF REVEALED HISTORY   116

PART II. CHRISTIAN LITERATURE

Chapter 8
TRACES OF EARLY CHRISTIAN REVEALED HISTORY   124

Chapter 9
SHEPHERD OF HERMAS   128
     The Preeminent Church   129
     Similitudes   131
     Revealed History in the *Shepherd of Hermas*   136

Chapter 10
ASCENSION OF ISAIAH   137
     Apocalyptic History in the *Ascension of Isaiah*   137
     Inspired Prophetic History: The Vision of Isaiah   141
     Revealers of History: The Prophetic School
       Behind the *Ascension of Isaiah*   144
     Revealed History in the *Ascension of Isaiah*   147

Chapter 11
ODES OF SOLOMON   148
   Hortatory Historical Odes   151
   Historical Odes Beginning with a Claim
       to Inspiration   157
   Other Historical Odes   166
   Revealed History in the *Odes of Solomon*   168

Chapter 12
LUKE–ACTS   171
   The Resurrection Narratives   172
   The Lucan Scheme of Revealed History   181
   The Missions Speeches   183
   Speeches Supporting Elements of the Lucan Scheme   192
   Luke and Revealed History   205

Chapter 13
THE GOSPEL OF JOHN   209
   Historical Revelation in John   211
   The Goal of Historical Revelation:
       Grasping the Revelation in Jesus   227

Chapter 14
EARLY CHRISTIAN USE OF REVEALED HISTORY:
   FORMS AND IMPLICATIONS   237

Chapter 15
CONCLUSION   242

Appendix: Sources behind *2 Baruch* 53–74   249
Bibliography   251
Index of Biblical References   262
Index of Authors   273

Acknowledgments

This study originated in research undertaken at Duke University. I am deeply grateful to D. Moody Smith, the ideal supervisor, for giving generously his experience and knowledge yet freely allowing the work to go its own way. Orval Wintermute, Franklin Young, James Price and George Kennedy, graciously and promptly lent their aid as it was required. Although James H. Charlesworth moved to Princeton Theological Seminary before this work was well underway, I have learned much from him also. I am grateful to the faculty and administration of Hampden-Sydney College for a summer grant which supported the revision of the original manuscript into this book. Greatest thanks go to my wife Jackie, who not only typed the manuscript and designed foreign character sets but also willingly made this work her own. She now has entered a graduate programme in Mathematics. Perhaps I can soon return the favor! I want my children, John, Kristin and Nathan, to realize how much fun I have had with them, not least in the years given to writing this book.

ABBREVIATIONS

AB	Anchor Bible
AGAJU	Arbeiten zur Geschichte des antiken Judentums und des Urchristentums
AOT	*The Apocryphal Old Testament* (ed. H.F.D. Sparks; Oxford: Clarendon, 1984)
APOT	*Apocrypha and Pseudepigrapha of the Old Testament* (2 vols.; ed. R.H. Charles; Oxford: Clarendon, 1913)
BBB	Bonner Biblische Beiträge
BZ	*Biblische Zeitschrift*
CBQ	*Catholic Biblical Quarterly*
CBQMS	Catholic Biblical Quarterly Monograph Series
FRLANT	Forschungen zur Religion und Literatur des Alten und Neuen Testaments
ICC	International Critical Commentary
JBL	*Journal of Biblical Literature*
JJS	*Journal of Jewish Studies*
JSHRZ	Jüdische Schriften aus hellenistisch-römischer Zeit
JSJ	*Journal for the Study of Judaism*
JSOT	*Journal for the Study of the Old Testament*
JTS	*Journal of Theological Studies*
LCL	Loeb Classical Library
Nov. T.	*Novum Testamentum*
NTA	*New Testament Apocrypha* (2 vols.; ed. Edgar Hennecke, Wilhelm Schneemelcher, and R.McL. Wilson; Philadelphia: Westminster, 1963/1964)
NTD	Das Neue Testament Deutsch
NTS	*New Testament Studies*
OTP	*The Old Testament Pseudepigrapha* (ed. James H. Charlesworth; Garden City, NY: Doubleday, 1983/85)
RSR	*Recherches de science religieuse*
SBLDS	Society of Biblical Literature Dissertation Series
SBLSP	*Society of Biblical Literature Seminar Papers*
SBT	Studies in Biblical Theology
SNTSMS	Studiorum Novi Testamenti Societas, Monograph Series
Supp. Nov. T.	Supplements to *Novum Testamentum*
WBC	Word Biblical Commentary
WMANT	Wissenschaftliche Monographien zum Alten und Neuen Testament
WUNT	Wissenschaftliche Untersuchungen zum Neuen Testament
ZNW	*Zeitschrift für die neutestamentliche Wissenschaft*
ZTK	*Zeitschrift für Theologie und Kirch*

Chapter 1

INTRODUCTION

Since Westcott, students of the Fourth Gospel have commonly assumed that John depends on revelation directed toward the past words and deeds of Jesus. 'The evangelist possesses the audacity to incorporate revelations of the Christ who speaks to him through the Spirit into his portrayal of the historical appearance of Jesus.'[1] 'Thus the Gospel as such is a product of revelation by the Spirit who brings to remembrance the words of Jesus. The Spirit assures the legitimation of the Johannine tradition concerning the words and deeds of Jesus.'[2] Recently others have begun to take seriously the interest in the past evidenced in many apocalypses. Collins divides Jewish apocalypses broadly into two types: accounts of other worldly journeys and historical apocalypses which contain reviews of history.[3] G.I. Davies, Christopher Rowland, and Carol Newsom each point out and begin to describe features of this apocalyptic concern for history,[4] but as yet no extended study devoted to the historical apocalyptic material exists.[5]

---

1. 'Der Evglst. hat die Kühnheit besessen, die Offenbarungen des durch den Geist zu ihm sprechenden Christus in seine Beschreibung der geschichtlichen Erscheinung Jesu mit aufzunehmen' (Hans Windisch, *Johannes und die Synoptiker* [Leipzig: Hinrichs, 1926], 148).

2. 'Denn das Evangelium als solches ist eine Offenbarungsform des Geistes, der an die Worte Jesu erinnert. Der Geist sichert die Legitimation der im JohEv enthaltenen Tradition über die Worte Jesu' (Ulrich B. Müller, 'Die Parakletenvorstellung im Johannesevangelium', *ZTK* 71 [1974], 51).

3. John J. Collins, *The Apocalyptic Imagination: An Introduction to the Jewish Matrix of Christianity* (New York: Crossroad, 1984), 5-6; cf. John J. Collins, ed., *Apocalypse: The Morphology of a Genre* (Semeia 14; Missoula, MT: Scholars Press, 1979), 28.

4. G.I. Davies, 'Apocalyptic and Historiography', *JSOT* 5 (1978), 15-28; Christopher Rowland, *The Open Heaven: A Study of Apocalyptic in Judaism and Early Christianity* (New York: Crossroad, 1982), 136-55; Carol Newsom, 'The Past as Revelation: History in Apocalyptic Literature', *Quarterly Review* (Nashville, 1984), 40-53.

5. Neglect of this field of study stems from a negative evaluation of history in apocalypses. This negative evaluation, prevalent in the middle of this century, is still

If revelation directed toward understanding the past occurs in works as disparate as the Gospel of John and the historical apocalypses, they probably represent only the tip of an iceberg. Initial soundings suggest that revealed history was employed at least throughout the Mediterranean world and eastward into Mesopotamia.[1] Judging from its widespread use, claims to reveal the past were an effective rhetorical technique, a successful tool for persuasion. This rhetorical *topos* was effective because based on a widely accepted but seldom articulated epistemology: the ancient universe greatly exceeded human experience. Heavenly components made all events mysterious; unaided human intellect could no more grasp past or present events than future ones. In such a world an attempt to understand the past implied a claim to divinely bestowed insight.

Since only the future is mysterious to us, we tend to limit revelation to prediction. Modern students conclude that the long rehearsals of past events in many apocalypses exist only to convince readers that the implied authors can accurately predict the future or that the apocalyptic interest in eschatology rules out significant interest in history.[2] Interest in revelation and history is scarcely noticed in most ancient non-apocalyptic works. How does taking seriously the ancient conviction that accurate apprehension of the past requires revelation help in understanding these and other ancient works? Do Josephus' claims to inspiration in the *Jewish War* significantly affect his work? How significant for the interpretation of *Jubilees* is its claim to be dictated by an angel of the presence? How do revelations about the past function in the *Ascension of Isaiah*, the Fourth Gospel, Daniel, *4 Ezra*, the Animal Apocalypse or *2 Baruch*? How important is it to Luke–Acts that spirit-filled witnesses tell what Jesus did?

Although, in an age which assumed revelation as an everyday possibility, many authors undoubtedly perceived themselves inspired

widely influential. See for instance Bultmann's conclusion that apocalyptic interest in eschatology ruled out significant interest in history (Rudolf Bultmann, 'History and Eschatology in the New Testament', *NTS* 1 [1954], 5-16). Rössler attempted a corrective, but the usefulness of his work is limited. See Dietrich Rössler, *Gesetz und Geschichte. Untersuchungen zur Theologie der jüdischen Apokalyptik und der pharisäischen Orthodoxie* (WMANT 3; Neukirchen: Neukirchener Verlag, 1960). Reid has recently investigated historical material in Daniel and *1 Enoch* but follows a different muse from mine. See Stephen Breck Reid, *Enoch and Daniel: A Form Critical and Sociological Study of Historical Apocalypses* (Bibal Monograph Series 2; Berkeley, CA: Bibal, 1989).

1. See below.

2. Rudolf Bultmann, 'History and Eschatology in the New Testament', *NTS* 1(1954), 5-16.

by divine gifts of insight, I have not inquired into their religious experience. Instead I have investigated the rhetorical effects of their claims to relate past events by revelation. How does the author's attempt to disclose the hidden realities of the past function in the argument of his or her work? Asking this question has led to the isolation of several newly recognized literary forms. More importantly it has led to a deeper appreciation of the purposes for which the authors wrote and of the arguments which they employed.

Although I hope primarily to gain deeper understanding of individual books, the potential significance of this study transcends this concern. If many ancient Jews and Christians expected the best history to be based on revelation, a new factor emerges in the background of works not explicitly based on revealed history. Study of the Gospels and the traditions behind them must consider the possibility that not only might prophetic words of the risen Christ have entered the tradition, but prophets may have consciously shaped the tradition according to revelations about the past. Reviews of history in such works as the *Testaments of the Twelve Patriarchs* or the *Assumption of Moses*, which do not explicitly claim inspiration, will have to be evaluated in a new context. The abrupt switch from the theology of Jesus to that of Paul might be based on the activity of early Christian prophets who perceived heavenly significance behind the past activity of the earthly Jesus. Such implications of widespread interest in revelation directed toward the past exceed the scope of the present study. It is first necessary to establish revealed history as a pervasive force in the first century. This study will bring to light a neglected element in the historical consciousness of ancient Judaism and early Christianity and will shed new light on the thoughts and intentions of some works in which it is found.

Searching antiquity for revelations concerning the past is like casting the net on the other side of the boat; the net threatens to break before it can be brought ashore. So frequent and varied are such revelations that they defy adequate organization or analysis within the length of a single study. The necessity for limitation soon becomes painfully clear. After a brief examination of the scope of inspiration directed toward the past in the ancient world, limits will be established for the rest of the inquiry and a few terms will be defined.

While works as local as the *Potter's Oracle*[1] in Egypt or the Babylonian apocalypses[2] contained revealed history, the universal popularity of revelation directed toward the past shows most clearly when it appears in widely disseminated works. The *Iliad*, the staple of Greek education from grammar school up and the *locus classicus* for much of Greek culture and religion, appeals to the Muses for understanding of the past. What the *Iliad* was for Greek culture, the *Aeneid* rapidly became for Latin; Virgil recounts the history of Rome as a revelation from dead Anchises to Aeneas. The works of Sophocles, though never so widely read as the two epics, nevertheless made it into Quintilian's list of books that every budding orator should read;[3] *Oedipus the King* portrays Teiresias as possessing divine knowledge of the past.

Although the opening invocation to the Muses does not clearly call for inspiration concerning past happenings,[4] subsequent invocations in the *Iliad* specifically request revelation concerning events of the Trojan War:[5]

> Tell me now, you Muses who have your homes on Olympus.
> For you, who are goddesses, are there, and you know all things,
> and we have heard only the rumour of it and know nothing.[6]
> Who then of those were the chief men and the lords of the Danaans
> I could not tell over the multitude of them nor name them,
> not if I had ten tongues and ten mouths, not if I had
> a voice never to be broken and a heart of bronze within me,
> not unless the Muses of Olympia, daughters
> of Zeus of the aegis, remembered all those who came beneath Ilion.
> I will tell the lords of the ships, and the ships' numbers (2.484-93).[7]

---

1. L. Koenen, 'Prophezeihungen des "Töpfers" ', *Zeitschrift für Papyrologie und Epigraphik* 2 (1968), 195-209.

2. See A.K. Grayson and W.G. Lambert, 'Akkadian Prophecies', *Journal of Cuneiform Studies* 18 (1964), 7-30.

3. Quintilian 10.67.

4. *Iliad* 1.1-7.

5. The following is quoted from *The Iliad of Homer* (trans. Richmond Lattimore; Chicago: University of Chicago, 1951), 89.

6. Ἔσπετε νῦν μοι, Μοῦσαι Ὀλύμπια δώματ' ἔχουσαι—
  ὑμεῖς γὰρ θεαί ἐστε, πάρεστέ τε, ἴστέ τε πάντα,
  ἡμεῖς δὲ κλέος οἶον ἀκούομεν οὐδέ τι ἴδμεν—(2.484-86).

Greek text for the *Iliad* from *Homer, The Iliad* (trans. A.T. Murray LCL; New York: Putnam's, 1924).

7. εἰ μὴ Ὀλυμπιάδες Μοῦσαι, Διὸς αἰγιόχοιο
  θυγατέρες, μνησαίαθ' ὅσοι ὑπὸ Ἴλιον ἦλθον
  ἀρχοὺς αὖ νηῶν ἐρέω νῆάς τε προπάσας (2.491-93).

The author(s) remarks that though the Muses know who took part in the attack on Troy and their strength, the knowledge had long since faded from human memory. He can only tell the 'lords of the ships and the ships' numbers' if the Muses reveal them to him. For accurate information about the past the author chooses to rely on inspiration.[1]

It is unlikely that Virgil seriously claims inspiration for the catalogue of future Roman heroes contained in Book 6,[2] yet he clothes it so naturally with the trappings of inspiration that he seems to portray a kind of revelation widely practiced and understood. Aeneas, visiting Hades, receives a lecture by his father Anchises, who tells the stories of various shades he sees. Although the deeds described are in Aeneas' future, they uniformly lie in Virgil's past. Virgil uses the device of revealed history to add punch to his own interpretation of Roman history, especially to show his view of Roman greatness:

> Roman, remember by your strength to rule
> Earth's peoples—for your arts are to be these:
> To pacify, to impose the rule of law,
> To spare the conquered, battle down the proud (6.1151-54).[3]

Further revelations from the Sibyl and other shades in the underworld reveal events past even to Aeneas.

Oedipus the King turns on the ignorance of events in the past. To find the truth about past actions, Oedipus retains Teiresias, holy prophet (σεμνόμαντις, 556)[4] of Thebes. In a powerful scene, full of the irony for which the play is famous, Oedipus interrogates Teiresias. From the beginning it is clear that Teiresias has divined the truth, but he refuses to express it. When forced to reveal the true events of the past he does so reluctantly:

> I say you are the murderer of the king
> whose murderer you seek (362).

> I say that with those you love best
> you live in foulest shame unconsciously
> and do not see where you are in calamity (366-67).[5]

---

1. A further brief reference to such inspiration directed to the past occurs in *Iliad* 16.112-13.

2. *Aeneid* 6.970-1202.

3. Virgil, *The Aeneid* (trans. Robert Fitzgerald; New York: Vintage/ Random House, 1984), 190.

4. Greek text: Sophocles, *Oedipus Rex* (ed. R.D. Dawe; Cambridge: Cambridge University Press, 1982).

5. Sophocles, 'Oedipus the King' (trans. David Grene in *Greek Tragedies*, vol. 1, ed. David Grene and Richmond Lattimore; Chicago: University of Chicago, 1960), 126.

Though disbelieved, he is vindicated in the end. Long before anyone else knows, Teiresias, the mantic seer, has discerned that Oedipus killed his father and married his mother.

These examples from some of the most widely read works of antiquity suffice to show how familiar the device of inspired history would have been to educated Greeks and Latins at the end of the first century CE. It seems fair to assume, and further delving would certainly show, that revelation about the past played a part in the lives of the less educated as well. The activity of Teiresias probably reflects the expectation of the general public; the fifth-century BCE audience of Sophocles' play would hardly have been surprised for a mantic seer to have discovered the hidden sequence of past events.

Further investigation into popular hellenistic ideas of revealed history cannot be attempted here. Constraints of space require a focus on works closely related to John and the historical apocalypses in which revelation of the past has already been noted. The authors of the historical apocalypses and the Fourth Gospel were Jews or Christians as well as partakers of hellenistic culture. To use imagery taken from Venn diagrams, they belong in a circle containing Jews, a circle containing Christians, or in the overlap between them containing Christian Jews. Of course both circles are circumscribed by the larger circle of hellenistic culture. This investigation will be limited to productions of Judaism and Christianity that participate positively or negatively in the hellenistic-Roman world and are roughly contemporary with or earlier than the Fourth Gospel and the Jewish apocalypses in which the phenomena of revelation directed toward the past was first noted. Since surviving relevant Jewish works start responding to the hellenistic world about 200 BCE and since disasters of the Bar Kochba revolt enervated Jewish apocalypticism and curtailed the production of Jewish apocalypses, 200 BCE and 130 CE are logical dates to define the bounds of the study. Because John and the apocalypses are literary works only literary productions will be considered, though it is likely that magical texts and inscriptions would also yield relevant material. In sum, the following criteria have been used to determine which texts should be studied. Writings studied must

1. be literary works;
2. be of Jewish or Christian origin;
3. have been written between 200 BCE and 130 CE;
4. be of significant length;
5. have clear reference to the author's past;
6. have clear claim to inspiration.

The one or two items not derived from the above reasoning should be self-explanatory.

These criteria clearly include or exclude the vast majority of relevant texts. Strangely enough the criterion most difficult to apply is the one that looks the clearest. Anyone who has ever wrestled with dating a document knows how difficult a task it is and how much easier it is to fix a range of probability than to assign a narrowly defined date. Several works have been included even though the range of probable dating extends beyond this period. Their inclusion reflects my judgment that these works may reasonably be assigned within the period between 200 BCE and 130 CE.

As with any criteria, the above list leaves certain works on the borderline between inclusion and exclusion. A discussion of these has the double advantage of explaining why a given work is excluded or included and how the criteria have been applied.

The *Testament of Levi* contains a long review of the history of Israel including an interesting reinterpretation of Daniel's seventy weeks and reference to a future 'new priest' (*T. Levi* 14–18). However, Levi does not claim inspiration for his 'predictions' but bases them on the wisdom he has gained from the books of Enoch. In keeping with the testamentary form he passes on his wisdom to his children. Since this review of history lacks a claim to inspiration it will not be treated here.

Similarly the long review of history in the *Testament of Moses* (chs. 2–10) makes no explicit claim to inspiration. Like Levi, Moses delivers the sum of his wisdom to his successor (Joshua). Unlike Levi he does not authorize his knowledge by appeal to the books of Enoch. The source of his knowledge is not stated though he does refer to his own authority as mediator of the covenant (1.14). While Moses' reputation as the revealer *par excellence* would argue that anything he uttered might be considered revelation, the claim to inspiration in the *Testament of Moses* is too tenuous to hold the weight of an argument for the presence of revealed history.

Although Charles dates *2 Enoch* to the first century and concludes it was written by an Alexandrian Jew, both of these conclusions are open to question. This unique work is so difficult to date and contains so many non-Jewish features that F.I. Andersen, in his excellent study and translation, is unwilling fully to commit himself either to its early date or to its Jewish origin.[1] Although this text contains a bizarre creation account revealed to Enoch, uncertainty regarding its date and

1. F.I. Andersen, '2 (Slavonic Apocalypse of) Enoch', *OTP* 1.94-97.

regarding the community which produced it militates against its inclusion here.

The Apocalypse of Weeks (*1 En.* 93.1-14) outlines important events throughout history which Enoch has read in the heavenly books. Its clear claim to inspiration and reference to the past would argue for its inclusion, but its brevity and sketchiness argue against it. Since an analysis of the Apocalypse of Weeks would add little to the chapter on apocalyptic history where it would belong, it will be omitted.

The several recensions of the *Life of Adam and Eve* contain two occurrences of revelation directed toward the past. The Latin version contains an interesting variation on a revelation of the primordial history: the devil tells Adam the circumstances of his fall. God banished the devil and his angels from heaven because they had refused to worship the image of God in Adam. The adversary who opposed Adam and Eve determined that they, as the occasion of his fall, should share his lot (*LAE*, 12–17). Receiving information about the past from the devil instead of God offers a perspective on revealed history unique in the literature. Though the Latin version's information from the devil contains a tradition about the fall which is certainly old, no such certainty attaches to the framework of revelation in which it is placed.[1] The anecdote about the devil's talk is probably later. I am aware of no other information imparted by the devil in the period and the jumbled textual history of the *Life of Adam and Eve* does not inspire confidence.

The Greek version of the *Life of Adam and Eve*, frequently called the *Apocalypse of Moses*, in its title claims the authority of revelation: 'Account and Life of Adam and Eve, the first-created, revealed by God to His servant Moses, when he received from the hand of the Lord the tables of the law of the covenant, instructed by the Archangel Michael'.[2] However, all other versions lack this title. No attempt to recall the heavenly origin of the account occurs in the rest of the book. The claim of the *Apocalypse of Moses* to inspiration, though attesting familiarity with prophetic history at some point in its textual transmission, is too tenuous for inclusion here.

I have used the terms 'revealed history', 'historical revelation', 'historical prophecy', 'revelation of the past', 'inspiration directed

---

1. This theory of Satan's fall has a continued relation to revealed history. Jesus reveals a similar account to his disciples in the fourth-century Coptic work, *The Installation of the Archangel Michael*. See Robert G. Hall, 'The Installation of the Archangel Michael', *Coptic Church Review* 5 (1984), 108-11.

2. Translation of Alexander Walker, *Apocryphal Gospels, Acts, and Revelation* (Ante-Nicene Christian Library 16; Edinburgh: T & T Clark, 1870), 454.

toward the past', and 'inspired history' virtually interchangeably. All of them refer to accounts of the past which are based on information received from gods or their messengers. On the other hand, 'prophetic history', 'historical sermon', and 'apocalyptic history' are technical terms naming specified genera of revealed history. These genera and their several species are defined in the appropriate places in the text. 'History' is used loosely to refer to any record or account of events past to the author no matter how mythological or farfetched.

Since Christians of this period adapted Jewish forms to their needs, this study will begin by working out a morphology of Jewish inspired history. When complete, this morphology will be utilized and adapted to explain similar Christian works. A surprising variety of Jewish texts meet the criteria for inclusion in this study. *Jubilees*, the Animal Apocalypse from *1 Enoch*, the Cloud Vision from *2 Baruch*, much of Abraham's heavenly trip in the *Apocalypse of Abraham*, Daniel, *4 Ezra*, portions of the *Sibylline Oracles*, Judith, the *Biblical Antiquities* of Pseudo-Philo, and the *Jewish War* by Josephus all rely on revelations of the past. Analysis of each of these follows in the next few chapters. Their use of revealed history will be studied and, where possible, classified according to type. This study will seek to describe the goals, techniques, and objects to which Judaism of the period applied revealed history. It will also view each of these works from a new vantage point. Understanding the use these authors make of revealed history should spark fresh insight into their writings.

PART I

JEWISH LITERATURE

Chapter 2

PROPHETIC HISTORY

The use by the Jews of the term 'Former Prophets' to denote the books of Joshua, Judges, Samuel, and Kings, though the precise significance and antiquity of the term is unknown, argues some connection between prophecy and the writing of history. At some point in the history of Judaism, interpretation of these historical books aligned them with prophecy. Though few if any modern students of Judaism have investigated this correlation of prophecy with history writing, Jacob Neusner distinguishes the Mishnaic conception of history from that in earlier forms of Judaism by juxtaposing prophecy and history. 'So for all forms of Judaism until the Mishnah, the writing of history is a form of prophecy. Just as prophecy takes up the interpretation of historical events, so historians retell these events in the frame of prophetic theses.'[1] In this statement Neusner maintains a distinction between the prophet and the historian. Prophets interpreted events; historians wrote on the basis of these prophetic interpretations. At least one ancient historian, Josephus, identified the two; the best historians are prophets.

In *Against Apion* (1.Proem.1-10 §§1-56) Josephus finds it necessary to argue for the accuracy of the sources he used in compiling the *Antiquities of the Jews*. In contrast to the late and slovenly practices of Greek record keeping, Josephus describes the care shown by the Jewish priests for their genealogical records of two thousand years (*Ag. Ap.* 1.Proem.7 §§30-36). In contrast to the Greek historians who for their knowledge of ancient history are reduced to conjecture (*Ag. Ap.* 1.Proem.3 §15), Josephus describes how the Jewish historians were prophets who received the knowledge of the most ancient events through inspiration from God (*Ag. Ap.* 1.Proem.7 §37). This juxtaposition of prophecy and history by a first-century Jewish

---

1. Jacob Neusner, 'Beyond Myth, after Apocalypse: The Mishnaic Conception of History', *Response* 14 (1984), 17.

historian is a good place to begin inquiry into the background of inspiration directed toward the past.

Although Josephus writes to defend the accuracy of Jewish history writing rather than to describe how a prophetic historian wrote, certain aspects of his conception emerge. By contrasting the prophet to one who writes of his own free will (*Ag. Ap.* 1.Proem.7 §37),[1] Josephus makes it clear that the prophet writes history at God's behest. One cannot just decide to write history; one must be appointed to it as a prophet. Josephus portrays prophetic historians operating in two ways. They 'learn the most remote and ancient history through inspiration from God'[2] and they 'write a clear account of events of their own time just as they occurred'. Josephus reserves the first of these two functions for Moses who wrote history from the beginning of the world to his own death. The remaining thirteen prophetic historians, all of the second type, wrote history from the death of Moses until Artaxerxes, each prophet recording history for the time of his own experience (*Ag. Ap.* 1.Proem.8 §§39-40). These books by the prophets are regarded as the judgments (δόγματα) of God and if need be Jews will die for them (*Ag. Ap.* 1.Proem.8 §42). Because the succession of prophets was interrupted, Jewish history since the time of Artaxerxes, though generally reliable, enjoys less prestige (*Ag. Ap.* 1.Proem.8 §41).

Historical writing such as that described by Josephus, the primary concern of which is to recount past events and which has revelation as one of its components, will be called *prophetic history*. Since the two kinds of prophetic history distinguished by Josephus occur in writings of ancient Judaism, his distinction will be retained. Prophetic histories which relate events experienced by the historian but interpreted by revelation will be called interpretive prophetic histories. Prophetic histories in which events as well as their interpretations are received by revelation will be called inspired prophetic histories.

---

1. 'The freedom of choice to write is not for all. . . but only the prophets relate history' (μήτε τοῦ γράφειν αὐτεξουσίου πᾶσιν ὄντος. . . ἀλλὰ μόνων τῶν προφητῶν. . . συγγραφόντων). The texts and translations used for the works of Josephus are those of H.St.J. Thackeray in Josephus, *Against Apion* (LCL; New York: Putnams, 1926). For another brief discussion of these passages see Louis H. Feldman, 'Prophets and Prophecy in Josephus', *SBLSP* (1988), 431-33.

2. τὰ μὲν ἀνωτάτω καὶ παλαιότατα κατὰ τὴν ἐπίπνοιαν τὴν ἀπὸ τοῦ θεοῦ μαθόντων.

Interpretive Prophetic History: Josephus

After describing the task of prophetic historians Josephus immediately turns to his own work. As the prophets recorded the history of their own experience so Josephus in the *Jewish War* has written an account of events he has experienced (*Ag. Ap.* 1.Proem.9 §47). Does Josephus consider himself an inspired writer of history? Wherever this question has been asked, the answer has tended to be in the affirmative,[1] but discussions of the question have hardly extended beyond articulations of a hunch. A broader assessment of the evidence is needed.

While his assertion that the line of prophetic historians has failed may link Josephus with the rabbinic doctrine that prophecy ceased with the canon,[2] Josephus does not imply that inspiration analogous to that of the prophets has ceased. Although he habitually reserves the title προφήτης for the canonical prophets,[3] he portrays a string of post-canonical figures who act very much like prophets.[4] On the one hand Josephus wishes to make clear the distinction between canonical and subsequent writings and consequently between inspiration of the canonical period and inspiration of the subsequent period. On the other he does not wish to lessen the importance of inspiration; a non-canonical grade of inspiration continues, supporting many of the functions of the old prophecy even if it does not quite deserve the name. Josephus clearly asserts the failure of the old prophetically guaranteed history.[5] Subsequent histories were not eyewitness accounts by prophets worthy to continue the old prophetic succession.[6] Presumably Josephus includes his own writing under this stricture. Yet, properly speaking, Josephus does not make a doctrinal assertion

1. David E. Aune, 'The Use of ΠΡΟΦΗΤΗΣ in Josephus', *JBL* 101 (1982), 420; J. Blenkinsopp, 'Prophecy and Priesthood in Josephus', *JJS* 25 (1974), 241.

2. Blenkinsopp, 240, 262. Gary Lance Johnson, 'Josephus: Heir Apparent to the Prophetic Tradition?', *SBLSP* 22 (1983), 337-46. Feldman (431-33) rightly concludes that prophets capable of writing an inspired text have ceased according to Josephus. As we shall see Josephus does not imply cessation of history writing based upon inspired insight into the past.

3. Blenkinsopp, 262; J. Reiling, 'The Use of ψευδοπροφήτης in the Septuagint, Philo, and Josephus', *Nov.T.* 13 (1971), 156. Aune (419-21) finds two counterexamples, but they are clearly exceptions which prove the rule; see Johnson, 339.

4. For instance, *J.W.* 1.3.5 §§78-80; 2.7.3 §113; 2.8.12 §159. See Blenkinsopp, 256.

5. Willem Cornelis van Unnik (*Flavius Josephus als historischer Schriftsteller* [Franz Delitzsch Vorlesung, neue Folge; Heidelberg: Lambert Schneider, 1978], 48) rightly points out that this passage asserts a break in the succession of prophetic historians, rather than a failure of prophets.

6. Blenkinsopp, 240.

that inspiration directed toward history ceased, but an empirical observation: there did not happen to be any more prophets writing the histories of their own times. The chain of prophetic history was broken. Since for Josephus the failure of canonical prophets does not imply the failure of inspiration, Josephus does not preclude the possibility that later historians might be inspired to write history.

Josephus certainly portrays himself as a recipient of revelation in the *Jewish War*,[1] describing several kinds of prophetic experiences. Once he describes the appearance, as if in a dream, of someone standing beside his bed speaking an oracle of assurance[2] (*Life* 42 §209). Interestingly enough, at this point in his life he is promised protection from the Jews and encouraged to fight the Romans! The other passage which offers a glimpse into Josephus' experience of inspiration records quite the contrary imperative. The celebrated account of the revelation to Josephus in the cave under fallen Jotapata (*J.W.* 3.8.3 §§350-54) mentions five or six separate components in the experience of revelation. Josephus received the substratum of revelation through ominous images in nightly dreams. At the moment of crisis God called the dreams to remembrance (ἀνάμνεσις...εἰσέρχεται, §351). Fortunately Josephus was gifted with a strong charism of discerning the meaning of dreams and ambiguous utterances of God (§352). He was a priest, heir of the priestly knowledge of the scriptures and the priestly charismatic ability to interpret them (§352). Hence at that moment he was inspired (ἔνθους γενόμενος)[3] to interpret the scriptures (§353). The reception and interpretation of dreams which he admires in Daniel,[4] that inspired interpretation of scripture he

---

1. While some view Josephus' appeal to inspiration in the cave at Jotapata as hypocritical (e.g. F.F. Bruce, 'Josephus and Daniel', *Annual of the Swedish Theological Institute* 4 [Leiden: Brill, 1965], 159), recent students of Josephus rarely question his claim to inspiration. That Josephus prophesied the rise of Vespasian is incontestable, witnessed as it is by Dio Cassius (epitome 66.1) and Suetonius (*Vesp.* 5). Such divination was accepted in the hellenistic world by Jews and Romans; see van Unnik (42) and the discussion by Tessa Rajak, *Josephus: The Historian and his Society* (Philadelphia: Fortress, 1983), 185-95.

2. David E. Aune so classifies it in *Prophecy in Early Christianity and the Ancient Mediterranean World* (Grand Rapids: Eerdmans, 1983), 143.

3. Josephus uses this same phrase for the prophesying of Saul and the prophets (*Ant.* 6.4.2 §56; 6.5.2 §76); van Unnik, 43.

4. Josephus had special admiration for Daniel because he could interpret dreams (*Ant.* 10.10.2 §194, cf. §189). Marinus de Jonge, 'Josephus und die Zukunftserwartungen seines Volkes', *Josephus-Studien. Untersuchungen zu Josephus, dem antiken Judentum und dem Neuen Testament, Otto Michel zum 70. Geburtstag* (ed.

attributes to the Essenes (*J.W.* 2.8.12 §159),[1] the revelatory gift which he attributes to his priestly ancestry,[2] and the gift of anamnesis all coalesce in this one experience. Josephus has labored much to underscore the claim to revelation which alone justifies his surrender to the Romans.

The account of the revelation at Jotapata is first of all a call narrative. Josephus learns that God has chosen him to announce what is coming (3.8.3 §354); in obedience to God he must surrender to the Romans (3.8.5 §361). From now on Josephus lives for a different purpose: as the servant (διάκονος, 3.8.3 §354) of God he must deliver God's message (διαγγελία, *J.W.* 3.8.5 §361). Like the account of Paul's calling at Damascus,[3] the account of Josephus' call also contains an abstract of the message he is to proclaim.[4] He must announce the destinies of Roman kings (3.8.3 §351). He must announce that God will break his handiwork, the Jewish nation (3.8.3 §§351, 354), and that fortune belongs to the Romans (3.8.3 §354): God is on the Roman side.

With his call Josephus had received the burden of his future messages, but he had yet to declare them. With one exception in the prophecies that follow, Josephus carries out his mission to declare the destinies of the Roman kings and the Jewish people. The one exception is recounted as a flashback to the days before his call. Josephus had predicted the fall of Jotapata after forty-seven days and his own survival as a captive of Rome. Josephus tells this prophecy and its fulfillment before Vespasian and Titus, not strictly as part of his commission, though it furthers it, but only as a confirmation of his

---

Otto Betz, Klaus Haacker, and Martin Hengel; Göttingen: Vandenhoeck & Ruprecht, 1974), 207.

1. Since Otto Betz (*Offenbarung und Schriftforschung in der Qumransekte* [WUNT 6; Tübingen: Mohr-Siebeck, 1960], 106) it is common to notice also the parallels between Josephus as an inspired interpreter and the Teacher of Righteousness at Qumran. So Blenkinsopp, 247; Bruce, 159; Johnson, 340; Helgo Lindner, *Die Geschichtsauffassung des Flavius Josephus im Bellum Judaicum* (AGAJU 12; Leiden: Brill, 1972), 52.

2. Blenkinsopp (250-55) shows how important Josephus' priestly ancestry was to his concept of inspiration.

3. See especially Acts 26.15-18 and Gal. 1.11, 15. Otto Betz ('Die Vision des Paulus im Tempel von Jerusalem. Apg 22, 17-21 als Beitrag zur Deutung des Damaskus Erlebnisses', *Verborum Veritas, Festschrift für Gustav Stählin zum 70. Geburtstag* [ed. Otto Böcher and Klaus Haacker; Wuppertal: Brockhaus, 1970], 122) juxtaposes the revelatory experiences of Paul and Josephus.

4. The only content of the revelation at Jotapata that is actually new in the *Jewish War* is Josephus' call to announce this message; see Lindner, 57-58.

prophetic gifts (*J.W.* 3.8.9 §§406-407). His other prophecies spring directly from the revelation at his call. The messages revealed in summary form in his call are programmatic for Josephus' prophetic career as it is portrayed in the *Jewish War*.

Josephus first discharges his commission concerning the Roman kings (cf. *J.W.* 3.8.3 §51). At a private audience with Vespasian and Titus he announces that both will rule as Caesar. This typical recognition oracle[1] underscores the prophetic role of Josephus himself. Not only has he come as sent by God (ὑπὸ θεοῦ προπεμπόμενος) but he speaks as his messenger (ἄγγελος, *J.W.* 3.8.9 §400). By his obedience, Josephus saves his own head and confirms Vespasian in seeking the throne (*J.W.* 3.8.9 §400, 407; 4.10.7 §623). Referring to this incident, Vespasian later calls Josephus 'servant of the voice of God' (διάκονον τῆς τοῦ θεοῦ φωνῆς, 4.10.7 §626). Josephus successfully completed the first phase of his mission. By his obedience he changed the course of history.

Josephus must still announce that God has gone over to the Romans to break the Jewish nation (cf. *J.W.* 3.8.3 §354). Josephus discharges this remainder of his mission before the walls of beleaguered Jerusalem, announcing to those inside that, to be on God's side, they must surrender to the Romans (*J.W.* 5.8.4 §§375-419; 6.2.1 §§93-111). Although these speeches fulfill Josephus' call, Helgo Lindner argues that they are not prophetic. The charismatic trappings are gone; Josephus fails to refer to the experience of revelation at Jotapata.[2] Josephus does not announce the future but speaks of the past like an admonishing teacher.[3] Lindner is correct in his observations but not in his inferences. His observations can be interpreted differently. Josephus refrains from mentioning Jotapata not because he eschews the ethos of a prophet, but because he seeks an ethos greater, at least for Jewish audiences, than his own prophetic call could give. His own call, even in his eyes, looked very much like betrayal (*J.W.* 3.8.3 §354). Having in the *Jewish War* already established himself as a true prophet, in this speech he seeks to present himself in the role and with the ethos of the great prophet Jeremiah (*J.W.* 5.8.4 §§391-93).[4] He

---

1. Aune, *Prophecy*, 140-41.
2. Lindner, 57.
3. Lindner, 67.
4. Mayer and Möller think Josephus portrays himself in the situation of a classical prophet like Jeremiah (Reinhold Mayer and Christa Möller, 'Josephus—Politiker und Prophet', *Josephus-Studien. Untersuchungen zu Josephus, dem antiken Judentum und dem Neuen Testament. Otto Michel zum 70. Geburtstag*, [ed. Otto Betz, Klaus Haacker, and Martin Hengel; Göttingen: Vandenhoeck & Ruprecht, 1974], 283-84).

sounds like an admonishing teacher reflecting on Jewish history not because he has ceased to act as a prophet, but because a review of Jewish history coupled with exhortation for the present was viewed as one form of prophecy. Achior the Ammonite makes just such a speech before Holofernes in Judith 5.5-21, and Holofernes rebukes him for prophesying on behalf of the Israelites (Jud. 6.2).[1] Stephen, a man full of wisdom and the Spirit (Acts 6.10), makes just such a speech in Acts 7.[2] Thus Josephus, claiming the ethos of a Jeremiah, speaks the message God had given him at his call, casting it in a prophetic form. Josephus certainly conceived these speeches as prophecies in which he fulfills his prophetic commission.

That Josephus does not clothe these speeches with charismatic trappings underscores a significant characteristic of his understanding of inspiration. Josephus does not receive the kind of inspiration that puts the words of God in his mouth at the moment of utterance. At Jotapata he was inspired to see what God was going to do and he was commissioned to speak that message as opportunities arose. His later prophecies are his own rhetorical compositions in which he fulfills, to the best of his ability, the commission God has given him. The locus of inspiration is never in the speech or in the act of speaking, but always in the past in the commission and message he received at Jotapata. Hence the speeches are prophecies without being, in themselves, charismatic.

Josephus fulfills his prophetic commission to declare that God is on the Romans' side by rehearsing the history of Israel. In the first speech (*J.W.* 5.9.4 §§376-419) Josephus argues that Jewish history proves that Israel can only conquer without taking arms. When the people renounced arms to depend upon God they were delivered—when they fought they were defeated. He also argues that the Jews in Jerusalem have sinned. They have defiled the Temple more grossly than their ancestors before the exile. As God was on the side of Babylon, so is God on the Roman side. Only by repenting and surrendering to the Romans can the Jews be on the side of God. What provokes Josephus' second speech before Jerusalem (*J.W.* 6.2.1 §§91-111) is the cessation of the daily offering in the Temple. The Jews have not only defiled the Temple, they have ceased obedient worship of God. They should imitate Jeconiah, who had turned from his sins by surrendering to

1. 'And who are you Achior... to prophesy (ἐπροφήτευσας) among us ... and tell us not to make war against the people of Israel because their God will defend them' (RSV).

2. Aune (*Prophecy*, 142) compares Josephus' speeches to Stephen's speech. See below Chapter 3, 'Inspired Historical Sermons'.

Babylon. Thus Josephus announces a prophecy which utilizes history selectively to place recent events in their proper historical context and so interpret them. Whether or not *Jewish War* as a whole relies on historical prophecy, Josephus acts as a prophetic interpreter of history before the walls of Jerusalem.

Thus the ingredients were present for Josephus to write his histories as a prophetic historian. Josephus knew that the best histories were written by prophets. Although the chain of prophetic historians was broken, his understanding of inspiration did not rule out subsequent inspired histories. He perceived himself as a prophet, though he does not use the term, called to tell the destinies of the Roman kings and to explain how in the war God was on the Roman side. In fulfilling the latter commission he made use of historical prophecy before the walls of Jerusalem. All this tinder needs but a spark to justify the conclusion that Josephus writes the *Jewish War* as part of his prophetic commission.

The spark is not hard to see. Josephus wrote the *Jewish War* under imperial patronage to persuade Jews to revolt no more against Rome and to persuade Romans to retaliate no further against Jews.[1] The weapons he takes up are, by now, familiar. He explains how those in control had rebelled through a false interpretation of the scriptures and a false reading of the signs of the times. The rebellion was based on false prophecy and an interpretation, embraced even by the wise, that the one who in those days would come to rule the world was a Jew. Josephus replaces this understanding of prophecy with his own, borne out by subsequent events. The ruler to rise from Jewish soil was Vespasian. God had ordained Roman rule for their period of history. To rebel against the Romans was to rebel against God. God had destroyed Jerusalem for its many sins. Thus he explains the catastrophe to the Jews and excuses the rebellion to the Romans.[2] Since the false prophecy had been laid to rest by the same events which confirmed the true prophecy delivered by Josephus,[3] Romans need fear Jews no

1. David Daube argues that Josephus considered himself, like Daniel, the prophetic servant of a foreign king and helper of his fellow Jews. Now after the campaign his chief service to Titus was in writing the *Jewish War*. Since he considers the writing of history especially appropriate for a prophet, is it not likely that he considers his task a prophetic one? Cf. David Daube, 'Typology in Josephus', *JJS* 31 (1980), 18-36; refined by Johnson, especially 346.

2. For this reconstruction of Josephus' purpose I have relied heavily on David M. Rhoads, *Israel in Revolution, 6–74 CE* (Philadelphia: Fortress, 1976), 11-14.

3. Josephus repeatedly points out how his own prophecy is fulfilled and how that of the false prophets is not. For false prophets, see *J.W.* 6 §§285-315 and the discussion in de Jonge, 208-10. Since once a prophet's predictions prove true his

longer because Jews no longer would rebel. Therefore the purpose of the *Jewish War* exactly corresponds to the message with which Josephus was inspired and entrusted in the cave at Jotapata. Josephus is still fulfilling his call to declare the destinies of the Roman kings and to announce that God is with the Romans to break the Jewish nation. Josephus writes the *Jewish War* to fulfill his prophetic commission.

Although Josephus in the *Jewish War* has written history based upon revelation, he would not claim that his work was inspired. As with the prophecies declared in Palestine the locus of inspiration remains at Jotapata rather than in the writing of the book. He had received revelation concerning the true significance of events as they had happened (God is with the Romans; Vespasian is the savior from Palestine). Like the prophetic historians of old he had experienced the events he records. He reflects on the revelations and the events, all of which occurred in the past, and writes a history based on both. Perhaps in Josephus' mind here lies the difference between those histories authored by prophets in the old prophetic succession and his own work; the *Jewish War* is prophetic in the sense that it is based on inspiration, not in the sense that it is itself an inspired work. Nevertheless, Josephus both attests for the late first century the view that really good and true history is inspired history and has, in the *Jewish War*, produced a history based upon both revelation and experience.[1]

---

ministry as a prophet is validated (Deut. 18.22 much stressed by Josephus; see de Jonge, 206-207), Josephus' account in *Jewish War* is validated by the fulfillment of his prophecy.

1. Although the reference is too brief to do more than tantalize, Josephus (*Ant.* 1.239-41), quoting Alexander Polyhistor, calls another Jewish historian named Cleodemus Malchus a prophet. 'Cleodemus the prophet (προφήτης), also called Malchus, recorded the history of the Jews, just as Moses their lawgiver had done.' It is tempting, with Aune ('ΠΡΟΦΗΤΗΣ in Josephus', 420-21), to suppose that Cleodemus Malchus wrote history in his capacity as a prophet. Certainly the parallel between the work of Cleodemus and Moses may be read to imply that Cleodemus wrote prophetic history, for Josephus (*Ag. Ap.* 1.Proem.7 §37) specifically says that Moses wrote history as a prophet. Yet while the juxtaposition of Cleodemus with the figure of Moses and the word προφήτης might argue that Josephus perceived Cleodemus as a writer of prophetic history, the reference to Cleodemus is too brief and, given the fact that it occurs in a quotation of a quotation, is too distant to draw any firm conclusions regarding Cleodemus as a practitioner of prophetic history. The translation of the fragment of Cleodemus is taken from R. Doran, 'Cleodemus Malchus', *OTP* 2.887.

Inspired Prophetic History: Jubilees

The book of *Jubilees* describes a revelation Moses received on Mt Sinai from an angel of the presence.[1] Since the angel recounts the saga of creation, the lives of the antediluvian patriarchs, the acts of Noah and his sons, the righteous deeds of the three patriarchs of Israel, and the events of the exodus down to Moses' ascent up the mountain, *Jubilees* qualifies as prophetic history. Since the angel reveals events as well as their interpretation, *Jubilees* is an inspired prophetic history. *Jubilees* describes that revelation to Moses which Josephus isolated as the only example of his first class of prophetic historians: in *Jubilees* Moses 'learns the most remote and ancient history through inspiration from God'.[2]

The author probably wrote *Jubilees* immediately before or after the inception of the Maccabean wars[3] to oppose Gentiles and those Jews

---

1. It is unclear who is writing the book. Sometimes Moses and sometimes the angel receives the command to write (Moses: *Jub.* 1.5, 7, 26; 2.1; 23.32; 33.18. The angel: 1.27; 30.12, 21; 50.6, 13). This confusion only concerns the transcription of the account, for the angel is clearly portrayed as the author of the book in the sense that the material originates with him. The first person in *Jubilees* refers consistently to the angel (Klaus Berger, *Das Buch der Jubiläen* [JSHRZ 2.3; Gütersloh: Gütersloher Verlagshaus Gerd Mohn, 1981], 329, n. 2.18). If, as is probable, Moses writes the book, he only transcribes what the angel dictates to him. VanderKam's solution, assuming that the Greek translation failed to distinguish the hiphil and qal forms of כתב (the angel dictates [hiphil] what Moses writes [qal]), is plausible though conjectural (James C. VanderKam, 'The Putative Author of the Book of Jubilees', *Journal of Semitic Studies* 26 [1981], 215-17). Alternatively, perhaps both Moses and the angel write the book, the angel producing another heavenly book as he dictates, Moses transcribing its earthly copy. Heavenly tablets are produced or added to from time to time in *Jubilees* in response to historical developments (*Jub.* 6.28-29; 16.9; 30.19-20; 31.32). It should not be surprising if the angel in charge of the heavenly tablets were commanded to compile a new heavenly book for Moses and if Moses were enjoined to transcribe his own earthly copy. The angel writes the 'book of the first law' (*Jub.* 6.22). If as seems most likely this title refers to the Pentateuch (R.H. Charles, *The Book of Jubilees or the Little Genesis* [London: A. & C. Black, 1902], 53 n. 27; Orval S. Wintermute, 'Jubilees', *OTP*, 2.38), this also is a heavenly book with an earthly copy (against Michael Testuz, *Les Idées religieuses du livre des Jubilés* [Genève: E. Droz, 1960], 102). Whether written by an angel, or dictated by him to Moses, *Jubilees* is described as a book of the highest revealed character. For an interesting discussion of the heavenly tablets see Charles, *Jubilees*, 24-25 n. 10. Testuz, in another useful discussion, links the heavenly tablets too closely to foreordination (8, 52 54, 59).

2. Josephus, *Ag. Ap.* 1.7.37, cf. 1.8.40.

3. Nickelsburg and Schwarz, noting the prevalence in *Jubilees* of issues raised during the Antiochene persecution, date *Jubilees* to the bleak period immediately preceding the Maccabean revolt. VanderKam dates it right after the early successes of

who wished to be like them over issues related to hellenization. In its own terms it was probably written by one of that young generation who returned to the law (*Jub.* 23.26; cf. 1.23) to urge others to do likewise. The author writes a book to call Israel back from entanglement among the Gentiles to the 'good old days' of the patriarchs, Abraham, Isaac, and Jacob, when the separation from the Gentiles first occurred.

The ascription of the book of Genesis to Moses almost requires the conception of inspired prophetic history.[1] How else could he have written what occurred at creation or described antediluvian events? As heavenly trips suit Enoch so revelations of past events suit Moses. Of course, revelations of the law also suit Moses. The author of *Jubilees* combines the revelation Moses received concerning the law with the revelation he received concerning history. The resulting mixture of prophetic law and prophetic history is characteristic of the book of *Jubilees*.[2]

Jubilees does not merely report the past; it delves into history with a purpose. It seeks to establish correct attitudes and practices in the present by showing how they are firmly established in the heavenly and earthly warp and woof of history. For *Jubilees*, attitudes, practices, and decrees that were established in the past determine the present. At some time in the past heavenly decrees have slipped into the makeup of the universe. Hence they can be ignored only at great peril. In *Jubilees*, the angel reveals to Moses both the heavenly decrees and their entrance into the world to constitute it. Revelations of these decrees are of five types:

1. Revelations of law
2. Revelations of jubilees
3. Revelations concerning present difficulties

Judas Maccabeus. *Jubilees* seems to fit better in the period advocated by VanderKam since the issues which precipitated the revolt are still important but the reality of persecution is not pressing. *Jubilees* might be a little later than VanderKam thinks but not later than 140 BCE. See G.W.E. Nickelsburg, *Jewish Literature between the Bible and the Mishnah* (Philadelphia: Fortress, 1981), 82; Eberhard Schwarz, *Identität durch Abgrenzung* (Europäische Hochschulschriften 29.23.162; Frankfurt am Main: Peter Lang, 1982), 99-129; James C. VanderKam, *Textual and Historical Studies in the Book of Jubilees* (Harvard Semitic Monographs 14; Missoula, MT: Scholars Press, 1977), 283-84.

1. See Christopher Rowland, *The Open Heaven: A Study of Apocalyptic in Judaism and Early Christianity* (New York: Crossroad, 1982), 51-52; Berger, 279.
2. Berger, 280, 283.

4. Revelations of exhortation
5. Revelations of the future.

Each type will be treated in turn.

Revelations of Law
The book of *Jubilees* heightens the authority of the law by an appeal to its antiquity and to its heavenly origin.[1] The angel reveals to Moses the heavenly institution of a law along with the ancient circumstances of its earthly institution. Once a law from the heavenly tablets is enacted on earth, it is determinative for all subsequent history. What is engraved on the heavenly tablets and put into practice by the ancient and godly ancestors of Israel must be observed. This derivation of support for keeping the law from a combination of its ancient and heavenly origins relies upon the device of inspired prophetic history. The angel must both reveal the law's ancient heavenly promulgation and locate its earthly institution squarely within the life of a patriarch.

Such juxtapositions of the law's heavenly ordination and earthly institution pervade *Jubilees*. The law of purification after childbirth is written on the heavenly tablets because Adam entered the garden of Eden seven days after creation, but Eve after fourteen (*Jub.* 3.10).[2] Laws against murder are written on the heavenly tablets in connection with Cain's slaying of Abel (4.4-5). Noah promises in a covenant before God not to eat blood (6.10). Abram gives a tithe and the Lord ordains it as an ordinance forever (13.25). God commands Abraham to circumcise his children (15.11); when Abraham obeys, circumcision is said to be inscribed on the heavenly tablets (15.26). Even the two highest orders of angels, those privileged to keep the sabbath with Israel, are born circumcised (15.27) . In the story of Jacob's marriage to Leah and Rachel it is said to be ordained on the heavenly tablets that the younger sister must not marry before the elder (28.6). The rape of Dinah forbids marriage to the Gentiles—a law engraved on the heavenly tablets (30.9). Such a list is sufficient to show how the author of *Jubilees* establishes a variety of laws by their heavenly origin and the antiquity of their application. Statutes ordained in heaven and instituted on earth cannot be lightly disregarded.

Such examples well illustrate the importance of ancient and heavenly institution in *Jubilees*, but only a more detailed study can reveal how

---

1. See Wintermute (38), who classifies ways the authority of the law is supported in *Jubilees*. R.H. Charles (*Jubilees*, 37 n. 18) speaks of the author's 'beloved practice of antedating an event or usage he wishes to commend to his countrymen'.
2. Testuz, 48.

the ancient earthly and heavenly moments of a law's institution intertwine. Consider the following examples. The sabbath, the most important of the feasts in *Jubilees* (2.27, 30, 32), was instigated by God on
the seventh day of creation as a heavenly celebration only for the
highest orders of angels and the seed of Jacob (2.17-21). Of special
interest to the author is the antiquity of the sabbath command (on the
seventh day of creation), its celebration by the two highest classes of
angels, its foreordained celebration by Jacob and his children, and
their implied participation with angels in united heavenly and earthly
worship on the sabbath. The author offers all of these characteristics
of the sabbath as reasons his contemporaries should observe it, and all
of them are known by revelation of the past. Perhaps because *Jubilees*
has followed the priestly writers' lead in tying sabbath observance to
creation, the element of heavenly institution dominates. Yet the past
heavenly decree also fixes its earthly institution for the children of
Jacob. The heavenly command clearly precedes its first earthly
observance.

If the heavenly moment dominates this discussion of the sabbath, the
element of earthly antiquity dominates the account of the feasts instituted in Noah's day. The earthly feast of weeks or oaths[1] was ordained
in the heavenly tablets in response to a historical event: Noah's
sacrifice after the waters subsided when God ratified a covenant with
him (*Jub*. 6.17). From this origin it gains its significance; those who
keep the feast 'renew the covenant in all (respects), year by year'
(6.17).[2] After a lapse following Noah's death, Abraham and his sons
kept it, though it had lapsed again by Moses' days. The angel commands Moses to reestablish its observance (6.18-19). Since these
figures who kept the feast all received covenants, perhaps all of the
covenants are to be renewed at the feast. The angels kept the feast
renewing the covenants from creation (6.18), but human beings only
when they received and kept the covenants. *Jubilees* establishes the
significance of the feast by revealing its historical roots in the giving
of the covenants. It uncovers the ancient and enduring heavenly celebration of the feast by inspiration directed toward the past. Although
angels kept the feast of covenants from the beginning, it was ordained
for human beings only in response to Noah's institution of the feast.

---

1. In *Jubilees* the underlying שבועות probably means 'oaths' rather than 'weeks'
(Solomon Zeitlin, *The Book of Jubilees, Its Character and Significance* [Philadelphia:
Dropsie, 1939], 5-7; taken up by Testuz, 146).

2. This and all quotes of *Jubilees* follow Wintermute's translation. For the Ethiopic
text of *Jubilees* I have relied on R.H. Charles, *The Ethiopic Version of the Book of
Jubilees* (Oxford: Clarendon, 1895).

Here heavenly institution both precedes and follows earthly institution.[1]

Noah also institutes feasts at the beginning of each quarter of the year, probably on the four intercalated days of the calendar,[2] in commemoration of various steps in his deliverance from the flood (6.23-29). Noah apparently has the initiative; he establishes these feasts and then they are inscribed on the heavenly tablets (6.28-29).[3] Again the reasons to keep the feast—antiquity of establishment, heavenly ordination and significance—are all derived from inspiration concerning the past.

It is unnecessary to go into detail regarding the establishment of other feasts or fasts. The connection of the feast of the seven days with the sacrifice of Isaac (18.19), of the day of atonement with Jacob's grief over Joseph (34.18), and of passover with the exodus (49) follow the pattern of the three feasts outlined above. In each case the feast should be kept both because of its origin in antiquity and its ordination in heaven. The heavenly ordination and inception of the feast may precede the earthly inception of the feast or the heavenly ordination of the feast may follow its earthly ordination and initial celebration. Earthly observance may instigate or be instigated by heavenly decree. That the past earthly and heavenly components of these revelations so thoroughly intertwine shows how necessary an understanding of heavenly events is to an understanding of past earthly events and how necessary an understanding of past earthly events is to heavenly. Heaven and earth belong to the same world in *Jubilees*. A past event includes both heavenly and earthly components and can only be understood by revelation. Furthermore, the significance and necessity of observing a statute results as much from the circumstances of its first earthly observance as from its heavenly ordination. Those who

---

1. A similar intertwining of heavenly decree and earthly institution establishes the solar calendar. The true reckoning of days and years was first revealed to Enoch and written down by him for subsequent generations (4.17-18). Yet the calendar also derives from Noah's institution of the quarterly feasts (6.29). Hence the solar calendar stems from two of the more important figures of antiquity and also stems from heaven in connection with the heavenly recording of Noah's command (6.29) or as the angels made it known to Enoch (4.18). The heavenly decree both causes and is consequent upon the earthly institution of the solar calendar.

2. A deduction from the similar calendar in *1 Enoch*, but *Jubilees* only says on the first day of the month.

3. Berger, 359 n. 6.29: 'Die Gebote stehen nicht seit Ewigkeit auf den himmlischen Tafeln, sondern werden aufgrund bestimmter Ereignisse auf Erden auf die Tafeln gesetzt (geschrieben)'. Zeitlin (4-5) notices that only one of these feasts, that of the seventh month, is in the Pentateuch.

observe such laws can only know their full gravity by inspired prophetic history.

Revelations of the Jubilee Reckoning

The Ethiopic title to *Jubilees* emphasizes the book's division of history, *'The Account of the Divisions of the Days of the Law and the Testimony for Annual Observance according to their Weeks* (of years) *and their Jubilees throughout all the Years of the World'*.[1] The Damascus Rule (16.1-4) proves the antiquity[2] of this perception of *Jubilees* by quoting it under the title 'The Book of the Division of the Times according to their Jubilees and their Year-weeks'.[3] The proper division of history according to a sabbatical pattern is a prime concern for the author. History is divided into periods based on ever widening units following the sabbatical pattern: seven years form a basic unit; seven of these seven-year periods form a jubilee; the jubilee of jubilees comprises 49 × 49 years. The author dates everything by jubilees and year-weeks. The book ends at the jubilee of jubilees (*Jub.* 50.4). One of the chief accomplishments of the book of *Jubilees* is the revelation of the sequence of jubilees which orders the world. This sequence is shown to be part of the divine order by the correspondence of the most significant historical events with the most significant dates of the jubilee reckoning. The author discloses this particular aspect of the divine order by the entire flow of history revealed to Moses.

The jubilee reckoning of Wiesenberg permits a more precise grasp of the significance of the jubilee of jubilees in the scheme of the book. Although the jubilee is 49 years, the jubilee year (in which slaves are freed) is simultaneously the 50th year and the first year of the next jubilee.[4] Hence the exodus occurs on the 49 × 49th year. The entrance into the land occurs after the end of the first jubilee of the next jubilee of jubilees period, that is at the end of the 50th jubilee. The wilderness wandering occurs during the 50th unit of 49 years which is simultaneously the first jubilee of the second jubilee of jubilees and the 'jubilee

---

1. *zentu nagara kufulē mawa'elāta hege walasma'e lagbera 'āmatāta latasab'otomu la'iyobēlāstihomu westa kwelu 'āmatāta 'ālam.*

2. The earliest existing copy of CD is dated paleographically to 75–50 BCE (VanderKam, *Textual Studies*, 258).

3. ספר מחלקות העתים ליובליהם ובשבועותיהם (CD 16.3-4), my own translation. Hebrew text from Eduard Lohse, *Die Texte aus Qumran* (München: Kösel, 1964), 98. For a discussion of the relation between CD and *Jubilees* see VanderKam, *Textual Studies*, 255-58.

4. Ernest Wiesenberg, 'The Jubilee of Jubilees', *Revue de Qumran* 3 (1961), 16-17.

jubilee' of the first jubilee of jubilees.[1] Hence Israel is freed from Egypt and returned to its land in the jubilee jubilee just as Israelite slaves were to be freed in the jubilee year and returned to their land (Lev. 25.8-55; 27.14-24).[2] Such elaborate calculation along with the emphasis on sabbath and calendar argues for the importance of this division of years in the author's system, yet precisely what he wants to accomplish with these dates is less than clear.

Testuz believes that the author uses his elaborate chronological scheme to divide world history into ages.[3] While *Jubilees* presents insufficient data to support the tripartite division of world history attempted by Testuz, the coincidence of the jubilee of jubilees with the exodus, giving of the law, and entry into the land seems to indicate the beginning and end of an era.[4] Yet the preoccupation with years in a sabbatical pattern entails more than the revelation of a change of ages pivoting around the exodus events. As the observance of sabbaths and feasts is important for the author, so is the observance of the jubilee year. When the author declares that the keeping of the sabbath surpasses the importance of keeping a day in the jubilee year (*Jub.* 2.30), he implies that observance of the days of the jubilee is also important. The angel warns Moses that his people will err regarding the times of months, sabbaths, feasts, and jubilees (*Jub.* 6.37). This verse probably describes errors the author perceives and seeks to correct in his own time. Some at least of the author's contemporaries are keeping the jubilee at the wrong time.[5]

The most extensive discussion of the jubilee year and its significance occurs in the last chapter of the book (50.1-5), yet this passage is a difficult one. The angel declares how he had acquainted Moses with the law concerning the sabbath before reaching Sinai, presumably to

---

1. Wiesenberg postulated two editions of *Jubilees*, one locating the 49×49th year at the time of the exodus, one at the time of the entrance to the land. Reckoning the jubilee jubilee as the 50th jubilee accounts for emphasis on both exodus and entrance without the necessity of postulating editorial work.

2. Wiesenberg, 29.

3. Testuz, 172-75.

4. Wintermute, 39.

5. *B. 'Arakhin* 12b-13a records a rabbinic debate over the proper reckoning of jubilees. At issue is the length of the jubilee period (49 or 50 years) and the beginning point. Contrary to *Jubilees* the debate seems to settle on the 50-year reckoning. Since by this reckoning the Temple would have been destroyed on a jubilee year, the debate concludes that the jubilee periods commenced 14 years after the entrance into Canaan, again contrary to *Jubilees*. On the 49-year reckoning upheld by *Jubilees*, the Temple did not succumb on a jubilee year. Some such debate over the proper reckoning of jubilees must lie behind the book of *Jubilees*.

ensure that Israel would begin keeping sabbath right away (50.1). However, revelation concerning sabbaths of the land waited till Sinai and the general revelation of the law, presumably because there was no immediate need to observe these sabbaths (50.2). The 'sabbaths of the land' (*sanbatāta medr*) are the years the land is to lie fallow (see הארץ שבת, Lev. 25.6), according to Leviticus 25 every seven years. The 'sabbaths of years' (*sanbatāta 'āmatāta*, 50.2) probably also refer to these years of rest for the land. Jubilee years are special instances of these year sabbaths just as in Leviticus 25. The angel thus moves away from a discussion of sabbath days (50.1) to a discussion of sabbath years (50.2). It is clear that the angel has already given Moses legislation about these sabbath years. It is also clear that Moses does not yet know which years are sabbath years and which are not. 'And I also related to you the sabbaths of the land on Mt Sinai. And the years of jubilee in the sabbaths of years I related to you. But its year I have not related to you' (50.2). But it is necessary to know which is the jubilee year once the people possess the land. 'And the land will keep its sabbaths when they dwell upon it. And they will know the year of jubilee' (50.3). Immediately there follows:

> On account of this I ordained for you the weeks of years, and the years, and the jubilees (as) forty-nine jubilees from the days of Adam until this day and one week and two years. And they are still forty further years to learn the commands of the Lord until they cross over the shore of the land of Canaan (50.4).

The calculations in this verse have already been discussed. 'On account of this' ties v. 4 to the preceding verse. Since the people must know which year is the jubilee year and which years are the sabbaths of years, the sabbaths of the land, the angel has revealed the proper years. Telling the weeks of years and the jubilees from the time of Adam till the present is an accurate summary of the book of *Jubilees*. Hence in this verse the angel tells a purpose behind all the elaborate calculations of years in the book; *Jubilees* reveals a 'calendar' for the years of the world (cf. title) just as *Enoch* reveals the calendar for a single year. These calculations reveal which years are the jubilee years and 50.4 shows that the first week of years, at the end of which the land is to lie fallow, begins with the conquest of Canaan.

Jubilees 50.2b seems to overthrow this interpretation. 'But its year I have not related to you until you enter into the land which you will possess.' The obvious interpretation of this statement, in Ethiopic[1] as in English, assumes that Moses will not know which is the year until he

---

1. *wa'āmatosa 'inagarkuka 'eska 'ama tebwe' u westa medr 'enta te' enxazu.*

enters the land. Since, however, the angel proceeds to reveal the year to Moses on the mountain, this plain sense must be incorrect. The surrounding verses are helpful. The angel revealed the proper day for the sabbath because Israel needed to keep it even in the wilderness. But the sabbaths of the land are essentially tied to the land and could not be celebrated in the wilderness; hence the angel did not say 'this is the year' and would not until Israel entered the land. 50.2b might be paraphrased thus, 'I have not told you "This is its year" until you enter the land'.

This revelation of the proper sequence of years for the world, while certainly not the only purpose for *Jubilees*, is one of its major ones. *Jubilees* does not consider events in their jubilees through all the years of the world as might at first appear from the title. Wintermute's translation of *lagbera 'āmatāta* as 'for annual observance' is a masterstroke.[1] *Jubilees* reveals the division of history into jubilees and weeks of years for all the history of the world by revealing the courses of the ancient jubilee divisions, tying them to events to show their significance, and finally pushing the proper reckoning of jubilees and numbers of jubilees into datable times so that the correct divisions could be calculated until the end of the ages. *Jubilees* establishes the correct identification of years as sabbaths of the land and jubilees by a revelation of the past showing the correct scheme of years for that portion of history which was beyond memory. It divides the years into weeks of years and jubilees for correct observance of the years throughout all the years of the world as the title says.

The author establishes the authority of his reckoning of the years in precisely the same way as he does for the other laws concerning time. He ties its institution to antiquity both by fitting all of ancient history into its pattern and by tying its revelation to Moses. He gives it heavenly authority by having the angel speak from the heavenly tablets and perhaps record *Jubilees* itself on a new heavenly tablet. Thus the author grounds the division of the years on that same unity of revelation about the past and about heaven which characterizes his use of

---

1. Wintermute, 52. Charles (*Jubilees*) renders 'of the events of the years'; Berger (312), 'für die Ereignisse der Jahre'. It is not unusual to point out the discrepancy between this title and what *Jubilees* presents, for it does not recount events throughout all the years of the world but only through the giving of revelation on Sinai (John J. Collins, *The Apocalyptic Imagination: An Introduction to the Jewish Matrix of Christianity* [New York: Crossroad, 1984], 65). If, as is argued below, *Jubilees* seeks to establish the proper years for the keeping of the jubilee years and for the proper reckoning of time, the title fits the book. It seeks to establish the proper manner of keeping the years for all the years of the world as the title says.

historical inspiration elsewhere. But to the arguments from ancient and heavenly ordination, the author has added a further proof of the importance of the jubilee reckoning. All history is structured according to this particular calculation of jubilees; only by observing this reckoning of the jubilees will the proper correspondence between human obedience and divine order be maintained.

Revelations Addressing Various Difficulties
In *Jubilees* the revelation of the past is not directed only toward establishing the law or correcting observance of jubilees but also toward addressing present difficulties confronting the author. This use of revelation of the past can be illustrated by some of the steps taken by the author to explain the Gentile threat of military and cultural conquest of Israel.

The angel devotes a large portion of the historical revelation to a detailed account of the division of the earth among the sons of Noah. This rather dry lesson in geography puts the current enemies of Israel in their place and gives Israel clear title to the land. Noah's sons try to divide the earth but can only do so perversely[1] (*Jub.* 8.9). When they appeal to Noah, he divides among them by lot under angelic supervision (*Jub.* 8.10-11). The apportionment thus receives the approval of heaven and the sponsorship of a patriarch. Shem, Ham, and Japheth subdivide their portions among their children (9.1-13) in the presence of Noah their father (9.14), and all of them, Noah's sons and grandsons, call a curse down upon themselves should they fail to honor the land's division:

> So be it and so let it be to them and to their sons forever in their generations until the day of judgment in which the LORD God will judge them with a sword and with fire on account of all the evil of the pollution of their errors which have filled the earth with sin and pollution and fornication and transgression.

Major enemies of Israel in the author's day, Javan (Greece, *Jub.* 9.10), Mizraim (Egypt, 9.1), and Canaan (9.1), each receive a portion of the earth and subscribe to the curse. In seeking to rule the land of Israel all three transgress the agreement and call the curse down upon themselves. The author specifically attaches this curse to Canaan (10.30) who early despised his own portion to settle in Palestine. Israel, as the seed of Shem, has clear title to the land of Canaan and has

---

1. *'ekuy* (or *'ekay*, see Charles, *Ethiopic*, 31) is better rendered 'evilly' or 'in an evil (manner)' with Wintermute (see Berger, 370, 'im Bösen') than 'secretly' with Charles (*Jubilees*, 68).

all the sanction of antiquity, heaven, and solemn curse on its side in battling the more recent incursions of Egypt and Greece. Similar curses, called down by Isaac, support Israel against the Philistines and the Edomites (24.28-33; 36.9-11).

VanderKam has argued that the accounts in *Jubilees* of the battles of Jacob against the Amorites and against Esau are retroversions of the battles of Judas Maccabeas against Antiochene Syria and Edom.[1] While his thesis is conjectural, it fits well the thrust of *Jubilees* against the enemies of Israel in the author's time. As Jacob's victory over the Amorites fulfills the curse against the Canaanites, so Jacob's victory over Esau fulfills the curse against Edom. As the curse was fulfilled in Jacob's days, so it is in Maccabean times. Maccabean Israel, in bringing these curses against Syria and Edom, begins to live like the patriarchs. The author writes *Jubilees* to encourage just such imitation of the progenitors of Israel. The author uses inspired history not only to urge such imitation, but also to show how it has already begun.

Jews of the author's time not only battled against foreign armies but also against foreign culture, especially hellenistic culture with its claims of Greek superiority. *Jubilees* reveals that real superiority belongs not to the Greeks but anciently to Shem and through Shem and Abraham to Israel.

Noah delights that Shem's portion of the earth includes three of God's dwellings, the Garden of Eden, Mt Sinai, and Mt Zion, in fulfillment of Noah's blessing on Shem (8.18-20; cf. 4.11-12). In coordination with the nearness of God, Shem receives from his father the books of remedies against Mastema and his evil spirits which were given to Noah by the angels at God's behest (10.10-14). Although the children of Shem desert God and at Babel lose ability to read the books, both these deficits are restored in Abraham who returns to God (11.16-17) and is taught Hebrew, the language of heaven and creation, by the angel who spoke with Moses (12.25-26). Instructed by the angel Abraham began to read the books of his fathers (12.27). He passed this wisdom to Isaac and Isaac to Jacob.[2] Jacob, to whom it was given to read and, by inspired memory, to transcribe heavenly tablets (32.21-26), handed the books over to the care of Levi. 'And he gave all of his books and his father's books to Levi, his son, so that he might preserve them and renew them for his sons until this day' (45.16). The vaunted culture of the Greeks, produced under the inspiration of demons

1. VanderKam, *Textual Studies*, 217-41.
2. Nowhere is this explicitly stated, but it is implied. Abraham exhorts his children by the words of Enoch and Noah (21.10). Joseph recalls what Jacob read to him from the words of Abraham (39.6).

(12.20; 15.31-32) and out of touch with the ancient wisdom written under the tutelage of angels, cannot compare with the true and ancient wisdom which belongs to Israel.[1]

Revelation concerning Noah's division of the land and concerning the heritage of ancient heavenly wisdom in Israel directly addresses problems in the author's own day. Isaac's curse of the Philistines (24.28-33) or his curse which falls on Esau and his sons when they violate the injunction of brotherly love (36.9-11) belong to the same use of revealed history. Such passages, by a revelation of heavenly and earthly complexes of past events, reveal the real nature of things in the author's present. The enemies of Israel—Greece, Egypt, various Canaanite tribes (Amorites-Syria), Edom, Philistines—look strong enough, but all lie under various longstanding curses. Greek culture may have a kind of flashy appeal, but it is produced since the flood under demons as a by-product of Noah 's sons' departure from the truth and has no root in reality or in antiquity.

Revelations of Exhortation

The overall purpose in *Jubilees* is to persuade Israel to keep the law in the author's day. Such a deliberative intent requires exhortation to keep the law as well as reasons to observe it. The author derives reasons to keep the law from its heavenly origin and its ancient institution. He exhorts through hortatory interjections into the narrative spoken by the angel and in the testamentary speeches attributed to the progenitors of Israel.

The testamentary speeches (Noah, 7.20-60; Abraham, chs. 20–21; Rebecca and Isaac, 35.1–36.18) provide an opportunity for the author to address his readers directly, since the testaments address the children of the various patriarchs or matriarchs who are speaking and the book of *Jubilees* addresses their children living in the author's present. In the speeches the implied audience coincides with that of the book as a whole.

To this power of direct address the testaments add the authority of a parent exhorting his or her children,[2] the authority of the speech of a respected figure of the past, and the authority of the figure's accumulated learning. Noah and Abraham exhort according to what they know from their fathers. The device of inspired history undergirds these speeches by making their claim to authenticity plausible and

---

1. Endres also argues that *Jubilees* opposes hellenizing Jews (J.C. Endres, *Biblical Interpretation in the Book of Jubilees* [CBQMS 18; Washington: CBA, 1987], 236-37).
2. See Wintermute, 38.

emphasizing their importance, as if to say, 'Not only did Abraham say these things and derive them from his father, but an angel of the presence singled them out as important for Moses to deliver them to us'.

When the angel himself exhorts Moses to warn the people, other devices are brought to bear. Of course the angel is backed by the authority of his heavenly position, but since he regularly exhorts by bringing out the heavenly significance of some law exemplified in or called forth by human action, his exhortations are at the same time interpretations of human history by heavenly principles. The angel shows how history is ruled by divine law—the same law being delivered to Moses—and therefore how important it is to keep it. The angel constructs an inspired view of history by his exhortation and undergirds his exhortation by his inspired view of history.

Revelations of the Future

Like the apocalypses, *Jubilees* combines historical revelations with revelations of the author's present and future. The author is clearly interested in the future and in how the determined plan of God touches his present, but in *Jubilees* the historical concern[1] has such strength that it relegates the eschatological sections to a subordinate though important role. Like the exhortations, the eschatological sections (chiefly 1.7-25 and 23.11-32) apply the historical material to the present. The historical material reveals how the law is inscribed in heaven and built into the fabric of history and of creation. It also contains exhortations to keep the law, found chiefly in the testamentary speeches. The eschatological material offers another reason to keep the law. The author's present marks the rise of a new generation which by seeking the law will bring in the age of blessing (23.26-27). Now it is more urgent than ever to keep the law, for the time of healing, when God will circumcise the hearts of his repentant children and create in them a holy spirit, is here (1.22-25).[2] The eschatological material establishes rapport with readers in the author's present and applies the

---

1. G.I. Davies classifies *Jubilees* an apocalypse. 'What may be said is that it is a member of the group in which the "historiographical" moment has the position of dominance that in some other apocalyptic works belongs to the eschatological one' (G.I. Davies, 'Apocalyptic and Historiography', *JSOT* 5 [1978], 21-22). Rowland (51-52) and, more hesitantly, Collins (45-46) place *Jubilees* among the apocalypses. See Testuz, 12.

2. See Wintermute, 47: 'The first concern of the eschatological passages in *Jubilees* is to teach that God is now about to restore a proper relationship with his people and to call the readers to obedience'.

revelation of law in history to them. The eschatological material in ch. 1 serves as a powerful and winning proem, introducing the theme of keeping the law in the context of God's gracious will to his people. God has not forsaken them (1.6) for all their sins, but will aid those seeking to keep the law in the present (1.23). In ch. 23 the eschatological material shows how those who seek the law in the author's present will fall heir to, and even surpass, the blessings of the patriarchs. Since both of these passages encourage that emulation of the patriarchs which the author seeks to teach, it is unnecessary to excise them as interpolations with Testuz and Davenport.[1]

Conclusion
Jubilees uses the device of revealed history to make several points. The author discloses the true significance of laws, feasts, and times by discovering their heavenly connections and ancient circumstances of establishment on earth. The inspired glance at the past also reveals the heavenly and ancient authority of the law, recommending it to the author's contemporaries. When disclosing the proper pattern of jubilees, it uncovers data about the past not previously known, enabling the proper calculation of sabbatical years in the present. In its consideration of Israel's present enemies and cultural status, the historical revelation reveals the ancient and heavenly parameters of the present situation; when retroverting present battles into ancient ones it shows how these ancient, heavenly parameters are presently operative. Most if not all of these functions of revealed history in *Jubilees* cast light on constituents of the author's present; they exhort, encourage, and enlighten the author's contemporaries. Since the heavenly and earthly acts of the past determine the present, revelation about the past reveals the obligations and privileges of Israelites in the author's day.

All of the uses of revealed history in *Jubilees* presuppose and issue from a particular aspect of the author's world view. The universe, whether heavenly or earthly, is a unity. What happens on earth affects what happens in heaven even to the extent of determining what happens on the heavenly tablets, and, of course, the heavenly tablets determine what happens on earth. Moral, natural, and historical law are nearly indistinguishable; human beings are to observe the sabbath in the same way as the sun keeps its course or as the events of history follow God's plan. To keep the law is to be at harmony with the natural, historical, moral, heavenly and earthly universe all at once.

---

1. Testuz, 41; Gene L. Davenport, *The Eschatology of the Book of Jubilees* (Leiden: Brill, 1971), 14-15, 19.

Actions of human beings determine the law just as the law determines
human action. Human actions become part of the natural, historical,
and moral unity as they are determined by it. Hence true history can
only be written by revelation, for only by revelation can the heavenly
and earthly natural, historical, and moral components of human action
be known.

According to *Jubilees*, one of the duties of the Levites was to preserve and renew the ancient books. Wintermute, noting the Levitical
connections of the work, remarks:

> If our author defines his own vocation at any point, it must be here. He
> undoubtedly saw himself as one of a chain of priestly writers going back
> to Levi. The idea of renewing ancestral books probably implied a license to
> do more than just make new copies. He was commissioned to bring
> ancient traditions up to date.[1]

That the author chooses to recast his traditions in the form of
prophetic history shows much about both his view of history and his
view of prophecy. The best history, showing the heavenly connections
and eternal significance of actions in the past, could only be known by
revelation; revelation directed toward the past seemed a natural form
of prophecy. His book uniquely combines a pervasive historical interest with an exaggerated claim for inspiration. His fusion of revelation
and history antedates that of Josephus by some 250 years.

Jubilees *and the* Jewish War *as Works of Prophetic History*

These two works of prophetic history attest the importance of revelation concerning the past for the writing of annals. For Josephus, the
revelation that Vespasian is the deliverer from Palestine and that God
is for the moment on the Roman side provides the perspective without
which the revolt and its subsequent suppression cannot be understood.
Jubilees requires revelation of the past to support the unity of heavenly
and earthly constituents which it finds for any past occurrence. As
different as these two writings are they both base a chronicle of past
events upon revelation.

Since such a chronicle can claim insight into the divine structuring
of the past, each writing assumes that its depiction of the past throws
light on important components of the present. Josephus' revelation at
Jotapata not only serves as the basis for understanding events of the
Jewish War but also urges collaboration with the Romans as the present duty of his nation. *Jubilees* grounds commands, exhortations, and

---

1. Wintermute, 45.

encouragements for the present on the glimpse into the structure of the universe afforded by its revelation of the past. Prophetic history is thus a deliberative rhetorical technique; one means among others for persuading one's contemporaries to a particular course of action.

Each work shows willingness to interpret or rewrite history on the basis of the insight provided by revelation. *Jubilees*, because of the higher concept of revelation implied by inspired prophetic history, can rewrite the tradition it has received from the Pentateuch and presumably also from other sources. It can add speeches and incidents as well as reshape received material on the basis of its insight into the heavenly and earthly components of events already well known to its audience. The resulting narrative shows the significance and application of each of these well-known incidents to the author's community. The device of prophetic history updates older historical material and makes it relevant to the situation of the author's contemporaries by its fresh interpretation of the past. Josephus is heavily influenced by Greek rhetoric and the Greek genre of historical writing which require that he prove his thesis by recounting events in such a way as to support it. But Josephus has received his thesis for the *Jewish War* by revelation. Therefore, in showing how events suit his thesis he bares the divine order which shaped the past and determines the present and future. So sure is Josephus of this divine order that he also, when he touches on received tradition, is able to rewrite it. His speeches before Jerusalem show every bit as much freedom in reshaping historical traditions of his people as does *Jubilees*. It should be assumed that Josephus' narration of the events he has experienced, while broadly accurate, has been shaped by the thesis he received by revelation at Jotapata.[1]

Jubilees and the *Jewish War* illustrate the use of revelation in the ancient Jewish practice of writing history. To include both writings, the term 'history' must be construed loosely. Interpretive prophetic history is more compatible with modern views of historiography than is inspired prophetic history. Few would dispute that Josephus is a historian. Few would claim that title for the author of *Jubilees*. Yet despite their wide divergence in purpose, style, and technique, both authors turn to revelation to clarify the divine order behind past events. *Jubilees* and the *Jewish War* show over how wide a spectrum revelation was considered important for chronicling the past. Together

---

1. *Jubilees* and the *Jewish War* are what Mendels calls 'creative histories' (D. Mendels, '"Creative History" in the Hellenistic Near East in the Third and Second Centuries BCE: The Jewish Case', *JSP* 2 [1988], 13-20).

they justify positing prophetic history as a category of ancient Jewish history writing.

Chapter 3

INSPIRED HISTORICAL SERMONS

Judith, Pseudo-Philo (*Liber Antiquitatum Biblicarum*), and Josephus (*Jewish War*) place in the mouths of prophetic figures historical speeches which follow a common form.[1] These speeches divide neatly into two parts. (1) God, an angel, or an inspired person recounts past events, then (2) draws some conclusion from them. In the first part (the historical résumé) the more finely honed examples begin to make an intelligible point by themselves. The second part, the consequence, clearly expresses the main point of the speech, grounding it squarely on the historical evidence presented in the résumé. Speeches in this form with a claim to inspiration will be called inspired historical sermons.[2] For the sake of brevity I will occasionally call them sermons or historical sermons.

Ezekiel

Inspired historical sermons did not first appear within the period of time covered by this study (200 BCE–130 CE). Three sterling examples occur in Ezekiel (chs. 16, 20, 23). Each of these three prophecies

1. Other examples of this form occur in Dan. 5.17-28 and *4 Ezra* 14.23-35 and are treated in the chapters devoted to these books.
2. Speeches in this form have been noticed and loosely defined earlier. Eissfeldt includes them along with speeches which would not qualify as inspired historical sermons under his category of sermons. See Otto Eissfeldt, *The Old Testament: An Introduction* (trans. Peter R. Ackroyd; New York: Harper and Row, 1965). Thyen would include many of these in his Jewish-hellenistic homilies but does not note the relation between consequence and historical review or the connection to prophecy. See Helmut Thyen, *Der Stil der jüdisch-hellenistischen Homilie* (FRLANT 47; Göttingen: Vandenhoeck & Ruprecht, 1955). Inspired historical sermons are a subset of the forms isolated by these authors. Kliesch calls similar speeches in Acts Salvation-Historical Credos, confessions of faith concerning what God has done in history analogous to Deut. 26.5-10, but has not noted their tie to prophecy or the connection of consequence between the two parts. See K. Kliesch, *Das heilsgeschichtliche Credo in den Reden der Apostelgeschichte* (BBB 44; Köln-Bonn: Hanstein, 1975).

draws a similar consequence from the historical review. On the basis of the sinful propensity of Israel revealed in the historical résumé, God sentences the people to exile, purification, and redemption. The three passages are outlined side by side as follows.

	Ezekiel 16	*Ezekiel 20*	*Ezekiel 23*
Preamble	Make known her abominations (16.2).	I will not be inquired of by you. Let them (know their father's) abominations (20.3-4).	
Historical Résumé	16.3-34 Say 'Thus says the Lord God to Jerusalem' (16.3).	20.5-29 'Say to them, "Thus says the Lord God"' (20.5).	23. 2-21
	God saves Jerusalem at her birth (16.3-7).	Israel in Egypt (20.5). a. God's call (5-6). b. God's command (7). c. Israel's rebellion (8a).	God marries two lecherous sisters (Samaria and Jerusalem) in Egypt (23.2-4).
	God marries Jerusalem (16.8-14).		
	Jerusalem's initial unfaithfulness (16.15-22).		The first commits adultery with Assyrians. God delivers her over to her lovers and they slay her (23.5-10).
	Jerusalem's aggravated unfaithfulness with Egyptians, Assyrians, and Chaldeans (16.23-29).	Israel in the wilderness: first generation (20.8b–13a) a. God's thought of wrath rejected for the sake of his name (8b-9). b. God's act in Exodus (10). c. God's command (11-12). d. Israel's rebellion (13a).	The second multiplies adulteries with the Assyrians and the Chaldeans but turns from them longing for her former lovers in Egypt (23.11-21).
	Jerusalem's behavior more scandalous than a harlot's since she hires her lovers (16.30-34).		
		Israel in the wilderness: second generation (20.13b-21a).	

a. God's thought of wrath rejected for the sake of his name (13b-14).
b. God's judgment: They shall not enter the land but I shall not destroy them (15-17).
c. God's command to their children (18-20).
d. Their rebellion (21a).
Israel from the wilderness to Ezekiel's present (20.21b-29).
a. God's thought of wrath rejected for the sake of his name (21b-22).
b. God's judgment: I will scatter them (23-24).
c. Give them over to misleading statutes since they have rejected mine (25-26).
d. Again your fathers rebelled, this time with the high places (27-29).

Consequence: a Sentence	16.35-42	20.30-43	23.22-34
	'Wherefore, O Harlot, Hear the word of the Lord . . .' (16.35).	'Wherefore, say to the houses of Israel, "Thus says the Lord your God . . ." ' (20.30).	'Therefore, O Oholibah, "Thus says the Lord God . . ." ' (23.22).
	Because of your iniquities (16.36).	I will not be inquired of by you (20.30-31).	God will bring your lovers the Babylonians against

	I will give you to your lovers who will overthrow you (16.37-42).	You shall never be a nation worshiping idols like other countries (20.32).	you (23.22-31). You shall have your sister's cup (23.32-34).
		I will rule over you, bring you back to the wilderness of the exile to judge and purge you (20.33-38).	
		Worship idols if you wish, but only the faithful will return and worship me as my people in Zion (20.39-43).	
Concluding Summary	Because you have enraged me, I will requite these things on your head (16.43).	You will know that I am God when I deal with you for my name, not according to your deeds (20.44).	Because you have forgotten me, bear the consequences of your lewdness (23.35).
Further Amplification in the Form of a Second Historical Sermon[1]	Historical résumé (16.43-52). Consequence: a sentence (16.53-63)		Historical résumé (23.36-44). Consequence: a sentence (23.45-49)

For the purposes of describing the inspired historical sermon as a form, it is sufficient to observe the connection between the historical résumé and its consequence. In each of these passages from Ezekiel the historical résumé justifies the action God proposes in the consequence. Because Judah has invariably rewarded God's grace with disobedience, God sentences his people to exile and restoration. In rhetorical terms, an inspired historical sermon always takes the form of an expanded epicheireme of the form, 'x has occurred, therefore y'. Of course, both x and y may be complex.

---

1. Although these amplifications are in form inspired historical sermons, their historical content is not clearly defined. They are mentioned only because of their close relation to the preceding.

In addition to serving as excellent formal examples of the inspired historical sermon, these sections of Ezekiel well illustrate one of its subspecies. Any inspired historical sermon in which God or his agent rehearses history to justify a sentence passed upon an offender I will designate as judicial. In the form '*x* has occurred, therefore *y*', *x* represents misdeeds of an offender perhaps amplified by depictions of the goodness of the one offended or by other material, and *y* represents a sentence passed against the offender.[1]

Ezekiel uses the form with flexibility and power. Through the allegory of chs. 16 and 23 and the repetitive pattern of ch. 20, the historical résumés render the consequence inevitable even before it is explicitly drawn. In two cases (16 and 23) a second judicial historical sermon amplifies the effect of the first.

Liber Antiquitatum Biblicarum

Many less sophisticated inspired historical sermons in the judicial mode occur in *Liber Antiquitatum Biblicarum*.[2] In 15.5-6 God speaks such a judicial sermon against the people who have refused to enter the land because of the terrifying report of the spies. Although God converses with Moses, his speech justifies to the patriarchs the delay in entering the land.

Historical Résumé	Behold this is the seed to which I have spoken, saying, '*Your seed will stay a while in a land not its own, and I will judge the*
God's grace	*nation whom it will serve*'. And I fulfilled my words and made their enemies melt away and set the angels beneath their feet and placed the cloud as the covering for their head. And I commanded the sea, and when the abyss was divided before them, walls of water stood forth. And there was never anything like this event since the day I said, '*Let the waters under the heaven be gathered together into one place*', until this day. And I brought them forth, but I killed their enemies. And I brought them before me to Mt Sinai, and I bent the heavens and came down to kindle a lamp for my people and to establish

---

1. Theoretically a judicial inspired historical sermon might support the defense instead of the prosecution. Thus *x* would represent an exonerating historical account and *y* a statement of innocence. I am not aware of a good example of such a judicial sermon for the defense in sources from Judaism, but see Mt. 25.34-39 and certain speeches in Acts.

2. Dated right before 70 CE by Pierre Bogaert, 'La Datation', *Pseudo Philon: Les Antiquités Bibliques* 2 (ed. D.J. Harrington *et al*, SC 230; Paris: Cerf, 1976), 74. D.J. Harrington thinks the most likely date is 'around the time of Jesus' ('Pseudo-Philo', *OTP* 2.299).

	laws for creation. And I taught them to make sanctuaries for me that I might dwell in them (15.5b-6a).
People's sin	But they abandoned me and did not believe my words, and their mind grew weak (15.6b).
Consequence: a Sentence	And now behold the days will come, and I will do to them as they wished, and I will cast forth *their bodies in the wilderness* (15.6c).[1]

The historical résumé follows a pattern found in several judicial sermons in *LAB*. God first speaks of his grace at length to make the people's rebellion all the more heinous when it is mentioned. The same pattern, a lengthy amplification of God's grace preceding a brief allusion to sin, occurs in the historical résumé of a judicial sermon put in the mouth of Samuel (*LAB* 53.8-10).

Historical Résumé	And God said to him, 'I have indeed enlightened the house of Israel in Egypt and have chosen for myself then as a prophet Moses my servant and have done wonders through him for my people and have taken revenge on my enemies as I wished. And I brought my people into the wilderness and enlightened them as they looked on. And when one tribe rose up against another, saying, "Why are the priests alone holy?" I did not wish to destroy them and I said to them, "Have each one present his staff, and he whose staff will flower—him I have chosen for the priesthood". And when all had handed in the staffs as I had commanded, then I commanded the ground where the tent of meeting was that the staff of Aaron should flower in order that his family be made manifest all the days' (53.8-9a).
God's grace to priests	
Sin of priests	'And now those who have flowered have defiled my holy things' (53.9b).
Consequence: a Sentence	'Therefore behold the days will come, and I will trample on the flower that was born then and will stop them who transgress the word that I have commanded Moses my servant, saying, "*If you come upon a bird's nest, you shall not take the mother with young*". So it will happen to them that mothers will die with daughters and fathers will perish with sons' (53.10).

The consequence, which as in all inspired historical sermons gains its rationale from the historical résumé, here is reinforced by an appeal to Mosaic law. A variation in the pattern occurs in the judicial sermon found in *LAB* 44.6-15. This prophecy contains God's response

---

1. All quotations of *LAB* are from Harrington, 297-377.

to the sinful worship inaugurated by Micah (Judg. 17). Since it is too long to quote in full, there follows an outline of its contents. God is speaking.

Preamble	I will root out the human race because. . .
Historical Résumé	God gave the law on Sinai to which the people assented (*LAB* 44.6). Yet the people have made idols, profaned God's name and the Sabbath. The author turns some commands of the Decalogue to the service of his accusations concerning idolatry (44.7).
Consequence: a Sentence	A sentence against the human race, Jacob, Benjamin, and Israel for following Micah. Micah and his mother also receive sentence (44.9—first sentence in 10).
A Second Consequence (deduced from the historical prophecy)	Let the human race know that they cannot get away with provoking me with their sins (remainder of 44.10).

In this speech, a judicial sermon (*LAB* 44.6-9) with its own historical résumé (*LAB* 44.6-7) and consequent sentence (*LAB* 44.8-9), supplies the premises of a yet larger epicheireme with its conclusion in *LAB* 44.10. The judicial sermon justifies God's sentence against Benjamin, Micah, and Israel. The author of *LAB*, who is about to record the outworking of the sentence, views the sentence itself as having already occurred. Indeed it does lie in his past and in the past of his readers. Both he and they are quite familiar with the historical events stemming from it. Therefore, he builds a second inspired historical sermon which utilizes both the historical résumé and the consequent sentence of the judicial sermon as its own historical résumé and which draws its own consequence from God's dealings with the sin of Micah and all of its ramifications. At first the larger sermon also seems to be judicial. Its consequence contains several sentences, 'If they do this I will do this.' Yet the historical résumé of the larger sermon is not used to justify these as sentences but to show how God habitually works. The consequence reaches an inductive conclusion: 'As God requited the sin of Micah, so will he requite your sin. What you sow you shall reap.' Since the historical résumé of the larger sermon does not justify a sentence God intends to carry out, but inductively grounds a principle by which God governs the world, it does not qualify as judicial but belongs to a different group.

I am inclined to call this second group 'inductive historical sermons'. In these inspired historical sermons, the consequence follows from the historical résumé by induction and seeks to establish some general principle of God's working. Since other kinds of sermons may reason inductively to a general principle, what this definition leaves out is as important as what it contains. An inductive inspired historical sermon seeks to do no more than establish a general principle. If it inductively establishes a principle from history in order to support some other end such as exhortation, it is no longer an inductive sermon.

LAB contains another example of the inductive form. After seeking and receiving inspiration in a night vision, Joshua speaks to the people (*LAB* 23.3-13).

Historical Résumé	The righteousness of Abraham and the promises bestowed in his vision (23.4-8).
	Accordingly Isaac is born and Jacob goes to Egypt and is enslaved (23.8-9a).
	I remembered your fathers, sent Moses and delivered you by mighty deeds, gave you my law and cities to dwell in (23.9b 11a).
	I fulfilled the covenant which I spoke to your fathers (23.11b).
Consequence: an Induction	If you obey, I will set my heart on you forever. . . The consequence is mainly a series of promises (23.12-13).

As God richly blessed your fathers according to the promises given righteous Abraham, so God will richly fulfill these promises he gives to you if you obey him. The historical résumé undergirds the consequence by an inductive train of reasoning. God's future faithfulness is supported by his faithfulness in the past.[1]

A final form of the inspired historical sermon had gained rather wide currency in the first century. Hortative sermons base exhortation upon a historical résumé. The historical review offers reasons urging the action advocated in the consequence. They follow the form 'Since x has occurred, do y', where x and y can be complex. *LAB* contains one sermon which may be classified as hortative (18.5-6). The prophecy is addressed to Balaam urging him not to seek to curse the Israelites.

---

1. In *LAB* Deborah's victory song has the form of an inspired historical sermon. The historical résumé (32.1-11) offers reasons for the praise in the consequence (32.12-17). This song would characterize an epideictic sermon were the claim to inspiration more explicit.

Historical Résumé	And he said to him, 'Is it not regarding this people that I spoke to Abraham in a vision, saying, "*Your seed will be like the stars of the heaven*", when I lifted him above the firmament. . . until *he blessed him*' (18.5-6a).
Consequence: an Exhortation	'And do you propose *to go forth with them to curse* whom I have chosen? But if you curse them, who will be there to bless you?' (18.6b).

Although the consequence does not contain a command or recommendation but a threat, the clear purpose of the speech is to deter Balaam from going with the messengers from Balak (cf. the beginning of 18.7). Since the historical résumé offers reasons to dissuade Balaam from a particular action, this is a hortative sermon.

Judith

At first glance Achior's speech (Jud. 5.5-21) does not look like a prophecy of any kind. Since Achior as king of the Ammonites is a traditional enemy of the Jews, he seems an unlikely candidate to speak for the God of heaven. No claim to inspiration occurs in the speech or in the text immediately surrounding it. Yet Holofernes accuses Achior of prophesying falsely, 'And who are you, Achior, and you hirelings of Ephraim, to prophesy among us as you have done today and tell us not to make war against the people of Israel because their God will defend them?' (Jud. 6.2). Closer inspection reveals further prophetic constituents of the scene. Achior's speech contributes to a deliberation for war. In Hebrew thought this is a classic situation for prophetic activity as in the deliberations before Ahab and Jehosaphat (1 Kgs 22).[1] Indeed the deliberations for war in Judith 5–6 seem modeled on those in 1 Kings 22. In both scenes the question concerns the advisability of fighting in a particular situation. As the false prophet, Zedekiah son of Chenaanah, urges to fight, so Holofernes, prophet of the god Nebuchadnezzar (cf. Jud. 6.2), argues for attacking the Jews. His speech even concludes with a parody of a Hebrew prophetic formula, 'So says King Nebuchadnezzar, the lord of the whole earth. For he has spoken; none of his words shall be in vain' (Jud. 6.4).[2] As Micaiah ben Imlah warns against the engagement, so Achior

1. See Erich Zenger, *Das Buch Judith* (JSHRZ 1.6; Gütersloh: Mohn, 1981), 475 n. 2b.
2. Holofernes also parodies Israelite hymnic speech. Compare Jud. 6.2, 'Who is God but Nebuchadnezzar?', with Ps. 18.31, 'Who is God but the Lord?' (Ernst Haag, *Studien zum Buch Judith. Seine theologische Bedeutung und literarische Eigenart* [Trierer Theologische Studien 16; Trier: Paulinus, 1963], 34).

prophesies against attacking the Jews. As Micaiah is rewarded with imprisonment until the King of Israel returns in peace (1 Kgs 26–28)—Ahab certainly intended to kill him when his words proved false—so Achior is handed over to the Jews that he might perish with them when his words prove false (Jud. 6.5-9). The conclusion of the speech is reminiscent of the advice of Balaam, another Gentile prophet.[1] It is probably justifiable to regard Achior's speech as a prophecy; it is certain that Achior's speech follows a prophetic form.

If a prophecy, it is clearly a hortative historical sermon. The historical résumé offers reasons why Holofernes should not attack the Jews.

Proem	'Let my Lord now hear a word from the mouth of your servant, and I will tell you the truth about this people that dwells in the nearby mountain district. No falsehood shall come from your servant's mouth' (Jud. 5.5).
Historical Résumé	Judith 5.6-19. The Hebrews turned to a peculiar God (5.6-8). He blessed them (5.9-10). He delivered them mightily from oppression in Egypt (5.11-14). He gave them a land (5.14-16). When righteous they prospered. When unrighteous, they suffered defeat and deportation (5.17-18). Lately they have repented and returned to God and their sanctuary in Jerusalem (5.19).
Consequence: an Exhortation	'Now therefore, my master and lord, if there is any unwitting error in this people and they sin against their God and we find out their offense, then we will go up and defeat them. But if there is no transgression in their nation, then let my lord pass them by for their Lord will defend them, and their God will protect them, and we shall be put to shame before the whole world' (5.20-21).

Since the historical résumé supports an exhortation, Achior's speech is a hortative sermon.

The Jewish War

The first speech of Josephus before the walls of Jerusalem (*J.W.* 5.8.4 §§375-419) and its claim to inspiration have already been discussed in the section on Josephus. It remains only to question whether, despite certain distinctive features, it is not a hortative inspired historical sermon.

Its present form, whether due to Josephus himself or his Greek secretaries, fits well the categories of classical rhetoric. Josephus opens

---

1. See Num. 31.16 and especially *LAB* 18.13; Josephus, *Ant.* 4.6.6 §129.

with a proem of the kind known as the direct approach which contains
the proposition for the speech: 'Ah miserable wretches, unmindful of
your own true allies, would you make war on the Romans with arms
and might of hand? What other foe have we conquered thus, and when
did God who created, fail to avenge, the Jews, if they were wronged?'
Josephus intends to urge the Jews in Jerusalem to lay down their arms
by arguing that the Hebrew race has never gained victory by force.
Josephus turns to a series of topics taken from Jewish history designed
to show how God delivered the people without arms, and how
whenever they took up arms they were defeated. He also argues from
the relative righteousness of the Romans and the relative sinfulness of
the Jews that God is now on the Roman side. Josephus closes with a
peroration urging the Jews to confess their sins and, by surrendering,
to repent. The following diagram analyses this interesting speech both
as a classical deliberative oration and as a hortative sermon.

Proem	Jews gain victory not by might of arms but by the power of God (*J.W.* 5.8.4 §§376-78).	Proem
Historical Résumé	I. Refusal to use force in reliance on God implies victory (*J.W.* 5.8.4 §§379-90).	Topics
	a. Abraham did not use force when Sarah was carried off by Necho (5.8.4 §§379-81).	
	b. The fathers who were delivered from Egypt refrained from the use of arms (5.8.4 §§382-83).	
	c. The ark was returned by the Philistines without resort to weapons (5.8.4 §§384-86).	
	d. Sennacherib was overthrown when hands were raised in prayer not in arms (5.8.4 §387-88).	
	e. Exiles in Babylon did not fight but were freed by Cyrus in his gratitude to God (5.8.4 §389).	
	f. Summary transition: 'In short, there is no instance of our forefathers having triumphed by arms or failed of success without them when they committed their cause to God; if they sat still they conquered as pleased their Judge, if they fought they were invariably defeated' (*J.W.* 5.8.4 §390).	
	II. Armed resistance implies defeat (*J.W.* 5.8.4 §§391-400).	
	a. Zedekiah, disregarding Jeremiah's warnings, gave battle to the king of Babylon and was defeated. Josephus likens himself to Jeremiah (5.8.4 §391-93).	

b. The Jews fought Antiochus Epiphanes but were miserably defeated though Antiochus had mocked God (5.8.4 §394).

c. The Romans themselves under Pompey besieged Jerusalem and conquered when the Jews fought (5.8.4 §395-97).

d. When the Jews fought Rome under Antigonus, Jerusalem again was sacked by Rome (5.8.4 §398).

e. Summary transition: 'Thus invariably have arms been refused to our nation, and warfare has been the sure signal of defeat. For it is, I suppose, the duty of the occupants of holy ground to leave everything to the arbitrament of God and to scorn the aid of human hands, can they but conciliate the Arbiter above' (5.8.4 §§399-400).

III. Weighing sins of the Jews and the Romans (5.8.4 §§401-14).

a. You have outraged God, polluted the Temple, etc. (5.8.4 §§401-403).

b. Romans have been relatively righteous (5.8.4 §§404-406).

c. God delivered early, when he saved the city—unlike the case with Pompey, Sossius, Vespasian, and Titus All this succeeded and even now the springs, which had dried for you flow for Titus as they did for the Babylonians when they took the city (5.8.4 §§407-11).

d. Summary transition: 'My belief, therefore, is that the Deity has fled from the holy places and taken his stand on the side of those with whom you are at war' (5.8 .4 §§412-14).

Consequence: an Exhortation

'Yet a way of salvation is still left you, if you will: and the Deity is easily reconciled to such as confess and repent. Oh! iron-hearted men, fling away your weapons, take compassion on your country even now tottering to its fall, turn round and behold the beauty of what you are betraying: what a city! what a Temple! what countless nations' gifts! Against these would any man direct the flames? Is there any who wishes that these should be no more? What could be more worthy of preservation than these—ye relentless creatures, more insensible than stone! Yet if you look not on these with the

Peroration

> eyes of genuine affection, at least have pity on
> your families, and let each set before his eyes
> his children, wife and parents, ere long to be the
> victims either of famine or of war. I know that I
> have a mother, a wife, a not ignoble family, and
> an ancient and illustrious house involved in
> these perils; and maybe you think that it is on
> their account that my advice is offered. Slay
> them, take my blood as the price of your own
> salvation! I too am prepared to die, if my death
> will lead to your learning wisdom' (*J.W.* 5.8.4
> §§415-19).

Josephus has cast his speech in a form perfectly acceptable to an
educated Greek reader. The Greeks frequently employed historical
illustrations in deliberative oratory. Yet Josephus has also remained
faithful to his Jewish models. He interprets Jewish history to make his
points and considers the past sins of his people and of the Romans
squarely in the tradition of the inspired historical sermon. Since the
historical résumé provides grounds for the exhortation in the
consequence, Josephus employs the hortative form.

Inspired Historical Sermons and Revealed History

Like other kinds of inspired glances at the past, inspired historical
sermons use the past to inform the present. The shift to the present is
sharp, explicit, and direct and takes the form of a consequence drawn
from the preceding historical revelation. The consequence can be one
of at least three kinds. In the judicial sermon the consequence is a
sentence; in the inductive sermon, a regular pattern; in the hortatory
sermon, an exhortation. In every case the history is contoured around
the consequence so that the consequence follows naturally from it. This
reshaping of the historical material may, as with the speeches of
Josephus or Ezekiel, involve far-reaching reinterpretation of events,
or it may take up a more standard interpretation of events as in *LAB*
or Judith. Since the goal of the whole prophecy is the readers'
acceptance of the consequence and since acceptance of the consequence
turns on acceptance of the interpretation of history, the historical
revelation is of prime importance. The claim to inspiration, important
as it is to the prophecy as a whole, is especially important in under-
girding this interpretation of history by a powerful ethos. Inspired
historical sermons are another form of historical revelation.

Chapter 4

APOCALYPTIC WORLD HISTORIES

Although the topic is somewhat neglected in works on apocalypticism of the last century, apocalyptists show a substantial interest in history.[1] Tabulated by numbers of words alone, apocalyptic portrayals of the past frequently tend to exceed in length apocalyptic portrayals of the future.[2] Since apocalypses characteristically claim to be revelations (ἀποκάλυψις) they promise to produce many examples of inspired history.[3] Several apocalypses recount events of the past before considering the present and future. Any vision report, vision and interpretation, or report of a heavenly trip which begins by recounting events in the apocalyptist's past before moving to the present and future will be called an apocalyptic history. There are at least two kinds of apocalyptic history. (1) Apocalyptic histories which review world history from creation to consummation, such as *1 Enoch* 83–90, *2 Baruch* 53–74, and the *Apocalypse of Abraham* 21–32, shall be called apocalyptic world histories. (2) Apocalyptic histories, such as those in Daniel, which review a segment of world history shall be called limited apocalyptic histories. This chapter will consider apocalyptic world histories, and the next will consider limited apocalyptic histories.

The initial justification for considering *1 Enoch* 83–90, *2 Baruch* 53–74, and *Apocalypse of Abraham* 21–32 together rests on their subject matter. Each relates a more or less complete world history from creation to consummation. Of course each organizes its

1. But see G.I. Davies, 'Apocalyptic and Historiography', *JSOT* 5 (1978), 15-28; John J. Collins, ed., *Apocalypse: The Morphology of a Genre* (Semeia 14; Missoula, MT: Scholars Press, 1979); Christopher Rowland, *The Open Heaven: A Study of Apocalyptic in Judaism and Early Christianity* (New York: Crossroad, 1982), 136-55.

2. Rowland, 137.

3. What I call 'apocalyptic histories' are sometimes called 'historical apocalypses'. I reserve 'historical apocalypse' to designate a whole work. 'Apocalyptic histories' may be part of a larger work.

presentation of world history according to its own principles and each uses world history to answer its own questions and to address its own situation. I shall examine how each of these apocalyptic world histories uses revealed history and then draw some more general conclusions concerning the use of revealed history in them.

1 Enoch 83–90

The Book of Dreams (*1 En.* 83–90), which reports two dream visions Enoch received before his marriage, contains one of the earliest and most extensive apocalyptic reviews of history. In the first dream he sees the earth destroyed and Mahalalel, his grandfather, receives the interpretation: all the sin of the earth must sink to destruction in the abyss. After praying that a righteous remnant might be spared, Enoch receives a second dream vision, the Animal Apocalypse, which portrays human history allegorically. Human beings are depicted as various animals, and angels are depicted as stars or men. There seems little reason to doubt the section's unity.[1] In all probability its author wrote during the early success of Judas Maccabeus to support the Maccabean cause.[2]

The components of revealed history clearly belong to the Animal Apocalypse. Enoch recounts it as a revelation given to him in a dream (85.1-3; 90.40-42). After recounting his vision Enoch describes the content of his revelation, 'All the deeds of men in their order were shown to me' (90.41).[3] Since the apocalyptist has written concerning all the 'deeds of men' from Adam to the messiah in the new Jerusalem, and since the whole vision is portrayed as a revelation, it is reasonable to conclude that the author was as interested in revelation about the past as about the future. The Animal Apocalypse contains revealed

1. Most authors assume its unity. See R.H. Charles, *The Book of Enoch* (Oxford: Clarendon, 1912), 179; James C. VanderKam, *Enoch and the Growth of an Apocalyptic Tradition* (CBQMS 16; Washington, DC: Catholic Biblical Association, 1984), 161; Barnabas Lindars thinks the dream visions circulated separately (Lindars, 'A Bull, a Lamb, and a Word: 1 Enoch XC.38', *NTS* 22 [1976], 483-84).

2. Charles, *Enoch*, 182; Josef T. Milik with Matthew Black, *The Books of Enoch: Aramaic Fragments of Qumrân Cave 4* (Oxford: Clarendon, 1976), 44.

3. In context, 'Everything will come to pass and be fulfilled; and all the deeds of men in their order were shown to me' (90.41). Although the context contains an allusion to Enoch's future, most of the events referred to are in the real author's past. The reference to Enoch's future expresses the certainty of the vision, not its content. The vision's content is described as 'all the deeds of men in their order'. I have used Knibb's translation except where noted. See Michael A. Knibb with Eduard Ullendorf, *The Ethiopic Book of Enoch*, II (Oxford: Clarendon, 1978).

history. What situation does the apocalyptist seek to address with this revelation about the past?

There are several clues. Various characters in the apocalypse express the author's own feelings and ideas. The interpretation Mahalalel gives Enoch's first dream (83.7-9) expresses the author's fears for his own time and his solution to them. Neither Mahalalel nor the apocalyptist can doubt that the sins of the earth must be destroyed in the abyss. For Mahalalel facing the deluge and for the apocalyptist under the persecutions of Antiochus IV, the possibility is very real that even the righteous will not survive. It may be assumed that Mahalalel's solution is the same as the author's: let believers pray that a remnant be left.

Enoch then voices the prayer. He begins his prayer with praise (84.2-4), concurs with God's plan of judgment (84.4), and makes his request, 'And now, my Lord, wipe out from the earth the flesh which has provoked you to anger, but the flesh of righteousness and uprightness establish as a seed-bearing plant forever' (84.6). Certainly this is just the prayer the apocalyptist wants to make as he sees judgment falling not on the wicked but upon the righteous in the days of Antiochus Epiphanes.[1]

The author himself indicates how well this prayer fits his own day. Enoch, who watched the deluge with equanimity although it had originally called forth his prayer,[2] cries out and groans at the inception of the period of Israel's distress in which the apocalyptist lives (89.67, 70). The recording and delivering angel, probably Michael,[3] throughout the period of Israel's trial repeatedly shows God how righteous sheep are destroyed (89.70, 76) and, in an echo of Enoch's earlier prayer, implores that God intervene and spare those sheep not appointed for destruction (89.76). Thus the concern over the destruction of the righteous with which the Book of Dreams commences echoes the author's concern for his own day. One of the fears faced by this apocalypse is God's indifference to the extermination of the righteous.[4]

The apocalypse addresses this rhetorical problem not only by revelations about the future, but also by revelations about the past. The

1. The prayer's answer is the Animal Apocalypse which promises that, throughout history, God will preserve a remnant (VanderKam, 170).
2. The 'great day of judgment' (84.4) is the deluge (Charles, 85; VanderKam, 121).
3. See Charles, 201.
4. See Charles, 181, 200 for a similar analysis of the problem facing the apocalyptist.

apocalypse reveals the correct division of world history into periods or ages under differing administrations and conditions.[1] The apocalyptist consoles and encourages the righteous, afflicted as they are, by properly distinguishing the ages according to the revelation given him.

A conscious parallelism is drawn between the judgment at the flood and that judgment culminating in the days of Antiochus.[2] In both cases the righteous face destruction with the wicked, the sin which clamors for judgment is both human and angelic, destruction comes upon both the human and angelic agents of evil, and the righteous remnant is saved. Thus the first answer given by the Animal Apocalypse is based upon revealed history. An inspired perception of the apocalyptist's recent past coupled with an inspired perception of the antediluvian past reveals the similarities of the two ages. As God delivered a righteous remnant in the earlier age so he will in the later.

The previous example illustrates how the apocalypse consoles the righteous by juxtaposing similar ages; it also seeks to encourage by distinguishing dissimilar ages. The righteous of the apocalyptist's day are keenly aware that the pattern enunciated in the Deuteronomic History no longer works. Repentance no longer leads to an intervention of God on Israel's behalf. An inspired glimpse at occurrences in the heavenly realm can explain the silence of God by showing a change in heavenly administration, a turning over of the ages which was quite invisible without the benefit of revelation. In the earlier period of Israel's history God personally shepherded Israel, rewarding the righteous and judging the wicked, but now Israel is shepherded by the seventy angels of the nations.[3] The angelic

---

1. While the apocalypse as a whole speaks eloquently of this concern to divide history into ages, at one point that concern may be explicit. Knibb translates 90.41, 'All the deeds of men in their order were shown to me'. The last phrase, 'in their order' (*baba keflu*) is literally 'according to its division'. Ephraim Isaac ('1 [Ethiopic Apocalypse of] Enoch', *OTP* 1.72) translates 'each according to its type', presumably referring to different kinds of deeds. A third possibility better fits the content of the vision. The seer claims to have received a revelation concerning the proper division of human activity: 'Every work of man in its division was shown to me.' His vision reveals what human deeds fit under each administration or age in history. The divisions of human deeds refer to the different periods of history revealed in the apocalypse. The title to *Jubilees* uses the same root (*kufālē*) to refer to divisions of time.

2. Nickelsburg, *Jewish Literature between the Bible and the Mishnah*, 91.

3. While some still hold that the shepherds represent human figures, Charles argued very persuasively that they were angels (Charles, *Enoch*, 200). Most interpreters follow Charles. For the contrary view see Stephen Breck Reid, '1 Enoch: The Rising Elite of the Apocalyptic Movement', *SBLSP* 22 (1983), 154.

shepherds prove unfaithful to their commission, hence the lack of justice in the present age.[1] Once again the apocalypse consoles with revelation about the past.

According to Enoch's revelation the world has just or is just about to roll over into the next age. Already God has begun to intervene, the last battle and the judgment are near. Once again the righteous can count on God's help. They can fight under Judas Maccabeus confident of God's intervention as of old. Here, of course, the apocalypse moves into encouraging by a revelation of the future,[2] but the revelation of the future derives its punch from a revelation about the past. The revelation about the past age under the angelic shepherds allows the author both to explain the previous experience of the righteous and to encourage them to act out of step with their experience. Yes, God had not helped them, but now the age was changing. Their old experience no longer held true.

Quite apart from the interplay between the ages, the revelation about the instatement of the seventy shepherds consoles the righteous. Not God, but the shepherds are responsible for the long reign of injustice. What appeared to be evil really is. They can resist the shepherds and their Gentile henchmen secure in the knowledge that, despite appearances, God will reward them.

These examples show how important the revealed reinterpretation of the past is to the purpose of the apocalypse. A further consideration illustrates how central revelation about the past is to the apocalyptist's understanding of history. As Daniel 9 witnesses, Jeremiah 25 had imposed a framework on history following the exile.[3] The framework had three tiers. Since the people provoked God by refusing to listen to

---

1. A complex of traditions lie behind the image of the shepherds (Nickelsburg, 92). That God ruled Israel but angels ruled the nations may have been a commonplace in the apocalyptist's day (cf. *Jub.* 15.31-32; Sir. 17.17). If so, to depict God handing Israel over to the nations' angels was a drastic explanation of Israel's troubles.

2. This discussion assumes an interpretation for *1 En.* 90.13-19 first put forward by Milik (44) then refined in different ways by Nickelsburg (93-94) and VanderKam (163). Charles sought to make sense of the passage by pairing supposed doublets so that only one battle occurs (see R.H. Charles, 'Book of Enoch', *APOT* 2.258). It is better not to rearrange the text but to postulate two battles, one in the real author's immediate past, one in his immediate future. Thus the Animal Apocalypse encourages Maccabean warriors to expect God's help in an eschatological battle followed by the judgment. See also Martin Hengel, *Judaism and Hellenism*, I (Philadelphia: Fortress, 1983), 187.

3. What follows relies heavily on VanderKam's discussion of an unpublished paper by Carol Newsom, 'Historical Résumé as Biblical Exegesis' (VanderKam, 165-67).

the prophets (Jer. 25.4-7), he delivered them into the hands of the nations. Desolation serving the Gentiles would last seventy years (Jer. 25.11-12), after which God would pass the cup of wrath over to the nations. They and their shepherds would be judged, overthrown, and destroyed (Jer. 25.15-38). The apocalyptist of *1 Enoch* 83–90 placed the judgment of the nations and their shepherds in the future (90.17-27) and the refusal to listen to the prophets just previous to the fall of Samaria (*1 En.* 89.51-54).[1] He can fix these parts of the framework in time because God had revealed to him the true significance of the seventy years by revealing to him what had happened in the past in the heavenly realm. God had appointed each of the seventy angelic rulers of the nations to rule over Israel for a period. Jeremiah's seventy years are in reality these seventy periods. This revelation of what had happened in the past not only explains the terrible experience of post-exilic Israel, but also suggests the proper understanding of Jer. 25.15-38. The shepherds to be destroyed are these very angelic shepherds. As the deluge wiped out both human evil and the angelic evil which caused it, so the next judgment will destroy both the nations oppressing Israel and their wicked angelic rulers. The revelation the author received about the past not only explains the past and present experience of Israel but also, by correctly interpreting Jeremiah 25, constitutes the basis for the apocalyptist's understanding of Israel's future freedom when the ages revolve again and God once more directly shepherds the sheep.[2] The revelation on which all others hinge is a revelation of the past.

Formally, *1 Enoch* 83–90 is a vision report. Enoch narrates his vision and appends a brief note concerning its significance. The revelation divides history into the following divisions or ages.

Division 1 Adam to deluge	Division 2 Noah to Final Judgment
1. Human sin (*1 En.* 85).	1. Human sin, specifically Israel's rejection of prophets and neglect of holy place (*1 En.* 89.9-58).
2. Angelic evil ('watchers'; fallen stars, *1 En.* 86).	2. Angelic sin (70 shepherds, *1 En.* 89.59–90.16).

---

1. The reign of the shepherds begins not with the exile but with the arrival of Assyria (Charles, *Enoch*, 201; Hengel 1.187; François Martin, *Le Livre d'Hénoch* [Paris: Letouzey et Ané, 1906], xxix).

2. Revelation by interpretation of scripture is common in apocalypses. VanderKam (167, see also 142, 190) connects this with mantic activity.

3. Enoch's (putative author's) present at inception of God's intervention (*1 En*. 90.14-16).

3. Real author's present at inception of God's intervention (*1 En*. 87.3).

4. God judges angelic shepherds (*1 En*. 90.17-26).

4. Judgment on angelic evil (*1 En*. 87–88). Enoch's (putative author's) present at inception of judgment against angels (*1 En*. 87.3).

5. God judges human beings (*1 En*. 90.26-28).

5. Judgment on human evil (Deluge *1 En*. 89.1-8).

Division 3
Righteous Israel in the New Temple
(*1 En*. 90.29-42)

The parallels within the scheme are obvious. As argued above, part of the author's argument hinges on the parallels. As God judged the world in the first age, delivering it from human and angelic evil, so he will judge the second age, delivering Israel from human and angelic evil. Especially significant is the movement toward angelic evil in each age. For heirs of Enochic tradition, the antediluvian angelic fall evokes an aura of consummate evil. This angelic evil wrecked everything, imposing on humanity a burden of fear too great to bear. Hence, attributing the recent dismay of Israel to angelic evil has considerable explanatory power. Wickedness in heavenly places can explain why God's promises of goodness to those who are faithful have failed. It can also offer hope: as God could not tolerate heavenly evil in the watchers so he will not in the shepherds. Even now he is preparing and supporting a faithful remnant against the shepherds. He will ultimately overthrow corrupted angels and humans and establish a righteous Israel in the Temple.

Hence the revelation about the past establishes a recurring pattern in world history. The first division of the past, from Adam to Noah, elaborates the pattern. The second division reveals the current features of the pattern and locates the present within it. Knowing where they fall in the pattern enables the righteous both to understand the present and to act faithfully in it.

Hence revealed history was necessary. A revelation about the future could not explain God's current silence in the face of the destruction of the righteous. Their experience had rightly shown them that they could not expect God to work, but a revelation about the heavenly component of their past experience could restore their hope in God. Only a glimpse of what had happened in the heavenly realm could explain the humanly incomprehensible events down below and nerve them for the present fight.[1] This is not to belittle the future component of the revelation. It, too, is important, but its importance should not diminish the decisive role played in this apocalypse by revelation about the past.

2 Baruch 53–74

Essential elements of revealed history also occur in *2 Baruch* 53–74. Baruch sees a cloud which alternately rains black and bright waters. After Baruch prays for an interpretation of the vision, Ramiel, the angel in charge of true visions, comes to explain the revelation. Twelve black and bright waters complete the history of the wicked and the righteous from Adam to the Second Temple. These are followed by a final pair of black and bright waters which constitute the consummation. By far the greater part of the interpretation (106 out of 135 verses or 79%) recounts events in the real author's past; 96 of the 135 verses are in the past of Baruch, the putative author (the imperfects begin at 67.7). Since the claim to inspiration is clear and the reference to the past extensive, this section of *2 Baruch* is of prime importance for an investigation of inspired history.

Analysis of this intriguing historical revelation is complicated by the author's probable use of a source for the vision and its interpretation.[2] Yet the author of *2 Baruch* has freely altered the source to express his concept of the messiah. The many echoes between the interpretation and the rest of *2 Baruch* also betray his hand. Since the source has been thoroughly worked into its present context, it is rash to base too much on its use of inspired history.[3] An understanding of inspired

---

1. Reid (153) may support this statement by his description of the Animal Apocalypse as a product of 'mantic historicism'. However, his definition of 'mantic historicism' needs further clarification to be greatly useful here.

2. For a discussion of this source see Appendix A. Violet regards *2 Bar.* 71.2 as the close of the interpretation and notes that what follows can stand on its own. He conjectures that *2 Bar.* 72–74 is a Jewish apocalypse perhaps appended by the author of *2 Baruch*. Charles thinks the passage is dislocated. Bogaert thinks it introduces and emphasizes what follows. See Bruno Violet, *Die Apokalypsen des Esra und des Baruch in deutscher Gestalt* (Die griechischen christlichen Schriftsteller der ersten drei Jahrhunderte; Leipzig: Hinrichs, 1924), 309-13; R.H. Charles, *The Apocalypse of Baruch Translated from the Syriac. Edited with Introduction, Notes and Indices* (London: A. & C. Black, 1896), 114; Pierre Bogaert, *Apocalypse de Baruch: traduction du syriaque et commentaire* (Sources Chrétiennes 144-45; Paris: Les Editions du Cerf, 1969), 2.126.

3. See Appendix A.

history in the cloud vision and its interpretation requires an understanding of the author's purpose in *2 Baruch* as a whole.[1] To read *2 Baruch* straight through is to realize that its author seeks not primarily to explain God's incomprehensible action at the fall of Jerusalem[2] but to persuade his suffering people to cleave to the law and to obey it. After the various revelatory dialogues with God or with an angel Baruch returns to address the people (*2 Bar.* 31.1–32.8; 44.1–46.7; 77.1-17). These addresses provide the opportunity of molding the reader's response to the revelatory material. In each case Baruch does not communicate or explain the revelation he has just received, but he exhorts the people to keep the law.[3] Therefore, in all the bewildering array of visions and revelatory dialogue, the author's chief purpose is to persuade his suffering readers to obey the law. The revelatory material presents reasons to keep the law or diffuses arguments against keeping it. *2 Baruch* concludes with its longest exhortation, the Letter to the Nine and a Half Tribes (78–87), which draws together various themes from the book and enlists them squarely behind exhortation to keep the law. Since such an epilogue offers the final opportunity to stress what the author wishes to express, it is best to conclude that he seeks to persuade his people to keep the law.[4] *2 Baruch* also begins with emphasis on obeying the law. The

1. Although R.H. Charles (*Baruch*, lv-lvii), perceived *2 Baruch* as a conglomerate of many sources, most interpreters find the apocalypse a literary unity: Bogaert, 1.80-81; Violet, lxxiii-lxxiv; M.R. James, 'Notes on Apocrypha', *JTS* 16 (1915), 405; John Strugnell, review of *L'Apocalypse Syriaque de Baruch: Introduction, traduction du syriaque et commentaire*, by Pierre Bogaert, in *JBL* 89 (1970), 485; Gwendolyn B. Sayler, *Have the Promises Failed? A Literary Analysis of 2 Baruch* (SBLDS 72; Chico, CA: Scholars Press, 1984), 5. Klijn seeks to retain stress on the unity of *2 Baruch* while reopening the question of the author's use of several sources (A.F.J. Klijn, 'The Sources and Redaction of the Syriac Apocalypse of Baruch', *JSJ* 1 [1970], 65-76).

2. Explaining the fall of Jerusalem, important at the book's beginning, quickly recedes behind other concerns. See Wolfgang Harnisch, *Verhängnis und Verheißung der Geschichte. Untersuchungen zum Zeit- und Geschichtsverständnis im 4. Buch Esra und in der syr. Baruchapokalypse* (FRLANT 97; Göttingen: Vandenhoeck & Ruprecht, 1969), 73.

3. Charles (*Baruch*, lvi), uses the disparity between revelation and exhortation as fuel for his elaborate source theory. See Klijn, 75.

4. My argument assumes the text of *2 Baruch* as it presently exists. Bogaert and Murphy assume that the Letter to the Nine and a Half Tribes (*2 Bar.* 78–87) belongs to the work; Violet (lxxv) and Sayler (98-101) argue that *2 Baruch* originally ended with ch. 77. The decision is difficult. On the one hand, ch. 77 makes a satisfying end to the apocalypse; on the other the Letter effectively summarizes arguments central to *2 Baruch* and shares themes and tone with the addresses of Baruch to the people. If

first chapter contains God's scathing indictment against the two tribes for forsaking the law. In the second chapter the obedience of Baruch and his few righteous friends so mightily protects Jerusalem that God must command them to leave before he can destroy the city. Thus the book opens with paired statements positively and negatively emphasizing the effectiveness of the law; there is great power for good in keeping it, great peril in disregarding it. Since the apocalyptist begins with a forceful statement of the law's power, ends with a lengthy exhortation to keep the law, and scatters shorter exhortations to keep the law at strategic points throughout the narrative, it is reasonable to conclude that the author's foremost goal is to persuade his readers to observe the law.[1]

The author expresses objections to keeping the law in several clutches of questions, two uttered by Baruch, one by the people. God's announcement of the destruction of Jerusalem elicits from Baruch the first barrage of questions: So Jerusalem is destroyed; what now? If Israel is blotted out who will praise you and who will listen to your law? What is to become of all you said to Moses about us? (*2 Bar.* 3.5-9). As the last question shows, the author is especially concerned over how the promises to those keeping the law can be fulfilled after the destruction of Jerusalem.[2] Moses promised that God would execute

---

retained, the Apocalypse (1–77) and the Letter (78–87) continue a pattern well established in *2 Baruch*; as each revelatory section concludes with exhortation by Baruch to the people with him, so the whole apocalypse concludes with an exhortation by Baruch to Jews everywhere. Although the Letter circulated independently, both the Syriac manuscript and the unpublished Arabic manuscripts of *2 Baruch* contain the Letter to the Nine and a Half Tribes. See P.J. Van Koningsveld ('An Arabic Manuscript of the Apocalypse of Baruch', *JSJ* 6 [1975], 205-207), who also points out that the Arabic appears to differentiate more clearly than the Syriac between chs. 1–77 and the Letter. I am inclined to attribute the sense of completeness found in both the Letter (78–87) and the Apocalypse (1–77) to the switch in literary form and to include the Letter as the epilogue to *2 Baruch*. Needless to say I am much more impressed by the unity of theme and purpose between the Letter and what precedes than I am by the contradictions between them found by Sayler, 98-101. See F.J. Murphy, *The Structure and Meaning of 2 Baruch* (SBLDS 78; Atlanta: Scholars Press, 1985), 28-29.

1. Klijn (68) thinks the leading theme of the work is contained in 14.1-7; 'Why do sinners flourish and are the righteous ones taken away?' Sayler (38) asserts that the primary issues of *2 Baruch* are 'the vindication of God as just and powerful in the wake of the destruction; and the survival of the faithful Jewish community in the aftermath of the destruction'. These issues are certainly addressed by *2 Baruch*, but they undergird persuasion to keep the law. See below.

2. Harnisch, 75-76; Sayler, 41: 'At stake is the continued efficacy of the covenant which God made with his people through Abraham and Moses.'

judgment according to the law. Those who obeyed the law would prosper in the land; those who disobeyed would not. Without the land, where is the promise to those who keep the law? The author replies with the doctrine of the heavenly Jerusalem and the promise of messianic deliverance and reward at the consummation. God is not just concerned with the collective obedience of the people, rewarding them with the land, punishing them with its removal. He also is concerned with individual obedience,[1] rewarding those who obey with the heavenly Jerusalem at the last day, punishing others with torment. The fall of Jerusalem does not imply that the law no longer is in force. It is still of paramount importance to keep the law.

The promise of God judging by the law at the consummation is the dominant reason the apocalypse offers for keeping the law after the fall of Jerusalem. Yet the author recognizes, perhaps forced by opposing detractors of the law, that the promise of future judgment alone cannot rehabilitate the promise of the law. Baruch raises another series of objections even after he recognizes God's justice at the consummation. How could judgment on the nations at the last day be worse than what has come on Israel? At the last day most of the sinners will have already died in prosperity. What justice will be served by judging the few that are left (*2 Bar.* 14.1-3)? While Israel has many sinners it also has many righteous. The Gentiles have no righteous. How can God righteously judge against Israel and for the Gentiles by delivering Israel into Gentile hands (*2 Bar.* 14.4-8)? Baruch, without himself questioning the justice of God, concludes that God's justice is incomprehensible (*2 Bar.* 14.8-9). While the judgment at the consummation can serve as a reason for keeping the law and as a partial vindication of God's righteousness, it cannot exonerate God of injustice or undergird the promise of the law in the present. In the present the justice of God has gone awry. The promise to Moses that God would judge by the law has failed. Historical explanation as perceived by the historical books (Deuteronomic history) is not working. The apocalyptist must counter such skeptical thinking if he is to persuade his people to keep the law.[2]

A third series of questions stems from a crisis in leadership.[3] The righteous people of Baruch's flock seem less concerned about the righteousness of God and the promise of the law than about the

---

1. Harnisch, 78, 87.
2. See the helpful discussion of *2 Baruch* 14 in Harnisch, 79–86.
3. Anitra Bingham Kolenkow, 'The Fall of the Temple and the Coming of the End: The Spectrum and Process of Apocalyptic Argument in *2 Baruch* and Other Authors', *SBLSP* (1982), 249.

question, 'Who will lead them and teach them the law when Baruch is gone?' (*2 Bar.* 32.8–33.3; 46.1-3; 77.13-16). Two sections (48.31-37; 70.3-5) describe what seems to be the apocalyptist's present as a time of poor leadership. The mean and unknown rule the renowned and noble. The foolish speak and the wise are silent. Such descriptions may recall the law-abiding leaders of the Jewish War who, though manifestly wrong, had taught that the law supported their cause. Indeed theirs was the obvious interpretation of the law: God would deliver the land. How can we try to keep the law if we have no one who can correctly interpret it?

Therefore Baruch and his flock express two different responses to the seeming failure of the promise of the law. One directs the question against the law itself, the other against the interpreters of the law. The one asks 'What good is it to keep the law since its promise has failed?' The other asks 'What good is it to keep the law since it is difficult to interpret and we have no way of knowing whether what we do pleases God?'

How does the cloud vision and its interpretation use inspired history to counter such objections against the present usefulness of obedience to the law? The cloud vision (*2 Bar.* 53–74) comprises the final revelatory section of the book. It contains *2 Baruch*'s last and most complete answer to the problems which discourage obedience to the law. One of the most desirable objects of revelation in *2 Baruch* concerns the 'courses of the times' (*dwbrhwn dzbn'*, καιρων ταξεις in the Greek fragment of *2 Bar.* 14.1). This phrase, found in *2 Bar.* 14.1; 20.6; 56.2, refers to the way God has structured history. Insight into the 'courses of the times' would allow one to see as God sees[1] and vindicate the promise of the law and the righteousness of God (*2 Bar.* 24.3-4). Few attain it (48.2-3). *2 Baruch* first uncovers the courses of the future times (14.1; 20.6) supporting the necessity of keeping the law and vindicating God's justice by revealing the consummation. Then the cloud vision and its interpretation reveal the courses of the times from creation through consummation (56.2). It can thus explain not only the final outworking of God's justice and the law's promise, but also the present confusion in which justice and the law's promise have seemed to fail and in which teachers and their interpretations of the law have been found wanting.

Chapter 69 contains the key to understanding the interpretation given by Ramiel. It divides history into two parts. The first twelve black and bright waters describe twelve periods of human deeds; the

1. Harnisch, 264.

last two black and white waters describe what God himself would do at the consummation (68.3-4). The first twelve periods, while they are ordained by God from the beginning, rely on human initiative. Human sin or human righteousness determines the character of the period (56.3; 69.3-4).[1] Where human beings depart from the law they constitute a black-water period and retribution follows. Where human beings cleave to the law they constitute a bright-water period and receive blessing. Thus Ramiel reveals how throughout the twelve periods the promise of the law is fulfilled and the justice of God executed. The intention to show God's justice according to the promise of the law appears most strongly in the doubtful cases of Manasseh and Josiah. Ramiel produces a wealth of bizarre detail to show how Manasseh, who though wicked enjoyed a long reign, received personal requital in the present and future and called forth the decree of wrath on Israel which issued in the exile (*2 Bar.* 64–65). Similarly, Josiah, who though righteous died early, is assured of future personal reward beyond many. That the exile closely follows his righteous reign is explained partly as a result of Manasseh's wickedness, partly as a result of Israel's continued wickedness even under his reign, for he was the only one righteous in his time (*2 Bar.* 66.1, 5). Thus God rigorously executed the promise of judgment by the law in the first twelve periods. In them the faithfulness of God to his promise is unassailable. The revelation about history shows that for the first twelve periods the promise to Moses about the law had worked out in clear, thoroughly predictable ways.

The consummation begins with a period of black waters (*2 Bar.* 70). Since the character of this period is determined not by human action but by the action of God, it appears unjust. Nothing in the bright twelfth waters has called down such a judgment of God. No sinful action of Israel or its rulers has caused it. The waters are black and judgment comes just because God has decreed it so. God is intent on turning the world upside down. Those to whom rule and wealth and wisdom belong are deposed and the base and impious and foolish take their place (70.3-5). In a world purposely turned upside down it is hardly surprising that no one can discern the righteousness of God or the fulfillment of the promise of the law. But, by revelation, Baruch has discovered that the present confusion results from an indiscernible shift of the courses of the times in the recent past.[2] The consummation

---

1. F.J. Murphy (110-11) interprets similarly.
2. The author's present lies somewhere in ch. 70. Bogaert (1.87) rightly refers calamities in this chapter to the Jewish War but draws overly specific conclusions from the very general descriptions of *2 Bar.* 70.8 (Bogaert 2.125).

has begun. Therefore the seeming injustices, painful as they are, are only the final outworking of God's righteous judgment on the wicked. God initiates the final judgment and fulfillment of the promises of the law by suspending that judgment and plunging the world into disorder. What seems to break the law's promise of wrath on the disobedient actually brings its highest fulfillment as will soon appear. The last black water does not reply to the present or immediately past sins of Israel as most of the other black periods did. Rather the last black waters reply to all the sins of the world. The period of confusing judgment shall soon be followed by final joy as a reward to the righteous.

In this way the author is able to show how the righteousness of God holds true at all periods of history, not just in the final tally at the last judgment. In the first twelve periods God's righteousness quickly executed the promise of the law; the Deuteronomic explanation for history fitted perfectly.[1] For the present brief period it does not seem to work, but that is only because God has begun to redress all the sins of the world, not just respond to specific recent human actions. A broader view, which takes into account all of history, can explain what is happening in the present as the outworking of a larger pattern of God's justice administered under the law.

This historical revelation also explains the crisis in leadership. The first twelve black and bright waters emphasize leadership, good or bad, and its power to determine the character of the time.[2] Wicked leaders (Adam, Jeroboam, Manasseh) produce bad times; righteous leaders (Abraham, Isaac, Jacob, Moses, David and Solomon, Hezekiah, Josiah) produce good times. During these times a leader who was law-abiding could count on God's blessing. His choices were clear and the result certain. However, the readers of 2 Baruch had seen lawful leaders bring disaster in the Jewish War by counting on God blessing the righteous. Again the inception of the consummation explains why acting in trust that God would defend the righteous had not worked. First, God had placed the base and foolish in positions of political leadership (2 Bar. 70.3-4). Second, the leaders had misapplied the promises in the law because they had failed to perceive the change in the course of the times. Since those to whom 2 Baruch was addressed were not in positions of political leadership and since God was even now revealing to them the change in the course of the times, they need not fear that their interpretation of the law would lead them astray. With the help of the cloud vision they could cleave to the law and

1. Harnisch, 260.
2. Kolenkow, 250.

expect that the law should beget its own interpreters (*2 Bar.* 77.15-18; see also 46.4-7) until the messiah begin to reign and the problem of leadership be solved forever.

The final solution given by *2 Baruch* to the crisis in leadership and to the seeming failure of the law's promises stems from revelation about the past. The first twelve black and bright waters vindicate the promises of the law as it applied to the leaders and to the people. They sum up the past in twelve periods, showing how the promises of Moses had worked out in them according to the principles of Deuteronomic history. The vision and its interpretation then lay those twelve periods and their ways of realizing the promise of the law to rest with respect and show how the present differs because God has brought in the consummation. Though later obvious to all, in *2 Baruch* the consummation begins so naturally that the closest observer cannot see its inception (*2 Bar.* 28.4; 27.15; 48.32, 38). Yet, to understand the enigmas of the present, it is necessary to see that the consummation has already begun. The cloud vision and its interpretation reveal this important but imperceptible event of the recent past. Thus *2 Baruch* uses revealed history to make two points. The heavenly view of the first twelve periods upholds the promises and interpretation of history contained in the law. The heavenly view of the last black waters explains the confusion of the present by revealing an event in the recent past; the consummation has begun. That the basis for keeping the law includes also revelation about the future (*2 Bar.* 70–74) and that in *2 Baruch* as a whole the future solution receives more prominence than the past do not lessen the importance of these revelations of the past.

Apocalypse of Abraham 21–32

In the *Apocalypse of Abraham*, God whisks Abraham to the seventh heaven to see the picture which represents God's plan for creation (22.2). Since this picture depicts everything which has or will come into existence at God's word, Abraham sees past as well as future events—the garden with Adam and Eve, the fall of Jerusalem and its cause, as well as the end of the age. The *Apocalypse of Abraham* claims inspiration concerning the past. Though the apocalypse exists only in Old Church Slavonic, a translation from the Greek which in turn was probably a translation from Hebrew, and as a fully independent work only in one manifestly corrupt manuscript, its broad outlines are clear. Since it dates from the beginning of the second century

CE,[1] the *Apocalypse of Abraham* belongs in a study of apocalyptic world history.

The most obvious problem addressed by the *Apocalypse of Abraham* concerns the destruction of the Temple in Jerusalem. Yet to Abraham's anguished question, 'Why must it be so?' (*Ap. Ab.* 27.6), the author has a ready answer: it was destroyed because of false worship in the Temple (27.7; cf. 25.1-4). The author has depicted Jewish worship in the Temple as the equivalent of idolatry, murderous offering of boys to an idol which represented the anger of God (25.1-4). Like the inhabitants of Qumran, the author probably rejected the Temple worship practiced in Jerusalem before 70 CE.[2] Therefore the immediate reason for the destruction was hardly a mystery and was quickly resolved by a revelation concerning the author's past: the Jews had continually offered idolatrous worship in the Temple.

The author seems much more perplexed by what underlies this obvious problem. If God has chosen Israel why would God permit the Jews to err against him (26.1) and so bring on themselves this catastrophe? Throughout the book the author seeks to face this problem of Jewish apostasy.

The first revelation of the past concerns the sin of Adam and Eve. They are pictured embracing one another eating the grapes which Azazel feeds them. God interprets the picture (23.10-11), and Abraham's questions (23.12, 14) further specify its meaning: human beings, in their thoughts and works, are under the dominion of Azazel and God has willed it so. To Abraham's questions as to why God made humanity so flawed, God answers that he has granted Azazel dominion over all who desire evil (23.13) and that he has placed the desire for evil in their hearts because of what they were going to do to Abraham's descendants (24.1).[3] With one stroke, and that a revelation

---

1. Ryszard Rubinkiewicz and H.G. Lunt, 'The Apocalypse of Abraham', *OTP* 1.683 n. 16 (added by James H. Charlesworth). I have followed the versification in this edition of the *Apocalypse of Abraham*. Cf. James R. Mueller, 'The Apocalypse of Abraham and the Destruction of the Second Jewish Temple', *SBLSP* (1982), 341-50; L. Ginsberg, 'Abraham, Apocalypse of', *The Jewish Encyclopedia* (New York: Funk & Wagnalls, 1901), 92; G.H. Box and J.I. Landsman, *The Apocalypse of Abraham* (New York: Macmillan, 1919), xv.

2. A. Rubinstein, 'A Problematic Passage in the Apocalypse of Abraham', *JJS* 8 (1957), 45-50. I agree with Rubinstein that this verse answers Abraham's question, but I think the burden is on Abraham's children, not on the Gentiles.

3. The four 'ascents', 'descents', or 'entrances' (*Ap. Ab.* 27.3) are usually interpreted of the four empires (see Box and Landsman, 74 n. 7; A. Pennington, 'The Apocalypse of Abraham', *AOT* 387 n. 27.2). I interpret them as the four hostile

about the past, the author has both explained human sin and vindicated God's justice in the face of the oppression of his people.

The historical revelation of the Garden of Eden reveals that all humanity, by God's will, is under the dominion of Azazel and desires evil. Another historical revelation, a catalogue of sins, beginning with Adam but moving to generalities, shows how the rule of Azazel works out throughout history (*Ap. Ab.* 24–25). This catalogue ends with a description of the false worship which precipitated the various Gentile incursions into the Temple and brought about its destruction (25–27).[1] As a historical revelation had shown how all humanity to Abraham were under Azazel, so a historical revelation shows how many of Abraham's descendants forsook their freedom as Abraham's seed. Abraham had turned from idolatry to God, thus receiving the promise. Apostate Jews had turned from God to idolatry's equivalent, offering false worship even in the Temple. They had returned under Azazel's dominion, forsaking their heritage, and so lost their privileges (cf. *Ap. Ab.* 31.6-8). Thus the *Apocalypse of Abraham* explains both human sin and Jewish apostasy by the work of Azazel and evil desire, both of which are willed by God.

Although most students of the work reluctantly excise much of 29.3-13 as a Christian interpolation,[2] I find most of the chapter original.[3] Abraham sees a figure arise from among the heathen. Gentiles worship him; Azazel supports him. Some from among Abraham's descendants worship him as well, but others insult and even strike him (*Ap. Ab.* 29.4-7). This man who is worshiped continues the theme of idolatry connected with Azazel. As, at God's behest, Azazel has led human

Gentile penetrations of Jerusalem under Nebuchadnezzar, Antiochus IV, Pompey, and Titus.

1. See Ryszard Rubinkiewicz, 'La vision de l'histoire dans l'Apocalypse d'Abraham', *Aufstieg und Niedergang der römischen Welt* II.19.1 (Berlin, New York: Walter de Gruyter, 1979), 143-44. Marc Philonenko and Michael Stone accept the theory of a gloss with misgivings. See Belkis Philonenko-Sayar and Marc Philo-nenko, 'Die Apokalypse Abrahams', *JSHRZ* 5.5 (Gütersloh: Gütersloher Verlagshaus Gerd Mohn, 1982), 417, 450 n. xxix; Michael E. Stone, 'Apocalyptic Literature', *Jewish Writings of the Second Temple Period* (ed. Michael E. Stone, Compendia Rerum Judiacarum ad Novum Testamentum 2.2; Philadelphia: Fortress, 1984), 415.

2. However, the identification of the man with Azazel as a son of Abraham must be a Christian gloss aimed at finding Christ in the text. 29.10 is so confused that it must have suffered some excision as well. For arguments supporting these findings see Robert G. Hall, 'The "Christian Interpolation" in the Apocalypse of Abraham', *JBL* 107 (1988), 107-10.

3. See the alternate reading in Rubinkiewicz and Lunt, 704 n. 1.

beings into idolatry from the beginning, so in the last period (the twelfth), Azazel sets up another idol, a human being. Yet there is a difference: this idol liberates Abraham's descendants from the Gentiles (29.8) by testing them (29.13). The man who is worshiped provokes a division between the righteous Hebrews who insult and strike him and those idolatrous Hebrews who join the heathen in worshiping him (29.12-13). Once judgment had fallen on all the Hebrews because of the idolatry in the Temple (27.7); now judgment falls upon the heathen of Abraham's seed (29.14)[1] but blessing on the remnant who strive in God's glory for the deserted Temple and who will live in the age of justice (29.17-21).

The heathen man with Azazel probably represents the Roman Emperor. Suetonius mentions with sympathy a Jew who had successfully hidden his nationality for many years to avoid paying the tax imposed after the Jewish War.[2] Such Jews must have in worshiping the Emperor joined their Gentile neighbors. Since the *Apocalypse of Abraham* rigorously opposes idolatry in every form, its author would probably repudiate even those who avoided worshiping the Emperor by paying the tax, for the tax supported the worship of Jupiter Capitolinus.[3] Hadrian's plan to refound Jerusalem as Aelia Capitolina, with temples to Jupiter and to himself sharing the former sight of the Jewish Temple, may have sparked the Bar Kochba Revolt.[4] First readers of the *Apocalypse of Abraham* would have little need to puzzle over the identity of the man with Azazel.[5]

The vision of the man who is worshiped and its interpretation disclose the significance of events in the author's immediate past and present. The destruction of the Temple and the apostasy of many Jews, tragic from the earthly perspective, from the heavenly perspective are triumphant. God destroys the idolatrous Temple to make way for a new pure Temple to be founded again after the 100-year period. God raises up the man with Azazel to purify the people by provoking separation between idolatrous and loyal Hebrews. Apostate Jews remain with the heathen under Azazel's influence, but the newly cleansed children of Abraham enter God's blessing by eschewing idolatry as Abraham their forefather had done (*Ap. Ab.* 6–8).

1. Hall, 108-109.
2. Suetonius, *Domitian* 12.2.
3. Josephus, *J.W.* 7.218; Dio 66.7.2.
4. Dio 66.12.1-2; Mary Smallwood, *The Jews under Roman Rule from Pompey to Diocletian* (Leiden: Brill, 1981), 428-38, 459.
5. Hall, 109.

The *Apocalypse of Abraham* 21–32 thus contains a review of the history of the world similar to those in *1 Enoch* 83–90 and *2 Baruch* 53–74, although less complete. In its depiction of the garden of Eden (*Ap. Ab.* 21–24.2), the *Apocalypse of Abraham* explains the origin of human sin in the activity of Azazel and explains the activity of Azazel as punishment for the way the Gentiles have treated righteous Jews. The catalogue of sins (*Ap. Ab.* 24–26) depicts the result of Azazel's activity on human deeds. Most significantly, it locates the idolatrous worship by Jews in the Temple squarely within the stream of deeds flowing from Azazel's dominion in the Garden of Eden and in human history. The description of the fall of the Temple explains it as punishment for the Jews' idolatrous Temple worship under the dominion of Azazel (*Ap. Ab.* 27–29.4a). The vision of the man who is worshiped, its interpretation, and the ensuing discussion describe the separation of righteous Jews from the dominion of Azazel and their consequent blessing (*Ap. Ab.* 29). Chapters 30–32 amplify some of the material in ch. 29. The revelation of the past is essential to explaining the author's present. Only revelation can show the power of the dominion of Azazel and the past and present means of separating the righteous Jews collectively from it. Of course the depiction of the future, by showing the result of sorting the righteous from the wicked, also interprets the present, but the relevance of the future does not lessen the importance to the author's message of the revelation about the past.

Apocalyptic World History

This review of *1 Enoch* 83–90, *2 Baruch* 55–74, and *Apocalypse of Abraham* 21–32 has turned up several findings of significance for the apocalyptists' use of revealed history. Revelations about the past play an indispensable role in addressing the rhetorical situation facing the apocalyptists. Such revelations explain why faithful Jews who have languished in the years before Antiochus Epiphanes should now join Judas Maccabeus expecting God to act (*1 En.* 83–90), the apparent failure of the promise of the law after the fall of Jerusalem in the disordered present (*2 Bar.* 55–74), or the dominance of Azazel and how God is at work in Jewish apostasy (*Ap. Ab.* 21–32).

Certain kinds of arguments based on revealed history tend to recur. Revelation of a former pattern in history reinforces the author's interpretation of the present and future (*1 En.* 83–90; *2 Bar.* 55–74). Changes from one age to another explain anomalies and encourage action (*1 Enoch, 2 Baruch*). Revelations of heavenly administrations explain historical events and conditions (*1 Enoch*'s revelation of the shepherds, *Apocalypse of Abraham*'s revelation of the dominion of Azazel).

Uniformly these apocalypses reveal crucial components of history which are imperceptible to a human observer. The *Apocalypse of Abraham* shows how the worship of Jews as well as Gentiles lies under the dominion of Azazel and how Jewish apostasy of the recent past, by separating faithful from unfaithful Jews, frees the faithful from Azazel's dominion. *2 Baruch* reveals how an imperceptible switch in ages from normal course of events to consummation both explains the anomalies of the recent past (disasters surrounding the fall of Jerusalem and the following disorder among Jews) and fulfills in a larger scale the promise of the law so faithfully adhered to in earlier history. The Animal Apocalypse (*1 En.* 83–90) discloses a recurrence of an ancient pattern (human sin, angelic sin, judgment) and explains misfortunes of the Jews from late monarchy to Antiochus Epiphanes as the earthly manifestation of a change in heavenly administration. Though hidden from human observation, all of these past events and conditions are required for an accurate understanding not only of the past but also of the present and future. Revelation of the past is a necessary component of an accurate view of world history. For these apocalyptists, history written without revelation is doomed to error.

In addition to similarities in the use of revealed history, these three apocalypses share formal characteristics. Of course, according to form critical distinctions commonly applied to apocalyptic literature, these three historical apocalypses differ. The Animal Apocalypse is a vision report, *2 Baruch* 53–74 a vision and angelic interpretation, the *Apocalypse of Abraham* a heavenly trip. But each of them considers world history as a whole. Each applies world history to a present problem. Each contains revelations past to the putative as well as to the real author, divides history into periods, locates the present shortly after a switch in ages, reinterprets history familiar to the readers, and ends in a consummation in which afflictions precede blessing. The three organize their presentation of world history according to a common pattern:

1. Commonly received history is told to reveal a historical pattern or condition (*1 En.* 85–86; *2 Bar.* 56–66; *Ap. Ab.* 21–23).
2. The pseudonymous author is placed in a situation analogous to the real author's (*Ap. Ab.* 24; *1 En.* 87; *2 Bar.* 67):

   Abraham alone escapes from idolatry and service to Azazel as the author of the *Apocalypse of Abraham* and his faithful compatriots escaped idolatry by repudiating any vestige of emperor worship.

Baruch endures the destruction of the first Temple as the real author of *2 Baruch* endures the destruction of the second.

Enoch experiences the inception of judgment against the watchers as the real author of *1 Enoch* 83–90 experiences the inception of judgment against the angelic shepherds.

3. Telling commonly received history to reveal a pattern continues (*2 Bar.* 68; *1 En.* 88–90.16; *Ap. Ab.* 25–28).
4. The righteous endure affliction (*Ap. Ab.* 29.1-12; *2 Bar.* 69–71; *1 En.* 89.59–90.16).
5. The real author's present stands at the inception of God's intervention (*1 En.* 90.14-16; *Ap. Ab.* 29.13; *2 Bar.* 70.6).
6. Affliction becomes delivering judgment (*2 Bar.* 72; *1 En.* 90.17-28; *Ap. Ab.* 29.14-16; 31.1-8).
7. God blesses the righteous (*2 Bar.* 73–74; *1 En.* 90.29-42; *Ap. Ab.* 29.17-21).

Though they exist among essential differences, such similarities in content, type of argument, and form are sufficient to distinguish apocalyptic world history as a genus of revealed history.

Chapter 5

LIMITED APOCALYPTIC HISTORY: DANIEL

The book of Daniel utilizes a second kind of apocalyptic history: instead of explaining confusing past events by fitting them into a scheme of world history as a whole, Daniel considers only the period which causes the confusion. The apocalyptist reduces events of the confusing period to a series of patterns which authenticate expectations for the future.

The book of Daniel contains six different reviews of history, each of them explicitly claiming inspiration. One of these, a judicial historical sermon uttered by Daniel to Belteshazzar, condemns Belteshazzar to ruin at the hands of the Medes and Persians (Dan. 5.17-28). The other five (Dan. 2.27-45; chs. 7; 8; 9; 10–12) share several characteristics. Each of them casts its entire review of past events as predictions for the future, each rehearses events from the period beginning with Nebuchadnezzar and ending with Antiochus IV Epiphanes, and each promises the destruction of Antiochus and his kingdom and the deliverance of the faithful.[1] All but the vision interpreting Jeremiah's seventy years depend on the system of four world empires explained most clearly in chs. 2 and 7. Since, despite such similarities, each of these five visions reveals its own peculiar perspective on events from the period of the empires, each vision requires its own analysis.

---

1. Collins finds a sequence common to chs. 7; 8; 10–12: history prior to Antiochus IV, Antiochus' revolt against God, supernatural intervention, eschatological state of salvation (not in 8). See John J. Collins, *The Apocalyptic Vision of the book of Daniel* (Harvard Semitic Monographs 16; Missoula, MT: Scholars Press, 1977), 133. Chapter 9 contains most of these elements as well, though in abbreviated form.

Daniel 2

Although the vision of King Nebuchadnezzar, if not its interpretation, possibly arose as a Babylonian oracle of imperial history,[1] it has an important function in the book of Daniel. This vision and its interpretation (Dan. 2.31-45) divide history from the exile to the author's present into a sequence of four empires and expect an eternal kingdom established by the God of heaven. Though sketchy, the interpretation offers enough detail to assure Daniel's first readers, even should they miss the allusion to the well-known four-kingdom scheme,[2] that they lived in the fourth kingdom right before God's intervention. Such a vision lays emphasis on the near deliverance of Daniel's readers, but it also makes an important historical point. The puzzling period from the exile to Daniel's present, in which the people of God endure foreign rule, is defined as the era of the empires. God grants empire to each people in turn and has restricted the rule of the nations to a fixed length in four divisions. This vision serves as an introduction to the other historical visions by delimiting the period to be explained[3] and by outlining an explanation.

Daniel 7

The vision in ch. 7 takes up the scheme of four empires from ch. 2 and invests them with imagery taken from the myth of the chaos monster.[4] Each of four beasts, like Leviathan, arises from the sea, and each of them, as the myth requires, calls forth a heavenly reaction. Hence a repetitive historical pattern emerges and is echoed in the structure of the passage. After each beast is described, a switch to the divine pas-

1. John J. Collins, 'The Court-Tales in Daniel and the Development of Apocalyptic', *JBL* 94 (1975), 221-22.
2. For an excellent assessment of the ancient view that Greece is the fourth in a series of world empires see David Flusser, 'The Four Empires in the Fourth Sibyl and in the Book of Daniel', *Israel Oriental Studies* 2 (1972), 148-75.
3. Rössler argues that Daniel is interested in history as a whole since monstrous empires arise from primeval chaos. Koch thinks Daniel organizes history into three great world epochs: independent Israel, world empires, eternal kingdom. Collins rightly rejects Koch's view noting that the visions in Daniel hardly glance at the history of Israel. The historical interest in Daniel is limited almost exclusively to the period of the four empires. See Rössler, *Gesetz und Geschichte. Untersuchungen zur Theologie der jüdischen Apokalyptik und der pharisäischen Orthodoxie*, 56; Klaus Koch, 'Spätisraelitisches Geschichtsdenken am Beispiel des Buches Daniel', *Historische Zeitschrift* 193 (1961), 1-32; Collins, *Apocalyptic Vision*, 158.
4. For an elaboration of Daniel's use of the chaos myth see Collins, *Apocalyptic Vision*, 96-106.

sive[1] indicates the decision of the heavenly court. This pattern is introduced in the accounts of the first three beasts.[2]

	Dan. 7.4	Dan. 7.5	Dan. 7.6
Apparition's Description	The first was like a lion and had eagle's wings.	And behold, another beast, a second one like a bear. It was raised up on one side; it had three ribs in its mouth between its teeth;	After this I looked, lo, another like a leopard, with four wings of a bird on its back; and the beast had four heads;
Heavenly Decision in Divine Passive	Then as I looked its wings were plucked off, and it was lifted up from the ground and made to stand upon two feet like a man; and the mind of a man was given to it.	and it was told, 'Arise, devour much flesh'.	and dominion was given to it.

The heavenly decision confirms the power of the second and third beasts, at least for a time, and gives tacit approval to their reign. The metamorphosis of the first beast also reveals that it rules with heavenly authority. In the Animal Apocalypse a beast becoming a man implies a high degree of privilege and heavenly acceptance; the man has become an angel.[3] Here also the transformation of the first chaos monster into a man tokens a switch for the better and implies a certain legitimacy. When the eternal godly kingdom comes it also is represented by a man

1. James A. Montgomery, *A Critical and Exegetical Commentary on the book of Daniel* (ICC; Edinburgh: T & T Clark, 1927), 288.
2. The quotations of Daniel are from the RSV.
3. Noah (a bull) and Moses (a sheep) become men; *1 En.* 84.4; 89.36. Commentators frequently link the first beast's humanization with Nebuchadnezzar's rehabilitation in Daniel 4. See André Lacocque, *The Book of Daniel* (Atlanta: John Knox, 1979), 139. This view is rejected by R.H. Charles, *A Critical and Exegetical Commentary on the Book of Daniel* (Oxford: Clarendon, 1929), 177. Montgomery (287) sees the humanization as a mitigation of hubris. Nebuchadnezzar and Babylon receive relatively good press in Daniel. Collins argues that the vision in ch. 2 is Babylonian since 'the identification of Nebuchadnezzar with the head of gold appears far more appropriate for a Hellenistic Babylonian than for a Jew of any period'. See John J. Collins, *The Apocalyptic Imagination: An Introduction to the Jewish Matrix of Christianity* (New York: Crossroad, 1984), 76. The present instance shows a positive evaluation of Nebuchadnezzar in the visions as well as in the tales and may undercut Collins's reasoning.

(Dan. 7.13-14). The first kingdom not only is permitted to rule but also most closely approximates that kind of rule approved by God. In each case, then, the heavenly court grants provisional and limited approval to the first three beasts.[1]

Although the fourth beast differs from the others (Dan. 7.7) and is so dreadful that it recalls no natural animal, it also is described according to the recurrent pattern.

Apparition's Description	After this I saw in the night visions, and behold, a fourth beast, terrible and dreadful and exceedingly strong; and it had great iron teeth; it devoured and broke in pieces, and stamped the residue with its feet. It was different from all the beasts that were before it; and it had ten horns. I considered the horns, and behold, there came up among them another horn, a little one, before which three of the first horns were plucked up by the roots; and behold, in this horn were eyes like the eyes of a man, and a mouth speaking great things (Dan. 7.7-8).
Heavenly Decision in Divine Passive	And as I looked, the beast was slain, and its body destroyed and given over to be burned with fire. As for the rest of the beasts, their dominion was taken away, but their lives were prolonged for a season and a time (Dan. 7.11b-12).

While in this case the pattern is interrupted by the sitting of the heavenly court, the interruption does not weaken the pattern but reinforces it. Since this application of the pattern most directly affects the intended readers of Daniel, the author gives a glimpse of the heavenly court as it renders the decision. Like prophecy, apocalyptic thought assumes that what happens on earth results from deliberations in the heavenly council (Job 1–3; 2 Kgs 22; Rev. 5). Since the sentence upon the fourth beast lies in the future and is not yet visible on earth, the glimpse of the heavenly court undergirds the certainty of the coming sentence and emphasizes its importance.

The pattern again recurs in the description of the eternal kingdom:

Apparition's Description	I saw in the night visions, and behold, with the clouds of heaven there came one like a Son of man, and he came to the Ancient of Days and was presented before him (Dan. 7.13).

---

1. Such an understanding comports well with the view of the first three kingdoms in Daniel 2–6. In these chapters representatives of the first three empires honor Daniel, receive his advice, and even acknowledge the God of Heaven. No such softening influence ameliorates Antiochus' reign of terror. Koch, 'Spätisraelitisches Geschichtsdenken', 13–14; cf. Martin Noth, 'The Understanding of History in Old Testament Apocalyptic', *The Laws in the Pentateuch and Other Studies* (Edinburgh: Oliver and Boyd, 1966), 201-202.

| Heavenly Decision in Divine Passive | And to him was given dominion and glory and kingdom, that all peoples, nations, and languages should serve him; his dominion is an everlasting dominion, which shall not pass away, and his kingdom one that shall not be destroyed (Dan. 7.14).[1] |

Here again a future event is guaranteed by reference to the heavenly court (7.13).

The vision seeks to assure readers of Daniel that the enormities of the fourth beast will call forth judgment and consequent deliverance. It is this future application of the pattern that receives emphasis in the interpretation (Dan. 7.19-27). The revelation of the past (Dan. 7.2-9) contributes to this assurance for the future by establishing the pattern.[2] Every chaos monster calls forth a heavenly decision. Daniel's contemporaries need not fear that the present empire, for all its terror, will be overlooked. The revelation also contributes to this assurance by distinguishing the fourth beast from the former three. The first three beasts, though true chaos monsters and hence opposed to God, were tame enough to receive dominion for a time. The last chaos monster is so terrible and, led by the little horn, works such enormities that a different kind of heavenly decision is called for and given. As the last beast fulfills its potential as a chaos monster in opposition to God, so it is overthrown by God as the chaos monster myth requires. The revelation of history in Daniel 7 establishes a pattern of divine intervention and assures Daniel's first readers that as the depredations of the fourth empire exceed those of the earlier, so the heavenly decision against it will be more severe. The last empire shall never rule by divine fiat but shall be destroyed.

Daniel 8

In ch. 8, the portrayals of Antiochus IV Epiphanes, Alexander the Great, and the Medo-Persian kings follow a well-defined pattern. An

---

1. 'His dominion...be destroyed' is a non-verbal sentence in Aramaic and should be understood to continue the passive construction.

2. Newsom thinks that the apocalyptist deduces what has happened in the future from such a pattern in the past. Without ruling out her insight I prefer to emphasize the effect of the pattern on the reader. The author constructs an inductive argument; predictions for the future are more believable if they continue a pattern known from the past. See Carol A. Newsom, 'The Past as Revelation: History in Apocalyptic Literature', *Quarterly Review* 4 (Nashville, 1984), 43-44.

apparition of each is described, a few mighty deeds are enumerated, the apparition magnifies itself[1] and is no more.

	Dan. 8.3-4	Dan. 8.5-8	Dan. 8.9-11a
Apparition's Description	I raised my eyes and saw, and behold, a ram standing on the bank of the river. It had two horns; and both horns were high, but one was higher than the other and the higher one came up last.	As I was considering, behold, a he-goat came from the west across the face of the whole earth, without touching the ground; and the goat had a conspicuous horn between his eyes.	Out of one of them came forth a little horn, which grew exceedingly great toward the south, toward the east, and toward the glorious land.
Apparition's Action Emphasizing its Power	I saw the ram charging westward and northward and southward; no beast could stand before him, and there was no one who could rescue from his power.	He came to the ram with the two horns, which I had seen standing on the bank of the river, and he ran at him in his mighty wrath. I saw him come close to the ram, and he was enraged against him and struck the ram and broke his two horns; and the ram had no power to stand before him, but he cast him down to the ground and trampled upon him; and there was no one who could rescue the ram from his power.	It grew great, even to the host of heaven; and some of the host of the stars it cast down to the ground, and trampled upon them.

---

1. הגדיל can be used of God in a good sense, 'do great things'. When used of humans it usually implies hubris, so in Dan. 8.4, 8, 11, 25 (Montgomery, 329).

Apparition	He did as he	Then the he-goat	It magnified
Magnifies itself	pleased and	magnified himself	itself, even up to
Apparition's	magnified	exceedingly.	the prince of the
Demise	himself. [At the	[When he was	host. [A time
	hand of the he-	strong, the great	limit set for the
	goat] (See 8.7,	horn was	horn's enormi-
	above right.)	broken.]	ties] (Dan. [8.8].
			8.13-14). 'By no
			human hand he
			shall be broken'
			(Dan. 8.25, in the
			interpretation).

Although the descriptions of the little horn's enormities against the Prince of the host (8.11-12) might seem to interrupt the pattern, they actually confirm it. They amplify the theme of self-exaltation, showing specific ways the little horn magnified itself.

It follows that one of the prime goals of inspired history in this chapter is to reveal this pattern in history. God makes a kingdom rise, gives it power for a time, then, when it exalts itself against him, he topples it. This thesis is proved by a series of historical examples. The Medes and Persians did great things, magnified themselves, and were overthrown by Alexander. Alexander worked mighty deeds, magnified himself, and was cut off in his prime. Now Antiochus has entered the lists, has succeeded even in warfare against the heavenly host, but has exalted himself directly against God so that his enormities have made even soldiers of the heavenly host cry out the plaintive 'How long?'[1] Given the evidence of Epiphanes' hubris (8.11-12) and the pattern revealed in history (8.3-8), it hardly requires a prophet to forecast his fall.

Although the revelation of this pattern and the future relief promised in it comprises the primary goal of revealed history in this vision, other goals are also met. The specific catalogues of the sins of Antiochus (8.11-12, 24-25) locate the sufferings of Daniel's readers squarely in God's plan and reinterpret them. The enormities of Antiochus do not show his superiority to God but bring about his sure and speedy downfall. The device of revelation, by proving that the recurring cycle of hubris and judgment is based upon the heavenly view of history, ensures its accuracy.

---

1. Although G.R. Beasley-Murray and others reject Collins's contention that Antiochus IV here and elsewhere battles the heavenly host, I am inclined to accept it. See G.R. Beasley-Murray, 'The Interpretation of Daniel 7', *CBQ* 45 (1983), 53; Collins, *Apocalyptic Vision*, 139-40.

Daniel 10–12

The complex vision in Daniel 10–12 contains the longest and most detailed of Daniel's reviews of history. The detailed accounts of the wars of the Ptolemies and Seleucids are not organized according to a neatly recurring pattern of words and phrases. Perhaps the facts, as the author wished to present them, could not be squeezed into such a mold.[1] But though no such pattern recurs in the text, a refrain of failure indicates the author's purpose. However powerful a king may become he is always frustrated before reaching his objective.

The last Persian king becomes strong only to provoke Greece against himself (11.2). The Greek king has great dominion only to be broken (11.3-4). The kings of the south and north make an alliance by marriage which does not endure (11.5-6). The king of the south , though attacked by the king of the north, wins a great victory but cannot prevail (11.7-13). Violent Hebrews raise themselves up but fail (11.14). A king of the north prevails against the king of the south yet fails to establish a marriage alliance or take coastlands and stumbles seeking to regain fortresses in his own land (11.15-19). Then an exactor of tribute is broken in a few days (11.20). As in the other visions, that portion of history concerning Antiochus IV Epiphanes receives most extensive treatment. His plots against strongholds are good only for a time (11.24). He does indeed succeed against the king of the south, but only so that the king of the south may not stand (11.25). When the two kings try to out-maneuver each other at the council table, their lies are to no avail (11.27). On a second campaign to the south Antiochus is frustrated by the Kittim (Rome) and rebounds to make war on the holy covenant. Though his successes against the covenant are enumerated at length (11.30-35) as are his future successes against the king of the south (11.36-39) and elsewhere (11.40-44), his blasphemous hubris assures that he also will be frustrated: 'yet he shall come to his end, with none to help him' (11.45).

Certainly one purpose of the historical review in this chapter is to demonstrate this cycle of royal failure. For all their power the kings never reach their goals. Their plans are doomed to frustration. When applied to the ravages of Antiochus against the covenant, the expected frustration of his plans can only imply relief for Daniel's constituency. The inspired history of Daniel reveals this cycle of frustration to encourage the wise contemporaries of the author and those who listen to them.

---

1. Newsom (48-49) also notices the lack of a pattern in the historical review in this chapter.

Other forms of encouragement arise along the way. The depiction of Antiochus' war against the covenant puts forward a view of what has happened which must differ from the perceptions of the Jewish hellenizers. These hardly perceived themselves as forsaking the covenant (11.31) or being seduced with flatteries to violate it. Yet Daniel's interpretation of their activity receives the authority of revelation. The revelation of history also provides a rationale for the sufferings of the wise and a warning to those who follow them to do so sincerely (11.33-34).

The review of history receives yet further significance from its setting within the vision. It is framed with indications of heavenly activity (10.2–11.1; 12.5-13). Before rehearsing history the angel who converses with Daniel reveals the heavenly battle which is reflected in earthly events. The angel has been withstanding (frustrating?) the prince of Persia and can come to enlighten Daniel only when relieved by Michael (Dan. 10.13-14). He and Michael will resist the prince of Persia and, when he is finished, the prince of Greece. Whether the angel speaking with Daniel arises to strengthen Darius the Mede or (more likely) to strengthen Michael (11.1),[1] his activity brings about the switch in empire. Having gained a glimpse of this heavenly activity we know the source of that recurring frustration of mighty kings which the review of history reveals. Michael and the angel conversing with Daniel have thwarted them by exertion in the heavenly fight. At the final frustration of Antiochus IV such heavenly intervention is explicit. Following the earthly succession of rulers, Michael himself arises to awaken the dead to everlasting life or contempt and to form a new kingdom in which the wise become like the angels.

Therefore this revelation of history not only reveals the cycle of failure to which the greatest kings of the earth are subject, but also

---

1. Commentators have generally dealt with the difficulties of 10.20–11.1 by theories of dislocation or interpolation. Montgomery's rearrangement of the verses more or less captures the sense of the passage whether or not the text ever followed the order he gives. See Montgomery, 416-17; Lacocque, 212. I am not convinced by Montgomery that לֹו should be changed to לִי in 11.1 or that 11.1a 'In the first year of Darius the Mede' is a gloss. DiLella thinks 11.1 was added by the final editor of Daniel who also incorporated Daniel 9 to identify the angel of chs. 10–12 with Gabriel. See Louis F. Hartman and Alexander A. DiLella, *The Book of Daniel* (AB 23; Garden City, NY: Doubleday, 1978), 266, 285-86. If DiLella is correct Dan. 11.1 still belongs to the final form of Daniel and should be interpreted as such, but a reference to Gabriel's appearance to Daniel in ch. 9 hardly fits the context of heavenly conflict. It seems better to regard 11.1 as an explanation for the fall of the Babylonian empire and the succession of Darius to the throne; when reinforced by the angel speaking, Michael was able to overthrow the Babylonians and instate Darius.

reveals its cause. The schemes of kings, including those of Antiochus IV, can never prosper for they are frustrated by the heavenly warfare waged by Michael and that angel speaking to Daniel. The greatness of Michael's helper (10.2-9), made all the greater by Daniel's faintness in his presence (10.7-9; 15-19), increases confidence in his ability to frustrate kings. Hence the descriptions of the angel and of Daniel's faintness with which the vision commences are integral to the historical revelation. By returning to contemplate the great figure of the angel (12.5-8), the vision concludes with a final assertion of his ability to carry out that frustration of emperors which he portrayed.

Daniel 9

Like other reviews of the past in Daniel, the interpretation of Jeremiah's seventy years (9.24-27) covers the period from the exile through Antiochus IV. Yet compared with the other visions it lacks interest in historical detail. The first sixty-two weeks of years are passed over almost without comment; the deeds and destruction of Antiochus IV are described in only two verses, so condensed as to be very difficult to interpret. Probably this vision's greatest significance as a revelation of the past stems not from the details it discusses but from its extension of Jeremiah's seventy years to seventy weeks of years which cover the entire period of historical interest in Daniel.

The book of Jeremiah twice mentions this seventy-year period. Jer. 29.10-11 promises return to Jerusalem and blessing for her after seventy years are completed for Babylon; Jeremiah 25 describes the seventy years as the period of Babylonian dominance and of God's judgment against Israel and the other nations (Jer. 25.9-11). During this period God causes each nation in turn to drink the cup of his wrath, bringing anguish on kings and people alike (25.17-26, cf. 30-38). At last in the 70th year (9.12) Babylon must drink Yahweh's cup (25.26). God has summoned a sword against the whole earth.[1]

The inspired interpretation of Jeremiah's seventy years moves freely between the promise of blessing after the seventy years (Jer. 29.10-11) and the promise of disaster within the seventy years (Jer. 25). By expanding the seventy years the interpretation in Daniel 9 explains the whole period from exile through Antiochus IV as the 'troubled time' (9.25) before the blessing promised to Jeremiah. The 'desolations of

---

1. I owe the link between Jeremiah 25 and Daniel to an unpublished paper by Carol A. Newsom, 'Historical Résumé as Biblical Exegesis', summarized by James C. VanderKam in *Enoch and the Growth of an Apocalyptic Tradition* (CBQMS 16; Washington, DC: Catholic Biblical Association, 1984), 165-67.

Jerusalem' (9.2) include the author's time, for right up to the end of this period desolations are decreed (9.26) perpetrated by the desolator (9.27). Hence the wise of the Danielic community still await the coming hope and blessing promised by Jeremiah. They still live, as had their parents before them, in the period of Jerusalem's desolation. Therefore, the inspired interpretation of Jeremiah's seventy weeks explains the present desolation of Jerusalem and its past weakness, a historical revelation of considerable significance. Of course it also reveals just how near is the blessing on Jerusalem since once again Jeremiah's seventy years are almost spent.

Since the other visions in Daniel portray so clearly the fall and struggle of nations and empires during the seventy weeks of years, perhaps insight into the true meaning of Jeremiah's seventy years is the root from which the other visions spring. If so, the book of Daniel not only extends the seventy years of Jeremiah to seventy weeks of years, but also extends the passing of God's cup of wrath described in Jeremiah 25 from one cycle within one empire to four such cycles (Daniel 2 and throughout). Hence the succession of empires enacts God's judgment in history. Daniel's constituency has been living during the last judgment and indeed right before the crisis. Since all the empires must be punished, the last must end with direct intervention from God. Then and only then follows the blessing at the end of the seventy weeks of years.

Daniel's inspired interpretation of Jeremiah's seventy years explains the past and present weakness and desolation of Jerusalem as well as the dizzying succession of kings and empires and the hardships they bring. All of the kings are in God's plan. All of them are bringing God's delivering judgment that much nearer and indeed all of them, by struggling against it, bring about that judgment which is the chief characteristic of the present period. Such revelations of the true significance of the past and present would surely prove useful to Daniel's community of the wise.

A Judicial Historical Sermon: Daniel 5.17-28

In response to Belteshazzar's puzzlement over handwriting on the wall, Daniel utters a judicial historical sermon against him:[1]

Preamble	David renounces the King's gifts but declares he will read and interpret the message (Dan. 5.17).

---

1. Commentators frequently note the 'prophetic' character of this speech or relate it to Nathan's rebuke of David. Cf. Hartman and DiLella, 189; Montgomery, 261.

Historical Résumé	Three historical premises set up the consequence: 1. God gave Nebuchadnezzar greatness (Dan. 5.18-19). 2. Nebuchadnezzar exalted himself against God and God humiliated him (Dan. 5.20-21). 3. Belteshazzar exalted himself against God though he knew all this (Dan. 5.22-23).
Consequence: a Sentence	Daniel reads and interprets the words mina, minas, shekel, half minas;[1] God has numbered and ended your rule; you have been weighed in the balance and found wanting; your kingdom is divided and given to the Medes and Persians.

Each element of this tightly knit speech supports the consequence. The preamble asserts Daniel's prophetic independence from the king and intimates the condemnatory character of the coming oracle. The historical résumé proves by example that God exalts rulers to power, that he casts them down when they exalt themselves, and that Belteshazzar has knowingly exalted himself. What can follow but the consequence? God has taken the kingdom from Belteshazzar and given it to the Medes and Persians.

This judicial historical sermon incorporates much that is important for Daniel as a whole. Its conclusion fits the four empire scheme which dominates Daniel's inspired history. Pride, as that which brings God's judgment against rulers, is a central theme of Daniel and finds expression in the visions[2] as well as in the tales. Hence this inspired historical sermon reveals and enacts a general historical principle of great importance to the book of Daniel.

Daniel as Limited Apocalyptic History

Insight into the mysterious and significant period of history embracing Nebuchadnezzar and Antiochus IV is thus an important component of the message of Daniel. Such insight into the past can only be gained

---

1. While the interpretation of these terms as monetary weights is now generally accepted, their specific references are debated. Lacocque thinks they evaluate the relative worth of the four kingdoms: Babylon and Medes are worth a mina each, Persia worth a shekel, Alexander and his successors are worth several half minas (half indicating division between Seleucids and Ptolemies). See Lacocque, 102-103. Others more plausibly relate the words to a succession of rulers usually identifying Nebuchadnezzar with the mina, Belteshazzar with the diminutive shekel, and interpreting פרסין as a dual, identifying the two halves with the Median king and the Persian king. For variations of this theory see Hartman and DiLella, 190; Charles, 136. On any understanding both these words and their interpretation pass sentence on Belteshazzar.

2. Hubris is especially important in ch. 8, in virtually every appearance of Antiochus IV, and in several of the tales.

from the God who reveals mysteries (Dan. 2.28).[1] Daniel 9 reveals the true significance of Jeremiah's seventy years: the entire period from Nebuchadnezzar to Antiochus IV manifests God's judgment on the nations including Israel. Daniel 2 reveals that this period contains four cycles of judgment, that is, four empires. Daniel 7 distinguishes the fourth from the other three; to the first three the heavenly court grants a measure of support and legitimation, but to the last, so much worse than the others, only destruction. Daniel 8 reveals a pattern of hubris; as earlier (and greater) kings exalted themselves only to be cast down, so Antiochus and his kingdom must fall. Dan. 5.17-28 reveals a similar principle and applies it to the succession of empire from the Babylonians to Medes. Daniel 10–12 reveals the cycle of frustration which dogs all the kings, especially the Diodochoi. It reveals the heavenly source of their frustration and, consequently, the inevitability of frustration for Antiochus IV. As a true perception of the importance of history in Daniel should not rule out but rather support the significance of eschatology, so a correct apprehension of the revelation of the future in Daniel should affirm and not overlook the importance of a revelation of the past.

That Daniel serves kings of Babylon, Media, and Persia is underscored both in the tales and in the visions. Since the succession of empires in the four-empire scheme structures the action of the tales as well as of the visions and since the four-empire scheme with its various interpretations is the prime object of revelation in Daniel's application of revealed history, it follows that the entire book of Daniel is built upon an inspired glance at the past. Of course, Daniel differs from the apocalyptic world histories in that the revelations of the author's past are cast as revelations of the future. Daniel sees what will be. It thus might be asked whether Daniel deals with true revelations of the past at all, but such an objection has less substance than at first appears. The apocalyptist responsible for the book of Daniel sought to understand his past in order to understand his present and future, to give himself, and his contemporaries, hope. That he chose to express his understanding of the past in the form of revelations shows his epistemology of history. An accurate grasp of what has happened cannot come from human observation and speculation alone. Understanding the past requires a grasp of what has happened in the heavenly places (the heavenly court in Dan. 7, the activity of Michael and his helper in Dan. 10–12), of the pronouncements of the heavenly court

---

1. Probably the picture of Daniel in 2.27-30 accords with the self-perception of the author of Daniel and of the other משכלים. See J.J. Collins, *Apocalyptic Imagination*, 72.

(Dan. 5; 7; 8; 10–11), and of the true nature of empire explained mythologically (the myth of the chaos monster, especially Dan. 7 and 8). Accurate insight into the past must be based upon an inspired interpretation of Jeremiah's seventy weeks (Dan. 9). Understanding the past depends on revelation whether the device of pseudonymity requires casting the material as a revelation of the future or of the past. Daniel, with his interpretation of dreams, inspired interpretation of scripture, revelatory visions, and intercourse with angels, is depicted as the ideal wise man. Since the apocalyptist responsible for the book of Daniel is probably one of the wise who make many understand in the days of Antiochus IV (Dan. 11.33), inspired interpretations and revelatory visions are probably part of his own repertoire as well. That he should have cast some of his revelations concerning the past as revelations concerning the future, in accordance with his choice of pseudonym, does not make them any less revelations of the past.

The book of Daniel then is built upon a revelation of the past. Daniel employs revealed history to establish a recurring pattern within a puzzling and distressing period. The pattern, once established for the past, undergirds the apocalyptist's interpretation of the present and his expectations for the future. Daniel also reveals the principles behind the pattern: the inevitable reward for the hubris of kings, the inevitable overthrow of empires unmasked as chaos monsters, the inevitable frustration of kings opposed by angelic warriors. These principles are important historical revelations in their own right. No one who has perceived the true nature of these empires through the powerful imagery of the chaos myth will ever view them in quite the same light again. In the same way the principles of hubris and the heavenly frustration of kings, while allowing the kings to retain their terror, put that terror in a more comfortable context. Readers, who have seen these principles bring about the fall of the first three empires (or of predecessors of Antiochus within the last empire) according to the revealed patterns, will be encouraged to believe that the pattern and the principles will bring about the fall of Antiochus as well.

Thus Daniel writes large one of the arguments from revealed history already found in the apocalyptic world histories. Like the apocalyptic world histories, Daniel seeks by revelation to bring new insight to a troubled period of Jewish history in which older philosophies of history, such as the Deuteronomic historical principles, seem no longer to be operating. Unlike the apocalyptic world histories, Daniel considers only the period causing vexation; the author finds no need to place the vexing period into context in God's plan for the world from creation. Daniel sufficiently resembles *2 Baruch*, the

Apocalypse of Abraham, and the Animal Apocalypse to warrant classifying them all as apocalyptic histories. It differs from them
significantly enough to justify subdividing apocalyptic histories into
two types. *2 Baruch*, the *Apocalypse of Abraham*, and the Animal
Apocalypse, in that they seek to understand the puzzling period by
fitting it into the entire course of world history, are apocalyptic world
histories. Daniel, since it limits its interest to one period of history, is
a limited apocalyptic history.

Chapter 6

REVEALED HISTORY:
A FLEXIBLE TECHNIQUE FOR PERSUASION

The last four chapters considered Jewish works for which the author's
use of revealed history encouraged classification according to type or
form. The present chapter considers works which resist classification.
4 Ezra, though it makes marginal use of limited apocalyptic history
and inspired historical sermons, presents a bewildering array of
historical revelations. Revealed history constitutes a versatile weapon
in this apocalyptist's arsenal for dealing with difficult questions.
Sibylline Oracles 3, 4, and 5 also introduce new twists. Though
unquestionably Jewish, they rely heavily on Greek poetic and literary
forms. While at points they resemble the apocalyptic world histories,
classifying them as such before studying Greek use of revealed history
would be premature and probably inaccurate. The impossibility of
classifying the uses of revealed history in *4 Ezra* and the *Sibylline
Oracles* is probably as significant for understanding the ancient Jewish
use of revealed history as the possibility of classifying others. The
Sibylline books and *4 Ezra* demonstrate the flexibility of revealed history as a rhetorical technique. It was not limited to certain settings or
types of argument but was at home wherever it might bring
conviction.

4 Ezra

Like the book of Job, *4 Ezra* expands and elaborates the ancient
Hebrew form of the lament.[1] Ezra bemoans the desolation of Zion and

---

1. The lament form was applied by Harnisch to the introductory speeches of Ezra
in the first four visions. Thompson relates ch. 3 to Old Testament laments which
confess guilt but appeal to God for mercy. Others rightly see the situation of lament
controlling the questions asked and answered by the book: Harnisch, *Verhängnis und
Verheißung der Geschichte. Untersuchungen zum Zeit- und Geschichtsverständnis im
4. Buch Esra und in der syr. Baruchapokalypse*, 20-23; Alden Lloyd Thompson,
Responsibility for Evil in the Theodicy of IV Ezra (SBLDS 29; Missoula, MT:

the coming destruction of the many human beings who have disregarded the law. Biblical laments generally include a petition and *4
Ezra* is no exception. Ezra requests understanding of God's inscrutable
dealings with Israel[1] and seeks mercy for the mass of humanity
doomed to perish.[2] Although Ezra receives praise for identifying with
the wicked, his petition for mercy toward humanity is consistently
declined. This refusal echoes a pattern of denied intercessions for the
wicked in Jeremiah. As Jeremiah could not prevail to deliver
Jerusalem from disaster (Jer. 7.16; 11.14; 15.1), so Ezra cannot
deliver the mass of humanity from the destruction due its sin. Ezra's
request to understand God's dealings with Israel is also consistently
denied. The enlightenment Ezra seeks is too great for human comprehension. Uriel, who in *1 Enoch* runs the cosmos, never tires of
explaining that the understanding Ezra seeks exceeds his capacity
(4.10-12; 5.34-40) and surpasses what is fitting for a human being to
know (4.13-21). Yet to the request for understanding Uriel (and God)
eventually accedes after much persistence on Ezra's part,[3] for in the
climactic fourth vision Ezra receives that understanding which
surpasses knowledge. 'Speak, my lord; only do not forsake me lest I
die before my time. For I have seen what I do not know, and I have
heard what I do not understand' (*4 Ezra* 10.34-35).[4] The fifth and
sixth visions elaborate this unknowable knowledge, and in the final
vision Ezra transmits the sum of such knowledge in the twenty-four
exoteric and seventy esoteric books. Although Ezra cannot alter the
decision of the heavenly court condemning the wicked, he can prevail
to attain by apocalyptic vision that knowledge of God's dealings with

Scholars Press, 1977), 161; Jacob M. Myers, *I and II Esdras* (AB 42; Garden City,
NY: Doubleday, 1974), 125; Earl Breech, 'These Fragments I Have Shored Against
My Ruins: The Form and Function of 4 Ezra', *JBL* 92 (1973), 271.

1. This question opens the dialogue of the first three visions: 3.28-36; 5.28-29;
6.55-59.

2. See especially the long prayer 7.46–8.36.

3. Stone notes that Uriel's questions in 4.5-8 assume that human beings cannot
grasp knowledge traditionally imparted by apocalypses. Michael E. Stone, 'Lists of
Revealed Things in the Apocalyptic Literature', *Magnalia Dei: The Mighty Acts of
God* (ed. F.M. Cross, W.E. Lemke, P.D. Miller, Jr; Garden City, NY: Doubleday,
1976), 419-20. Stone concludes that *4 Ezra* engages in polemics against apocalyptic
understanding. I am inclined to draw the opposite conclusion; Uriel's reluctance
stresses the need for *apocalyptic* answers to Ezra's questions. See John J. Collins,
The Apocalyptic Imagination: An Introduction to the Jewish Matrix of Christianity
(New York: Crossroad, 1984), 160, cf. 168. Understanding central to *4 Ezra*: it is
better not to live than to suffer and not know why (*4 Ezra* 4.12).

4. All quotations from RSV.

Israel which is beyond human capacity. Such knowledge offers the only answer possible in this evil age to the petitions in Ezra's lament. *4 Ezra* is written to commend such apocalyptic knowledge to confused Jews thirty years after the destruction of Jerusalem. Hence the book ends by endorsing the twenty-four open, but especially the seventy hidden, books.

The argument in *4 Ezra* requires a number of reflections on history. The more extensive of these historical reviews, and perhaps the more interesting, occur in the context of Ezra's laments. In the longest (*4 Ezra* 3.1-27) Ezra rehearses the history of Israel from Adam to the fall of Jerusalem, showing the inevitability of failure in keeping the law.[1] This historical review constitutes the complaint or statement of trouble found in the classic lament form and is followed by the expected request (3.28-36). Similar laments precede each of the next two visions (5.21-30; 6.38-59) and a final lament introducing the fourth vision (9.29-37) is interrupted before the petition. Since, as laments, such reviews of history do not explicitly claim inspiration, they cannot be used as examples of inspired history.[2] Yet, though these laments must be discounted for the present purpose, inspired history does play an important role in *4 Ezra*. Uriel utters several brief speeches referring to past events as does God himself. The visions of the mourning woman, of the eagle, and of the man with the clouds each have their share of past reference, and the story of Ezra restoring the law and other books to Israel has no less than four distinct allusions to inspired history.

The historical revelations in the first three visions are all spoken by Uriel or God to Ezra and all try to explain the evil of this present age or the necessity of its remedy in judgment. That is, these historical revelations deny Ezra's petitions for the wicked. In 4.26-32 Uriel draws a series of conclusions from a declaration about the past,

---

1. Pieter G.R. deVilliers, 'Understanding the Way of God: Form, Function and Message of the Historical Review in IV Ezra 3.4-27', *SBLSP* (1981), 366.

2. Although these laments do not claim inspiration it is difficult to be certain that they are not conceived as inspired. Ezra reports that his mouth was opened (*mštgš hw'*, 9.27) before the fourth lament. The passive might suggest that it was opened by God though it may merely carry over the passive form 'my heart was troubled'. Myers (270) attributes it to an involuntary reaction of the seer. Yet this deep troubling of Ezra's mind always occurs in the presence of God and initiates dialogue with God or his representative (3.1-3; 5.21-22; 6.35-37; 9.26-29). The lament may be provoked in Ezra by God's presence. If so these laments are also inspired, but the claim to inspiration is too tenuous to establish the use of revealed history in *4 Ezra*. The Syriac text used throughout is that of R.J. Bidawid in *The Old Testament in Syriac according to the Peshitta Version*, Part 4, fasc. 3 (Leiden: Brill, 1973).

utilizing the style of argument, if not the form, of an inspired historical sermon. From the historical premise (an evil grain was sown in
Adam's heart and has produced much godlessness [4.30, cf. 28]), no
less than three separate inferences are drawn: (1) If an evil seed has
produced so much evil, how much good will many good seeds sown in
the new age produce? This more probable reading is based on the
Syriac. The Latin yields an opposite but equally valid conclusion: if
one grain produced so much evil, how much evil will the sowing of its
many descendent seeds produce?[1] In either case the historical premise
serves to make a point important to Uriel's argument. (2) Because evil
seed was sown in Adam's heart the present age is too infirm to bring
about the promise to the righteous. The historical revelation implies
the utter bankruptcy of the present age and the suffering of the
righteous in it (4.27). (3) The sowing of the bad seed in Adam implies
the destruction of the present evil age, for how can a field for good
seed be produced until the field for bad seed is destroyed? (4.29).
These three inferences from history underscore the evil of the present
age and the consequent necessity of judgment.

A less elaborate but similar deduction from historical premises
occurs in 6.1-6. Here God is speaking. God assures Ezra that he himself will visit creation with its end. The argument proceeds by analogy.
God planned his creation and himself executed his plan. In the same
way he will execute his creation's end since it is the last part of the
plan.[2] When Ezra reproaches God with the fate of the wicked who
both suffer now and in the future (7.18), Uriel replies with a discussion of the past. God commanded them what to do to live, but they disobeyed (7.21-24); hence God's ways are just (19-20, 25).

When Ezra, seeing the multitude of those who will be condemned,
thinks it would be better if no judgment followed death, the angel
replies that God created judgment first when he created the world with
Adam in it (7.70). Here a historical revelation again serves to base an

---

1. The thrust of the premise, which emphasizes that all evil stems from Adam,
favors the Syriac reading as does Ezra's question in 4.33 which presupposes some
mention of the goods of the new age. Of course the Latin's emphasis on the evil of
this age also suits the context. A scribe might have added *tbt'* in Syriac to clarify the
one interpretation or have excised it as too great a jump in subject. On balance I prefer
the Syriac. Syriac: Bruno Violet, *Die Apokalypsen des Esra und des Baruch in
deutscher Gestalt* (Die griechischen christlichen Schriftsteller der ersten drei
Jahrhunderte; Leipzig: Hinrichs, 1924), 17; G.H. Box, '4 Ezra', *APOT*, 2.566.
Latin: Myers, 165, RSV.

2. The last clause of v. 6 is omitted in the Syriac but should be retained. Cf.
Myers, 197; Box, 575; against Violet, 46.

inference. Ezra's prayers can never change God's purpose of judgment which is woven into the fabric of this age.

The final speech of Uriel before the climatic fourth vision which 'converts' the seer embraces the form as well as the content of a judicial historical sermon:

General Principle	He answered me and said, 'As is the field, so is the seed; and as are the flowers, so are the colors; and as is the work, so is the product; and as is the farmer, so is the threshing floor' (9.17).
Historical Résumé	For there was a time in this age when I was preparing for those who now exist, before the world was made for them to dwell in, and no one opposed me then, for no one existed; but now those who have been created in this world which is supplied both with an unfailing table and an inexhaustible pasture have become corrupt in their ways. So I considered my world, and behold, it was lost, and my earth, and behold it was in peril because of the devices of those who had come into it. And I saw and spared some with great difficulty, and saved for myself one grape out of a cluster, and one plant out of a great forest (9.18-21).
Consequence: a Sentence	So let the multitude perish which has been born in vain, but let my grape and my plant be saved, because with much labor I have perfected them (9.22).

This speech begins with series of analogies enunciating a general principle: what is produced depends on the ingredients and effort which produced it. The historical résumé applies this general principle. God made the world by himself without opposition. When those he created rebelled against him, he labored to save some. Therefore those for whom God labored will be saved but the rest will perish. Given the historical ingredients here revealed what other consequence could ensue?

Harnisch attributes to 9.18-21 an even greater historical component. The passage, by separating creation from 'this age', divides history into three periods: creation, this evil age, the age to come.[1] This age, corrupted by opposition to God, will be eradicated, though a remnant will be saved from it with great labor. Therefore let the many, the aberrant ones, perish. Though it rests upon an emendation to 9.18, Harnisch may be correct. If so, the negative answer given here to Ezra's intercession for the wicked turns even more clearly on a revelation of the past.

In the dialogues with Ezra (visions 1–3), Uriel (or God) frequently uses primordial history or an outline of salvation history to underscore

---

1. Harnisch, *Verhängnis*, 137-41.

the necessity and certainty of judgment. Since these histories are
spoken by Uriel or God, they are revealed histories; since they
uniformly draw consequences from historical premises they follow the
reasoning, if not the form, of inspired historical sermons. They constitute an important line of argument in the dialogues showing the
impossibility of salvation for those who disobey the law. It is
primarily these historical arguments which deny Ezra's petition for the
wicked.

Each of the three allegorical visions, those of the mourning woman,
of the eagle, and of the man, utilizes revealed history. The use of
revealed history in these visions follows no regular pattern but varies
from vision to vision. Like the inspired historical arguments considered above, they attest inspired history as a regular part of the
seer's repertoire.

Although the vision of the mourning woman emphasizes primarily
the glory of the heavenly Jerusalem, inspired history plays a significant
role in it. The most probable interpretation of the vision identifies the
woman with the heavenly and her son with the earthly Jerusalem.[1]
Uriel interprets the woman's thirty barren years as the 3000 years
before earthly Jerusalem was built,[2] the time of the son's rearing as the
time when God's presence was in the Temple,[3] and the son's death as
Jerusalem's destruction. This brief review of Jerusalem's history
portrays the true relation between the heavenly and earthly Jerusalems.
The vicissitudes of the earthly Jerusalem, though causing heavenly
Jerusalem to mourn, do not diminish her glory. As long as the
heavenly Jerusalem exists, as it always will, the possibility of a new
son, a new earthly Jerusalem, exists. Unknowingly, Ezra's speech to
the woman may foretell the reestablishment of the earthly Jerusalem in
the new age (10.16-17, 24).[4] Yet what the vision really seeks to get
across with its revelation of the past is that any historical Jerusalem
with a true Temple is at most a manifestation of the heavenly
Jerusalem. The wise, like Ezra, can take consolation in the glory of
heavenly Jerusalem regardless of the present state of her son.

Although Ezra's vision of the eagle is in form a limited apocalyptic
history, the function of its view of the past is difficult to pinpoint.
While it seems certain that the monstrous eagle represents Rome and
probable that its three heads represent the Flavian emperors, Ves-

---

1. Box, 605.
2. The numbers differ between versions. See Myers, 275.
3. Box, 607 n. 14.
4. Wolfgang Harnisch, 'Die Ironie der Offenbarung: Exegetische Erwägungen zur
Zionvision im 4. Buch Esra', *SBLSP* (1981), 94-95.

pasian, Titus, and Domitian, precise identification of the twelve wings representing kings or the eight wings remains doubtful.[1] Indeed the imagery is so complex and so few clues to interpretation are given that it seems unlikely for the point of the vision to be the portrayal of the historical sequence of emperors. In this case, despite the vision's historical content, all the emphasis falls on the future demise of Rome at the hands of the Davidic messiah.[2] The vision's assertions about the past appear limited to portraying the many internal struggles that marred Roman rule.[3] Despite the elaborate descriptions of the eagle the importance of history in this vision is minimal. It was not written to interpret history so much as to prove that the end of Roman dominance was near. The historical material is adduced primarily to bring the visions of Daniel up to date.

The vision of the man coming with the clouds also primarily concerns the future, yet it contains an excursus describing the history of the lost ten tribes (13.39-48). This excursus recounts events which can only be known by revelation since the ten tribes have been living apart from the rest of humanity. Primarily it assuages curiosity by revealing the manner of God's faithfulness to his faithful ones who were exiled in the days of King Hoshea.

In the last 'vision', in which Ezra restores the law to Israel, revelations of the past once again are central. Because of the many attempts early in this century to divide *4 Ezra* into component sources[4] and because of more recent preoccupation with themes of theodicy in the first four visions,[5] it is frequently overlooked how fitting a conclusion

---

1. Attempts to identify the eagle's wings are legion. Although it requires discarding the interpretation, Gry divides the twelve wings into pairs and speaks of six emperors. See L. Gry, *Les Dires prophétiques d'Esdras (IV Esdras)* (Paris: Geuthner, 1938), 1.xcviii. Probably those who try to identify twelve emperors are correct. See the valiant attempt by W.O.E. Oesterley, *II Esdras (The Ezra Apocalypse) with Introduction and Notes* (Westminster Commentaries; London: Methuen, 1933), 145. Yet there are difficulties with every interpretation so far adduced. The identification of the twelve wings is further complicated by a textual variant; the Latin, against the Syriac, does not require that all the wings actually rule (*4 Ezra* 11.20-21). The second wing with the long rule is almost certainly Augustus. See the summary of scholarship in Myers, 299-302, and note his discretion in refusing to try to identify all the wings.

2. Harnisch, 250, 254.

3. Civil war was viewed as a weakness even by the Romans. See Virgil, *Aeneid* 6.821-30.

4. Box, 549-52; Oesterley, xi-xix; Gry, xcviii-cxii.

5. Thompson, *passim*; Walter Harrelson, 'Ezra among the Wicked in 2 Esdras 3–10', *The Divine Helmsman: Studies on God's Control of Human Events, Presented*

Ezra dictating sacred books makes to the book as a whole. Klaus Koch
has argued convincingly that the goal of the first four visions is understanding the 'way of the Most High'.[1] It is a commonplace to notice
that vision four is a turning point in the book.[2] The fourth vision
commences with the lament and questioning characteristic of the first
three visions and concludes with apocalyptic vision and interpretation
characteristic of the latter half of the work. It is less common to notice
the reason for the switch from dialogue to apocalyptic vision: in
granting Ezra a glimpse of the true glory of Zion lamenting though
she be, God imparts to Ezra his first taste of the knowledge which surpasses human understanding. The experience sends Ezra reeling. Three
times Ezra expresses the reason for his stupor: he has seen the
incomprehensible (*4 Ezra* 10.28, 32, 34-35). He has attained the
knowledge—long sought and long denied—which passes human
understanding.[3] The vision of the eagle (vision 5) and of the man
(vision 6) continue this bestowal of the knowledge beyond human
comprehension. The final vision provides the capstone: Ezra is not
given merely a vision or two, but whole books containing 'the spring
of understanding, the fountain of wisdom and the river of knowledge'
(14.47). Such understanding answers the petitions in Ezra's agonized
laments. Even his prayers, righteous as they are, cannot change the
situation. Despite his efforts this age is evil and will remain so. It
cannot be bettered but must be destroyed to make way for the new age.
But divine understanding can lighten the load of the wise even in this
age and ensure their participation in the age to come. Ezra's dictation
of the twenty-four open and seventy secret books assures members of
the author's community that they have received revelation sufficient to
encourage them by living well to attain the glorious future age.[4]

Inspired history is an important component of the requisite divine
understanding. God reveals to Ezra that he (God) had delivered many

---

to Lou H. Silberman, ed. J.L. Crenshaw and S. Sandmel (New York: Ktav, 1980),
21-39.

1. Klaus Koch, 'Esras erste Vision. Weltzeiten und Weg des Höchsten', *BZ* 22
(1978), 46-75. He is followed closely by deVilliers, 363-65.

2. Harnisch, 'Ironie', 79, 88; Harrelson, 36; Michael E. Stone, 'Reactions to the
Destruction of the Second Temple', *JSJ* 12 (1981), 202.

3. Such knowledge is not merely cognitive but also experiential. Almost all of the
factual content of the last four visions has already been imparted by Uriel to Ezra, but
not the emotional impact. In the Zion vision Ezra sees with his eyes what before he
had only heard with his ears. Such deeper apprehension leads to a kind of
conversion. See Stone, 'Destructions', 202; Breech, 273-74; A.P. Hayman, 'The
Problem of Pseudonymity in the Ezra Apocalypse', *JSJ* 6 (1975), 56.

4. deVilliers, 365-66.

secrets to Moses on Sinai, instructing him to publish some and hide others (14.3-6). The goal of this historical revelation is to heighten the dignity and prestige of the forthcoming revelation to Ezra. God will uncover secrets to Ezra as he had to Moses and will command Ezra to publish some openly and impart some only to the wise. God also reveals the content of his words to Moses. I 'showed him the secrets of the times and declared to him the ends of the times' (14.5). Since these are in parallelism it is possible that the 'secrets of the times' and the 'ends of the times' refer to the same thing. Yet it is also possible that a distinction is made between them. If so, the 'secrets of the times' probably refer to mysteries of the past, present, and future and 'ends of the times' to mysteries concerning the coming cataclysm.[1] Because of the similar distinction (14.21) drawn between what God has done and what he will do and in view of the concern for the past in this apocalypse, it seems better to credit the difference between the two phrases: God showed Moses secrets of the times past, present, and future and also revealed to him the final catastrophe and the new age. Revelations of the past are an important component of that super-human knowledge which is the goal of this apocalypse to Ezra.

The same inference should be drawn from Ezra's prayer (14.20-22). Since the law has been burned, future generations will have to face the evil days without knowledge of what God has done (*'bd' d'bdt*, 14.21) and of what he will do (*mdm d'tyd 'nt dt'bd*). Ezra asks for the spirit that he might write 'everything that has happened in the world from the beginning' (14.22). Although this statement is connected with Ezra's request to restore the law, it is clearly as important to see what has been done in the past as to see what will be done in the future. To reveal both Ezra must write by the Holy Spirit (14.22).

Ezra's final address to the people exemplifies this important use of the past. Ezra's prayer sets his own speaking to the people in the present in parallel with the purpose of the books in the future. The books are not so necessary now since Ezra lives to reprove the people; after his death the books will be necessary (14.20). Since the books which are to replace Ezra's reproof are clearly inspired, the reproof they replace must also be inspired, and indeed Ezra speaks in the form of a hortative historical sermon:

---

1. In *4 Ezra* 'the end' refers to whatever eschatological event is decisive in the context. Michael E. Stone, 'Coherence and Inconsistency in the Apocalypses: The Case of the End in 4 Ezra', *JBL* 102 (1983), 241. Stone had anticipated his definition of 'the end' in 'The Concept of the Messiah in 4 Ezra', *Religions in Antiquity: Essays in Memory of Erwin Ramsdell Goodenough* (ed. Jacob Neusner, Studies in the History of Religions 14; Leiden: Brill, 1968), 298.

Address	Hear these words, O Israel (14.28).
Historical Résumé	At first our fathers dwelt as aliens in Egypt, and they were delivered from there, and received the law of life, which they did not keep, which you also have transgressed after them. Then the land was given to you for a possession in the land of Zion; but you and your fathers committed iniquity and did not keep the ways which the Most High commanded you. And because he is a righteous judge, in due time he took from you what he had given. And now you are here, and your brethren are farther in the interior (14.29-33).
Consequence: an Exhortation	If you, then, will rule over your minds and discipline your hearts, you shall be kept alive, and after death you shall obtain mercy. For after death the judgment will come, when we shall live again; and then the names of the righteous will become manifest, and the deeds of the ungodly will be disclosed (14.34-35).

Ezra bases his exhortation to future happiness on what God has done in the past. A proper knowledge of what God has done in the past urges obedience in the face of the judgment which ends this age. If the goal of *4 Ezra* is knowledge of the way of the most high, that knowledge has a past as well as a future component.

The inspiration accorded Ezra in this last vision shows one more unique feature directed toward the past. Ezra desires to rewrite the law which has been burned (14.21-22). God grants his request by giving him a drink to bring him understanding and to strengthen his memory. Ezra receives once again the revelation which Moses (14.3-5) and the prophets received. The seventy books might include those revelations initially given to the patriarchs and other ancient worthies.[1] Ezra thus receives revelation of a particular kind of past event: God brings to Ezra's memory what has already been revealed to others. Though the renewal of ancient books by inspired memory has a partial parallel in Jacob's remembrance of heavenly books (*Jub.* 32.21-26) and an echo in the Paraclete-memory of the Gospel of John (Jn 14.26), such instances are too diverse to define a genus of revealed history. Yet *4 Ezra* 14 suggests a possible link between revealed history and the perplexing phenomenon of pseudonymity: an author might perceive himself inspired to recount a revelation given in the past to a person long dead.

Although *4 Ezra's* one historical apocalypse hardly uses revealed history to make any discernible point, *4 Ezra* is rich in inspired history. In the first three visions inferences from revealed history

1. See the books of the fathers mentioned in *Jubilees*.

explain the denial of Ezra's petition for the wicked. Ezra's other question, concerning the desolation of Zion, is answered by revelation of the ways of God, past, present, and future. Revelations about the past show the goodness of creation, the wickedness of this age and its origin in human opposition to God, and the true distinction between the heavenly and the earthly Jerusalem. The definitive expression of the superhuman understanding occurs in the restoration of the twenty-four and seventy books. Not only do these books reveal the past as well as the future, but their bestowal is an act of historical revelation. Past revelations are revealed yet again to Ezra by a combination of heightened understanding and memory.

The most arresting aspect of revealed history in *4 Ezra* is its variety. The apocalyptist employs inspired historical arguments to show why the wicked must be condemned despite Ezra's petition. He uses two inspired historical sermons, one judicial, the other hortatory, as suits the occasion. Several passages are employed to reveal past events or conditions not otherwise known to the reader. The vision of the mourning woman, by revealing the historical relation between the heavenly and earthly Jerusalems, encourages those who have lost the earthly. By revealing the content of the revelations to Moses, the apocalyptist emphasizes the importance and the similarity of the revelations about to be given to Ezra. A revelation concerning the history of the ten lost tribes may serve to vindicate God's justice and covenant faithfulness but perhaps primarily satisfies curiosity. In the most remarkable of Ezra's historical revelations, Ezra, by receiving again what God disclosed to Moses, and probably to others also, discovers what God has done and will do. The mechanism of this revelation is inspired memory. This act of historical revelation assures that those who wish will have the understanding necessary to endure faithfully until the coming of the new age. Such flexible use of historical revelation to make points deeply significant for *4 Ezra* shows how central are revelations concerning the past to the author's apocalyptic repertoire. Revelations of the past, as of the future, may be applied at need in whatever way seems appropriate to answer the host of problems the apocalyptist sets out to face.

Sibylline Oracles

Although the corpus of *Sibylline Oracles* was authored by Christians as well as Jews, only Jewish works survive from the period of interest here. *Sibylline Oracles* 3–5 are clearly dated before 130 CE. While book 11 may well date to the turn of the era as Collins argues,[1] no consensus has yet been reached on the matter. Since any findings based on book 11 would be suspect because of the date, only books 3–5 will be considered.

While books 3–5 are uniformly Jewish, their form, concept of inspiration, and much of their content derives from Greek antecedents. Like all sibylline literature, the extant *Sibylline Oracles* are written in dactylic hexameter. Jewish, like pagan, sibyls speak reluctantly, compelled from great weariness to speak the words of the god.[2] When the famous collection of Roman sibyls was lost in fire, authorities collected fragments from various sources to renew the collection. In the same way books 3 and 5 should be viewed as collections of juxtaposed oracles rather than attempts to maintain a sustained argument.[3] Like their Greek models Jewish sibyls speak *ex eventu* prophecies.[4] Reviews of the past cast as predictions for the future characterize pagan as well as Jewish sibyls. A proper study of inspired history in these Jewish *Sibylline Oracles* would require investigation of the vast literature of pagan inspired history. Since such a study exceeds the scope of the present work it will be necessary to inquire how the Jewish exponents utilized these Greek forms of inspired history rather than to pursue the interesting but complex question of how these Greek forms function in and of themselves. For this reason, from the many passages of inspired history in the *Sibylline Oracles*, those chosen for analysis will show some special twist of interest to the Jewish author or editors.

The way these oracles utilize sibylline forms will be examined through several passages. *Sibylline Oracles* 3.401-88 shows how a Jewish author makes a point through an extended quote of a pagan sibyl—the Erythrean. In *Sibylline Oracles* 3.97-161 the author uses inspired history to reinterpret Greek mythology. *Sibylline Oracles* 4 uses inspired history and prediction, reminiscent of apocalyptic world

---

1. John J. Collins, 'The Sibylline Oracles', in *Jewish Writings of the Second Temple Period* (ed. Michael E. Stone; Philadelphia: Fortress, 1984), 373-76. In this Collins develops views of Alons Kurfess, *Sibyllinische Weissagungen* (Berlin: Tusculum, 1951), 338-39. See also Kurfess, 'Die Oracula Sibyllina XI–XIV nicht christlich, sondern jüdisch', *Zeitschrift für Religions- und Geistesgeschichte* 7 (1955), 270-71. Geffcken thinks book 11 was written in the third century CE. See Johannes Geffcken, *Komposition und Entstehungszeit der Oracula Sibyllina* (Leipzig: Hinrichs, 1902), 65-66.

2. Compare Virgil, *Aeneid* 6.78 with *Sib. Or.* 4.18; 3.1-7, 295-97.

3. John J. Collins, *The Sibylline Oracles of Egyptian Judaism* (SBLDS 13; Missoula, MT: Scholars Press, 1974), 4, 6, 9, 21, 24, 26.

4. Virgil, *Aeneid* 6.82-95.

history, to urge the Gentiles to repent and be converted. *Sibylline Oracles* 5 mixes inspired history with prediction so that the two can scarcely be distinguished.

A Fragment from the Erythrean Sibyl (3.401-88)

The character of the sibylline books as collections of oracles is conducive to interpolation. After the body of *Sibylline Oracles* 3 was written,[1] several political oracles were incorporated in the book to bring the collection up to date and to impart the distinctive sibylline flavor of prophecies against many specific cities.[2] These political oracles (lines 350-488), though all *ex eventu* prophecies, came from diverse backgrounds and are not necessarily Jewish. One of these (*Sib.Or.* 3.401-88) is probably excerpted from the Erythrean sibyl.[3] It is not hard to see why this piece would be attractive to a Jewish sibyllist. After announcing woes on Troy and describing events of the Trojan War (3.401-18), this oracle launches into an attack on the veracity of Homer. He is a false writer (ψευδογράφος, 319).[4] He will write the story of Ilium not truthfully but cleverly (οὐ μὲν ἀληθῶς ἀλλὰ σοφῶς, 423, 424). Writing falsely about everything he will make gods stand by the empty-headed heroes of the Iliad. (καί γε θεοὺς τούτοισι παρίστασθαι γε ποιήσει,//ψευδο γραφῶν κατὰ πάντα τρόπον, μέροπας κενοκράνους, 429-30). At the same time the Erythrean sibyl appreciates Homer's accomplishment. 'He will have much intelligence and will have speech well proportioned to his thoughts' (421).[5] His work will heap glory on the heroes and also on himself (431-32). Thus the Erythrean sibyl maintains a high appreciation for Homer's work while rejecting the substance of its portrayal of the battles of the gods and heroes before the walls of Troy. Given the high esteem accorded the Homeric epics in Greek culture, the concentration on his works at all levels of Greek education, and the formative role they played for official Greek religion, the Erythrean sibyl's attitude toward Homer would prove attractive and useful for a faithful hellenized Jew of the first century. Such a person could only appreciate the nice balance between rejecting the substance but affirming the art of the Homeric poems. This balance fits well the

---

1. Collins dates between 163 and 45 BCE, 'The Sibylline Oracles', *OTP*, 1.355.
2. Collins, *OTP*, 1.359.
3. Geffcken, *Komposition* 13; Collins, *OTP*, 1.357; H.C.O. Lanchester, 'The Sibylline Oracles', *APOT*, 2.386.
4. The Greek text is that of Johannes Geffcken, *Die Oracula Sibyllina* (Leipzig: Hinrichs, 1902).
5. English translations are those of Collins, *OTP*, 1.317-472.

polemic against pagan religion which occurs throughout the Jewish sibyls. Since this oracle already circulated among pagans and was known by them,[1] its inclusion validates the other oracles against pagan religion by reminding readers that sibyls were widely known to have said such things. Hence this particular inspired glance at the past solved a knotty problem for those Jews who wished to reconcile Hebrew and Greek culture. The works of Homer should be appreciated for their craft and language, but no qualms were necessary in rejecting all the stories about the gods' dealings with the heroes as mere embellishment on Homer's part. Incidentally, willingness to accept an oracle from a pagan source may indicate that Jewish sibyllists seriously thought that God had spoken through these ancient Gentile women. The view, prevalent in the medieval church, that the Hebrew prophets were counterbalanced by Gentile sibyls may not so drastically differ from the attitude of the sibyllists themselves.

Sibylline Oracles 3.97-161

Collins assigns this oracle concerning early antediluvian history to the original collection made between 161 and 145 BCE.[2] Certainly it traces conflict over kingship back to the beginning and provides a context for the oracles concerning the end which make up much of the book,[3] yet this oracle also uses inspired history to effect rapprochement between Greek and Hebrew mythology.

The story begins with the overthrow of the tower of Babylon and the strife consequent upon the confusion of tongues (3.97-109). Attention turns to a genealogy of Gaia and Ouranos closely paralleled in Hesiod's *Theogony* (421ff.). Cronos and Rhea and their children, Zeus, Poseidon, Pluto, and Hera as well as Aphrodite, Demeter, Hestia, and Dione all appear, but as human beings not as gods (3.110-55). The oracle concludes with the death of these descendants of Titan and Cronos and a list of succeeding kingdoms down to Rome.

The fall of the tower occurs in the tenth generation of articulate men after the flood (3.108-109). Since Gaia and Ouranos and their children are called the first articulate human beings (τοι πρώτιστοι μερόπον ἀνθρῶπων), the discussion of Cronos and Titan is best seen as a flashback to the time before the fall of the tower. Gaia and Ouranos correspond to Noah and his wife, Cronos, Titan, and Iapetus to their

---

1. Varro quoted in Lactantius, *Div. Inst.* 1.6; Pausanias 10.2.2.
2. Collins, *OTP*, 1.354.
3. Collins, *OTP*, 1.354; *Egyptian Judaism*, 27.

children.[1] As in the Noah stories of *Jubilees* the land was divided between three children by oath.[2] As in *Jubilees* these oaths were broken, bringing strife upon the earth.[3] The feud between Cronos and Titan and their children begins the practice of warfare which is rewarded with God's judgment against them (154-58). This judgment starts the succession of world kingdoms and should probably be equated with the fall of the tower.[4]

This revelation of the past provides a point of contact between Greek and Hebrew mythology, accounting for the Greek stories of the gods on the basis of human history. The stories of the gods are placed squarely in the run of Hebrew history in the time of Noah and his descendants. Those beings the Greeks worship are shown to be unequivocally human and, as all human beings, squarely under God's control. Yet this revelation of the past also provides ground for appreciation of the Greek stories. True they are not stories about gods, but they have their place. The revelation provides a context in which Jews may appreciate Greek stories as well as explaining to Greeks the error of worshiping their gods.[5]

The oracle also explains the run of history as a succession of empires and emperors striving for mastery over the world once the equitable divisions made soon after the flood were transgressed. In the allusion to the flood and to the judgment at the tower, God's intervention in human affairs is promised.

Sibylline Oracles 4
Book 4 of the *Sibylline Oracles* is an interesting exception to the rule that sibylline books are collections of oracles. In its present form book 4 is a unity supporting a single message. This is not to say that the book does not have several discrete oracles in it. Flusser has rightly identified a hellenistic anti-Macedonian oracle in 4.49-101[6] and Collins

---

1. Valentin Nikiprowetzky, *La Troisième Sibylle* (Etudes Juives 9 Paris: Mouton, 1970), 113, 116, 117.
2. Nikiprowetzky, 103.
3. Compare 3.114-20 with *Jubilees* 8.10-30; 9.14-15; 10.29-33.
4. Nikiprowetzky, 105.
5. See Collins's understanding of the purpose of *Sibylline Oracles* 3: 'In fact the whole purpose of the sibylline enterprise would appear to be to develop the common ground shared by Egyptian Jews and their environment. In this a framework is established within which the Greeks might learn to appreciate Judaism in terms of their own values and ideals, but also the Jews might learn to appreciate what they held in common with the Greeks' (*Egyptian Judaism*, 54).
6. David Flusser, 'The Four Empires in the Fourth Sibyl and in the Book of Daniel', *Israel Oriental Studies* 2 (1972), 150-53.

may rightly seek its original conclusion in 4.174-92.[1] The Jewish author may have taken over this oracle with an addition concerning Rome already in place or may have added it herself. Regardless of the origin of the material, the final Jewish author has forged a unity with clearly defined goals in which inspired history plays a major role.

As the author of book 4 chose the Greek form of sibylline prophecy to carry her message, so she also organized it according to the canons of classical rhetoric. Book 4 may be analysed as a deliberative speech. *Sibylline Oracles* 4.1-23 serves as a kind of proem, introducing the sibyl as speaker and establishing her ethos; she speaks by authority of the one great God who is too great for a temple among human beings. Beginning with such a powerful ethos, though capable of supporting any message the sibyllist wishes to express, may contain an element of risk. Although a negative attitude toward an earthly temple is attested in Jewish Christian sects (notably Elchasites and Ebionites, cf. Stephen's speech in Acts) and surfaces occasionally in the Old Testament (Isa. 66; 2 Sam. 7), it is not the general Jewish attitude either before or after the destruction of the Temple in 70 CE.[2] Neither would the majority of pagans be won by it. No evidence suggests a sizable body of Gentiles discontent with worshiping gods by sacrifices in temples.[3] On the other hand this proem does claim an exalted ethos for the sibyl as spokeswoman for the greatest of gods and develops one strand of Jewish thought as a possible answer to the destruction of the Temple. In the wake of this destruction it may have been necessary to vindicate God before giving his message. The destruction of the Temple does not indicate a defeated God, one with little right to speak. The cessation of earthly temple worship is of little consequence since God is too great for an earthly temple in any case. He is quite exalted above earthly events and rules them all. This proem also introduces the sibyl's subject as proems often do:

> He it is who drove a whip through my heart within,
> to narrate accurately to men what now is
> and what will yet be, from the first generation
> until the tenth comes (4.18-21).

Sibylline Oracles 4.24-49 advances a proposition: the pious will be happy, the impious tormented. Accompanying these assertions is a

---

1. John J. Collins, 'The Place of the Fourth Sibyl in the Development of the Jewish Sibyllina', *JJS* 25 (1974), 374.
2. Collins, 'Fourth Sibyl', 378-79.
3. Of course philosophers sometimes undercut traditional understandings of sacrifice. See Plato, *Euthyphro*, 14c-15c.

description of the pious as those rejecting earthly temples, refraining from wickedness, and glorifying the great God. This description of righteousness, coupled with the publication of judgment against the wicked on behalf of the righteous, implies exhortation: turn from wickedness and inherit happiness. Yet this exhortation is not explicit.

There follows a series of headings proving the proposition (*Sib. Or.* 4.50-192). The rise and fall of four kingdoms (Assyrians, Medes, Persians, Macedonians) is chronicled, followed by a longer treatment of Rome. As in Daniel a pattern is established. Time after time, a kingdom rises and falls. Rome will fall also. The count of generations soon reaches ten, six for Assyria, two for Media, one for Persia, and one for Macedonia. Since the tenth generation is the last in the present form of the oracle it must include Roman as well as Macedonian hegemony. The fall of Rome and end of the world loom in the immediate future.

The account of Roman rule is elaborated in several ways. For the first time earthly events are explained as the outworking of God's judgment on impiety. The Lord responds to the impieties of Patara with thunderings and earthquake (4.112-13).[1] War comes against Jerusalem because of abominable murder before the Temple (4.115). Vesuvius anticipates the final fiery catastrophe because Rome has turned against the pious (4.130-36). Yet in the main the moral thrust, so evident in the proposition, is reserved for the end of times when impiety is multiplied and God destroys the whole human race by a great conflagration (4.152-61, 171-78) and then raises and judges it. The righteous live again on earth but the unrighteous are covered with earth and live in Tartarus-Gehenna.

The proof is complete. The pious are blessed and the wicked punished as the proposition asserted. The historical revelation to the sibyl has shown how the entire process of history issues in this conflagration and final blessing of the righteous. The revelation concerning the blessing of the righteous and the distress of the wicked occurs as the exhortation implicit in the proposition is given urgent voice. The sibyl implores 'wretched mortals' to repent and be baptized and so avert the coming conflagration.[2]

> Ah, wretched mortals, change these things, and do not lead the great God
> to all sorts of anger, but abandon daggers and groanings, murders and
> outrages, and wash your whole bodies in perennial rivers. Stretch out your

1. As Collins points out, 'Lord' could denote Poseidon in the source, but in the present context 'Lord' must be the Great God. See Collins, *OTP*, 1.387, n. u.
2. Collins ('Fourth Sibyl', 377-80) connects this baptism with Jewish baptist sects in the Jordan Valley.

hands to heaven and ask forgiveness for your previous deeds and make propitiation for bitter impiety with words of praise; God will grant repentance and will not destroy. He will stop his wrath again if you all practice honorable piety in your hearts (*Sib. Or.* 4.162-70).

Probably this exhortation is the goal of the whole work even though it is only implicit in the proposition.[1] Book 4 thus imitates a deliberative speech. Despite the fall of the Temple and Gentile ascendancy it argues that all should repent and embrace the great God. Book 4 lacks a clear epilogue. Perhaps the author did not wish to dilute the portrayal of the judgment by a final summary.

The place and function of inspired history in the argument is not altogether clear. Although an exhortation follows the historical revelation, book 4 cannot be classed as a hortative historical sermon, since the exhortation does not follow clearly from the history as a consequence. In form the fourth Sibylline book is very close to apocalyptic world history, yet since pagan sibylline prophecy frequently related all of world history under a scheme of ten generations or empires, it would be over-hasty to identify it with a form isolated from Jewish apocalypses. Furthermore, in the apocalyptic world histories revelations of the past play a more significant role in the argument than they do here in the *Sibylline Oracles* 4. As the proposition indicates, book 4 is written to portray the blessing on the righteous and the curse on the wicked at the end of time, rather than to reinterpret the past. Inspired history may have been included partially because it was the normal stuff of sibylline prophecy, but it has a more positive, though limited, role as well. By placing world history in the context of final judgment against the wicked and for the righteous, revealed history maintains the omnipotence of the Hebrew God despite the fall of the Temple and Gentile dominance of world history. By assuming the Gentile scheme of five world empires book 4, like Daniel, establishes a pattern. As the other empires have fallen so will Rome. By integrating these five empires within the common sibylline scheme of ten generations and allotting to the tenth generation both the empires of Macedon and Rome, the historical revelation implies the nearness of the coming judgment. Perhaps more importantly, by concluding Gentile history organized according to a well-known Gentile scheme with final judgment by the Jewish God, the sibyllist undergirds exhortation for Gentiles to repent and be baptized. Gentile like Jewish

---

1. Collins ('Fourth Sibyl', 377-78) finds in 4.152-72 the author's primary attempt to interpret his earlier material.

history climaxes in the judgment. It behoves Gentiles as well as Jews to be ready.

Sibylline Revealed History
Aside from the introductory oracle which is an epitome of book 11 and therefore possibly late, *Sibylline Oracles* 5 makes little use of inspired history. Book 5 is much more a collection of oracles than book 4. References to the past are frequently juxtaposed immediately with references to the future and probably serve primarily as validators for the predictions rather than serving a more positive role.

These Jewish *Sibylline Oracles* employ inspired history in keeping with that desire for rapprochement with Greek culture implied by the choice of a sibyl as pseudonym. In book 3 the sibyl reveals secrets about the past which permit the correct appreciation of the Homeric epics or of Greek mythology. Such historical revelations provide a basis upon which a faithful Jew can participate in the surrounding culture. Book 4, though not seeking a ground for participation in Greek culture, also uses the sibyl pseudonymously as a bridge between cultures. The sibyl, by showing God's control of Gentile world history, summons not only Jews but the whole human race to repentance by baptism. The historical revelations undergird this summons by integrating the widely accepted Gentile view of history in the ten-generation, five-empire scheme with a final judgment and call to repentance. Jewish sibyllists, whether from Egypt or Palestine, used sibylline historical revelations to establish continuity between Greek and Hebrew culture.

The Flexibility of Revealed History
4 Ezra and the *Sibylline Oracles* show clearly that the use of revealed history was not constrained within a few forms or types. The current world view implied a certain epistemology of history. If the counsel of God determines what happens and if every event has heavenly as well as earthly components, then revelation is necessary to understand past events. In such a climate of thinking a revelation about history is always welcome as premise to an argument or as a topic for persuasion. Hence revealed history could be used flexibly. Those who mastered the technique used revealed history in recognizable forms or outside of them. They hoped to be persuasive wherever belief in the historical activity of God and in the possibility of revelation coincided.

Chapter 7

Techniques of Revealed History

The initial, and accurate, impression left by the works studied so far is one of diversity. Jews between 200 BCE and 130 CE applied historical revelation to a variety of objects in a variety of ways to address a variety of problems. Such diversity of historical revelations implies that revealed history is not so much a genre as a technique. It was one of the weapons available in the first century CE for attacking the difficulties of the day, one technique in the first-century writer's repertoire for solving knotty problems. Its use was limited only by the problems addressed and by the author's ingenuity. Judging by its widespread employment it must have proved effective. As a technique revealed history has three aspects.

Revealed history is a rhetorical technique, a *topos*. One way of convincing readers to do or believe as they should was to show how mysteries of God's working in the past make those actions or beliefs imperative or desirable in the present. How better to encourage a potential Maccabean warrior than to reveal how present affliction on Israel is due to angelic oppression which a pattern in history shows is about to be overthrown (Animal Apocalypse)? What more conducive to keeping the law than its having been woven into the fabric of the universe as revealed in *Jubilees*? In the confusing time following the destruction of Jerusalem, God apparently had blessed the wicked Gentiles instead of the relatively righteous Jews. What could better uphold the principle of keeping the law than a revelation that the age had changed; that as God in history had always blessed the righteous but cursed the wicked, now he was doing so on a much broader scale (*2 Baruch*)? What could be more damning than the recitation of sins as they were perceived in the heavenly court? The sentence of a judicial historical sermon, based as it is on revelation of the past, is certain. Hence, whether the author's intent is judicial, deliberative, or epideictic, revelation of the past can be a powerful tool to effect conviction in the hearers.

Revealed history is also an epistemological technique. It provides a basis for knowledge of the past. Past events known by revelation are much more certain than those known merely by memory or tradition. Interpretations of events from revelation are much surer than those imposed merely by the human mind. Those understandings of the past which by revelation know the heavenly actions behind earthly events surpass in accuracy those based merely on events perceived by a human observer. The practice of revealed history grows out of a view of historical explanation different from the modern one. Those who believe that every event has heavenly as well as earthly components are dissatisfied with any history which cannot explain heavenly as well as earthly constituents of an event. For such a conception of historical explanation, an accurate grasp of events in the past requires revelation.

Revealed history is also a hermeneutical technique. Since prophets spoke by inspiration, they revealed more than human perception can grasp. How can Jeremiah's seventy years be understood when the events that fulfill them are invisible? The Animal Apocalypse reveals the heavenly events which fulfill the seventy years and hence, for the first time, accurately interprets Jeremiah's prophecy. Sometimes it is difficult to know whether the key which opens the scripture bases the revelation about history or whether the key is derived from a revelation about history. Does Daniel receive a revelation about history and hence understand Jeremiah, or does he receive a revelation about Jeremiah and hence understand history? Probably the latter at least as portrayed in Daniel 9. Yet evidence within the Jewish sources allows movement both ways. Revelations about history interpret scripture and revelations about scripture interpret history. And, as true revelations should, the two kinds complement and confirm one another. As only the one who by revelation has perceived what really happened can rightly understand the scripture, so only the one who by revelation has perceived what scripture means can understand what happened.

Despite its multiplicity Jewish historical revelations divide naturally into several genera and species. Prophetic histories record the past from the standpoint of revelation. Josephus, who in the *Jewish War* writes history based on a blend of revelation and experience, writes an interpretive prophetic history. *Jubilees*, which purports to be written or dictated by one of the angels of the presence, is an inspired prophetic history. These two species of prophetic history are distinguished by two characteristics: relation to inspiration and object of revelation. *Jubilees* has for its object events long since past to its putative as well as its real author, therefore it receives events and their interpretation by revelation and perceives itself as inspired. The *Jewish*

War relates events experienced by Josephus. Hence Josephus has the option, which he exercises, of limiting revelation to interpreting the events he remembers. He learns of no events or speeches by revelation and he does not consider his history inspired. Yet he bases his understanding of what happened in the Jewish War on a revelation of God's will in history.

Apocalyptic history aims not to chronicle past events so much as to reveal God's purposes, dispensations, and judgments for the run of history. Without exception apocalyptic histories occur in apocalypses; historical mysteries are disclosed in a vision, vision with interpretation, or a heavenly trip. All the apocalyptic histories studied spring from a historical crisis: the threat to Jerusalem under Antiochus IV or the destruction of Jerusalem in 70 CE. All of them address some aspect of a problem which plagued post-exilic Israel: what has become of the wisdom principle, 'God blesses the righteous but curses the wicked'? Where is the promise of Deuteronomy and the Deuteronomic History? Such questions are answered by showing how the deuteronomic principle held under the old heavenly administration but not under the new (2 *Baruch*, Animal Apocalypse), or by showing how even Israel is dominated by Azazel (*Apocalypse of Abraham*), or how the larger pattern of history fulfills the principle through those events which seem to deny it (Daniel, 2 *Baruch*). Apocalyptic history divides neatly into two species by object considered. Apocalyptic world histories describe the divisions of history and their dispensations from creation to consummation. Limited apocalyptic histories describe patterns of heavenly action within a period in which puzzling events have occurred.

Inspired historical sermons set out not to recount history but to draw a consequence. A historical review reveals the divine perspective on historical events. A consequence which follows from the historical sequence is then explicitly drawn. Historical sermons were classified according to the consequence drawn. Judicial historical sermons recount a series of sins which cry out for judgment. As a consequence, God passes a sentence against the offenders. Inductive historical sermons ground a general principle on the historical review. Hortative historical sermons base an exhortation on the revelations concerning the sequence of past events. Historical sermons probably originated as a form of prophetic speech. They are ordinarily addressed by a prophet to an audience or by God to a prophet.

Yet these genera do not exhaust the varieties of historical revelation encountered. The historical revelations in *4 Ezra* and the *Sibylline Oracles* fail to fit into the categories above. *4 Ezra* uses revelation directed toward the past so flexibly that it seems to produce a number of new categories all by itself. Ezra restoring the entire body of ancient wisdom to Israel by inspired memory is unique, though it is anticipated in *Jubilees*. The *Sibylline Oracles*, by adapting Greek forms of revealed history, also go their own route. Revealed history cannot be circumscribed within certain genera, useful as the genera may be. As a technique, it can be used wherever it is helpful.

As revelations of the past almost always apply to the present, so present realities almost always determine what is revealed. Interactions between past and present are of several kinds.

Patterns echoing the present are revealed in the past so that what happens in the past can serve as a model for what happens in the present and future. Patriarchal battles in *Jubilees* are virtually the same as Maccabean ones; the author wishes to show that as God once judged on behalf of Israel so he will judge now since the enemies and issues are the same. The Animal Apocalypse parallels antediluvian and postdiluvian times; as God overthrew ancient angelic oppressors (the watchers) so he will overthrow modern ones (the shepherds). Daniel reveals a series of patterns. As the heavenly court judged former empires so it will judge the present one (Dan. 7). As angelic powers frustrated all earlier kings so they will frustrate Antiochus IV (Dan. 10–12).

Revelations of the past establish laws, conditions, rights, or judgments which apply in the present. In *4 Ezra* Uriel by revelations of the past shows why the majority of human beings must perish. Josephus, in the *Jewish War*, proves that God has decided to favor the Romans. *Jubilees* discloses how Israel's right to the land is fixed in heaven and earth since the days of Noah, implying that Ptolemies and Seleucids overstep their authority. It reveals how laws indelibly etched on the heavenly tablets have also been set in the concrete of past history and must be kept, how the proper reckoning of time (jubilees) is absolutely tied to historical events and must be observed in the present. Judicial historical sermons show how the past justifies a present decision of the heavenly court.

Revelations of the past ground exhortations for the present. Hortative historical sermons urge present action as a consequence of a revealed interpretation of events. The Animal Apocalypse urges armed resistance to Antiochus IV, *2 Baruch*, continued allegiance to the law. *Jubilees* reveals testamentary speeches of patriarchs and matriarchs of Israel which are addressed to all of their descendants. *Sibylline Oracles* 4 exhorts Gentiles to avoid the judgment on the basis of revelations about Gentile history.

Revelations of the past solve present puzzles. *2 Baruch* solves the seeming failure of the deuteronomic principle (God blessing the right-eous) by revealing how a switch in ages has occurred; the consummation has already begun. Leadership which recognizes this will not err so drastically as that which brought about the Jewish War. The Animal Apocalypse, by revealing the reign of the unrighteous angelic shepherds, reveals why Israel has been unjustly oppressed. *4 Ezra* seeks understanding of the present difficulties; solutions start with the past revelation which distinguishes heavenly and earthly Jerusalem and end with Ezra's inspired dictation of the twenty-four and seventy books. *4 Ezra* also asks why most of humanity must perish and the answer given comes from revelation of the past. *Sibylline Oracles 5* and *Jubilees* seek to establish the correct relation between Greek and Hebrew culture—*Jubilees* by rejecting Greek culture as out of touch with ancient heavenly wisdom but in touch with the demonic, *Sibylline Oracles 5* by giving Greek culture qualified approval once its under-standing of the gods is safely defused by an accurate understanding of the past.

In all these ways the past determines the present and problems in the present have shaped the revelation about the past. This interaction between past and present is one of the prime characteristics of revealed history.

Revelation also justifies and grounds assertions made about the past. *4 Ezra* can recount the history of the lost ten tribes because Ezra has received it by revelation. *Jubilees* can attribute speeches to its charac-ters because it knows what happened in the ancient past; because it claims inspiration it can rework traditions in the Pentateuch. For Josephus revelation supplies the thesis to prove. Elsewhere revelation grounds the various patterns or changes in heavenly administrations invisible to a human observer (Animal Apocalypse, Daniel, *2 Baruch*). By revelation Daniel discovers the true nature of empires as chaos monsters. Revelation assures that *Jubilees* has correctly seen how laws have passed into the heavenly and earthly structure of the universe. Revelation underwrites the application of scripture to the past. In short, revelation guarantees the truth of many differing assertions made about the past.

Some mechanism of revelation must apply this guarantee. Every conceivable mode of inspiration undergirds the revealed histories studied. To the visions, visions with interpretations, and heavenly trips mentioned earlier (employed in Daniel, Animal Apocalypse, *2 Baruch*, *Apocalypse of Abraham*) must be added the conversations between Uriel and Ezra in *4 Ezra*, between God and Moses or others in *LAB*, between the angle and Moses on the mountain in *Jubilees*, the sibylline frenzy in the *Sibylline Oracles*, the inspired interpretation of scripture in the Animal Apocalypse and Daniel (interpreting Jeremiah's seventy years), in *4 Ezra* (interpreting Daniel), or in Josephus, the combination of dreams and timely remembrance at Jotapata in Josephus, or the inspired memory by which Ezra received again the ancient books.

Hence we end as we began with an assertion of the diversity of historical revelation. Authors used it in any way they wished. They utilized those modes of revelation most congenial to them and to their constituencies. They addressed the most pressing problems, the most puzzling questions, the most confusing or significant periods of history and revealed what they and their communities most needed to know. Revealed history was a technique to be utilized according to need.

PART II

CHRISTIAN LITERATURE

Chapter 8

TRACES OF EARLY CHRISTIAN REVEALED HISTORY

Early Christian literary works grew within the matrix of ancient Judaism. The principle that God brought about historical events and its corollary that only revelation could ground an adequate understanding of history were components of that matrix. When groping around to build their own distinctive view of what God had done, early Christians gladly grasped the manifold tools of revealed history. These tools sat naturally in the hands of those who perceived themselves as experiencing a renewed outpouring of the Spirit. They were not long in putting them to use.

Works of Paul and his followers already yield traces of revealed history. Paul's declaration about knowing Christ according to the flesh, difficult though it be,[1] surely assumes two ways of knowing Christ, one appropriate to the old creation, one appropriate to the new. Although Paul refers to the present if any time reference is discernible at all, he presupposes a basic tenet of revealed history: the truest perception of Jesus must be distinguished from the ordinary human one. More importantly, Paul mentions the wisdom he speaks with the mature (τελείοις, 1 Cor. 2.6) which is hidden from all (2.7) but revealed by the Spirit (2.10). This wisdom has a nominal past reference, for had the rulers of this age understood it, they would not have crucified the Lord of glory (2.8). Hence the wisdom from the Spirit includes an accurate apprehension of who Jesus was, the Lord of glory incognito. Yet historical revelation is far from the center of Paul's thought on this issue. Wisdom implies knowledge not of the past but of the things of God.[2] Paul defines the things of God in 1 Cor. 2.12 (cf. 2.9-10): 'We have received...the Spirit which is from God, that we might understand the gifts bestowed on us by God'. By wisdom Paul denotes a grasp of God's grace rather than of the past. The same is

---

1. Victor Paul Furnish, *II Corinthians* (AB 32A; Garden City, NY: Doubleday, 1984), 330-32

2. τὰ βάθη τοῦ θεοῦ (2 Cor. 2.10), τὰ τοῦ θεοῦ (2.11), τὰ ὑπὸ τοῦ θεοῦ χαρισθέντα ὑμῖν (2.12).

true in Gal. 1.12, 16 or Eph. 1.15-22; 3.7-13. Paul (or his followers) expects to receive insight from God into the continuing effects of Christ's deeds, rather than into what Christ did. Though these passages in which Paul claims prophetic insight may have the past in view, they fail to concentrate upon it.

Of course Pauline arguments frequently concentrate upon the past. Romans 9–11, 1 Cor. 10.1-5, 2 Cor. 3.7-18, Gal. 4.4-5, and similar passages reinterpret the past to make a point, but such arguments are not accompanied by claims to inspiration. Although Aune and others argue that a portion of Romans 9–11 (11.25-26) is an early Christian oracle[1] and passages such as 1 Cor. 7.40b might imply that Paul considers all his judgments inspired, to define revealed history on the basis of a tenuous link to revelation would build much on a weak foundation.

In sum, where Paul claims inspiration, concentration on the past is weak; where he concentrates on the past, claims to revelation are weak. Christian inspired history, once established, may help interpret Paul, but evidence from Paul is too equivocal to establish and explain the Christian use of inspired history. Yet at least this much can be inferred: the works of Paul and his followers attest the presence of presuppositions congenial to revealed history in the earliest literary remains of Christianity.

In his book, *Community of the New Age*, Kee proposes an interpretation of Mark suggestive for revealed history. The stress on secrecy echoes the experience of Mark's community which faces persecution by those who cannot perceive what God in Jesus has done and is doing.[2] The stories of the blind men who are healed (Mk 8.22-26; 10.46-52) and the concealing purpose of the parables (4.11) imply a distinction between those inside and those outside the community: to those inside God gives comprehension but to those outside only bewilderment. 'For Mark *understanding of reality is not achieved by availability of evidence but by revelatory insight*.'[3] The author of Mark nowhere claims inspiration for his book and Kee does not claim it for him. Kee thinks of the community members gaining from the second Gospel insight into their own present rather than into the past. Nevertheless, stress on gifts of understanding to perceive rightly the true

---

1. See David E. Aune, *Prophecy in Early Christianity and the Ancient Mediterranean World* (Grand Rapids: Eerdmans, 1983), 252-53, and the literature cited there.

2. Howard Clark Kee, *Community of the New Age: Studies in Mark's Gospel* (Philadelphia: Westminster, 1977), 66-67, 96.

3. Kee, 59 (his italics). For a similar hypothesis see Joel Marcus, 'Mark 4.10-12 and Marcan Epistemology', *JBL* 103 (1984), 557-74.

present significance of what Jesus said and did is relevant to revealed history even if it is not equivalent to it.

The close association between apocalypticism and revealed history heightens the expectation of finding interest in the past in the Apocalypse. The Revelation to John does refer to the past. Since the author's present almost certainly stands somewhere in the sequence of the seven seals, the scene from the throne room, in which the slain lamb is found worthy to open the book, must lie in the past. The difficult vision of the woman who bears the male child (ch. 12) must also contain references to the past. The child who will rule the nations with a rod of iron must be Christ (12.5). The progression in which the dragon persecutes the woman and her children first from heaven then, when thrown down from heaven, persecutes them on the earth may refer to the past. Yet to press the imagery into a historical sequence would be to destroy it.[1] The chapter seeks not so much to reveal the past as to assure the saints of victory despite continued persecution: they are protected (12.6, 14, 16), their endurance is effectual (12.10-11), the wrath of the Dragon only means his time is short (12.12). Other references to history (chs. 13, 17) are no clearer. The author of the Apocalypse is concerned with the present and future rather than the past. Past details are few and at the periphery of his interest.

Although the Pauline letters, Mark, and the Apocalypse never adopt that clear claim to inspiration and intent to consider the past necessary for inclusion in this study, they skirt the boundaries of revealed history. They presuppose knowing Christ or constituents of the present by revelation. The epistemology of Paul or John the prophet would support revealed history had their interest taken a more decisive turn toward the past. Mark, though interested in the past deeds of Jesus and though sharing the same epistemology, never clearly applies that epistemology to the past. Nevertheless their conceptions lead near enough to inspired history to encourage further inquiry; their concentration on revelation, Jesus, and what flows from his deeds and words evidence the presuppositions of inspired history in early Christianity. In Paul, these presuppositions can be traced in the earliest literary remains of Christianity.

Five Christian works meet the criteria for inclusion in this study. The Gospel of John is the only ancient Jewish or Christian work in

---

1. 'But that history [of Jesus] is remote from the author's present contemplation. . . The Apocalyptist's thought here is a wholly ideal conception, independent of time and every concrete manifestation. . .' (I.T. Beckwith, *The Apocalypse of John: Studies in Introduction with a Critical and Exegetical Commentary* [Grand Rapids: Baker, 1979 (1919)], 617, cf. 620).

which revelation of the past has been widely recognized. The inspired witnesses in Luke–Acts tell the story of Jesus; their accounts are relevant to revealed history. The *Odes of Solomon* are inspired songs which frequently treat the past deeds of Jesus and interpret the real meaning of the tradition about him. The *Ascension of Isaiah* reviews early church history and discloses the descent and ascent of Christ. The *Shepherd of Hermas* contains sundry relevant passages.

Conclusions from Part I will serve as a foundation for understanding these works. The various genera and species of revealed history will be retained, utilized, and developed. John and Luke–Acts are limited prophetic histories. The *Ascension of Isaiah* contains an inspired prophetic history. When juxtaposed with Josephus they argue for a blossoming of prophetic history at the end of the first century CE. Luke–Acts uses historical prophecy extensively and adds new species to the several already isolated. The *Ascension of Isaiah* and the *Shepherd of Hermas* utilize apocalyptic history. The *Odes of Solomon* evidences a new genus of revealed history: the inspired historical ode or song. Like *4 Ezra* or the *Sibylline Oracles*, the *Shepherd of Hermas* contains several passages of revealed history which resist classification. Since some of these works utilize more than one form of revealed history while some use none, since in this sample the two prophetic histories require much more extensive treatment than any of the other works, and since genera and species of revealed history have already been defined, Part II will not devote a separate chapter to each type of revealed history but will consider these five Christian works in turn. Within the parameters defined in Part I, these works will be studied with two questions in view: How do these works use revealed history? How does a grasp of revealed history help us understand them?

Chapter 9

SHEPHERD OF HERMAS

In its wide range of revelatory material,[1] the *Shepherd of Hermas*[2] contains several references toward the past. Frequently such references lack real historical interest; they merely allude to the past in order to clarify a revelation about something else. When the shepherd interprets Hermas' present afflictions as due to the present and past sins of his 'family' (*Herm.* Sim. 7)[3] all the weight of interest falls upon understanding the present. Similarly, the pictures of the church, the building of the tower (Vis. 3; Sim. 9), or the staffs from the willow tree (Sim.

---

1. Although Martin Dibelius doubts that *Hermas* reflects actual visionary experience for the most part (*Der Hirt des Hermas* [Handbuch zum Neuen Testament, Die Apostolischen Väter, 4 Tübingen: Mohr/ Siebeck, 1923]), the claim to inspiration is clear. The work reports visions in which heavenly messengers (chiefly an old woman and a shepherd) bring revelation. Much of the book is written by divine command (Vis. 2.1.3-4; 2.4.2-3; 5.5-7); portions of it are copied verbatim from heavenly books (Vis. 1.3.4; 2.1.3–2.3.4).

2. Although portions of *Hermas* may date in the 90s (Giet) or in the second half of the first century (Osiek), the majority of interpreters place it in the first half of the second century (Pernveden). Snyder dates it before the 140s because of the presbyterial organization and the persecution references. For similar reasons Dibelius dates it to the 120s or 130s. Reiling thinks the eleventh mandate reflects Christian prophecy of the middle of the first half of the second century. Although I recognize that the work probably took shape over a period of time (Giet, Osiek, Snyder), the middle of the first half of the second century seems reasonable as a date for most if not all of the material. See Dibelius, 421-23; Stanislas Giet, *Hermas et les pasteurs* (Paris: Presses Universitaires de France, 1963), 280-305; Carolyn Osiek, *Rich and Poor in the Shepherd of Hermas: An Exegetical-Social Investigation* (CBQMS 15; Washington, DC: CBA, 1983), 7, 12-14; Lage Pernveden, *The Concept of the Church in the Shepherd of Hermas* (Studia Theologica Lundensia 27; Lund: Gleerup, 1966), 13; J. Reiling, *Hermas and Christian Prophecy: A Study of the Eleventh Mandate* (Leiden: Brill, 1973), 2; Graden F. Snyder, *The Shepherd of Hermas; The Apostolic Fathers: A New Translation and Commentary* 6 (Camden, NJ: Nelson, 1968), 19, 22-24.

3. Dibelius (419-20, 423) argues, probably correctly, that this 'family' is the Christian community. See also Erik Peterson, 'Kritische Analyse der fünften Vision des Hermes', *Frühkirche, Judentum und Gnosis. Studien und Untersuchungen* (Freiburg: Herder, 1959), 275.

8) contain elements from the past. People before the time of Hermas had entered the church (that is, had been built into the tower or given the green staffs) and some must have already repented. Yet not the past, but the function and nature of repentance primarily concerns the author.[1] In a few instances Hermas shows deeper interest in the past; he wants to understand what has happened to the Son of God or to the apostles in their preaching. He wants to show the preexistence of the church. He wants to connect God in creation with the church and with his present doings. Such passages require examination.

The Preeminent Church

Several brief passages in the first two visions reveal the preeminence of the church over all created things (*Herm.* Vis. 1.1.6; 1.3.4; 2.4.1).[2] Each is introduced as the particular message the revealer was sent to bring.[3] While all three share similar ideas, two of them (Vis. 1.1.6; 1.3.4) resemble each other also in form. In this form a revelation about creation expressed in participles and subordinate clauses precedes the finite verb which expresses the message of the apparition for the present. The revelation in the subordinate clauses reinforces that in the finite clause.[4]

subordinate   ὁ θεὸς ὁ ἐν τοῖς οὐρανοῖς κατοικῶν καὶ κτίσας ἐκ τοῦ μὴ ὄντος τὰ ὄντα καὶ πληθύνας καὶ αὐξήσας ἕνεκεν τῆς ἁγίας ἐκκλησίας αὐτοῦ

finite   ὀργίζεταί σοι ὅτι ἥμαρτες εἰς ἐμέ (Vis. 1.1.6).

subordinate   Ἰδού, ὁ θεὸς τῶν δυνάμεων, ὁ ἀοράτῳ δυνάμει καὶ κραταιᾷ καὶ τῇ μεγάλῃ συνέσει αὐτοῦ κτίσας τὸν κόσμον καὶ τῇ ἐνδόξῳ βουλῇ περιθεὶς τὴν εὐπρέπειαν τῇ κτίσει

---

1. These visions might be historicized. A historical persecution exposed the weaknesses of the staffs or stones—but the text does not clearly warrant such an interpretation. Even the presence of persecution is debatable; cf. Snyder (10 n. 5, 23) who interprets Thegri as the power of Rome threatening persecution. Peterson interprets the monster as Gehenna. See Erik Peterson, 'Die Begegnung mit dem Ungeheuer', *Frühkirche, Judentum, und Gnosis*, 295. Dibelius (422) sees persecution as a factor.

2. Pernveden, 21.

3. Vis. 1.1.6 introduced by ἄκουσον τὰ ῥήματα ἅ σοι μέλλω λέγειν. 1.3.4 is the only part of the heavenly book which Hermas can remember. What he remembers or does not remember is part of the revelatory experience. He remembers what applies to the righteous. 2.4.1 is the only message of the young man in the night vision.

4. Text from Molly Whittaker, *Der Hirt des Hermas* (Die griechischen christlichen Schriftsteller, 48; Berlin: Akademie, 1956), 2, 3.

αὐτοῦ, καὶ τῷ ἰσχυρῷ ῥήματι πήξας τὸν οὐρανὸν καὶ
θεμελιώσας τὴν γῆν ἐπὶ ὑδάτων καὶ τῇ ἰδίᾳ σοφίᾳ καὶ
προνοίᾳ κτίσας τὴν ἁγίαν ἐκκλησίαν αὐτοῦ, ἣν καὶ
ηὐλόγησεν,

finite   ἰδοὺ μεθιστάνει τοὺς οὐρανοὺς καὶ τὰ ὄρη καὶ τοὺς
βουνοὺς καὶ τὰς θαλάσσας, καὶ πάντα ὁμαλὰ γίνεται
τοῖς ἐκλεκτοῖς αὐτοῦ, ἵνα ἀποδοῖ αὐτοῖς τὴν ἐπαγγελίαν,
ἣν ἐπηγγείλατο, μετὰ πολλῆς δόξης καὶ χαρᾶς, ἐὰν
τηρήσωσιν τὰ νόμιμα τοῦ θεοῦ ἃ παρέλαβον ἐν μεγάλῃ
πιστει (Vis. 1.3.4).

Though their revelations of the past have much in common these two
passages differ considerably in what they reveal about the present. The
first reveals God's anger with Hermas over his thoughts concerning
Rhoda (cf. 1.1.2). Its subordinate revelation of the past reinforces
God's anger by revealing his greatness in creation (he created what is
from that which is not) and his grace (he increased and multiplied
creation for the sake of his church). Such amplification shows the
enormity of sins against such a God. It also makes a positive point: as
in *4 Ezra* where the world is made for Israel, so in the *Shepherd of
Hermas* the world is made for the sake of the church.

The second passage in this form reveals God's continued care for his
church.[1] He is moving (μεθιστάνει) heavens, mountains, hills, and seas
to smooth the way of his chosen ones. If they faithfully keep God's
ordinances, he will give them his promise. The subordinate revelation
of the past reinforces this revelation of God's care in the present by
offering an inductive guarantee: as God exercised his power in
creation for the sake and pleasure of the church, so he now exercises
his power to tame creation for the sake of his chosen ones, if they only
remain faithful to receive his promise. The past care of God for the
church, evident in the beauty (εὐπρέπεια) of creation, guarantees
God's continued care to order creation for his chosen ones. Again the
world is made for the sake of the church.

In the former two messages, the revelation of creation for the sake
of the church played an ancillary role; in the third passage (Vis. 2.4.1)
it occupies center stage. In a dream a young man appears to Hermas to
reveal the identity of the old woman who had talked with him. She is

---

1. Dibelius (440), noticing this passage's independence from its context, suggests
that it derives from an independent source. However, its use of a form favorite with
the author militates against Dibelius's shrewd guess. In addition to *Herm.* Vis. 1.1.6
and 1.3.4, the same form also occurs in Man. 1.1 where the subordinate clause,
though referring to the creation, seems more a confession than a revelation of the
past. That in Man. 1.1 the finite verb precedes the subordinate is probably an
insignificant difference.

the church; she surpasses every created thing for not only was she created first,[1] but she is also the final cause of all.

Although two of these passages concentrate on the present rather than the past, the three together show an interest in the nature of the church. Since the author seeks to heighten the importance of the church by stressing the eternal purpose of God for it, he employs historical revelation: the church is the first creature, everything else is created for its sake.

Similitudes

The remaining references to the past, like the revelation concerning the old woman's age, interpret various features of Hermas' allegorical visions. Similitude 5 describes the ministry and exaltation of the Son of God; Similitude 9 elaborates the vision of the tower (Vis. 3) to explain more clearly the place of repentance in the church. As part of his interpretation the shepherd reveals the inclusion in the church of the righteous who died before the advent of the Son.

Similitude 9

Though only the description of the salvation of the dead (Sim. 9.15.4–16.7) and a brief description of creation and redemption through the Son (Sim. 9.12.1-4) clearly refer to the past, the entire similitude flirts with history. The tower representing the church is built first with Old Testament saints then with the prophets and teachers who preach the Son of God (Sim. 9.12.4). The building only begins when the Son was manifested in the last days of the consummation (Sim. 9.12.3). At a particular time the work of building stops; the Lord of the tower tests the stones and commands the angel of repentance to reclaim as many as possible of the stones that failed the test. But this offer of repentance is firmly fixed in history; it has occurred in Hermas' present. Now is the time when saints who repent can receive the promises; soon the repentance will be sealed forever (Vis. 2.2.4-8). After the time of second repentance the tower will be built in perfection. Viewed in this way not only the revelations of the building of the tower in Similitude 9 and Vision 3 but also that of the willow staffs (Sim. 8) are limited apocalyptic histories. They reveal the gift of righteousness and salvation in Christ, subsequent decay on the part of some Christians manifested when the Lord tests his own, an offer of repentance under heavenly supervision, the closing of the time of repentance, and the

---

1. The stress here is on preeminence, not preexistence; cf. Snyder, 39.

subsequent perfection of the church. Yet the real interest of these apocalyptic histories lies not in a revealed explanation of what God is doing in puzzling events of the past—the surprising event is the *present* offer of repentance—but in admonition to take advantage of the present mercy of God.[1] The author wishes to show how the present offer of repentance makes sense in what God is doing and how the present reprieve requires present action. Pursuing these, his real interests, has blurred the historical references. The church, built on the Old Testament saints, includes both those who have fallen asleep and those who are living. Hermas finds no need to explain the church as a historical entity in either a heavenly or an earthly sense. The second explanation of the tower (Sim. 9) concentrates on aspects of the revelation with no historical interest, explaining the twelve mountains as peoples with differing traits, the various stones as different kinds of Christians. The author, in adapting it to his own ends, has de-historicized the form 'limited apocalyptic history'.

Several passages in these limited apocalyptic histories contain further admonitory interest in the past. The revelation about the great age of the new gate (Sim. 9.12.1-3) reveals that the Son of God who gave counsel at creation has lately been manifested in the last days of the consummation; hence all must enter the tower through him (Sim. 9.12.4-8). A more elaborate revelation about the past concerns the incorporation of the righteous who died before the manifestation of the Son of God (Sim. 9.15.4–16.7). These had been constant companions of the maidens (virtues) until death, but, not knowing Christ, they had descended to the deep (βαθός) in death. Apostles (prophets, Sim. 9.15.4) and teachers, who had fallen asleep in the faith of the Son, had preached to them. Then all, the first saints and prophets of Old Testament as well as Christian prophets, apostles, and teachers, had ascended together from the βαθός, this time baptism,[2] to enter through the gate of Christ and be laid as the foundation of the tower. The church is founded on Old Testament worthies. Like *Odes of Solomon* and other early Christian literature, *Hermas* is concerned with what happened to the Old Testament saints, but the revelation in *Hermes* shows apostles and teachers, not Christ, bringing news of the Son to them. Perhaps this difference reflects the passing of first-generation Christians. It also reveals what happened to the first gen-

---

1. Note Giet's ahistorical summary of the parable's meaning; 'Le sens général de la *Parabole* est clair: tous les péchés ne sont pas pardonnés, parce que certains supposent des dispositions qui détournent de la pénitence ceux qui les ont commis; mais tous sont susceptible de l'être' (Giet, 243).

2. Dibelius (626) discusses the twofold reference of βαθός.

eration at death. Since they had listened to the word of the Son of God they did not really die but descended living to preach to those in the deep and thus bring them out alive with them through baptism to be built into the church (Sim. 9.16.6-7). With this revelation Hermas shows the necessity of baptism and entrance through the Son for all. Though the church excels in age any other creation, it has only lately begun to be built in its proper form.

Although these prophecies employ the form of limited apocalyptic history, Hermas has mastered the form and made it serve his interest in the present. They reveal a pattern underlying historical events as limited apocalyptic histories ordinarily do, yet interest centers not on past elements of the pattern, which are hardly unusual, but on the surprising offer of repentance in the present. The historical pattern heightens the plausibility of the offer of repentance by placing it in a familiar setting. Incorporated into these apocalyptic histories are revelations of past events: the preaching of the apostles to the dead and the counsel of the Son at creation. Hermas knows the power of revealed history and utilizes it with flexibility even where his own concern centers on the present.

Similitude 5
The fifth similitude contains the most extensive development of christology in the *Shepherd of Hermas*. Since Hermas considers what Christ did, what his reward was, and who he was, this similitude qualifies as inspired history. The interest in history, as always in the *Shepherd*, serves hortatory concerns. Questions concerning proper fasting, understanding Jesus, and living well with the Spirit so intertwine as to leave the impression of confusion. Attempts to disentangle the resulting knot has led to theories of sources, redaction, or interpolation[1] which contribute to an understanding of the text as it now stands.

Dibelius isolates two parables and three distinct interpretations.[2] Quite apart from raising questions of traditional history, Dibelius's analysis goes a long way toward clarifying this difficult section. Following his lead, the fifth similitude begins to take shape. An introductory dialogue between Hermas and the shepherd questions the proper role of fasting and offers an initial response: true fasting is keeping God's commands (Sim. 5.1). The shepherd tells a parable to

---

1. Dibelius, 564-65. Koester thinks the sections on fasting (Sim. 5.1, 3) are interpolations (Helmut Koester, *Introduction to the New Testament 2: History and Literature of Early Christianity* [Hermeneia: Foundations and Facets; Philadelphia: Fortress, 1982], 260).
2. Dibelius, 564, cf. 571.

illustrate his point (Sim. 5.2) and offers its first interpretation (Sim. 5.3): God rewards those who do more than he commands; true fasting includes giving to the poor. In another dialogue Hermas overcomes the shepherd's resistance to divulging fuller understanding of the parable (Sim. 5.4), then the shepherd interprets the parable christologically (Sim. 5.5.1–6.4a). In the final interpretation, he grounds an exhortation to live spotlessly with the Holy Spirit on the christological understanding of the parable (Sim. 5.6.4b–7.4). Hence the Similitude portrays a conversation in two parts. The shepherd comes to correct Hermas' understanding of fasting—the parable and its initial interpretation belong to this first phase of the conversation. Hermas not unnaturally supposes that any parable spoken by a heavenly messenger must contain yet greater secrets and presses for further understanding. The resulting dialogue both moves the conversation into its second phase and enhances curiosity concerning the revelation to follow; what is wrung from the angel with such difficulty must have considerable value. Only the second phase of the conversation reveals the past. It reveals the Son's obedience, exaltation, and something of who he was and is.

The two christological interpretations closely parallel one another in form. In each the shepherd volunteers christological interpretations of details in the parable (Sim. 5.5.1-3; 6.4b-8), then answers questions from Hermas (Sim. 5.5.4–6.4b; 5.7.1-4). The first part outlines an understanding of some details of the parable; the subsequent conversation emphasizes what the author hopes his readers will derive from it. Although distinguishing two christological interpretations aids in following Hermas' thought, it must not obscure the unity of the christological part of the conversation. These two interpretations are closely bound together in one interpretive discourse (Sim. 5.4.1–5.7.4) of the same form as that on fasting in Sim. 5.3.1-9.[1] The christological interpretations initially map the allegory, identifying features of the parable with heavenly or earthly counterparts (Sim. 5.5.2-3). Although this definition elicits wonder from Hermas (5.4), neither christological interpretation draws out the implications of the allegory. Instead both interpretations follow the author's interest. The author in the first interpretation concentrates on the great authority of the Son of God (Sim. 5.6.2-4a) and in the second interpretation on the perfect cooperation of flesh and Spirit in him (Sim. 5.6.4b-7).

---

1. Each interpretive discourse begins with a request for understanding (Sim. 5.3.1; 5.4.1-5) followed by an explanation and hortatory application of the parable (Sim. 5.3.2-9; 5.5.1–7.4).

In the first of these passages (Sim. 5.6.2-4a) the term 'Son' refers to the earthly Jesus even though he has authority over the angels and over the people whom God has created (5.6.2-3). His giving of the law (5.6.3) probably refers to the teaching ministry of Jesus; cleansing his people from sins with great labor and hardship probably refers to the passion (5.6.2).[1] No shift separates the authority over the angels and over God's people from those other earthly activities of the Son. Quite the reverse: all the features of the parable in this first interpretation belong to the time when the servant is still proving his worthiness to be fellow heir of God; that is, they occur before the slave's exaltation. Hermas wants to show that the slave who represents the Son of God (5.5.2) actually had great authority and power. Therefore both the authority and labor of the Son refer to Jesus in his earthly ministry. By historical revelation Hermas proves the great authority and power of the earthly Jesus. Even then Jesus had authority over the angels and stationed them to care for his people; even then he was lord of the people God created, lord of the vineyard.

In the second interpretation Hermas uses the term 'son' in a second sense. Here the Son is the Spirit. The servant represents the 'flesh' of the earthly Jesus. The divine council determines to elevate this flesh to the rank of fellow heir with the Spirit since the flesh had collaborated perfectly with the indwelling Spirit, acting with all strength and courage. This second interpretation then reveals the nature of Jesus, a Spirit-filled human being chosen by God for a great task. It also shows the rationale behind his exaltation to Godhead; he perfectly served the Spirit. In this case by historical revelation, Hermas teaches an adoption christology.

Quite clearly these are two different interpretations of the parable as Dibelius realized. The first interpretation follows the definitions of the allegory in Sim. 5.6.2-3. The son in the parable is the Spirit in reality; the slave in the parable is the Son of God in reality. Hence the actions of the slave represent the earthly actions of the Son of God. The second interpretation fuses the reality with the symbol which represents it. In the parable the son and the friends counsel with God; surprisingly in this interpretation not the Spirit and the angels but the Son and the angels counsel with God. Here the title 'son' can name the Spirit as well outside the parable as within it. No longer is the slave the Son of God, instead he represents the human being Jesus who was chosen to bear the Spirit who is the Son of God. Jesus becomes the Son of God by adoption.

1. Dibelius, 570-71.

Of course the different interpretations need not use symbols in the same way. Though these two christological interpretations use the imagery of the parable differently, their interpretations are not incompatible; they should interpret each other. Taken together they reveal the great authority of the earthly Christ, who he was and who he is. Jesus was the human being chosen by God to bear the Spirit, his Son, on a special mission. The human being fully cooperated with the Spirit to do the work of the Son of God, both in ruling angels and the people God created and in giving them a law and toiling to remove their sins. As a reward God adopted the human being, granting him equal status with the Spirit as God's heir. This is a historical revelation worthy of the name. As always the shepherd draws from it an exhortation: 'See how God rewards those who dwell in purity with the Spirit? Your own adoption follows the pattern established by Jesus.'

Revealed History in the Shepherd of Hermas

Although the *Shepherd of Hermas* uses the form of limited apocalyptic history in the vision and similitude concerning the tower (Vis. 3; Sim. 9) and in the similitude of the green branches (Sim. 8), the author has partially emptied it of historical concern. True, these apocalyptic histories reveal a historical pattern (gift of salvation in Christ, decline of some Christians, testing manifests this decline, guarded offer of repentance, time of repentance closes, church is perfect) but interest centers on the surprising element of the pattern: the present offer of repentance. The remainder of the pattern exists to ease the readers astonishment by placing the offer of repentance plausibly within the expected course of events. Elsewhere Hermas uses revealed history more incisively, but less clearly follows Jewish models. His work reveals that the world was created for the sake of the church and how the apostles and teachers descended to the abyss to preach to the righteous dead. A major focus of revealed history scrutinizes christology. Hermas reveals the adoption of Jesus as co-heir with the Spirit and reveals the great authority he had when in the form of a servant. A christological thrust will prove characteristic of Christian revealed history. The author uses revealed history with facility and flexibility, but in this work the past hardly claims a large share of the author's concern. The seer's chief interest throughout is in the possibility—and necessity—of the second repentance.

Chapter 10

ASCENSION OF ISAIAH

The *Ascension of Isaiah* twice resorts to revealed history—once rehearsing the descent, death, and ascension of Christ, along with subsequent church history to the completion of the world (3.13–4.22) and once detailing Christ's descent from the seventh heaven to earth and his subsequent ascent in glory to the right hand of God (10.1–11.35). Both passages explicitly claim inspiration: Isaiah delivers the second as a vision report to a select group including King Hezekiah (*Ascen. Isa.* 6.1–7.1; 11.36-40); the first begins by summarizing Isaiah's prophecy (*Ascen. Isa.* 3.13-31) and continues as Isaiah's first-person report of what will happen (4.1-16). The *Ascension of Isaiah* deserves careful attention since it devolves from an early Christian prophetic community for which revealed history was a prime (perhaps the prime) concern.[1]

How does the community behind the *Ascension of Isaiah* utilize revealed history? We will first look at an historical apocalypse (*Ascen. Isa.* 3.13–4.22), then examine the Vision of the Descent and Ascent of the Beloved (*Ascen. Isa.* 6–11). Finally we will explore the importance of revealed history to the community behind the *Ascension of Isaiah*.

Apocalyptic History in the Ascension of Isaiah

I have argued elsewhere that the *Ascension of Isaiah* derives from a prophetic school embroiled in conflict with other early Christian groups.[2] Members of the school, ordinarily scattered to disseminate their message, gather periodically to learn from senior prophets in the

---

1. Although students of the *Ascension of Isaiah* have yet to agree on its date, elsewhere I have argued that the recension represented in the Ethiopic arises early in the second century. Hence it lies within the range of this study. See Robert G. Hall, 'The Ascension of Isaiah: Community Situation, Date, and Place in Early Christianity', *JBL* 109 (1990), 289-306.

2. The next paragraphs summarize conclusions from my article: Hall, 'The Ascension of Isaiah: Community Situation'.

school (*Ascen. Isa.* 6). The senior prophet organizes the school hierarchically after one of the lower levels of heaven and 'opens the door' joining the school to the heavens. As the fragrance of the Spirit fills the room, members of the school take heavenly trips to see God. The highest revelation, which communicates the doctrine central to the school, concerns the descent and ascent of the Beloved. Since belief in this central doctrine is necessary for salvation, apprentice members of the school write down and pass on revelations given their elders. A host of adversaries confronting the school deny the validity of heavenly trips to see God, reject the descent and ascent of the Beloved, and vigorously oppose efforts to disseminate the school's message. Although these opponents hold church office (they are shepherds and elders [*Ascen. Isa.* 3]), the author depicts them as false prophets. Only a few of the true prophets remain and they can seldom get a hearing. The *Ascension of Isaiah* is a last-ditch effort to reach a reluctant audience with the essential message concerning the descent and ascent of the Beloved. The author uses limited apocalyptic history as one means of confronting this adverse rhetorical situation.

The historical apocalypse (*Ascen. Isa.* 3.13–4.22) in its present form stems from the final author of the *Ascension of Isaiah* but it incorporates a source (*Ascen. Isa.* 4.1-22) which the author has interpolated extensively and which he titles 'The Book of the Completion of the Days'.[1] Like the book of Revelation, events in 'the Book of the Completion of the Days' frequently bear an indistinct relation to history. Charles's observation on vv. 2-3 is accurate as far as it goes: 'It is quite correct that these words and the rest of v. 3 belong to the historical Nero. The rest of the passage has to do with the Antichrist only.'[2] These verses identify Nero, the murderer of his own mother and of the Apostle Peter, as the incarnation of Beliar. The following verses (4-13) describe this incarnation of Beliar, who, having deceived the whole world by signs and wonders, sets up his image for worship in all the cities and persecutes the church. Certainly emperor worship has supplied the model for the antichrist's actions in demanding worship (4.6-9, 11). As the use of the Nero myth implies, the false

---

1. Arguments for the presence of a source include change in subject matter and speaker, inclusion of a title, and a pattern of wording similar to that used in the introduction of a source at *Ascen. Isa.* 7.1. See Hall, 'Ascension of Isaiah: Community Situation', 289-292.

2. R.H. Charles, *The Ascension of Isaiah Translated from the Ethiopic Version, which, together with the New Greek Fragment, the Latin Versions and the Latin Translation of the Slavonic, is here Published in full* (London: A. & C. Black, 1900), 25.

wonders are those of the emperor cult (10).[1] As in Revelation and *Apocalypse of Abraham* persecution against the righteous is associated with such emperor worship. The mythical language thus describes the experience of the present in eschatological terms much like similar language in Revelation.[2] The persecuted community, reduced by many apostates, will be delivered by the glorious appearance of Christ and the armies from the seventh heaven. Thus the 'Book of the Completion of the Days' nominally employs limited apocalyptic history. Only the death of Peter and the rise of Beliar in Nero are clearly past; the majority of the imagery describes the present. The source confronts the present affliction of the church threatened by demands for emperor worship and turns to the past only long enough to point out the change in world history which explains it. With Nero, Beliar is incarnate. His incarnation continues in the later emperors.

Although a concern with emperor worship and persecution of Christians well suits the story line in the Martyrdom of Isaiah, the final form of the *Ascension of Isaiah* does not develop these parallels. Instead the final author develops parallels between Isaiah's prophetic community and that of his own.[3] The author includes the 'Book of the Completion of the Days' because of its palliative effect: it reassures the reader by including the author's more innovative historical interpretations (3.13-31; 4.16) within a widely accepted framework of early Christian expectation. The author's interest centers less on the imperial threat against Christians than on the picture he paints of the pristine time of the apostles (3.13-20) and of later disorder in the Church (3.20-31).

By expanding the older apocalypse the author of the *Ascension of Isaiah* creates a larger limited apocalyptic history with much greater interest in the past (3.13–4.22). The author first presents a brief inspired account of events paralleling those in the Gospels and Acts (3.13-20). In the scheme of this apocalypse these verses define what the author's opponents have rejected. They anchor doctrine of the descent and ascent of the Beloved in the prophetic activity of the apostles and derive the happy state of the church, with its many signs and wonders

---

1. Charles, 28 n. 10. See also Steven J. Scherrer, 'Signs and Wonders in the Imperial Cult', *JBL* 103 (1984), 599-610.
2. The community has fled or expects at any moment to flee to the desert (*Ascen. Isa.* 4.13; cf. Rev. 12).
3. This conclusion is based primarily on passages such as 1.1-13; 2.7-11; 3.1-13 where references to the Vision of the Descent and Ascent of the Beloved show the author's hand most clearly. See Hall, 'Ascension of Isaiah: Community Situation', 292-300.

and its profusion of prophets, from its adherence to the apostles' prophecy. When the church lived like the author's community in the days of the apostles, it lived in power and harmony. By centering the pristine days of the apostles on the Vision of the descent and ascent of the Beloved and by basing their apprehension of who Jesus is on prophecy (3.21)[1] rather than tradition, the author helps the reader accept the revelation about Jesus to be elaborated in chs. 6–11.

The next section (3.21-31) contrasts the church situation of the author's present with the ideal time of the apostles. Now wicked shepherds and elders seek riches instead of the glorious robes of the saints. As Manasseh listens to Beliar and persecutes Isaiah, these shepherds and elders listen to the spirit of error (3.28), abrogate the prophecy of the few remaining true prophets and feud with one another. The author draws on commonplaces concerning the church at the end of the first century[2] and applies them to his own situation: the church rejects the true prophecy of the author's school to follow the false prophecy of the wicked shepherds who speak whatever pleases them (3.30). This rejection of the true prophecy explains the widely recognized decline of the church as the result of its rejection of the message of the author's school.

The author uses limited apocalyptic history to undergird by revelation the doctrine of the descent and ascent of the Beloved, to establish by revelation the author's view that the happy early church had believed this doctrine and been blessed for it, and to pinpoint by revelation the problem with the present church: in rejecting the author's community and its revealed understanding of what occurred in Christ, the church has through pride forsaken the prophecy of the apostles and been forsaken by the Holy Spirit (3.21, 26). The rejection of the author's community and its doctrine immediately precedes the Beloved's approach (3.21). This summary of history functions much as a narration in an ancient speech influenced by classical rhetoric; it accounts for facts known by the readers in a framework favorable to the author's message. The limited apocalyptic history mollifies fears about the author's community and doctrine by tracing both to the time of the apostles and explains the present disorder and strife in the church as the natural result of rejecting the author's school. The

---

1. The Greek for the Ethiopic 'teaching' (*temeherta*) is προφητεία (3.21). Since διδαχὴ τῶν δώδεκα was a common phrase a scribe might easily have substituted it for the unusual προφητεία τῶν δώδεκα. Prophecy of the twelve apostles well suits the prophetic interest in the *Ascension of Isaiah*.

2. Michael A. Knibb, 'Martyrdom and Ascension of Isaiah', *OTP* 2.149.

author undergirds this interpretation of history by claiming prophetic inspiration for it.

The limited apocalyptic history (3.13–4.22) is but one way the author seeks to win a hearing from a reluctant audience. The author also carefully chose the Martyrdom of Isaiah as vehicle for the community's revelation. The characters are as stereotyped as those of a melodrama: Manasseh's wickedness is proverbial, his domination by Beliar obvious; but no more obvious than the righteousness of Isaiah and Hezekiah. Since everyone knew Isaiah had seen God and knew that Manasseh had persecuted Isaiah, the setup was perfect. The author had only to flesh out the story with details from the current situation. Manasseh acts like the opponents of the author's school; Isaiah, like one of the school's chief leaders. Although anyone embroiled in the events around the author's school could have seen the application of the story, the author's analysis of the past and present in this limited apocalyptic history (3.13–4.22) helps the reader to see these parallels in a proper light.

Inspired Prophetic History: The Vision of Isaiah

The limited apocalyptic history (3.13–4.22) gave much of its first section to revealing what Jesus did. The Vision of Isaiah concentrates on revealing heavenly and earthly deeds of Jesus. The historical revelation occurs in a heavenly trip: Isaiah, caught up to heaven, sees and hears God command the Beloved to descend all the way to Sheol incognito and to return in full glory (10.7-15). He then watches Christ obey (10.17–11.35).

The revelation discloses Christ's divinity and highlights his glory. Details of Isaiah's ascent to the seventh heaven underscore the Beloved's greatness. The accompanying angel restrains Isaiah from worshiping a splendid angel in the second heaven (7.21-22; cf. 8.5); Isaiah's mistake heightens the overwhelming glory of the Beloved whom Isaiah properly worships in the sixth and seventh heavens. All the glory from all the heavens streams visibly and audibly up to the Beloved, the Spirit, and the Father. The culmination of glory and praise on this 'trinity', together with the prohibition of worshiping other glorious heavenly beings, clearly places Christ on the divine side of the line between creatures and God.[1] When Christ and the Spirit turn to give praise to the Father their glory is hardly diminished.

---

1. Richard Bauckham, 'The Worship of Jesus in Apocalyptic Christianity', *NTS* 27 (1981), 335.

According to Bauckham, these details seek to safeguard monotheism without denying divinity to Christ.[1]

The inspired glance at the past also reveals how this divine Christ came to be a man and die. God commanded him to divest himself of his glory heaven by heaven, at each level transforming himself into the likeness of angels there. Below the lowest heaven he is to transform himself into the likeness of one of the powers of the air, on the earth into a man, then by death to enter Sheol. The prophet gives enough details of his life and death to identify the Beloved as Jesus before describing the resumption of his glory at the resurrection and his triumphant return worshiped by all—even by the disorderly angels in the air. The Beloved's ascent culminates in an increase of his glory, for now he sits instead of stands at the Father's right, and somehow has won the right for the Spirit and the saints also to sit in the Father's presence. This scheme discloses how such a glorious divine Christ could look human and die. If 11.2-15 is original, the vision explains the incarnation by a nativity; otherwise its explanation is closer to John or Philippians 2 than to Matthew or Luke.

Probably because controversy centered on the facts of Christ's divinity and descent and ascent, the author does not dwell on the soteriological effects of Christ's deeds. Yet hints of the community's soteriology show how it derives from the historical revelation. By manifesting his glory on his return, the Beloved compels homage from each heavenly level. The manifestation of the Beloved in glory orders even the most disorderly realm of the rebellious powers (11.23-24); summaries, probably referring to the same event, speak of the Beloved judging the powers (10.12-15;[2] cf. 1.5; 5.15-16). A similar effect occurs elsewhere: when the Beloved manifests his glory in Sheol he apparently overwhelms death; when he ascends he leads many of the righteous, who have yet to receive their garments, out of Sheol with him (9.13-18). Although for these resurrection to the seventh heaven and to existence in greater glory than the angels depends on the ascension of the Beloved, other righteous ones had received this privilege even before the descent (9.28). In one respect, however, all the saints await the ascent of Christ for full instatement in their exalted status; only when the Beloved ascends to his throne may the saints sit on their thrones and wear their crowns.

---

1. Bauckham, 332-35.

2. A difficult passage in the Ethiopic. Although Charles emends extensively I accept the interpretation of the rather free rendering in Flemming/Duensing/Hill. See Charles, 70-71; J. Flemming, Hugo Duensing, and David Hill, 'The Ascension of Isaiah', *NTA*, 2.659.

The historical revelation is remarkably free from exhortation. The single responsibility of its hearers is that they believe and keep Jesus' words (9.26); of course they must believe in his descent and ascent as well (3.18, cf. 2.9). At every level, Sheol, earth, firmament and upper heavens, it is crucial to perceive the glory of Jesus, for the manifestation of Jesus' glory sets right every level of the universe. Only those who perceive the glory hidden in the descending and ascending Christ can participate to their bliss in this reordered universe.

The Vision (*Ascen. Isa.* 7–11) reveals the glory hidden in the earthly Jesus. The revelation of the past discovers what would otherwise remain unknown about the earthly Jesus and the past events associated with him. It reveals dimensions of those events which by definition could be known by no human observer. The Beloved came incognito, deliberately masking who he was (the 'Messianic Secret' *par excellence*). The apostles perceived his glory at the resurrection and by prophecy preached it. The community's Christian prophets on heavenly trips were granted true understanding of the past which revealed who Christ was. It is important to perceive and overwhelmingly important to believe in the glory of Jesus revealed by the Spirit to the author's community.

Though clearly an apocalypse, the Vision of Isaiah lacks that movement to the present and future which would define it as an apocalyptic history. It does not seek to explain a confusing period of history by revealing God's activity in and around it as an apocalyptic history would; it seeks to chronicle a particular sequence of past events imperceptible to human observers. The Vision reveals the glory of Christ by showing heavenly events belonging to the incarnation. In intent if not in form or content it is closer to Gospels such as Luke and John than to the apocalyptic histories.[1] Since it reveals events never otherwise experienced by a human observer, the Vision of Isaiah lies even closer to *Jubilees* than to these two Gospels. Because both facts and interpretation are known by revelation and because its major purpose is to chronicle past (if heavenly!) events, the Vision of Isaiah can be classified as an inspired prophetic history. It should come as no surprise to discover inspired prophetic history in an apocalypse, for *Jubilees*, its other exemplar, can be viewed as an apocalypse.

---

1. Its original author may have had an understanding of inspiration somewhat akin to that behind the Johannine Paraclete. In the *Ascension of Isaiah* the 'angel of the spirit' reveals to Isaiah the glory of Christ, the things that belong to Christ, the things to come, and the true understanding of events in the ministry of Christ.

Revealers of History:
The Prophetic School behind the Ascension of Isaiah

The preceding analysis has already moved to consider the community behind the *Ascension of Isaiah*. Since this community defined itself in terms of the descent and ascent of Christ, the *Ascension of Isaiah* offers an excellent opportunity to see how revealed history functioned in a social setting.

The Vision of Isaiah (*Ascen. Isa.* 6–11) opens with a singular description of prophetic activity (6.1-17). The presence of Isaiah at the court of Hezekiah provokes a prophetic conference. Forty prophets from the surrounding country appear with a purpose: 'And they had come to greet him, and to hear what he said. And they hoped he would lay his hands on them and that they might prophesy and he would listen to their prophecy'[1] (6.4-5). Isaiah, as a senior prophet, not only is the chief speaker but also conducts a prophetic school, imparting the spirit of prophecy by the laying on of his hands and fine tuning prophetic sensitivity by listening to the prophets and correcting their deficiencies. During the conference, as Isaiah spoke with Hezekiah, 'they all heard a door opened and the voice of the Holy Spirit' (*Ascen. Isa.* 6.6). This peculiar imagery probably joins the worshiping hierarchy of prophets to the hierarchy of worshiping angels in heaven (cf. 6.9).[2] For this special event Hezekiah summons all the prophets and people and, as they all hear the voice of the Spirit, they worship. God, whose proper place is in the highest heaven among the holy ones (6.8), has, by the Spirit, granted them access to himself. At this point Isaiah is caught up in ecstasy to heaven. The people leave since they do not[3]

1. Translations come from R.H. Charles and J.M.T. Barton, 'The Ascension of Isaiah', *AOT*.
2. If the 'alien world' (*'ālam nakir*) refers to heaven, then God grants the prophets access to heaven. If 'alien world' refers to this age then the Spirit grants access to God by coming through the door himself to be with the assembly. I prefer the first option. *Ascen. Isa.* 6 describes the circle of prophets in the same order as one of the levels of heaven. Isaiah, by taking the king's throne sits in the position of the angel in charge. The open door may indicate participation in heavenly worship. Hezekiah's throne room has been joined to heaven as its lowest circle. With the open door compare the gates between heavens which open as Christ gives the password. Such a door opening between Hezekiah's throne room and the lowest heaven would seem a logical prelude to Isaiah's privileged ascent. See Rev. 4.1-2.
3. The Ethiopic text omits the negative. With Charles, Tisserant and Flemming/Duensing/Hill I have followed the Slavonic and late Latin. See Eugène Tisserant (*Ascension d'Isaïe. Traduction de la version éthiopienne avec les principales variantes des versions greque latines et slave. Introduction et notes* [Paris: Letouzey et Ané, 1909]).

believe that Isaiah has been caught up to heaven, but the prophets and some with the fragrance of the Spirit about them (6.17) stay to hear Isaiah's report. When Isaiah comes to himself he brings a message describing the heavenly joys of the blessed and the ascent and descent of Christ. The prophetic school, with its laying on of hands and correction by the senior prophet, the opening of the door at the coming of the Spirit, the consequent worship, the senior prophet's ecstasy, the departure of the people in disbelief, and the culminating report of the prophet to those on whom the Spirit rests, probably reflects the worshiping community behind the *Ascension of Isaiah*.[1] The *Ascension of Isaiah* issues from a lively school of Christian prophets which, though it does not rigidly exclude non-prophetic Christians, reserves its most precious revelations about the past activity of Christ for those whom the Spirit has readied to receive them.

Although prophets of this community see eternal judgments, torments of Gehenna, the prince of this world and his minions, the world's destruction, judgment of the angels, destruction of Samael, the heavenly robes of the saints, and words concerning faith in the Beloved,[2] the revelation most characteristic of this community is that of the descent and ascent of the Beloved. This revelation about the past is clearly of central importance: While other prophets receive other visions,[3] only the chief prophet Isaiah sees the vision of the descent and ascent of the Beloved (*Ascen. Isa.* 6); the rest of the school carefully records and passes on this revelation of the past (1.5). Frequently the author comments on the importance of the doctrine of the descent and ascent of the Beloved: Only those who believe in the ascension of Christ accompany Isaiah into the wilderness (2.9);[4] those who believe in Jesus' cross and in his ascension into the heaven from which he came will be saved (3.18); those who believe in the descending LORD[5] inherit the robes and crowns placed in the seventh heaven for the righteous (8.26). The doctrine of the descent and ascent is a major bone of contention; opponents of the author's school reject the doctrine of the vision. The elders and shepherds turn from the prophecy of the

---

1. This paragraph summarizes Hall, 'Ascension of Isaiah: Community Situation', 293-96.
2. This list derives from summaries of revealed things found in passages such as *Ascen. Isa.* 1.2-4, 5; 5.15-16.
3. See revelations to Hezekiah listed in *Ascen. Isa.* 1.2-4.
4. I presuppose the Ethiopic reading of this verse and its interpretation in Michael Knibb, 158 n. n.
5. Ethiopic, *'egzī'abehēr*.

apostles (3.21);[1] this prophecy includes the descent and ascent of the Beloved (3.18).[2] The anger of Beliar burns against Isaiah because of the vision of the descent and ascent of Christ which he has seen (3.13). Inspired by Beliar Belkira accomplishes Isaiah's death by accusing him of claiming to see God (3.6-13), a necessary component of the Vision.

The structure of the *Ascension of Isaiah* reflects the importance of the Vision to the author's community as well; fully half of the finished work describes this vision in detail. The remainder of the work clearly leads up to this vision. Details from the martyrdom are directed toward removing prejudices which might hinder readers from appreciating the vision to come. Since every one knew that Isaiah had seen God, Belkira's scriptural argument that no one could see God and live (3.7-10, undoubtedly frequently addressed to the author's compatriots) must be specious. The author has cast his own school in a favorable light by describing it as the school of Isaiah and has portrayed those who oppose the school as the likes of Manasseh and Belkira, a notorious king and a false prophet. By the time the reader begins the vision he or she is as prepared as possible to receive it favorably.

This community fights its battles under a banner of historical revelation; the revelation about the past activity of Christ is crucial for the *Ascension of Isaiah* and the community behind it. The motive behind historical revelation is christological: the reality of what Christ did cannot be perceived by human (or angelic) eyes. Only revelation can enable one to understand what really happened in Christ. Historical revelation is required for salvation since salvation depends on seeing the glory of Christ. Revelation about the past forms the theology—and the gospel—of the prophetic school behind the *Ascension of Isaiah*.

---

1. See p. 140 n. 1.
2. As Charles (21 n. 18) points out, the Ethiopic uses the word 'resurrection' twice in 3.18, *latenšä'ē fequr* (the resurrection of the Beloved) and *batenšä'ēhu asāb samāy* (in his resurrection to the seventh heaven). The Greek uses different words in these phrases: εἰς τὴν ἀνάστασιν τοῦ ἀγαπητοῦ and ἐν τῇ ἀναβάσει αὐτοῦ εἰς τὸν ἕβδομον οὐρανόν. The Ethiopic probably preserves the correct reading. Any scribe would expect an ascension into heaven rather than a resurrection into heaven and in Greek the change is slight: ἀναστάσει το ἀναβάσει. On the other hand a resurrection to heaven well fits ideas in the *Ascension of Isaiah* where at the resurrection Christ regains his former glory: he emerges from the tomb on the shoulders of the angels (as the Cherubim?) and is immediately recognized and worshiped in all the heavens in contrast to his descent when his glory was hidden. Thus when the twelve teach the resurrection in 3.18a, this includes the teaching of the ascent of the Beloved which is the distinctive doctrine of the community behind the *Ascension of Isaiah*.

Revealed History in the Ascension of Isaiah

The school behind the *Ascension of Isaiah* knew and utilized Jewish forms of revealed history. The Book of the Completion of the Days and the later apocalypse which incorporates it are apocalyptic histories. The school's preoccupation with the descent and ascent of the Beloved distilled an apocalyptic manifestation of inspired prophetic history. The *Ascension of Isaiah* also evidences something entirely new: a prophetic school concentrating on revelations of the past. This early Christian apocalypse derives from a vigorous, if embattled, prophetic school which found its highest calling in the propagation of revelations concerning the past heavenly and earthly deeds of the Beloved. Perhaps this school, in its willingness to live and die for its view of christological revealed history, was an isolated phenomenon, though 1 John may reflect similar battles, as we shall see. Yet taken together the *Ascension of Isaiah* and the *Shepherd of Hermas* attest the christological relevance of revealed history in the early second century. The spatial[1] and conceptual divergence between these works implies the importance of revelations concerning who Christ was and what he did for a wide spectrum of early Christianity. The *Odes of Solomon*, though close conceptually to the *Ascension of Isaiah*, provide yet another perspective, and a new form, to christological revealed history.

---

1. Affinities with *Odes of Solomon* argue a Syrian origin for the *Ascension of Isaiah*; *Shepherd of Hermas* of course stems from the environs of Rome.

Chapter 11

ODES OF SOLOMON

The *Odes of Solomon* are prophetic songs:[1] the odist regularly claims
inspiration (*Odes Sol.* 6.1-2; 12.1-3; etc.). Since all the odes probably
come from the same prophet, the claim to inspiration may be assumed
to refer to all of them. Since many portray past acts of God or the
messiah, they are important in any study of early Christian inspired
history.[2]

Consistent with their character as hymns, the *Odes of Solomon* make
few allusions to datable historical events. Dating must rely on the use
of the *Odes* by other authors or on the contacts of the *Odes* with various circles of thought. Harris and Mingana think the *Odes of Solomon*
were known by Ignatius and hence date the work late in the first
century.[3] The relevant passages from Ignatius are impressive but fall
short of proving that Ignatius knew the *Odes*. Evaluating contacts of
the *Odes of Solomon* with circles of thought has also proved suggestive
but inconclusive. The *Odes of Solomon* show marked, if complex,
relationships to the hymns of Qumran,[4] the New Testament christo-

1. D.E. Aune, 'The *Odes of Solomon* and Early Christian Prophecy', *NTS* 28
(1982), 435-60.
2. Sanders is almost alone in arguing that the *Odes of Solomon* are not Christian in
some sense of that term. He argues that they stem from a first-century amalgam of
Judaism and an Adonis cult (Jack T. Sanders, *The New Testament Christological
Hymns: Their Historical Religious Background* [SNTSMS 15; Cambridge: Cambridge University Press, 1971], 109-16).
3. Rendel Harris and Alfonse Mingana, *The Odes and Psalms of Solomon*, II
(Manchester: Manchester University Press, 1920), 42-43, 67-69.
4. Admitted by most interpreters. Advanced especially by Jean Carmignac ('Un
Qumranien converti au Christianisme: l'auteur des Odes de Salomon', *Qumran
Probleme* [ed. H. Bardtke, Deutsche Akademie der Wissenschaften zu Berlin.
Schriften der Sektion für Altertumswissenschaft 42; Berlin: Akademie, 1963], 75-
107) and by James H. Charlesworth ('Les Odes de Salomon et les Manuscrits de la
Mer Morte', *Revue Biblique* 77 [1970], 522-49; 'Qumran, John, and the *Odes of
Solomon*', *John and Qumran* [ed. J.H. Charlesworth; London: Chapman, 1972],
106-36).

logical hymns,[1] Johannine Christianity,[2] Ignatius,[3] *Ascension of Isaiah*,[4] and (Valentinian) gnosticism.[5] Of these the contacts with Valentinianism are least significant because they occur in precisely those areas where the gnostic system itself has contacts with the earlier literature. The remaining contacts would permit a late first-century or early second-century date.[6]

The *Odes of Solomon* have been called both 'gnostic'[7] and 'non-gnostic'.[8] Neither label seems particularly helpful; both attempt to define the *Odes of Solomon* in terms of later systems of thought.[9] Like

1. Sanders, 101, 103-104.

2. Generally admitted. See especially James H. Charlesworth and R. A. Culpepper, 'The *Odes of Solomon* and the Gospel of John', *CBQ* 35 (1973), 298-322.

3. Harris/Mingana, 42-43.

4. Charlesworth, 'The *Odes of Solomon*', *OTP* 2.733.

5. F.-M. Braun, 'L'énigme des Odes de Salomon', *Revue Thomiste* 57 (1957), 597-625. Kurt Rudolph, 'War der Verfasser der Oden Salomos ein "Qumran-Christ"? Ein Beitrag zur Diskussion um die Anfänge der Gnosis', *Revue de Qumran* 4 (1964), 523-55. Rudolph goes beyond Valentinian gnosticism to rely on Mandaean sources.

6. Late first or early second century: D.E. Aune ('Odes and Prophecy', 436; *The Cultic Setting of Realized Eschatology in Early Christianity* [Leiden: Brill, 1972], 174); Carmignac (92); Charlesworth and Culpepper (211); Charlesworth (*OTP*, 2.727); Harris/Mingana (69); Michael Lattke ('The Apocryphal *Odes of Solomon* and the New Testament Writings', *ZNW* 73 [1983], 294-301). First half of second century: Brian McNeil ('The Odes of Solomon and the Scriptures', *Oriens Christianus* 67 [1983], 111). Second century: W. Bauer ('The Odes of Solomon', *NTA*, 2.810); Rudolf (553). Second half of the second century: F.-M. Braun (613-15); Louise Abramowski ('Sprache und Abfassungszeit der Oden Salomos', *Oriens Christianus* 68 [1984], 90); J.H. Bernard (*The Odes of Solomon Edited with Introduction and Notes* [Texts and Studies 7.3; Cambridge: Cambridge University Press, 1912], 42). H.J.W. Drijvers has argued for a later and later date in the third century: 'The 19th Ode of Solomon: Its Interpretation and Place in Syrian Christianity', *JTS* 31 (1980), 337-55; 'The Odes of Solomon and Psalms of Man: Christians and Manichaens in Third-Century Syria', *Studies in Gnosticism and Hellenistic Religions Presented to Gilles Quispel on the Occasion of his 65th Birthday* (ed. R. van den Broek and M.J. Vermeren; Leiden: Brill, 1981), 117-30; 'Facts and Problems in Early Syriac-Speaking Christianity', *Second Century* 2 (1982), 157-75; 'Die Oden Salomos und die Polemik mit den Markioniten im syrischen Christentum', *Symposium Syriacum* 1976, (Orientalia Christiana Analecta 205; Rome: Pontifical Institute, 1978), 39-55.

7. W. Bauer, 809-10; R. Abramowski, 'Der Christus der Salomooden', *ZNW* 35 (1936) 45, 62-64; and especially Rudolph, 523-55.

8. James H. Charlesworth, 'The *Odes of Solomon*—Not Gnostic', *CBQ* 31 (1969), 357-69.

9. Aune, 'Odes and Prophecy', 436; less clearly Henry Chadwick, 'Some Reflections on the Character and Theology of the *Odes of Solomon*', *Kyriakon: Festschrift Johannes Quasten*, I (ed. P. Granfield and J.A. Jungmann; Münster: Aschendorff, 1970), 266-70.

the Qumran literature, the Gospel of John, and the *Ascension of Isaiah*, the *Odes of Solomon* use images and ideas which later became components of the gnostic systems. The *Odes of Solomon* should probably be regarded as early Christian prophetic hymns representing a Christianity very close to some forms of first-century Judaism but not at all averse to borrowing imagery from many facets of its religious environment.

The *Odes of Solomon* delight in connotative language. They prefer imagery, allusion, and wordplay to plain speech. The resulting difficulties, which have challenged all interpreters of these songs and account for their widely divergent interpretations, face this study as well. Therefore an investigation of inspired history in the *Odes of Solomon* cannot avoid the tedious but rewarding task of interpreting each relevant ode individually. Only after the pieces are discovered can the puzzle be assembled to form a picture of inspired history in the *Odes of Solomon*.

Several odes with clear reference to the past work of the messiah are spoken in the first person. Given the odist's expectation that the messiah should speak through his prophets' mouths,[1] first-person historical utterances of the messiah are no surprise, but they do raise a difficulty. How can we distinguish first-person utterances of the odist (of which there are many) from first-person utterances of the Christ speaking through him? Since for several odes the extent of the historical material is determined by where Christ begins to speak, distinguishing first-person utterances of Christ from those of the odist is crucial.[2] The following classification of the historical odes will separate those where Christ may speak in the first person from those in which he does not and will treat the latter first. Perhaps understanding

---

1. Then I arose and am with them
   and will speak by their mouths' (*Odes Sol.* 42.6).
Unless otherwise noted translations are from Charlesworth, 'Odes of Solomon', *OTP*, 2.725-72. Syriac text is from James H. Charlesworth, *The Odes of Solomon: The Syriac Texts* (Society of Biblical Literature Texts and Translations 13, Pseudepigrapha Series 7; Missoula, MT: Scholars Press, 1977).

2. Sanders (102, 108-109) and Rudolph (526-27) think it a mistake to distinguish too sharply between the odist and Christ in questionable cases. The odist is identified with Christ. R. Abramowski (52-57) speaks of two sons of God, one proper, one adopted, who ultimately are one. I also think that in some sense the odist is identified with Christ. He puts on Christ and what happens to Christ happens to him (see Chadwick, 269). Yet I think the 'I' of the odist can be distinguished from the 'I' of his messiah on the basis of content. Passages clearly spoken by the odist or clearly spoken by Christ can furnish criteria for distinguishing Christ from the odist in more questionable cases.

how the odist uses inspired history will aid in distinguishing the odist from Christ in the first-person historical sections.

Hortatory Historical Odes

Several historical odes begin with exhortation. The exhortation then gives way to reflection on some past action of Christ. Songs in this form will be called hortatory historical odes; *Odes* 8, 23, 39 and 41 are of this type.

Ode 39 reflects on the dangers of crossing a raging river and urges hearers to 'put on the name of the Most High' and so get across walking in Christ's footsteps. The first eight verses develop the image of the river. It is the Lord's power which overwhelms those who despise him (*Ode* 39.1-4). Verses 5-7 develop the antithesis: those with the sign of the Lord upon them cross in safety. Verse 8 gives a consequent exhortation: 'Therefore put on the name of the Most High and know Him and you shall cross without danger.' The last section of the ode (vv. 9-13) comprises a historical revelation. The Lord walked across the waters on foot; his footsteps became like a beam (*qys'*, the same word as 'cross'[1]) firmly fixed (*mtqn bšrr'*, fixed in truth)[2] making a sure way for those who follow him. Hence *Ode* 39 describes an aspect of the redemption of Christ worked in the incarnation: he has established a safe way over the judgment of God. If the 'beam' is an allusion to the cross so much the better. In addition to reflecting on the past in this way the odist has probably taken up the tradition of Jesus walking on the water and filled it with new content.[3] Hence, the revelation has two references to the past: it both reveals an aspect of the salvation won by Christ and it reveals new meaning in a well-known tradition about the earthly ministry of Jesus.

Ode 23 has with reason been called the most difficult song in the collection.[4] Its most difficult feature concerns a letter which descends from God and a wheel on which it lodges. The significance of the letter and wheel has hitherto eluded interpreters. The best that can be done is to acknowledge the difficulty and offer a conjectural solution.

Consider the following parallels and partial parallels.

---

1. Charlesworth, *OTP*, 2.768 n. g.
2. The need for parentheses shows the author's skill at word-play.
3. Hesitancy to permit this allusion seems unnecessary. Charlesworth (*Odes Syriac*, 137 n. 10) and Harris/Mingana (397) diffidently mention the parallel, but see Charlesworth, *OTP*, 2.768 n. 1, where the suggestion is made with greater confidence.
4. Harris/Mingana, 336.

> The word (*ptgmh*) of the Lord and his desires (*sbywhy*) the holy thought (*mhšbt'*) which he has thought concerning his Messiah (*Odes Sol.* 9.3).

> For the word (*mlt'*) of the Lord investigates that which is invisible and perceives his thought (*mhšbt'*, *Odes Sol.* 16.8).

> And worlds are by his word (*mlt'*)
> and by the thought (*mhšbth*) of his heart (*Odes Sol.* 16.19).

The last two parallelisms establish a correlation between God's thought and his word. The first establishes a similar correlation between God's word, his desires, and his thought and it ties all three concepts to his messiah. Since *mlt'* and *ptgm'* are probably interchangeable in the *Odes of Solomon*, it seems justifiable to conclude that the author closely associates (perhaps to a limited extent identifies) God's word (*ptgm'*, *mlt'*), thought (*mhšbt'*), and desires (*sbyn'*) with his messiah (*mšhh*). In *Ode* 23, the enigmatic letter is introduced in the following parallelism.

> And his thought (*mhšbth*) was like a letter and his will (*sbynh*) descended from on high (*Odes Sol.* 23.5).

Since the letter is likened to God's thought and identified with God's will by the parallelism, the letter probably serves as another image for the Word, God's messiah. Interpreting the letter so makes sense in the context of the *Odes of Solomon*, for the descent of the messiah frequently engages the author's imagination.[1]

The word 'wheel' occurs in none of the other odes. The wheel with the letter restrains its adversaries, mows them down, then fills in rivers and crosses them, uproots forests and makes a wide way. Elsewhere in the *Odes of Solomon* the messiah does similar things: the messiah builds a way across rivers (*Ode* 39); the messiah restrains adversaries (24.7, abysses; 42.11, Sheol and death). Perhaps the sign of the Kingdom (*mlkwt'*, 23.12) is equivalent to the name which rules (*mmlkw*, 23.22)—name of the Father, Son, and Spirit. The head which appears on the wheel is called the son of truth from the most high

---

1. A similar argument is used by H.J.W. Drijvers, 'Kerygma und Logos in den Oden Salomos dargestellt am Beispiel der 23. Ode', *Kerygma und Logos. Beiträge zu den geistesgeschichtlichen Beziehungen zwischen Antike und Christentum. Festschrift für Carl Andresen zum 70. Geburtstag* (Göttingen: Vandenhoeck & Ruprecht, 1979), 158-61. Harris and Mingana (338) also interpret the letter as a reference to the incarnation. Drijvers calls attention to the letter in the Hymn of the Pearl which, he thinks, represents Christ. Braun (608) and R. Abramowski (45, 64) also refer to the Hymn of the Pearl. There are of course many heavenly documents in the Pseudepigrapha. I am not certain that the letter in the Hymn of the Pearl is Christ, though that is one logical interpretation in its present context in the *Acts of Thomas*.

Father who proceeds to inherit everything and 'head' elsewhere also refers to the messiah (24.1). Probably these images, the letter and the wheel, refer to the incarnation of the messiah, a favorite theme of the odist.

Other details of *Ode* 23 can be explained on the assumption that it recounts the incarnation. The letter descending from the Father chronicles the descent of the messiah. Those who try unsuccessfully to grasp and read the letter parallel the disciples in Mark or John, who do not fully understand who Jesus is during the earthly ministry.[1] The wheel requires more elaborate conjectural explanation. The two most viable interpretations of the wheel explain it as the instrument of torture by that name reflecting the cross[2] or as an allusion to the wheels of the throne chariot in Ezekiel, Daniel, and the Angelic Liturgy (4Q Shir Shab).[3] According to the latter explanation the letter descends, is seen by many, and then is enthroned on the chariot of God. The sign of kingdom and providence (dominion? Dan. 7.9, 13-14) associated with the letter on the wheel (*Odes Sol.* 23.12) might confirm an interpretation as divine throne. A Johannine conception of the cross as Christ's glorification[4] would permit a union of the image of the throne chariot with the image of torture on the cross: the instrument of torture is Christ's throne.[5] The odist delights in such double references. *Ode* 23.13-14 describes victory over enemies won by the cross/enthronement. Probably the odist makes another double reference in the pair, head/feet. Head and feet may express top and bottom or may refer to the messiah as leader. I am inclined to view the head (23.16) as the messiah, the highest, and the feet as the lowest. Head and its throne wheel descending to the feet may refer to the *descensus ad inferos*, another favorite theme of the odist (cf. *Ode* 42). That the cross/throne should be the instrument of descent is appropriate. That the head, the Son of God, should appear at the head of those gathered for Sheol is fitting (23.18; cf. 42.14). The messiah inheriting everything (23.19) would refer to his ascent and enthronement in heaven. The enlargement of the letter written by God would refer to the work of prophets who, like the odist and those under the Paraclete

1. The motif of misunderstanding by the disciples fits well with the Odist's desire to understand the Beloved by revelation rather than by an appeal to apostolic tradition.
2. Braun, 608.
3. Charlesworth, *Odes Syriac*, 96 n. 8; Drijvers, 'Kerygma und Logos', 166.
4. Charlesworth rightly finds this concept in the *Odes of Solomon* (Charlesworth, *Odes Syriac*, 43 n. 5).
5. Drijvers ('Kerygma und Logos', 166) unites the throne and cross imagery.

in John and the Spirit in 1 Corinthians, can now read and understand the letter by divine help.

The foregoing paragraph is not offered as a definitive interpretation of this difficult ode. It is offered only to show how the paradigm suggested earlier, that the ode recounts the incarnation of the messiah, can be articulated over the ode as a whole. Such details as the prophetic interpretation of the letter postulated for the last two verses, though logical in themselves, sit far too loosely on the text to serve as evidence for revelation about the past. Yet we can conclude that *Ode* 23 probably refers to the incarnation and that it is therefore a historical ode. Since it begins with a declaration of the joy of the elect which serves as ground for an exhortation to walk in the knowledge of the Lord and his grace (such knowledge goes well with the interpretation of this ode as a reference to the incarnation), *Ode* 23 also belongs to the hortatory historical odes in which an exhortation to experience the love, knowledge, or praise of the Lord precedes an account of the past accomplishments of the messiah.

Ode 8 has one of the clearest changes of speakers in the *Odes of Solomon*. The ode begins with a series of exhortations referring to the Lord in the third person. Although Harris/Mingana and Charlesworth insert 'Christ speaks' after v. 7, first-person utterance does not begin until v. 9 and continues through v. 19. The last three verses return to exhortation and lack first-person speech. They should probably be regarded as words of the odist.

The ode primarily seeks to exhort hearers to live in the experience of deliverance (*Ode* 8.1-7, 20-22). Verse 8, which properly belongs to the exhortation, designates the subsequent verses in the first person as a special revelation:

> Hear the word of truth
> and receive the knowledge of the Most High.

The Father rather than the Son probably speaks the ensuing first-person speech, for elsewhere the breasts from which flow the holy milk are the breasts of the Father; the Son is the cup.[1] Other utterances of the first-person speaker are as consistent with the Father speaking as with the Son.

The Father speaks of his present love and care for his own, but also of what he has done for them in the past:

---

1. Cf. *Odes* 8.14; 19.2; 14.2. *Ode* 14.2 probably also refers the breasts to the Father.

And before they had existed,
I recognized them;
And imprinted a seal on their faces (8.13).

Hence the Father reveals what he has done in creating his own as well as what he is doing and will do for them. This revelation shows the basis for the experience of deliverance which the ode urges. A revelation of the past work of God in the believer grounds exhortation to live in the experience of God's work.

Ode 41 employs exhortation to introduce reflection on the earthly accomplishments of the savior. Framing a meditation on the grace received by his community are exhortations to praise the LORD and exult in him (41.1, 7). There follows a first-person section and then a third-person description of what the Word has done. The first-person section uses concepts elsewhere applied to Christ. Compare the two following parallels:

All those who see me will be amazed,
because I am from another race (41.8).

All who saw me were amazed
And I seemed to them like a stranger (17.6).

Christ clearly speaks the latter verse and Harris and Mingana logically argue that he must speak the former verse as well.[1] In *Ode* 41 the thought of God begetting the messiah precisely fits the Word christology stated elsewhere, as does the reference to wisdom in *Odes of Solomon* 41.9 (cf. Prov. 8.22).[2] Yet 'Let us exult with the exultation of the Lord' (41.7) should introduce some response of praise from the community as actually occurs later (41.11-15). A speech of Christ, initially at least, seems out of place. Perhaps, however, 41.8-10 can be both a speech from Christ and a praise from the community. 'Let us exult with the exultation of the Lord ' (41.7) means 'Let us join in the exultation which Christ exults [subjective genitive]'. The worshipers are to experience the joy Christ experiences.[3] The switch back to the

---

1. Harris/Mingana, 402.
2. Harris/Mingana, 402.
3. This is entirely comprehensible against the background of Qumran where members experience the joy of heavenly beings. See Aune, *Realized Eschatology*, 182: 'The Spirit of God is the agent who enables the cult leader and the congregation to participate in eschatological salvation through the proleptic experience of participating in the future heavenly worship of God within the setting of an earthly community assembled for worship. The participation of the congregation in this experience is demonstrated by the frequent shift from "I" to "we" in the *Odes*, the

third person corresponds to the exhortation to praise and the community's desire to praise the exultant one.

If Christ speaks in these verses (41.8-10), he reveals the past: his supernatural birth. The history of Christ continues in the third-person declaration that follows. The Word is identified as the savior who does not reject his own, the man who humbled himself, was raised and appeared in the perfection of his Father. The ode reveals the descent and ascent of the Christ as seen in Philippians 2 or in Johannine theology or the *Ascension of Isaiah* and comments on the result which is characteristic of the *Odes of Solomon*: light streaming from the Word. Perhaps to controvert those who expected multiple messiahs,[1] the odist reveals that the messiah is one. He was before the foundation of the world and gives life.

Ode 41 follows the pattern of the other hortatory historical odes: historical revelation follows exhortation to experience the Lord in love, praise, or deed. *Ode* 41 ends with what may serve as a description of itself: 'A new chant for the Lord from them that love him' (41.16). *Ode* 41, as indicated by its exhortation to praise, is almost certainly liturgical. The history and true significance of Christ is revealed to those who together exult with the Lord's exultation. The exhortation in *Ode* 8 also seems especially liturgical ('Open, open your hearts to the exultation of the Lord and let your love abound from the heart to the lips' [8.1]). Since both have 'I' sections, this locates first-person prophecy of the past squarely in the context of corporate worship.[2] An inspired account of past acts of God or Christ on behalf of the members of the community was part of their experience of worship. The prevalence of such passages in the *Odes of Solomon* shows how important this experience was. All four of these odes imply that exhortation as well as worship was regularly based on revelation of the past. The revelation might concern what God has done for the believer, but more frequently considered the saving acts of the messiah.

---

characteristic use of plural imperatives and the final "Hallelujah" (*Odes* 4.9f.; 6.5f.; 17.15; 18.7; 41.2-7, 11; 42.21-24).'

1. Charlesworth (*Odes Syriac*, 143 n. 8) and Carmignac (80) mention expectations of multiple messiahs at Qumran. Harris and Mingana (49) think of antidocetic arguments in Ignatius.

2. Aune, *Realized Eschatology*, 176, 188.

Historical Odes Beginning with a Claim to Inspiration

Several odes which may have a reference to the past begin with a claim to inspiration (*Odes Sol.* 6, 10, 12, 16, 36). These odes have two or three parts:

Type 1
A.	Claim to inspiration perhaps referring to the poet's odes or praises
B.	Historical references

Type 2
A.	Claim to inspiration, perhaps referring to the poet's odes or praises
B.	Historical references
C.	Conclusion making some kind of inclusion with A

Odes 6 and 12 are parallel in form. In each the odist alludes to the knowledge given him by God (*Odes Sol.* 6.1-7; 12.1-3), describes the past archetypal gift of knowledge (6.8-12; 12.4-12), and blesses those who have acquired (or acquired and dispensed) this knowledge (6.13-18; 12.13). Hence they belong to type two.

Ode 12 begins with the odist's claim of inspiration:

> He has filled me with words of truth,
> that I may proclaim him [or it].
> And like the flowing of waters, truth flows from my mouth
> And my lips declare his [its] fruits.
> And he has caused his knowledge to abound in me. . . (*Odes Sol.* 12.1-3a).

and ends with a blessing:

> Blessed are they who by means of him have recognized everything, and have known the Lord in his truth (*Odes Sol.* 12.13).

Between the claim to inspiration and the blessing, the ode reveals the past activity and present (eternal) characteristics of the logos (*ptgm'*). While the logos clearly does something in the past (12.4, 8-12), the nature of his activity depends on the translation of *'lm'* (12.4, 8). On first reading *'lm'* is attractively translated by 'aeons'.[1] Aeons, conceived as gnostic or protognostic divine beings, received power of speech from the logos (12.8) and became 'the narrators of his glory', etc. (12.4). This interpretation fits well the writer's concern for heavenly places and heavenly beings. As one who frequents paradise and joins in the heavenly praise there, he would naturally find the

---

1. Michael Lattke, *Die Oden Salomos in ihrer Bedeutung für Neues Testament und Gnosis*, I (Göttingen: Vandenhoeck & Ruprecht, 1979), 115.

instruction of the aeons by the Word a matter of interest and importance. The *'lm'* figure as subject or object in verses 9-11. They live in
love and harmony and know their creator by the activity of the Word.
Yet, if all these verses refer to aeons why the sudden reference to *br
'nš '* (a Son of man) in 12? Why is the dwelling of the Word in a man
important for revelation to aeons? If we allow *br 'nš '* to interpret the
verses above, Charlesworth's translation of *'lm'* as 'generations' seems
possible. The 'generations' refer to human beings, the 'interpreters,
narrators, confessors, preachers, teachers' (12.4) to various classes or
officers of God's people,[1] and the activity of the Word to his activity
on earth. Alternatively *'lm'* may be translated 'worlds' or 'ages'.
Creation declares the glory of God as in Psalm 19; one day speaks to
another, night pours forth knowledge to night (Ps. 19.2).[2] The ages or
worlds (conceived temporally or physically) are speaking to one
another (*Odes Sol.* 12.8). Although any of the three interpretations
seems possible, the last seems best. That the Word is father of the *'lm'*
(7.11) suits best the last interpretation for elsewhere in the *Odes of
Solomon* the Word acts in creation. *Ode* 16 considers the activity of
the Word in creation of the physical world and summarizes:

> The worlds are by his word
> and by the thought of his heart (*Odes Sol.* 16.19).[3]

Nothing in *Ode* 16 suggests the meaning 'aeons' for *'lm'*; it refers to
the physical universe as created by the Word (*mlt'*). In *Ode* 12 also the
author probably uses *'lm'* in the plural to refer to physical creation.

With any of these interpretations the odist claims inspiration, reveals
a past act of the Word, and then utters a blessing. If *'lm'* is translated
'aeons' the historical section reveals how the aeons long ago derived
knowledge and utterance from the Word. If *'lm'* in *Ode* 12 refers to
human beings (generations) then the historical section reveals the
earthly appearance of the Word. The odist is inspired to understand
more fully the gift of knowledge of speech from the incarnation. If
'lm' refers to creation the ode reveals how the Word at creation made
his creatures declare the glory of God. Since *Ode* 12 frames a historical revelation (12.4-12) with a claim to knowledge from God
(12.1-3) and a blessing on those who have such knowledge (12.13), it
conforms to the pattern (type 2) above.

---

1. Charlesworth, *Odes Syriac*, 62 n. 5.
2. Harris and Mingana (272) point out the parallel with Psalm 19.
3. Bernard (30) points out the parallel.

In *Ode* 6 the odist first speaks of his own inspiration; the Spirit (*rwḥh*) speaks through him as wind (*rwḥ'*)[1] speaks in the strings of a harp. He specifically connects his inspiration with the past:

> The Lord has multiplied his knowledge,
> and he was zealous that those things should be known
>   which through his grace have been given to us (*Odes Sol.* 6.6).

In the past by grace God has given certain things; knowledge of these things is given by the Spirit through the odist.[2] Verse 3 ('For he destroys whatever is foreign and everything is of the Lord') is enigmatic but probably refers to the odist and the purity of his inspiration. The Lord destroys any alien influence in the odist which might inhibit the ready, pure flow of the Spirit's words. Verses 4 and 5 raise the Lord's activity in v. 3 to the level of a general principle; from beginning to end the knowledge of God destroys anything contrary to him.

The historical section of this ode describes a stream of water which spreads over the whole earth and quenches the thirst of the thirsty (6.8-12). Elsewhere in the *Odes of Solomon* water denotes saving knowledge (11.4-9; 12.2-3) or destructive judgment (*Ode* 39). Both meanings figure here, for the same stream which brings refreshment to the thirsty (6.11) also carries everything away and shatters it (6.8). The general principle enunciated in 6.35 finds cosmic as well as individual expression. As the Lord has destroyed every alien thing that might hinder his expression through the odist (6.3) so the Lord who expressed his knowledge in the world purged from the world everything that hindered his expression. Whatever stood against the expression of this saving knowledge, whether human resistance (6.9) or the Temple itself (6.8), is carried away.[3] Such parallelism between

---

1. So Charlesworth (*Odes Syriac*, 28) followed by Lattke (*Oden in ihrer Bedeutung*, 90-91) restores the lacunae in the text. Harris/Mingana (234), '*yd*', 'hand'.

2. See 1 Cor. 2.12.

3. Is this a veiled (or not so veiled) allusion to Jesus' prophecies against the Temple as well as an allusion to their fulfillment? Other such allusions to tradition about Jesus figure in the *Odes of Solomon*. I am inclined to translate '*yty lhykl*' 'it carried off the Temple' with Harris/Mingana (233) rather than 'he brought (it) to the Temple' with Charlesworth (*OTP*, 2.738) and J.A. Emerton ('Notes on Some Passages in the *Odes of Solomon*', *JTS* n.s. 28 [1977], 507). The Coptic, which eliminates every hint at destruction in 6.8b, probably smoothes over this difficult text. See *Ode* 39.1 where *mytyn* refers to a river carrying one headlong. Perhaps the odist has roots in one of the types of Judaism (represented at Qumran, in *Sib. Or.* 4, *Apoca-*

the first and second parts of the ode confirms that the stream represents knowledge from God. The knowledge expressed through the odist has been expressed in an even fuller way in the past. The stream of knowledge spread and filled until the knowledge of the Lord covered the earth as the waters covered the sea.[1] Probably the gift of knowledge to the odist stems from this initial gift of knowledge in the past.

To what past event does this imagery refer? In the odes the messiah is the source of knowledge. Since Jesus prophesied against the Temple, its destruction can logically be viewed as a result of his utterance. The restrainers (v. 9) might naturally refer to those who sought his death. To any familiar with the Johannine vocabulary (and the odist shows many contacts with it) the depiction of a stream of knowledge flowing from Jesus seems plausible.[2] *Ode* 30 speaks of a spring flowing from the lips of the Lord from which the thirsty may drink (30.6). Hence the stream probably depicts the past and present effects of the incarnation of the messiah. If so, *Ode* 6 conforms precisely to the pattern already seen in *Ode* 12. It opens with a claim to inspiration (6.1-8), reveals an aspect of salvation which was poured out from the messiah (6.9-19) and concludes with a blessing of those who, like the odist, have been entrusted with dispensing this water for the thirsty to drink (6. 20-22).

Like *Odes* 6 and 12, *Ode* 16 begins with a reference to the inspiration of the odist and his inspired praises (*Ode* 16.1-9, esp. 5). The odist is especially inspired to tell the work of God and of his Word (16.6-7). In the historical section this translates into a consideration of creation. The odist describes both the ancient activity of the Word in creation and the order which is created by him—two themes which traditionally belong together in Hebrew poetry.[3] The ode concludes with a brief note of praise forming an inclusion with the beginning.

A. Odist inspired to praise (16.1-9)
B. Creating and resultant order (16.10-19)
C. Praise (16.20)

Hence 16 is also type two.

---

lypse of Abraham, and possibly in John and in Stephen's speech) which considered the Temple apostate.

1. Harris/Mingana, 238.
2. Jn 7.37-38. Harris and Mingana (238) point out patristic references to the Christ as a stream. Bernard (56) wrongly equates it with baptism (thirst seems to dominate, not dipping).
3. See Ps. 104.

Although the description of creating the world closely parallels Genesis 1 and Psalm 104 where the chief actor is God, the logical subject of the verbs in the historical section is the Word (*mlt'*)[1] from 1.8. Hence at the end the odist can say, 'And the worlds are by his word'.[2] While the sentences in which *mlt'* occurs assert nothing a non-Christian Jew would have been unwilling to say about the role of God's word in creation, the passage taken as a whole seems to require understanding the *mlt'* as the hypostatized Word, the Son, as elsewhere in the *Odes of Solomon*.

Hence in each of *Odes* 6, 12, and 16 a claim to inspiration introduces a revelation about the past activity of the Son. Perhaps this pattern can be of help in distinguishing the voice of the inspired odist from that of the inspiring Lord.

Several odes in which Christ may speak are in the first person from start to finish (10, 17, 22, 28, 36, 42). Gunkel thinks that all of these odes are spoken by the redeemer;[3] Harris and Mingana divide five of them (10, 17, 28, 36, 42) into sections in which the first-person pronoun refers initially to the odist and then to Christ.[4] Gunkel's position has simplicity to recommend it and as he elaborates it his interpretation seems plausible. The switch in pronoun reference postulated by Harris and Mingana is awkward. Since at least one ode (22) shows Christ speaking throughout, Gunkel's form is known to occur. Harris and Mingana have this much to recommend their interpretation: unannounced switches to Christ speaking do occur in odes which begin in the third person or in the plural. In each case the ode's reference to history depends on the presence and location of the switch.

Although Charlesworth follows Harris/Mingana in attributing the first three verses of *Ode* 10 to the odist and the last three to Christ,[5] Gunkel attributes the entire ode to Christ as speaker.[6] In favor of Gunkel's interpretation, no indication of a change in speaker distinguishes the first-person pronouns of vv. 1-3 from the first-person verbs and pronouns of vv. 4-6. Yet the use of first-person verbs demarks the first half of the ode from the second: never in the first half but regularly in the second half is the 'I' the subject of the verbs. Furthermore the first half closely parallels those claims to inspiration

1. Charlesworth, *Odes Syriac*, 72 n. 6.
2. Again '*lm*' but here nothing in the context suggests aeons. Harris and Mingana (286) point out that in Heb. 1.2 a nearly identical clause attributes creation to the Son.
3. Hermann Gunkel, 'Die Oden Salomos', *ZNW* 11 (1910), 291-328.
4. Harris/Mingana, 263, 290, 358, 384, 403.
5. Charlesworth, *OTP*, 2.744.
6. Gunkel (311), 'ein Dankleid des Christus für die geschehene Erlösung'.

in the odes discussed previously. In the earlier examples the claim to inspiration served to introduce inspired speech directed toward the past. Since in the *Odes of Solomon* inspired speech regularly takes the form of first-person utterances of Christ, it is hardly surprising to find an ode beginning with a claim to inspiration and ending with an inspired speech of Christ. Formal considerations then make a switch in speaker from odist to Christ plausible. Does the song make sense when interpreted so?

Given the many claims by the odist to inspiration, the first verse (10.1) is most naturally taken as spoken by the odist in his own person:

> The Lord has directed my mouth by his Word
> and has opened my heart by his Light.

The last verse, however, is most naturally taken of Christ:

> And the traces of light were set upon their [the Gentiles'] heart, and they
> walked according to my life and were saved,
> and they became my people forever and ever.

That the inspiration of the first half is directed toward capturing a captivity for freedom (10.3) and that the person speaking in the second half describes how he captured the world[1] seems at first to argue that the inspired person is the same as the speaker who captures. Yet since the odist and those in his community frequently are identified with the savior, it is fitting that the one inspired by the Word does what the Word did. Because *Ode* 10 is formally parallel to *Odes* 6, 12, and 16 and because the ode makes good sense when divided between Christ and the odist, I am inclined to follow Charlesworth and see a change of speaker between vv. 3 and 4. *Ode* 10 then, like the other odes in this category, introduces a historical revelation by a claim to inspiration. In the revelation, Christ reveals what he has done. He has captured the world for the Most High, making Gentiles his people.

Gunkel considers the whole of *Ode* 36 as spoken by Christ.[2] Charlesworth and Harris/Mingana divide this ode also into a portion spoken by Christ (*Odes Sol.* 36.3-8) and a portion spoken by the odist (36.1-2).[3] *Ode* 36 begins with an account of a heavenly trip instead of a claim to inspiration. The formal parallel useful in interpreting *Ode* 10 does not apply. Furthermore those verses sometimes ascribed to Christ contain elements frequently associated with heavenly travelers. In the *Ascension of Isaiah* (7.25; 9.27-42) the prophet 'ascends before

---

1. Here *'lm'* may denote 'people in the world'.
2. Gunkel, 299.
3. Charlesworth, *OTP*, 2.765; Harris/Mingana, 384.

the lord's face' (*Odes Sol.* 36.3; *Ascen. Isa.* 9.27-42), is made like 'the greatest of the great ones' (*Odes Sol.* 36.4; *Ascen. Isa.* 7.25; 9.30), became 'one of those who were near him' (*Odes Sol.* 36.6; *Ascen. Isa.* 9.42), and was inspired with the heavenly song (*Odes Sol.* 36.7; cf. 36.2; *Ascen. Isa.* 9.28). With Gunkel it seems best to assume that the speaker of vv. 1-2 is the same as that of vv. 3-8, but is the odist or Christ the heavenly traveler? The above parallels from the *Ascension of Isaiah* show that for one early Christian prophetic community the experiences described for the odist were quite within the reach of an inspired but quite ordinary human being. Since Syriac has no article, *br nš*, *brh d'lh'*, and *nhyr'* (v. 3) can be rendered 'a man', 'a son of god', or 'a light' respectively. *bd* probably should be translated 'although'. Hence v. 3, which in Charlesworth's translation seems so clearly to suggest Christ as speaker ('Because I was the Son[1] of Man, I was named the Light, the Son of God'), may be translated, 'Although I was a man, I was named light, a son of God'. All these titles fit well the redeemed in the *Odes of Solomon*. Since elsewhere in the *Odes of Solomon* the odist takes apocalyptic heavenly trips (*Odes Sol.* 11.16; 38.1-22) but Christ nowhere does,[2] it seems best to assume that the odist is the 'I' in *Ode* 36.[3] *Ode* 36 is an account of a heavenly trip rather than a revelation of the past.

Comparing *Ode* 42.1-2 to *Odes* 27 and 35.7 provides a clue to its interpretation:

> I extended my hands (*pšṭ 'ydy*) and approached my Lord
> because the stretching out of my hands is his sign,
> and my extension is the common cross
> that was lifted up on the way of the Righteous one (42.1-2).

> I extended my hands (*pšṭ 'ydy*)
> and hallowed my Lord;
> for the expansion of my hands is his sign
> and my extension
> is the upright cross (27.1-3).

> And I extended my hands (*pšṭ 'ydy*) in the ascent of myself
> and I directed myself near the Most High,
> and I was saved near him (35.7).

---

1. Charlesworth (*Odes Syriac*, 127-28 n. 4) points out the difficulty of assuming an adoptionist christology in the *Odes of Solomon* where the preexistence of Christ and Word is stressed. Reading this ode as referring to the odist rather than Christ removes the difficulties.

2. Even Gunkel (316-18) interprets *Ode* 38 as an 'ascension of the soul' rather than an ascension of the redeemer.

3. R. Abramowski (58) identifies the traveler as the adopted son.

Ode 35 probably refers to the odist's own experience or that of a member of his community.[1] Hence, in 35.7, the odist is the one who extends his hands. That the odist extends his hands in 27 is also the most natural reading. Since the extension of the hands mimics the cross (27.3), 'his sign' refers to the crucifixion. Because the third-person pronoun (his sign) refers to Christ, the first-person verb (I extended my hands) must refer to the odist. The same logic holds for 42.1-2. Hence in 42 a switch occurs from the 'ego' of the odist to the 'ego' of Christ.[2]

An understanding of this extension of the hands may offer ample rationale for the switch in pronoun reference between 42.2 and 42.3. *Ode* 35.7 connects the extension of the odist's hands with his ascension to be near God. Similarly 42.2 connects his extension with his being 'lifted up on the way of the righteous one'. The identification of the odist's extension with the cross (27.3; 42.2) links attitude of prayer (extended hands like a cross) with the ascent to be near God. As the messiah was glorified on the cross to be with God, so the odist, identifying with the crucified, glorified messiah, ascends in glory to be with God.[3] Spreading his hands in the proper attitude of identification with Christ, he is 'lifted up' (*'ttly*) as Christ was 'lifted up' on the cross. Thus the odist is lifted up on the way of the righteous one; by extending his hands, he takes the very path to God and glory taken by Christ from the cross.[4] The extension of the odist's hands identifies him with the glorification of Christ. In such a state it seems natural that Christ should speak through him (42.6). In the case of *Ode* 42, the cruciform attitude of prayer becomes a claim to inspiration.[5]

---

1. So Gunkel, 319; Charlesworth, *Odes Syriac*, 126 n. 11; Harris/Mingana, 382.

2. Gunkel (303) thinks *Odes Sol.* 42.1-2 refers to the crucifixion and hence is spoken by Christ.

3. As noted above the odist frequently takes heavenly journeys. Aune rightly connects such journeys with praise (*Realized Eschatology*, 179, 182). Connecting heavenly journeys with praise forms another link between the attitude of prayer (42.1-2) and stepping out on the way of the righteous one (42.2).

4. In *Ode* 39 those who know the messiah follow the path made by him.

5. Aune ('Odes and Prophecy', 446-47), comes to a complementary conclusion regarding a ritual sequence for congregational prophecy: 'The ritual sequence evident in this passage (*Ode* 37.1-4), with supplementation from other passages in the *Odes*, consists of the following elements: (1) assumption of the standing position (cf. 26.12 [*qwm*]; 7.16b-21), (2) raising the arms in a cruciform pattern (27.1-3; 35.7), (3) a petition for the ability to utter inspired song is addressed to the Lord (cf. 14.7-8), (4) the odist experiences "rest", i.e. the overwhelming consciousness of the presence of God, and (5) the odist utters an inspired song.'

After the reference to the way of the righteous one, Christ, speaking through the odist, describes one station on this way, the descent to Sheol and the deliverance accomplished there. As the odist is on the way of Christ's glory, so Christ led a multitude on that way from Sheol (42.11, 17-18). Hence the odist, identified with Christ, reveals the past deliverance worked by Christ on his path of glorification which began at the cross. He reveals past events which show the power of Christ's work and which can only be known by revelation. On examination *Ode* 42 proves to have a latent claim to inspiration followed by a historical revelation; it belongs to type one.

Odes 17 and 28 also contain implicit claims to inspiration:

> And the thought of truth led me
> and I went after it and did not err (17.5).

> As the wings of doves over their nestlings,
> and the mouth of their nestlings toward their mouths
> so also are the wings of the Spirit over my heart (28.1).

As for 17.5, truth plays a role parallel to an interpreting angel in *Ode* 38. Hence the claim that 'the thought of truth led me' is functionally equivalent to 'I was inspired'. The claim to being fed and nurtured by the Spirit (28.1) also fits well the ubiquitous claims to inspiration in the *Odes of Solomon*. Since both these odes move from this implicit claim to inspiration to a consideration of the history of Christ, like 42 they belong among those historical odes which begin with claims for inspiration.

These two odes may actually signal the beginning of Christ's speech:

> And all who saw me were amazed (*kl dḥz' wwny tmhw*),
>   and I seemed to them like a stranger (17.6).

> Those who saw me were amazed ('*tdmrw 'ylyn dḥzyn hww ly*),
>   because I was persecuted (28.9).

> All those who see me will be amazed (*ntdmrwn klhwn 'ylyn dḥzyn ly*)
>   because I am from another race (41.8).

Though the formula 'who saw me were amazed' differs in tenses and wording, the coincidence is striking. In *Ode* 41 the formula introduces a speech of Christ. Most likely it does the same in *Odes* 17 and 28.[1] In both of these latter odes the words from Christ describe his past acts. *Ode* 17 describes Christ's glorification and his release of those who were bound through the knowledge once acquired by Christ (17.8) but now given to those Christ freed (17.13). Probably Christ breaks his

---

1. Harris/Mingana, 293.

own servants out of Sheol. *Ode* 28 interprets Christ's execution using images drawn from Psalm 22.[1] The messiah was surrounded by mad dogs foolishly attacking their master for his goodness. They sought his death and thought they succeeded in bringing it about, but did not. The ode also refers to the messiah's miraculous birth (*Ode* 28.17). Hence both odes (17 and 28) begin with an implicit claim to inspiration and proceed to a revelation of Christ's past deeds. They belong to type one of that class of historical odes which opens with the claim to inspiration.

When the odist explicitly claims inspiration he frequently applies that inspiration toward an elucidation of what Christ has done in the past. He describes the activity of the Word at creation in *Ode* 16 and possibly *Ode* 12; he investigates the saving activity of the Word in *Odes* 6, 10, 17, 28, and 42. These odes show revelation of the past activity of the redeemer to be one of the prime concerns of the odist.[2]

Other Historical Odes

Four historical odes remain which resist the classifications above. *Ode* 22 is a song of triumph spoken by Christ, praising God for the deliverance from the grave worked by his hands. It reveals how God through Christ destroyed the seven-headed dragon, raised chosen ones from the grave, clothed them with flesh, and made them a kingdom in which to dwell. Since it reflects on the effects wrought by the descent and ascent of the redeemer and since it is spoken by the glorified Christ, *Ode* 22 is an important instance of historical revelation directed to understanding the power of redemption in Christ.

Ode 19 should perhaps be classified with those odes that begin with a claim to inspiration. The odist begins:

A cup of milk was offered to me,
and I drank it in the sweetness of the Lord's kindness (19.1).

The author then proceeds to unpack the metaphor (19.2-5):

---

1. Harris/Mingana, 360-61.
2. Aune ('Odes and Prophecy', 445) notices that the speeches of Christ focus on his soteriological role: 'his mysterious appearance, the persecution he endured which was frustrated by his resurrection, his task of calling forth believers whom he has predestined, his proclamation to the dead and their response to him'. These elements are all historical. He also notes that the *descensus ad inferos*, as important as it is in the *Odes of Solomon*, only occurs as spoken by Christ—logically so, for how could it be known but by revelation?

The Son is the cup;
The Father is he who is milked;
The Holy Spirit is she who milked him (19.2).

The milk is evidently a figure for salvation,[1] but salvation in the odes is so tied to knowledge and knowledge to revelation that to drink this milk may amount to inspiration. In any case the metaphor and its interpretation move immediately to a consideration of the history of the messiah just as those odes which begin with inspiration move immediately to a consideration of history.[2] The historical section of *Ode* 19 (vv. 6-11) considers the birth of the Son and concentrates on the Virgin who bore him. As in the other instances when an incident from Christ's life is elaborated,[3] the virginal conception and birth is invested with new meaning. The Virgin has taken on characteristics of virgin Wisdom.[4] She loves and proclaims like the virgin in 33.5ff. The tradition utilized goes beyond that in Matthew or Luke; various details recall the apocryphal gospels or *Ascen. Isa.* 11.2-15. Yet as in the other odes an incident in Christ's life is considered and given new meaning.

Ode 31 considers the activity of the messiah in the third person (31.1-5), exhorts (second person) the afflicted to grasp immortal life, and concludes with a historical reminiscence in the first person by Christ. The third-person section (31.1-5) describes the accomplishments of the messiah: chasms (*thwm'*) vanished; error erred deluged by the truth; the messiah 'opened his mouth and spoke grace and joy/ and recited a new chant to his name' (31.3), offering to God those who had become sons through him. In the first-person section, Christ sings his song, rehearsing the turmoil of his execution. The messiah humbly bore the bitterness of those assailing him to fulfill the promises to the patriarchs (*Ode* 31.8-13). Hence *Ode* 31 both considers an aspect of Christ's earthly existence and reveals the salvation won by it.

---

1. Drijvers, '19th Ode', 340.
2. Hence there is a break between 19.5 and 6. Charlesworth's translation obscures the break by adding an object to the verb *gpt*. 19.6a probably is merely a metaphor expressing conception as indicated by the parallelism in 19.6b. *gp* or *gwp* means to hunt or capture with a net. 'The Virgin's womb captures' should probably mean no more than 'it conceived'. To supply an object, though sometimes necessary in English, obscures the fact that in Syriac the verb is here used intransitively as is *nsbyn* in 5.b. In Syriac, what is received (19.5) is not necessarily the same as what is captured in 19.6.
3. See *Ode* 39, which elaborates the tradition of walking on water, and *Ode* 24, which considers Jesus' baptism.
4. Harris/Mingana, 307-309; cf. Chadwick, 269.

Ode 24 develops features drawn from traditions about the baptism of Jesus:[1]

> The dove fluttered over the head of our Lord Messiah
> because he was her head (*Ode* 24.1).

> But the chasms were submerged in the submersion of the Lord (24.7).

The ode reflects on the ancient myth of the battle with the chaos monster. The presence of the dove or Spirit at the baptism of Jesus and the announcement which flows from her causes the chasms (*thwm'*) to writhe in birth pangs. The submersion of Jesus in the baptism becomes typical of the chasms' (*thwm'*) attempt to devour the messiah. Hence the baptism typifies the descent of the messiah to Sheol. Since the abysses could not contain the messiah, though they sought to bring forth death they gave birth to life (24.8) and were themselves put to death (24.7). Hence like *Ode* 39, *Ode* 24 both describes the past victory of the messiah and its consequences and invests an event remembered from the tradition about Jesus with new meaning.

Revealed History in the Odes of Solomon

Of the forty-one surviving *Odes of Solomon*, thirteen contain historical sections. The device of inspiration directed to the past, which in the first century was used by so many facets of Judaism, proved useful also to the Christian Jew who wrote the *Odes of Solomon*. By utilizing this technique in a song the odist created a new form: the inspired historical ode. Though he uses the device flexibly, his historical odes tend to cluster around two basic forms: hortatory historical odes begin with exhortation which is then grounded on a revelation of the past; odes beginning with a claim to inspiration proceed to disclose the past and its significance.

With one exception the author of the *Odes of Solomon* directs revealed history toward discovering what the messiah, the Word, has done. That exception, *Ode* 8, in which the Father speaks of what he has done for his chosen ones, proves the rule for much of what he has done is associated with the messiah in other odes. For example, in *Ode* 8 the Father prepares his breasts for his people, in *Ode* 19 it is clear that the people drink the milk from the Son who is the cup. The *Odes of Solomon* fit into the pattern of christologically-centered revealed history already observed in the *Shepherd of Hermas* and the *Ascension of Isaiah*.

---

1. Harris/Mingana, 344; Bernard, 102.

Those odes which reveal what the Word-messiah has done divide broadly into two camps. They either consider the activity of the Word in creation (12, 16) or they consider the activity of the Word in salvation. By far the majority of the historical odes reveal various aspects of the salvation won by the messiah (6, 10, 17, 22, 23, 28, 31, 39, 41, 42). Opening a way, releasing prisoners, and imparting knowledge are the most frequently used metaphors.

Characteristic of the *Odes of Solomon* is the inspired investigation of traditional material from the career of Jesus. The birth of Jesus including the virginal conception (*Ode* 19), his baptism (24), his walking on the water (39), and his crucifixion (28, 42) have significance for the salvation accomplished by the messiah when properly interpreted by revelation. In the cases of the virginal conception, the baptism and the walking on the water, the tradition becomes a metaphor describing the deliverance won by Christ.

Perhaps the consideration of the incarnation as a whole (*Ode* 23) is but a variation of the previous class. Yet it reveals many things not clearly connected with tradition from reminiscences about the earthly Jesus—the preexistence and enthronement of the messiah, for instance, or his descent to Sheol. Aune has noticed that such a key concept for the *Odes of Solomon* as the *descensus ad inferos* only occurs when the odist-prophet is inspired to speak in the name of Christ.[1] Christ's accomplishments—in Sheol, at creation, in blazing a trail to heaven—derive from revelation about the past. The chief concern in these, as in tradition from Jesus, is to understand the salvation won by the messiah. The odist investigates the material to find what the Christ has done for his own—to find out the full significance of the incarnation. He is not so interested in what an observer would have seen as in the mysteries he could not have seen.

These revelations may be cast in third-person utterances about the messiah (6, 12, 16, 19, 23, 31, 39, 41) or in first-person speeches in which the messiah through the odist declares what he has done (10, 17, 22, 28, 31, 41, 42). In either case, as seen most clearly in *Odes* 8 and 41, the setting of this revelation is the worshiping community to which the author belongs.

For the odist, knowledge saves and knowledge is brought by the Word. One of the most important things to know is what Christ accomplished. Hence through the odist, the Word reveals to his faithful ones what he had won for them:

---

1. Aune, 'Odes and Prophecy', 445.

Then I arose and am with them
and will speak by their mouths (*Odes Sol.* 42.6).

The Lord has multiplied his knowledge,
and he was zealous that those things should be known
    which through his grace has been given to us (*Odes Sol.* 6.6).

The works studied so far attest revelation directed toward under-standing who Christ was and what he did. Two works, Luke–Acts and John, have undertaken a greater task: they have cast recollections of Jesus into full-blown interpretive prophetic histories similar to that found in Josephus' *Jewish War*.

Chapter 12

LUKE–ACTS

Luke bases his understanding of Jesus and God's plan in history on the Holy Spirit's activity in the past and present. The Holy Spirit revealed the plan of God in the scriptures, carried it out in the ministry of Jesus and proclaimed it in the witness of the early church. This continuity of the Spirit's activity provides the assurance (ἀσφάλεια, Lk. 1.4) which Luke offers Theophilus and his readers. So argues Ulrich Luck in an intriguing article published in 1960.[1] In dependence on Luck, Fitzmyer speaks of the Spirit 'authenticating the proclamation about him [Jesus] in Acts' or of 'the Spirit-filled guarantee for the Jesus tradition'.[2] Minear grounds the authority of the eyewitnesses claimed by Luke not in their recollection alone but in their capacity as prophets:

> There are many 'eyewitnesses and servants of the Word' to be encountered within Luke–Acts, beginning with Zechariah in Luke 1 and ending with Paul in Acts 28. All have been given by the Spirit their endowment for future witnessing.[3]

---

1. Ulrich Luck, 'Kerygma, Tradition und Geschichte Jesu bei Lukas', *ZTK* 57 (1960), 51-66. Luck can speak as if the Spirit gives insight into the past: 'Das bedeutet aber, daß er den eigentlichen Zugang zur Geschichte Jesu nicht in einem heilsgeschichtlichen Schema begründet sieht, sondern allein durch das πνεῦμα erhält' (64). 'Daraus ergibt sich für ihn gerade unter theologischem Gesichtspunkt die Frage nach der Vergangenheit, in der sich die πράγματα ereignet haben, die sich ihm durch den Geist als μεγαλεῖα τοῦ θεοῦ (Apg 2,11) erschließen' (65).
2. Joseph A. Fitzmyer, *The Gospel According to Luke I–IX* (AB 28; Garden City, NY: Doubleday, 1981), 13.
3. Paul S. Minear, 'Luke's Use of the Birth Stories', *Studies in Luke–Acts* (ed. Leander E. Keck and J. Louis Martyn; Philadelphia: Fortress, 1980 [repr. 1966]), 117. Minear develops this theory further in *To Heal and to Reveal: The Prophetic Vocation According to Luke* (New York: Seabury, 1976), 81-147, especially 84-85, 127-43.

These opinions and the arguments behind them may not establish the use of inspired history in Luke–Acts, but they forcefully raise the possibility: Is Luke–Acts prophetic history?

Since Luke no more than Josephus announces his intention to write prophetic history, answering this question must rest on inferences. If we can show that Luke portrays persons inspired to understand the past and can also show that Luke–Acts shares the message and task of these inspired persons, we can infer that the author writes a chronicle based on revelation. I think he does: like his contemporary Josephus, Luke writes an interpretive prophetic history. I will first show from the resurrection narratives how Jesus reveals the plan of God to the disciples, making them his witnesses. Then I will show how this revelation supplies a scheme around which Luke organizes his work. Finally I will analyse a series of speeches, predominently inspired historical sermons, which support this scheme. At the conclusion of each section I will pause to assess the place of revealed history in Luke's work.

The Resurrection Narratives

Luke's account of the empty tomb and of the resurrection appearances highlights the bewilderment of the disciples. The women go to the tomb expecting only to anoint the body of Jesus. When they see the empty tomb, they still do not grasp what has happened. Even after they are reminded of the passion predictions of Jesus and have heard angels affirm that he is alive, Luke refrains from saying they believed (24.1-9).[1] When the apostles hear about the empty tomb and the angels' message that Jesus is alive, 'It seemed to them as nonsense (λῆρος) and they did not believe them' (ἠπίστουν αὐταῖς, 24.10-11). When Peter's curiosity galvanizes his own visit to the tomb, his confirmation of the women's words begets not understanding but astonishment (24.12).[2] Cleopas and his companion know everything necessary for understanding, but they cannot put together the incomprehensible facts (24.19-24). Luke describes them as sad (σκυθρωποί [24.17], contrast the χαρᾶς μεγάλης [24.52]), as foolish and slow of heart to believe (24.25). Even after Jesus had interpreted the scriptures to show that

1. Richard J. Dillon, *From Eye-Witnesses to Ministers of the Word: Tradition and Composition in Luke 24* (Analecta Biblica 82; Rome: Pontifical Institute, 1978), 52.

2. The majority of recent commentators accept v. 12 as authentic. See Fitzmyer, 28a.1547; I. Howard Marshall, *The Gospel of Luke: A Commentary on the Greek Text* (New International Greek Testament Commentary; Grand Rapids: Eerdmans, 1978), 888.

the Christ had to suffer and enter his glory and had appeared to them in the breaking of bread, Luke refrains from saying they understood. Instead their hearts burned while he opened the scriptures to them (Lk. 24.32). Presumably they could still 'disbelieve for joy and wonder' (24.41) with the others when Jesus proves that he is not merely a spirit (24.36-43). Only when Jesus gives the final revelation opening their *minds* to understand the scripture (24.45) can the disciples grasp what has really happened: 'And they returned to Jerusalem with great joy, and were continually in the Temple blessing God.'[1]

This resolution of the disciples' befuddlement climaxes a carefully developed motif of concealment: the disciples' failure to grasp the true significance of what had happened in the death of Jesus occurs repeatedly in Luke. After Jesus had revealed that the Son of man would be delivered into human hands,[2] Luke declares that the disciples did not understand: οἱ δὲ ἠγνόουν τὸ ῥῆμα τοῦτο, καὶ ἦν παρακεκαλυμμένον ἀπ' αὐτῶν ἵνα μὴ αἴσθωνται αὐτό, καὶ ἐφοβοῦντο ἐρωτῆσαι αὐτὸν περὶ τοῦ ῥήματος τούτου (Lk. 9.45).[3] They failed to understand the passion in the divine plan because it was hidden from them (divine passive). God was concealing his plan. The motif emerges with equal clarity at Lk. 18.34. Again after a passion prediction Luke comments: καὶ αὐτοὶ οὐδὲν τούτων συνῆκαν, καὶ ἦν τὸ ῥῆμα τοῦτο κεκρυμμένον ἀπ' αὐτῶν, καὶ οὐκ ἐγίνωσκον τὰ λεγόμενα (Lk. 18.34). On the basis of these and other passages Wrede argued that Luke converted Mark's messianic secret into a passion's secret,[4] and certainly the divine passives on the stem κρύπτω imply a heavenly secret God has not yet made known.[5] In the final scene of Luke, Jesus uncovers what had been hidden: in Acts the disciples declare what before the could not understand.

Hence, though Cleopas (24.21) and the others (Acts 1.6) had perceived enough from the events and the scriptures to hope for the

---

1. For a similar interpretation see William S. Kurz, 'Hellenistic Rhetoric in the Christological Proof of Luke–Acts', *CBQ* 42 (1980), 180 ; David L. Tiede, *Prophecy and History in Luke–Acts* (Philadelphia: Fortress, 1980), 31-32. Above all see Dillon, *From Eyewitnesses to Ministers of the Word*, IX, 19, 99, 127, 133, 135, 144, 216.

2. Notice the emphasis: θέσθε ὑμεῖς εἰς τὰ ὦτα ὑμῶν τοὺς λόγους τούτους (Lk. 9.44).

3. Again notice the emphasis by repetition.

4. William Wrede, *The Messianic Secret* (trans. J.C.G. Greig; Greenwood, SC: Attic Press, 1971), 170, 179; cf. Dillon, *From Eyewitnesses to Ministers of the Word*, 24.

5. Dillon, *From Eyewitnesses to Ministers of the Word*, 23. Notice the similar use of the passive in Lk. 24.16.

deliverance of Israel,[1] the import of what had happened could only be known by revelation. The plan of God which would bring that hope to fruition was hidden and could not be perceived even with hindsight. The resurrected Jesus reveals this secret plan only after its central event has occurred.[2] At least at this crucial point Luke relies on revealed history.

What does the resurrected Christ reveal? From Luke's point of view he reveals the past; in terms of narrative time he reveals both the past and the future. The revelation occurs in three progressively deepening phases. Angels communicate to the women that Jesus is alive and remind them of Jesus' words concerning his passion and resurrection (Lk. 24.5-7), Jesus appears to Cleopas and the other disciple to interpret scripture for them (24.25-27, 30-32), and Jesus appears to the eleven and the others to remind them of Jesus' words (24.44) and to open their minds to understand the scriptures (24.45-49).

The angels' words to the women have several references to the past. First they reveal that he has been raised (24.6),[3] a revelation of a past event which the women had not witnessed but which could account for the empty tomb. The rhetorical question 'Why do you seek the living among the dead?' reveals the present effect of the past event: Jesus is alive. The revelation of past occurrences unwitnessed by human beings is a major use of revealed history.[4] Second, the angels remind the women of Jesus' words. Such inspired memory has also figured in other revelations about the past.[5] The angels both summarize the content of Jesus' predictions concerning death and resurrection[6] and apply these words to the women's present confusion. Jesus' words explain the events which have led to the astonishing empty tomb. By noticing that the women remembered what Jesus had said, Luke shows that they were beginning to grasp what had happened. Hence a revela-

---

1. As noted by Wrede (168-69), Luke has altered Mark's portrayal of the twelve as dullwitted and imperceptive. Not their own slackness but God's will has withheld the knowledge from them until the proper time.

2. The foregoing paragraph owes much to Wrede, 164-80. For the idea of hiddenness resolved in revelation see 164, 167, 172. See also Hans Conzelmann, *The Theology of St. Luke* (New York: Harper & Row, 1960), 162.

3. With Fitzmyer, 28a.1545, I prefer this translation of ἠγέρθη to 'he has risen'.

4. The Animal Apocalypse of *1 Enoch* reveals the rule of the wicked angelic shepherds. In *Jubilees* the angel reveals to Moses the story of creation, etc.

5. *Jub.* 32.21-26; *4 Ezra* 14; Jn 14.26; Josephus *J.W.* 3.8.3 §351; cf. Acts 11.16 where memory aids revelation but is not clearly inspired.

6. Notice that Luke does not have the angels quote Jesus. In fact the reference to crucifixion goes beyond anything Jesus has said in the Gospel. Revelation by reminding can both interpret and specify the saying recalled.

tion about the past begins to explain what until now had been hidden from the disciples. The key to grasping that Jesus was the Christ (cf. Acts 17.3) is a revelation about the past.

On the journey to Emmaus Luke begins by showing how Cleopas and his comrade have all the data necessary to comprehend what has happened.[1] They know Jesus was a mighty prophet, like Moses powerful in word and deed,[2] and from him they expect the redemption of Israel (24.19-21). They know his rejection and execution by their rulers. They know the tomb is empty and that angels have announced Jesus to be alive. They have the scriptures which announce all these things (24.23-25). Yet none of the pieces fit together. They know all the events but not what has really happened in them. Only further revelation can prompt insight into their significance. Luke turns to inspired history.

The revelation to Cleopas and the other disciple has two components corresponding to the two elements composing the angels' announcement to the women. As the angels had announced that Jesus had been raised and was alive, so Jesus himself is revealed alive in the breaking of the bread at Emmaus. As the angels make sense of the past events by bringing to remembrance words of Jesus, so Jesus on the walk to Emmaus makes sense of the events by 'opening the scriptures' (24.32). Both inspired memory and inspired interpretation of the scriptures elucidate the past events by fitting them into God's plan.

While the use of scripture in the infancy narratives perhaps warns against the restriction of τὰ περὶ ἑαυτοῦ (24.27) to the events surrounding the passion, in the Emmaus incident the scriptural reinterpretation of events centers on the passion. It was necessary (ἔδει) for the messiah to suffer and enter into his glory (24.26). The two infinitives παθεῖν and εἰσελθεῖν are here governed by the imperfect ἔδει. Fitzmyer concludes that like the 'suffering', 'entering his glory' has already occurred.[3] Possibly he is right, yet it seems more likely that 'entering his glory' refers to the ascension, which in Luke occurs in the next scene (Lk. 24.50-51).[4] In either case both

---

1. Dillon, *From Eyewitnesses to Ministers of the Word*, 127, 132.
2. Compare Lk. 24.19 and Acts 7.22.
3. Fitzmyer, 28a.1566.
4. The association of the ascension with Son of man motifs (Acts 1.9) increases the likelihood that εἰσελθεῖν εἰς τὴν δόξαν αὐτοῦ (Lk. 24.26) refers to the ascension, since Jesus has already joined 'Son of man' with 'coming with glory' (ὁ υἱὸς τοῦ ἀνθρώπου... ἔλθῃ ἐν τῇ δόξῃ αὐτοῦ, Lk. 9.26) and since in Daniel one like a Son of man comes on the clouds to receive dominion and honor (Dan. 7.14; 9.13-14. δόξα figures in the LXX; Theodotion uses τιμή; MT יקר). Cf. Alfred

'suffering' and 'entering into his glory' describe revelations of the past. By showing how the scriptures make it necessary for the messiah to suffer, Luke explains an event past even to Cleopas; by showing how scriptures make it necessary for the messiah to enter his glory, Luke explains an event in his own past, though perhaps in the future of Cleopas. In the context, the emphasis falls on the events past to Cleopas. The data, so bewildering to the two disciples, all in the past, make sense as soon as it is clear from the scriptures that the messiah must suffer and enter into his glory. Such a revelation, based on inspired interpretation of the scriptures, makes sense both of the rejection and execution of Jesus by the rulers and of the confusing report that the tomb was empty and Jesus was alive. For the first time these disciples were glimpsing recent events as viewed in the counsel of God.[1]

Luke speaks of Jesus not only interpreting (διερμήνευσεν, Lk. 24.27) the scriptures but also opening (διήνοιγεν, 24.32) them. διανοίγω in Luke frequently denotes the revelation of what is hidden. In Acts 7.56 the heavens open to reveal the Son of man standing by the throne of God. In Lk. 24.16 the two disciples' eyes were held (οἱ ὀφθαλμοὶ αὐτῶν ἐκρατοῦντο) so they could not recognize Jesus. In Lk. 24.31 their eyes were opened (αὐτῶν διηνοίχθησαν οἱ ὀφθαλμοί) and they recognized him.[2] The suffering of the Son of man written in the prophets is hidden (κεκρυμμένον, Lk. 18.31-34) from the twelve as Jesus' own words are concealed (παρακεκαλυμμένον, 9.44-45). In Lk. 24.25 they are foolish and slow to believe what the prophets have spoken. Hence when Jesus opens (διήνοιγεν, 24.32) the scriptures[3] he reveals the plan of God behind the death and resurrection of the messiah which has been hidden in them.[4] By

Rahlfs, ed., *Septuaginta* (Stuttgart: Deutsche Bibelstiftung, 1938) 914. Cf. 1 Tim. 3.16, an early creedal piece which speaks of ἀνελήμφθη ἐν δόξῃ, uniting Luke's ἀνελήμψις with his εἰσελθεῖν εἰς τὴν δόξαν.

1. Kurz, 180.

2. Cf. 2 Kgs 6.17 LXX where Elisha opens the eyes of his servant to see the heavenly chariots that have been there all along.

3. Potential disciples must always have the scriptures opened (Acts 17.2-3; cf. 8.30-35).

4. Those who start from the speeches in Acts sometimes come to the opposite conclusion: 'There is no secret. You need no enlightenment in order to find what the Scriptures say about the Messiah-Jesus. . . There is nothing like a veil upon the Scriptures or on the hearts of the readers so that they cannot understand them, as we read in 2 Cor. 3.12-18' (Jacob Jervell, 'Sons of the Prophets: The Holy Spirit in the Acts of the Apostles', in *The Unknown Paul* [Minneapolis: Augsburg, 1984], 101). In the same vein see Donald Juel, 'Social Dimensions of Exegesis: The Use of Psalm

inspired interpretation of the scriptures Jesus reveals how the seemingly inexplicable recent events fit perfectly this long-hidden plan of God.

The revelation given in the Emmaus episode springs from the same motivation as the historical apocalypses. Such apocalypses seek by revelation to explain some recent disaster on Israel as part of the greater deliverance God is bringing. All makes sense when God's plan is revealed by the apocalyptist. In the same way Jesus reveals how God had worked in a recent disaster, his own death. All becomes clear when God's plan is revealed.[1] To reveal this divine plan Jesus resorts to a technique well known from the apocalyptic histories: inspired interpretation of scripture to explain past events.[2] Of course in contrast to the apocalyptic histories the revelation here is only briefly summarized, only hinted at, but this is by Luke's design. After all, Luke will expound this message fully in the speeches in Acts.

16 in Acts 2', *CBQ* 43 (1981), 552. Such statements give insufficient attention to Lk. 24 with its explicit portrayal of a secret in scripture which Christ reveals. See also the despair of the Ethiopian Eunuch and the claims to inspiration for the speeches in Acts (see below). Peter in Acts 2, for instance, speaks as a prophet—he has received revelation and call from Jesus (Lk. 24.44-49) and has just received the Spirit which makes God's servants prophesy (Acts 2.17-18). As he interprets the scripture he does not merely give his opinion but speaks with the authority of revelation. Certainly the truth is evident for all to see in scripture and Peter's argument does depend on logic and common sense (Acts 2.29), but Peter's hearers would never see that truth if Peter, speaking as prophetic witness, had not revealed it to them. Common sense is not logically incompatible with revelation. Luke's probable rhetorical training would lead him to present revelation (or anything else) as persuasively, and hence logically, as possible.

1. Schubert, in a series of articles elaborating Luke's 'proof from prophecy theology' has shown the importance of the plan or counsel of God ἡ βουλὴ τοῦ θεοῦ) in Luke–Acts. Luke emphasizes the 'definite plan and foreknowledge of God (Acts 2.23, cf. context) which is disclosed to and through the prophets and is fulfilled in Jesus'. Paul Schubert, 'The Structure and Significance of Luke 24', *Neutesta-mentliche Studien für Rudolf Bultmann zu seinem siebzigsten Geburtstag am 20. August 1954* (Beihefte zur Zeitschrift für die neutestamentliche Wissenschaft und die Kunde der Älteren Kirche 21; Berlin: Töpelmann, 1954), 182. See also Schubert's articles, 'The Place of the Areopagus Speech in the Composition of Acts', *Transitions in Biblical Scholarship* (ed. J.C. Rylaarsdam; Chicago: Chicago University Press, 1968), 239-46; and 'The Final Cycle of Speeches in the Book of Acts', *JBL* 87 (1968), 1-16. Tannehill speaks of Jesus revealing the plan of God in Luke 24. R.C. Tannehill, *The Narrative Unity of Luke–Acts, Vol. 1: The Gospel according to Luke* (Philadelphia: Fortress, 1986), 279-98, especially 297, 293-94.

2. See the reinterpretation of Jer. 27 in the Animal Apocalypse and in Dan. 9 or the reinterpretation of Daniel in *4 Ezra* 11.

The climax of revelation occurs when Jesus appears to the gathered disciples. Again the revelation has two parts: Jesus shows himself to the disciples, proving that he is alive (24.36-43) and then explains what has happened (24.44-49). The first part assures the disciples that Jesus has really risen, is in fact alive; hence the concern to show Jesus' physical presence. Its only reference to the past confirms that the resurrection has really occurred. The second part concludes the interpretation of the past begun in the earlier revelations.

The words with which Jesus opens the revelatory discourse are difficult.[1] Probably Fitzmyer's rendering points in the right direction, 'Now this is what my words meant which I addressed to you while I was still with you: All that was written about me in the law of Moses, in the Prophets, and in the Psalms must see fulfillment.'[2] The meaning of that first phrase comes close to the colloquial 'This is what I have been trying to tell you'. Jesus will interpret his own words by interpreting the scriptures. This final utterance of Jesus unifies both modes of revelation used in the preceding resurrection narratives: inspired memory and inspired interpretation. Like the angels he calls to mind what he had already said; as he did on the road to Emmaus, he interprets the scriptures. His own words and the scriptures contain the same message concerning the recent events.

Although at one point Luke shows Jesus connecting what is written in the prophets with his coming passion and death (Lk. 18.31-34) the fulfillment of the scriptures can hardly be termed the sum of Jesus' message even in Luke.[3] Hence Luke shows Jesus not merely recalling, but interpreting, his own words. This fulfillment of scriptures is the key which unlocks the real meaning in all the words of Jesus. Without a revelation of God's plan, Jesus' words, like the scriptures, cannot adequately be understood.[4]

Verse 44 should probably be regarded as the exordium of a speech: it sums up what Jesus is going to say. The next utterance of Jesus (24.46-49) again sums up the most important points of the speech and

---

1. Οὗτοι οἱ λόγοι μου οὓς ἐλάλησα πρὸς ὑμᾶς ἔτι ὢν σὺν ὑμῖν (Lk. 24.44a). See the discussions of Marshall, 904; Alfred Plummer, *Gospel According to St. Luke* (5th edn; ICC; Edinburgh: T & T Clark, 1922), 561.

2. Fitzmyer, 1578, cf. 1582.

3. With Fitzmyer (1578, 1582) and others I take the ὅτι as the referent of the οὗτοι; cf. Marshall, 904; Plummer, 561.

4. Luke in the birth narratives carefully ensures that his readers see Jesus fulfilling scripture before Jesus ever speaks (see the articles by Schubert). They therefore read Jesus' words with at least some of the insight necessary to understand them. Surely this is part of what the preface means by expounding everything in order.

applies them directly to the hearers as is appropriate to the peroration of a speech. 'Thus' (οὕτως, 24.46), difficult otherwise,[1] well introduces a peroration and probably refers back to the missing body of the speech. Luke (v. 45) does not summarize the points of the speech as might be expected but instead indicates the effects of the speech on the hearers: their minds are opened to understand the scriptures. With this speech Jesus removes the 'mental block' with which God had guarded the secret of passion and resurrection (9.45; 18.34).

The passages emphasize inspired interpretation of scripture. Most of each summary concerns what is written (γεγραμμένα, Lk. 24.44; γέγραπται, 24.46). The exordium stresses the sources: Moses, Prophets, Psalms—all well utilized in the speeches in Acts and the canticles of the birth narrative. The peroration contains some of the most interesting material for the present study. As in the earlier revelations, the scriptures are shown to explain the baffling events of the recent past (24.46).[2] But in addition to παθεῖν and ἀναστῆναι, γέγραπται governs another infinitive as well: κηρυχθῆναι. The scriptures not only show how the recent baffling events fit in the plan of God but also how the plan of God will shape the disciples' future. 'It is written. . . that repentance and forgiveness should be preached in his name to all the Gentiles' (24.47). From the standpoint of the speech this preaching lies in the future, but from the standpoint of Luke himself it lies in the past and is recounted in Acts. In its own way the mystery of Gentile inclusion qualifies as past revelation.

The speech commissions those present as witnesses of 'these things'. In this context 'these things' (τούτων) refers to the whole plan of God revealed in scripture as Jesus opens their minds. It includes what God has done and what he will do.[3] The scene has many features of a prophetic call. Jesus reveals to the disciples the counsel of God (24.44-47); he ordains them witnesses of this plan (48); and he promises to send power upon them to accomplish their task (49). The eyewitnesses, through the revelation of God's plan in the past events which they witnessed and in future events they will bring about, have become

1. Marshall, 905.
2. Luck (63) remarks that in opening the door to the scriptures Jesus has opened the door to his own history.
3. 'In the statement of v. 48, ὑμεῖς μάρτυρες τούτων, the demonstrative pronoun clearly refers to all the aspects of scripture fulfillment in vv. 46-47, and that includes a *future* component, the world-mission, which is certainly not yet factual reality! This makes it quite clear that it is of the paschal "opening" of the scriptures first that the third-day observer is made witness' (Dillon, *From Eyewitnesses to Ministers of the Word*, 216; cf. Luck, 61).

ministers of the word.[1] These ministers of the word, empowered by
the Spirit, announce the plan of God in their speeches in Acts and
further it with their actions.

In Luke the resurrected Christ appears to his disciples to reveal the
plan of God hidden in the scriptures and in recent events. He or his
angelic servants interpret the enigmatic events and words of Jesus well
known to human observers but not comprehended by them. This revelation uncovers the proper understanding of the scriptures and of the
plan of God as it has worked out in Jesus, specifically that the messiah
had to suffer and be raised and that repentance and forgiveness should
be proclaimed to the Gentiles. Because human observation cannot
penetrate to *was eigentlich gewesen ist*, the disciples are commissioned
as witnesses not merely of what they have perceived about the earthly
Jesus as human observers, but also of the interpretation of those events
as Christ revealed it to them. Several qualifications equip such witnesses: (1) They should have seen the raw data of the events
summarized in Lk. 24.18-24 or Acts 1.21-22. (2) They must have
received revelation from the risen Christ as to the significance of these
events in the counsel of God. In Luke 24 this revelation takes the form
of inspired memory and inspired interpretation, primarily of the
scriptures but also of Jesus' own words. (3) They must be empowered
by the Spirit. Since Paul, who lacks the first of these, is nevertheless
called to witness to what he has seen and heard just as are the apostles
(Acts 22.15; 26.16), the inspired understanding of the past events takes
precedence over the experience of the events themselves.[2]

The author of Luke–Acts himself is just such a witness. His whole
work declares what Christ reveals in Luke 24 and ordains witnesses to
speak: 'Thus it is written that the Christ should suffer and be raised
from the dead on the third day and that repentance and forgiveness of
sins should be preached to all the Gentiles' (24.46-47). Luke grounds
his work on revealed history. He seeks to show how the plan of God
works out in the events of Jesus' ministry and in the proclamation to
the Gentiles. His purpose resembles that of the author of a historical
apocalypse such as *2 Baruch*. Luke, like the apocalyptist, wants to
explain puzzling recent events as part of God's plan. Both want to
show that what has happened does not negate principles of scripture
but fulfills them. Both use revelation directed toward the past to show
how the baffling events fit into the totality of God's plan. Luke seeks to

---

1. Dillon, *From Eyewitnesses to Ministers of the Word*, 217.
2. This qualifies, but does not diminish the importance of the eyewitness motif in
Luke–Acts. Notice that, like John and Josephus, Luke holds the eyewitness and
inspiration motifs together.

explain the death of the messiah and the rejection of Israel, *2 Baruch* the destruction of Jerusalem, but both rely on the same technique and build on similar presuppositions, the techniques and presuppositions of revealed history. Yet unlike *2 Baruch*, Luke–Acts is not an apocalypse. Their authors had similar purposes but they chose different genera of revealed history to accomplish them. Since Luke–Acts maintains resolutely the intent to chronicle the past, it is not apocalyptic but prophetic history.

The Lucan Scheme of Revealed History

The resurrection narratives revealed the startling fulfillment of scripture in the passion and resurrection of Jesus, the correct understanding of his words and deeds, especially of his death and resurrection, and the blessing about to come on the Gentiles through repentance and forgiveness. Such elements constitute a pattern frequently repeated throughout Luke–Acts. Since Luke grounds this historical pattern in revelation from the resurrected Christ, further defining the pattern and tracing it through Luke–Acts will help in assessing the Lucan use of revealed history. After studying this pattern in the missions speeches, we will turn to the speeches of Simeon in the temple and of Jesus at the synagogue at Nazareth.

As hinted earlier, the missions speeches in Acts amplify the terse summaries of historical revelation found in the resurrection narratives. Luke uses these speeches to flesh out the program outlined in Luke 24. Since these speeches and others in Acts do not merely rely on the historical revelation given in the resurrection stories but also qualify as revealed histories in their own right, a consideration of inspiration in the speeches in Acts will precede a more detailed look at the missions speeches and how they elaborate that plan of God revealed by the newly resurrected Jesus.

A number of speeches in the first third of Acts do claim inspiration. Peter's speech at Pentecost (Acts 2.14-36, 38-39) follows immediately the announcement that they 'were all filled with the Holy Spirit' (Acts 2.4). Peter's speech to the High Priest and the council (4.8-12, 19-20) is introduced, 'Then Peter, filled with the Holy Spirit, said to them' (4.8). Peter, again before the high priest speaking for all the apostles, claims the Holy Spirit as witness alongside of himself and the others (5.32). Stephen, a man full of faith and of the Holy Spirit (6.5), speaks with irresistible wisdom and Spirit (6.10). At the beginning of his defense his face looks like the face of an angel (Acts 6.15), a probable claim to inspiration.[1] Cornelius expects Peter to speak what is 'commanded by the Lord' (Acts 10.33). Paul, sent out by the Holy Spirit (13.2, 4), filled with the Holy Spirit (13.9), addresses a 'word of exhortation' (λόγος παρακλήσεως, 13.15) to the synagogue.[2] Historical speeches by Paul or other Christians in the rest of Acts do not explicitly claim inspiration; neither do several speeches in the early portions of Acts. However, Luke probably expects his readers to take all the Christian speeches as inspired.[3] He ceases mentioning this inspiration because he considers it adequately established,[4] for every Christian who gives a speech is introduced at some point as speaking filled with the Spirit.[5] Indeed in Luke from the time of Pentecost every Christian has the Spirit, and the Joel quote reveals the descent of the Spirit to have brought prophetic speech and prophetic experience to the servants of God (Acts 2.17-21).[6] Some at least of the speeches in

---

1. M.-E. Boismard, 'Le martyre d'Etienne. Acts 6.8–8.2', *RSR* 69 (1981), 183. See also the glory of Moses' face after his ascent of the mountain and the progressive change in Isaiah's countenance in the *Ascension of Isaiah*.

2. Παράκλησις in Luke is connected to early Christian prophecy by E.E. Ellis, 'The Role of the Christian Prophet in Acts', *Prophecy and Hermeneutic in Early Christianity: New Testament Essays* (Grand Rapids: Eerdmans, 1978), 131-33.

3. See Leo O'Reilly, *Word and Sign in the Acts of the Apostles: A Study in Lucan Theology* (Analecta Gregoriana 243; Rome: Pontifica Universita Gregoriana, 1987); Richard J. Dillon, 'The Prophecy of Christ and His Witnesses according to the Discourses of Acts', *MTS* 32 (1986), 544-56.

4. John Kilgallen, *The Stephen Speech: A Literary and Redactional Study of Acts 7.2-53* (Analecta Biblica 67; Rome: Pontifical Institute, 1976), 114. See also Dillon, *From Eyewitnesses to Ministers of the Word*, 212, 216.

5. Cf. for Peter, Paul, Stephen above. James' suggestion (15.15-21) is declared inspired following his speech. 'It seems good to the Holy Spirit and to us' (Acts 15.28).

6. Jervell (110-11) limits the activity of the Spirit to the παρρησία with which words were spoken: 'The words of the gospel do not come from the Spirit, but the way they are spoken is given by the Spirit.' However, the verse he quotes (Acts 4.13; cf. 4.8) to establish his claim, though capable of bearing his interpretation, probably implies some knowledge given by the Spirit. The most obvious reason to marvel at perceiving that Peter and John were uneducated (ἀγράμματοι) is that they have spoken wisely. Jervell (100, 112-14) wants to establish scripture, not revelation by the Spirit or Jesus, as the source of the gospel, but Luke would see no reason to maintain such a distinction. The Spirit, who once spoke the plan of God in the scriptures (Acts 1.16) now speaks the same plan of God through the apostles (Acts 5.32). In Lk. 1 and 2 the Spirit clearly inspires messages of the gospel (Lk. 1.41 and 67, ἐπλήσθη πνεύματος ἁγίου; 2.27, ἦλθεν ἐν τῷ πνεύματι). Similar phrases introduce speeches in Acts (Acts 4.8, Πέτρος πλησθεὶς πνεύματος ἁγίου; 6.5, Στέφανον, ἄνδρα πλήρης πίστεως καὶ πνεύματος ἁγίου; 6.10, τῷ πνεύματι ᾧ ἐλάλει; 13.9-10, Παῦλος, πλησθεὶς πνεύματος ἁγίου,... εἶπεν).

Acts must fulfill the promise of Jesus that when the disciples were delivered before synagogues or kings, Jesus, or the Spirit, would give them στόμα καὶ σοφίαν ᾗ οὐ δυνήσονται ἀντιστῆναι[1] (Lk. 21.14-15; cf. 12.11-12). Further, those Christians who speak are witnesses who have received revelation from the risen Christ and been ordained by him,[2] either before the ascension (Lk. 24)[3] or, in the case of Paul and perhaps Stephen, by a vision of Christ in heaven (Acts 7.52; 9.1-9; 22.6-16; 26.12-18).[4] Certainly in the case of Paul, perhaps in that of Stephen, 'to witness to what they have seen and heard' is primarily to announce what has been revealed to them of God's plan.[5] Even though what Peter or James have seen and heard includes acts of Jesus, the main content of their speeches concerns what Jesus revealed to them in Luke 24. Those historical speeches in Acts spoken by such 'witnesses' should be considered inspired; they are products of inspired history.

The Missions Speeches

The 'missions speeches'[6] are hortative historical sermons: they draw a hortatory consequence from a review of history in the context of a

1. The description of Stephen almost quotes the passage in Lk. 21.15. Καὶ οὐκ ἴσχυον ἀντιστῆναι τῇ σοφίᾳ καὶ τῷ πνεύματι ᾧ ἐλάλει (Acts 6.10). Jervell (109, 114) doubts the application of this saying of Jesus to speeches in Acts, but even he has to admit its use in Acts 4.8, 6, 10 and ch. 7. His skepticism seems unjustified.

2. Minear sees the Gospel of Luke as preparation for charismatic ministers who are the eyewitnesses and ministers of the word: 'Ever since his account of the baptism of John, Luke had his eye on the preparations of the apostles as prophetic seers and sayers' (Minear, *To Heal and to Reveal*, 84). 'Luke thought of the twelve as prophets, in the Gospel as apprentices and in Acts as fully authorized' (p. 122). See also pp. 85, 127, 133, 136, 143. Fitzmyer (28, 119) comes to a similar conclusion.

3. The two sides of revelation, instruction by the risen Christ and inspiration by the Spirit, hold Luke and Acts together, the first showing continuity with what preceded, the second with what is to follow. See Raymond E. Brown, *The Birth of the Messiah: A Commentary on the Infancy Narratives of Matthew and Luke* (Garden City, NY: Doubleday, 1977), 242.

4. One consequence of the threefold account of Paul's vision is to establish beyond doubt his right to speak 'what he has seen and heard' (cf. 22.15).

5. Paul is chosen to 'know God's will' (Acts 22.14). Schubert, 'Final Cycle', 2. Stephen's speech hardly mentions Jesus.

6. The list of 'missions speeches' varies by interpreter. Schubert ('Areopagus Speech', 235) lists those in chs. 2, 3, 10, and 13 as here. Gerhard Schneider (*Die Apostelgeschichte* [Herders Theologischer Kommentar zum Neuen Testament 5; Freiburg: Herder, 1980], 1.96) calls the same speeches and that in ch. 4, 'Missionsreden vor Juden', even though Cornelius and his household (ch. 10) are Gentiles. Wilckens, in his discussions of the missions speeches, treats 2.14-39; 3.12-

claim of inspiration. The historical review has two parts: (a) an interpretation of acts of God relevant to the situation of the hearers, (b) an interpretation of events surrounding Jesus.

Peter's Speech at Pentecost

Proem	Men of Judea. . . give ear (2.14b).
Historical Review	(a) Peter interprets a recent event, the coming of the Spirit, by the Joel quote (2.15-21).
	(b) Jesus of Nazareth, attested by signs, you delivered up by the plan of God and killed. God raised him as David foretold. We are witnesses. Jesus, exalted at the right hand of God has sent the spirit you now see and hear (2.22-36).
Consequence	(Marked by a question from the audience.) Repent and be baptized every one of you in the name of Jesus Christ for the forgiveness of your sins; and you shall receive the gift of the Holy Spirit. . . (2.38-40).

Peter's Speech in the Temple

Proem	Men of Israel. (3.12)
Historical Review	(a) Peter begins with a recent event: lame man healed (3.12)
	(b) God glorified Jesus whom you delivered up, denied, and killed—the holy and righteous one, the author of life. But God raised him from the dead. Faith in his name has given this man health. In ignorance you fulfilled the prophets who said that Christ must suffer (3.13-18).
Consequence	Repent that your sins may be blotted out and that times of refreshing and Jesus the messiah may come. You must listen to the prophet like Moses, and all the prophets, lest you be destroyed from the people. God is blessing all the families of the Earth as promised Abraham, but he calls you first to turn from your wickedness (3.19-26).

Peter's Speech to Cornelius

Proem	
Historical Review	(a) Peter interprets a recent event: God has received God-fearing Gentiles (10.34b-35).

26; 4.9-12; 5.30-32; 10.34-43; and 13.16-38, including those here called missions speeches and those called defense speeches (Ulrich Wilckens, *Die Missionsreden der Apostelgeschichte. Form- und traditionsgeschichtliche Untersuchungen* [WMANT 5; Neukirchen: Neukirchener Verlag, 1961], especially 99).

(b) God sent Jesus throughout Judea after John—preaching, doing good, healing, and exorcizing. The Jews put him to death but God raised him and showed him to us. He commanded us to testify that he is the one to judge the living and the dead (10.36-42).

Consequence

To him all the prophets bear witness that everyone who believes in him receives forgiveness of sins through his name (10.43).[1]

Paul's Speech at Pisidian Antioch

Proem
Historical Review

'Men of Israel and you who fear God, Listen' (13.16b).
(a) Since in a synagogue, Paul starts by interpreting scriptural history, centering and ending on David whose line produced a savior, Jesus,[2] announced by John the Baptist (13.17-25).

(b) The message of salvation has been sent to us, for the rulers in Jerusalem fulfilled scripture, of which they were ignorant, by condemning Jesus, but God raised him from the dead and he appeared to those who are now his witnesses. We bring the good news: what God promised to the fathers he has fulfilled (13.26-37).

Consequence

Through this man forgiveness of sins is proclaimed to you, by him you are freed from what the law could not free you. Beware lest you scoff and perish (13.38-40).

Each of these speeches begins with the situation in which it is found in Acts. Each roots this situation in the history of Jesus. Each draws the hortatory conclusion: repent to receive forgiveness.[3] Within this

---

1. This verse does not explicitly admonish the hearers, but the speech is broken off. The verse, especially in the context of the other speeches in Acts, clearly implies exhortation. Though the point is debatable, I have considered 10.43 as the prelude to exhortation rather than as the conclusion of the historical review. Such an introduction to exhortation is found in Paul's speech to the synagogue at Antioch (13.38-40).

2. Jesus is here included in the history of Israel. The solemn resumption of the opening formula (compare 13.26 with 13.16) shows that for Luke the shift in subject matter occurs after this initial mention of Jesus.

3. Other attempts to describe the form of these speeches are compatible with the outline developed here. Dibelius notices the tie to the situation of the hearers (Martin Dibelius, 'The Speeches in Acts and Ancient Historiography', in his *Studies in the Acts of the Apostles* [New York: Scribners, 1956], 166). Wilckens (54) advances the following scheme.

    1. Introduction tied to the particular situation
    2. Jesus kerygma in two parts
      a. Jesus handled in a blameworthy manner by Jews

framework of similarities for each speech distinctive characteristics help delineate how inspired history is used.[1]

Peter's speech at Pentecost begins with the coming of the Spirit which had attracted the attention of the crowd. The Joel quote shows that the giving of the Spirit is part of God's plan, identifies the present as the day when 'all who call on the name of the Lord shall be saved' (Acts 2.21), and undergirds Peter's message (and all the other Christian speeches) with a powerful ethos: this message and others like it are prophecies stemming from the Spirit which has been poured out. Peter rehearses the history of Jesus to show how the death, resurrection, and exaltation of Jesus were part of God's plan (Acts 2.23, 25-31, 34-35),[2] how the gift of the Spirit results from the exaltation of Jesus (2.33), and how responsibility for the rejection and death of Jesus devolves squarely upon the hearers (2.22-23, 36). The consequence follows directly from this prophetic description of what underlies events known by all. They must repent of their rejection of the messiah, seek forgiveness, and receive the gift of the Holy Spirit (2.38); they must save themselves from the wicked generation which has rejected the messiah (2.41).

     b. God delivers Jesus: resurrection/ascension
    3. Call to return and receive salvation

Wilckens's outline is nearly identical to mine based on the historical sermon:

    1. Proem (not mentioned by Wilckens)
    2. Historical review
      a. Explanation of an act of God immediate to the hearers
      b. Explanation of God's act in Jesus
    3. Call to repent for forgiveness

Schweizer's scheme, though more elaborate, also fits well with my analysis. See Eduard Schweizer, 'Concerning the Speeches in Acts', *Studies in Luke–Acts* (ed. L.E. Keck and J.L. Martyn; Philadelphia: Fortress, 1980 [1966]), 208-16.

    1. Kliesch's term 'heilsgeschichtliches Credo' does not describe the hortative intent of these speeches as well as 'historical sermon' does. See Klaus Kliesch, *Das heilsgeschichtliche Credo in den Reden der Apostelgeschichte* (BBB 44; Köln-Bonn: Hanstein, 1975). See also H. Thyen, *Der Stil der jüdisch-hellenistischen Homilie* (FRLANT 47; Göttingen: Vandenhoeck & Ruprecht, 1955). Ellis and Bowker tie these speeches to synagogal preaching. E.E. Ellis, 'Midrashic Features in the Speeches of Acts', *Mélanges Bibliques en hommage au R.P. Béda Rigaux* (ed. A. Descamps and R.P. André de Halleux; Gembloux: Duculot, 1970), 303-12. J.W. Bowker, 'Speeches in Acts: A Study in Proem and Yelammedenu Form', *NTS* 14 (1967-68), 96-111.

    2. Schubert, 'Areopagus Speech', 241.

Peter's speech in the Temple follows a similar pattern of reasoning. The speech begins with the healing of the lame man which has attracted the attention of the crowd. He shows how this healing of the recent past derives from what God has done in Jesus: God has glorified his παῖς Jesus (3.13) by healing through faith in his name (3.16). But this same Jesus whom you denied and killed God raised from the dead. Hence repent (especially of denying the Holy One) and receive the messiah appointed for you to bring the times of refreshing when all is fulfilled. That all of the prophets, especially Moses, command obedience to Jesus (3.22-25) amplifies and undergirds the consequent exhortation. The promise to Abraham (3.25-26) shows the broadening of God's interest and the necessity of turning from wickedness to become a part of the new thing Christ is doing.

In the same way Peter, at the house of Cornelius, begins with a recent event: the visions he and Cornelius have seen which prove that God has received God-fearing Gentiles. The history of Jesus is told to show how God had vindicated Jesus by raising him and how the resurrected Jesus had revealed that he would judge the living and the dead, Jew and Gentile. The conclusion: all the prophets have shown that *everyone* who believes in this Jesus receives forgiveness of sins. Here the sins must be those all Gentiles are assumed to have. The history of Jesus, especially his resurrection to judge the living and the dead, grounds the extension of belief for forgiveness even to Gentiles.

Paul's speech at Antioch in Pisidia begins not with a recent act of God which must be explained to those who saw it, but with a series of long past acts of God well known to the audience. Since he speaks in a synagogue Paul begins by reviewing the history of Israel. Unlike Stephen's speech the historical review is positive;[1] Luke emphasizes God's acts of salvation[2] and his agents. God delivered the people from

---

1. Via, Richard, and Haenchen rightly note how the history of Stephen's speech dovetails with that of Paul at Antioch. Nevertheless the difference in emphasis in the two historical reviews (one *Heils-*, one *Unheilsgeschichte*) corresponds to the difference in the speeches' intents. Stephen's speech accuses the Jews, Paul's seeks to convert them. See E. Jane Via, 'An Interpretation of Acts 7.35-37 from the Perspective of Major Themes in Luke–Acts', *SBLSP* 14.2 (1978), 215; Earl Richard, *Acts 6.1–8.4. The Author's Method of Composition* (SBLDS 41; Missoula, MT: Scholars Press, 1978), 318; Ernst Haenchen, *The Acts of the Apostles: A Commentary* (Oxford: Blackwell, 1971), 408, 415.
2. Matthäus Franz-Joseph Buss, *Die Missionspredigen des Apostels Paulus im Pisidischen Antiochien* (Forschung zur Bibel 38; Stuttgart: Katolisches Bibelwerk, 1980), 47.

Egypt, cared for[1] them forty years in the wilderness, and give them a land. He gave them agents of salvation—judges until Samuel. When they asked for a king he gave them Saul, then David, a man after his heart. From this man's posterity, as promised, God raised up a savior, Jesus, who was announced by John as much more worthy than he. Sending Jesus is the latest act of God's care for Israel. At this point Paul switches to the history of Jesus. Those in Jerusalem, failing to recognize this savior, had him killed, but God raised him from the dead according to the scripture. From this the consequence immediately follows:[2] in Jesus God offers forgiveness; beware lest like your relatives in Jerusalem you resist God by rejecting his savior.

In each of these hortative historical sermons revelation about the past is crucial. The speeches require the hearers to adopt a new view of what has happened in the past. The hearers of the first three speeches know the facts about Jesus (2.22, 36; 3.13-14; 10.3-6) and have experienced some event which is part of God's plan but can make no sense of what they have seen and heard. The speech integrates the inexplicable recent event with the history of Jesus and demands a consequence. Those in the synagogue of Antioch know the facts of Israel's history but not what God has done in these days. Paul tells them the facts, including those that can be known only by revelation. In all these speeches the consequent exhortation to repent for forgiveness would lack force, indeed would lack sense, without the revelation about history.

These missions speeches derive their content from the revelation to the disciples in Luke 24.[3] The summary of the revealed message, delivered by the resurrected Jesus to those he ordained as witnesses (Lk. 24.45, 48), contains the following elements (Lk. 24.46-47).

1. It is written
2. that the messiah should suffer;
3. that he should be raised;
4. that repentance and forgiveness should be preached in his name;
5. that the proclamation should reach all nations.

Remarkably, each of the hortative historical sermons discussed above employs every one of these motifs.

---

1. Reading ἐτροφοφόρησεν instead of ἐτροποφόρησεν (Acts 13.18) as better fitting the notes of salvation in this part of the speech. The decision between the two is finely balanced.

2. Buss's division of the Antioch speech into five parts (Buss, 31) is compatible with its analysis as a historical sermon. See Buss, 24.

3. See Wilckens, 97; Via, 221.

Motif Number	Peter at Pentecost	Peter in the Temple	Peter with Cornelius	Paul at Antioch
1.	2.16-21, 25-32, 34	3.18, 21-26	10.43	13.23, 27, 32-41
2.	2.23	3.13-14, 18	10.39	13.27-29
3.	2.24-32	3.15	10.40-42	13.30-37
4.	2.38	3.19	10.43	13.38
5.	2.17,[1] 21, 39	3.25-26	10.34, 43[2]	13.46, 47[3]

Two other motifs essentially connected with the resurrection narratives round out Luke's scheme:

Each of the missions speeches explain rejection by the Jews of Jesus and of the revealed message about him (2.23, 36; 3.14-15, 17; 10.39; 13.27-29, 40-41, 46). The rejection of Jesus by Jews assumes increasing importance as Acts progresses but was not lacking earlier. Luke more than compensates for lack of the rejection theme in the resurrection narratives by his emphatic ascription of responsibility for Jesus' death to the Jews in the account of the passion. When the resurrection narratives reveal that Jesus must suffer and be raised, the suffering presupposes that rejection by Jewish leaders in the previous chapter.

Each of the missions speeches refers to the witnesses ordained in Luke 24 (2.32; 3.15; 10.41; 13.31) as an important element of its message. The speech to Cornelius even describes in detail the appearance to the eleven (10.40-43; cf. Lk. 24.36-49). Not only the message of the resurrected Christ but also the resulting body of enlightened witnesses comprise the gospel to be proclaimed everywhere. Luke explicitly ties the proclamation of the gospel in the missions speeches to the ordination of witnesses he has so painstakingly described at the consummation of his first book.

Therefore in the missions speeches Luke–Acts grounds a complex of ideas on revelation and uses them as a refrain: fulfillment of scripture, proper understanding of the words and deeds of Jesus, especially of his

1. 2.17, 'all flesh'; 2.21, 'all who'; 2.39, 'to you, your children and all those far off, whomever the Lord calls' indicate mission to the gentiles.
2. 10.43, 'all who'. The context clearly has Gentiles in view.
3. Though not in the speech these verses show how important turning to the Gentiles is in the context of proclamation to this synagogue. Perhaps Downing is right in including 13.46-47 in the speech (F. Gerald Downing, 'Ethical Pagan Theism and the Speeches in Acts', *NTS* 27 [1981], 554).

death and resurrection, rejection by many Jews, blessing on many Gentiles. Luke does not limit this complex of ideas to resurrection narratives and missions speeches; two speeches anticipate it early in the third Gospel and both explicitly claim inspiration.

The description of Simeon underscores his prophetic inspiration: 'the Holy Spirit was upon him' (Lk. 2.25); 'it had been disclosed to him by the Holy Spirit' (2.26); 'he came in the Spirit into the Temple' (2.27). Simeon foreshadows each of the elements in the refrain: fulfillment of scripture (2.32; cf. v. 29), proper understanding of Jesus' death (2.34-35), rejection by many Jews (2.34), blessing on the Gentiles (2.31-32).

The same elements recur in Jesus' speech at the synagogue in Nazareth. Scripture is fulfilled (4.21) giving a proper understanding of Jesus' words and deeds (4.18-19). The lynching scene foreshadows Jesus' death (4.29); does his escape foreshadow his resurrection (4.30)? His own people reject him (4.23-24, 28-29); blessing accrues to the Gentiles (4.25-27). Luke explicitly claims inspiration for this Nazareth speech. Jesus returns to Galilee in the power of the Spirit to teach in the synagogues (Lk. 4.14-15); Luke offers the sermon at Nazareth as an example of this inspired teaching.

The speech before the synagogue of Nazareth is often called a programmatic statement.[1] It serves as thesis statement not only for Luke but also for Acts.[2] Luke commits his entire work to showing how Jesus, though a prophet without honor among his own people (Lk. 4.24), nevertheless fulfilled their scriptures (4.18-21) and brought a blessing which reached to the Gentiles (4.25-27). The Gospel is devoted to showing the fulfillment of the passage quoted from Isaiah (Lk. 4.18-19): Jesus goes about preaching the good news, proclaiming release of the captives, and restoring sight to the blind (cf. 7.18-23). It also shows the failure of the Jews to honor Jesus (4.24), both in the ministry through stories of antagonism between Jesus and Jewish leaders and in the passion narrative which concentrates responsibility for the death of Jesus on the Jews. Acts portrays the continued rejection of Jesus by his own people (see Lk. 4.24) and the consequent bestowal of

1. Already in Wrede, 178.
2. While most interpreters see the Nazareth speech as programmatic for the ministry of Jesus (cf. Fitzmyer, 28, 526, 529), it is less common to see it as programmatic for Luke–Acts as a whole, but see Marshall, 178. Since Lk. 4.24-27 hints the rejection of Jesus by the Jews and his blessing of the Gentiles, which are major themes of Acts, the programmatic statement anticipates the full plot line of Luke–Acts—the fulfillment of scripture, ministry of Jesus, rejection by the Jews and blessing on the Gentiles.

God's blessing on the Gentiles (Lk. 4.25-27). This programmatic statement enunciates the historical principle of Luke–Acts:[1] God sent Jesus
to fulfill the scriptures; though rejected by his own nation, he gave
release[2] to the Gentiles who listened to the word about him. Hence the
speech at the synagogue of Nazareth outlines the remainder of Luke–
Acts; it contains the central principle around which Luke organizes his
history. Yet the speech at Nazareth is but one such summary of the
thesis of Luke–Acts. Simeon's speech, the resurrection narratives, and
the missions speeches establish the divine plan which is the thesis of
Luke–Acts and ground it on revelation: God has fulfilled scripture in
the words and deeds of Jesus, even in his death at the hands of his own
people and in his resurrection. Though many Jews have fulfilled his
plan by rejecting it, many Gentiles have done so by receiving it gladly.

As their inclusion in the missions speeches proves, for Luke this
revelation of the real significance of the events centering in Jesus is the
gospel. It is little wonder that Luke decided to write not only about
Jesus but also about the early church. The third Gospel shows how the
messiah Jesus, even in suffering and rising, fulfilled the scriptures.
Acts shows repentance and forgiveness preached, even to the Gentiles.
Both of these are necessary to that view of history revealed by the
resurrected Jesus to his disciples. Failure to write either Luke or Acts
would amount to failure to preach the whole gospel, 'the full counsel
of God' (Acts 20.27). Once again the connection between Luke's whole
project in Luke–Acts and revealed history is clear. Luke amplifies in
his work that same message which those witnesses, ordained and given
a revealed message by Christ and empowered and inspired by the Holy
Spirit, also proclaim. Luke–Acts is based on revealed history; it is
prophetic history.

Hence Luke carefully grounds on revelation that central principle by
which he interprets history. His action in doing so parallels very
nearly Josephus' method in the *Jewish War*. Both historians base their
interpretations of the events they recount on revelations of what God
was doing in the recent past, Josephus on the revelation given him at
Jotapata, Luke on a speech attributed to Jesus who gives an inspired
interpretation of Isaiah 61. By casting the central thesis of his historical work as a revelation Luke shows his sympathy with and
dependence upon inspiration concerning the past. His work is a
prophetic history.

---

1. See Fitzmyer 28.116.
2. ἄφεσις (twice in Lk. 4.18) figures prominently in the important Lucan category
'forgiveness of sins' (Lk. 1.77; 3.3; 24.47; Acts 5.31; 10.43; 13.38; 26.18). Dillon,
From Eyewitnesses to Ministers of the Word, 136-37.

Speeches Supporting Elements of the Lucan Scheme

The speeches studied have amplified each element of God's plan. Luke–Acts includes other speeches which elaborate one or two constituents of the plan. These speeches also qualify as historical revelations.

The canticles in Luke 1 and 2 are clearly inspired; they are spoken by angels (1.14-17, 32-37; 2.10-14), by people filled with the Holy Spirit (1.41-55, 67-79; 2.25-35) or by a prophetess (2.36-38).[1] Some of these reveal what is past even in terms of narrative time. Gabriel reveals that Elizabeth has already conceived (1.36); Elizabeth, in the Spirit, perceives what has happened to Mary (1.41-45); the angels reveal to the shepherds what has already happened in Bethlehem (2.10-12). Though short, these cases are far from trivial. They show not only Luke's readiness to use revealed history but also his expectation of gaining insight into past events by revelation. Elizabeth sings not only the fact but also the significance of Mary's pregnancy. The angel tells the shepherds not only the fact but also the significance of Jesus' birth:

> Be not afraid; for behold I bring you good news of great joy which shall come to all the people; for to you is born this day in the city of David a savior who is Christ the Lord. And this will be a sign for you: you will find a babe wrapped in swaddling cloths and lying in a manger (Lk. 2.10-12).

The shepherds will see only a baby, but the angel tells them what has really happened: God has given a savior. Luke utilizes these canticles and angelic pronouncements to reveal two aspects of the plan. They disclose the fulfillment of scripture in Jesus and reveal something of the proper understanding of what he will do. Though cast as prophecies of the future, in Luke's scheme they reveal a proper evaluation of the past and establish two elements of the scheme so important to his work.

Luke–Acts contains a number of historical sermons which are not missions speeches. Some of these occur as deliberations over what course of action the church should take. Peter's speech urging the election of an apostle to replace Judas and the speeches of Peter and James before the Jerusalem council (Acts 15) are of this type. Since they urge a particular course of action they are hortative historical sermons. Others fit within judicial process. Already we have identified the judicial sermon as an inspired historical sermon with a sentence as

---

1. Schubert calls these 'messianic prophets filled with the Holy Spirit' (Schubert, 'Structure', 178).

its consequence.[1] Luke–Acts utilizes the judicial sermon[2] but it utilizes more fully two other closely related kinds: in an apologetic historical sermon the consequence exonerates a defendant; in an accusatory historical sermon the consequence levels an accusation or prosecutes a case.[3] The speeches of Peter before the Jewish council (4.8-12, 19-20), before the same council (5.29-32), and before the elders of the church in Jerusalem (11.5-17) are all apologetic sermons. Stephen's speech (Acts 7.2-53) is an accusatory sermon. Logically enough, Luke uses those historical sermons which fit within judicial process primarily to support his theme of rejection by the Jews. They usually occur in cases where believers have been haled before Jewish courts.

Peter's second speech before the Jewish council (5.29-32) stands in inverted order; the consequence precedes the historical review.

Consequence   'We must obey God rather than men' (Acts 5.29).

---

1. See pp. 51ff. above.

2. *Jesus' Prophecy against Jerusalem*

Historical Review	'O Jerusalem, Jerusalem, killing the prophets and stoning those who are sent to you! How often would I have gathered your children together as a hen gathers her brood under her wings, and you would not!' (Lk. 13.34)
Consequence	'Behold, your house is forsaken. And I tell you, you will not see me until you say, "Blessed is he who comes in the name of the Lord" ' (Lk. 13.35)

Peter's Speech to Sapphira

Historical Review	'How is it that you have agreed together to tempt the Spirit of the Lord?' (Acts 5.9a)
Consequence	'Hark, the feet of those that have buried your husband are at the door and they shall carry you out' (Acts 5.9b).

3. Peter's speech to Ananias shows how easily the transition from accusatory historical sermon to judicial can be made. The historical review grounds two consequences, one a spoken accusation, one a sentence immediately enacted:

Historical Review	'Ananias, why has Satan filled your heart to lie to the Holy Spirit and to keep back part of the proceeds of the land? While it remained unsold, did it not remain your own? And after it was sold, was it not at your disposal? How is it that you have contrived this deed in your heart?' (Acts 5.3b-4a)
Consequence: an accusation	'You have not lied to men but to God' (5.4b).
Consequence: a sentence	Ananias falls down and dies (5.5a).

Historical Review	'The God of our fathers raised Jesus whom you killed by hanging him on a tree. God exalted him at his right hand as Leader and Savior, to give repentance to Israel and forgiveness of sins. And we are witnesses to these things, and so is the Holy Spirit whom God has given to those who obey him' (Acts 5.30-32).

The historical review, which explains what God has done in Jesus and in the apostolic witnesses, explains why Peter and John rightly disobeyed the Jewish authorities to obey God. The stasis is one of quality;[1] the defense rests on affirming that the action taken, though technically contrary to civil law, is actually right. It is better to obey God than human beings. The surprising order of consequence and historical review does nothing to change the logic of the speech. The context provides a good explanation for the variation; it permits a closer connection between the accusation ('You have not obeyed us', Acts 5.28) and Peter's reply. Beginning with the consequence permits Luke more easily to show how the historical review, which contains elements Luke always wishes to get across, is relevant to the charge.

In Peter's earlier speech (4.8b-12, 19b-20), Luke has masked the connection between historical review and consequence by placing between them a recess of the council to discuss the case. Nevertheless, while the historical review might stand on its own in the context as an answer to the question, 'By what power did you heal this man?', the consequence depends on the historical review for its logical force. Luke successfully counts on the memory of the reader to connect the historical review with the consequence.[2]

Historical Review	'Rulers of the people and elders, if we are being examined today concerning a good deed done to a cripple, by what means this man has been healed, be it known to you all, and to all the people of Israel, that by the name of Jesus Christ of Nazareth, whom you crucified, whom God raised from the dead, by him this man is standing before you well. This is the stone which was rejected by you builders, but which has become the head of the corner. And there is salvation in no one else, for there is no other name under heaven given among men by which we must be saved' (Acts 4.8b-12).

---

1. George A. Kennedy (*New Testament Interpretation through Rhetorical Criticism* [Chapel Hill: University of North Carolina Press, 1984], 120) further defines it as metastasis, a species of quality, transferring responsibility to God.

2. Josephus also divides single speeches by narration of action (Downing, 554).

Consequence   'Whether it is right in the sight of God to listen to you rather than to God, you must judge; for we cannot but speak of what we have seen and heard' (Acts 4.19b-20).

Peter's speeches before the Jewish council begin developing the antagonism between those who accept that view of history revealed by Jesus and those who do not. By including these historical sermons in the trial scenes, Luke shows that the interpretation of history which for him is the gospel distinguishes those Jews who conform to God's plan from those who do not. As Jews rejected the ancient prophets, as they rejected Jesus, the prophet *par excellence*, so they reject those witnesses who bear the revelation of the plan of God. Though these speeches contain the proper understanding of Jesus' life and death as well as Jewish rejection of it, their context emphasizes the theme of Jewish rejection. On the whole these speeches prove Peter and John to be right in their actions, the Jewish leaders to be wrong in their commands. These apologetic sermons show Jewish leaders rejecting the clearest expressions of God's plan as revealed to the disciples. To an even greater extent Stephen's speech dwells on rejection by the Jews.

Stephen's speech, an accusatory sermon, is one of the most interesting and difficult of the speeches in Acts. To many, the speech lacks unity of direction and does not fit its context. Although the context requires a speech of defense, Stephen's speech is really one of accusation; although the first part of the speech is a neutral portrayal of Israel's history, the last part of the speech turns toward invective.[1] However, when analysed as an accusatory historical sermon, Stephen's speech coheres well with its context and within itself.

Historical   A. When God called, Abraham obeyed and God gave him
Review   promises (7.2-8a):
                     1. Your posterity shall have this land, though you have
                     no posterity.

---

1. Dibelius, 167. Boismard (181-90) traces the speech's disunity to Luke's editing of a source. Robin Scroggs ('The Earliest Hellenistic Christianity' in *Religions in Antiquity: Essays in Memory of Erwin Ramsdell Goodenough* [ed. J. Neusner; Leiden: Brill, 1968], 182 n. 3) thinks the consequence is not original to the speech. Haenchen (286-90) argues that the speech has no bearing on the charges against Stephen and that the speech has no consistent theme. Jacques Dupont ('La structure oratoire du discours d'Etienne [Acts 7]', *Biblica* 66 [1985], 153-67) tries, I think unsuccessfully, to divide the speech based on rhetorical categories. His explanation of the abrupt change he feels at 7.35 as a switch from *narratio* to *argumentatio* falters even in his own article since he must switch back to the *narratio* for 7.44-50. However, Stephen's speech is not really patterned on Greek rhetorical form.

2. They will be aliens in a land that will enslave them 400 years.

3. I will judge the nation they serve.

4. They will come to worship me in this place (i.e. the land). All this is sealed by the covenant of circumcision.

B. First step in fulfilling the promises: the patriarchs (Acts 7.8b-16).

1. Patriarchs born—Abraham has a posterity (7.8b)

2. The patriarchs reject Joseph by whom God would deliver them and fulfill the next step in the promises to Abraham.

3.Hence the patriarchs by rejecting Joseph bring about the plan of God announced long before.

C. The time of the promise (7.17): Moses, the deliverer from Egypt (7.17-43).

1. The promised oppression (Acts 7.17-19).

2. The first rejection of Moses, the deliverer by whom God would fulfill his promise (7.20-29).

　a. Moses introduced as beautiful and well educated (7.20-22).

　b. Moses rejected as deliverer and judge.

3. The second rejection of Moses (7.30-43).

　a. God sends Moses to deliver the people from Egypt according to the promise (7.30-34).

　b. By this rejected deliverer and ruler God delivers the people, then appoints Moses as ruler (7.35-36).

　c. Moses gave further promises (of a prophet like Moses, 7.37) and laws, but the people refused to keep the laws, in their hearts returning to Egypt and worshiping false gods (Acts 7.37-43).

D. The final phase of the promise: worship in the land (7.44-50).

1. The tent, made according to the pattern God revealed to Moses, entered the land; worship occurred in it through the time of David (7.44-46).

2. Solomon built a rebellious house made with human hands in which the Lord of Heaven could not possibly dwell (7.47-50). Israel corrupted even this phase of the promise.[1]

---

1. Notorious difficulties surround any interpretation of this final section concerning the tabernacle and Temple. I have chosen the interpretation that best fits the context of the speech, which demands a rebellion by Israel concerning worship. The connotations of idolatry in χειροποίητος also support this interpretation. Interpreting the building of Solomon's Temple as rebellion, however, runs foul of the speech's

Consequence 'You stiff-necked people, uncircumcised in heart and ears,
you always resist the Holy Spirit. As your fathers did, so do
you. Which of the prophets did not your fathers persecute?
And they killed those who announced beforehand the coming
of the Righteous One, whom you have now betrayed and
murdered, you who received the law as delivered by angels
and did not keep it' (Acts 7.51-53).

The promise given to Abraham structures the entire historical review.[1]
The promise is given in the account of Abraham. The accounts of
Joseph and Moses show God working out his promise in spite of Israel
rejecting the deliverer sent to accomplish it. The account of the
tabernacle shows God's way of fulfilling his promise that they would
worship in the land (tabernacle) and Israel's rejection of it by building
a house. The historical review is designed to show how Israel,
inattentive to God's promise to Abraham, ceaselessly resisted its
fulfillment and implies that Israel always rejects the deliverers God
sends and always rejects the fulfillment of God's promises (as shown in
Joseph, Moses, Tabernacle). Hence the consequence: they are a stiff-
necked people, uncircumcised in heart and ears,[2] always resisting the

context in Luke–Acts, for Luke tirelessly emphasizes temple piety, but see 17.3
where Luke asserts that God does not live in temples made with hands. Perhaps the
difficulty with this section of Stephen's speech stems from Luke blunting the attack
on the Temple from his source and interpreting it in light of 17.3 which is perfectly
acceptable to him. As the speech stands in Acts, even the most culticly minded Jew
could read Stephen's words in an acceptable way. Few if any Jews of the first century would claim that God dwelt in the Temple. Solomon's dedication of the Temple
acknowledges this impossibility (1 Kgs 8.27; 2 Chron. 6.18). For all Luke's own
irenic attitude, however, he has not obliterated his source's attack on the Temple. He
has altered his source (unless the alteration had already occurred in his source) only
enough to make a less offensive reading possible. The best interpretation of the
speech, even as it now stands in Acts, still understands Solomon's building of the
Temple as a foolish departure from the worship in the land God had commanded
through Moses. Many think Stephen's speech hostile to the Temple: Kilgallen, 89,
94; A.F.J. Klijn, 'Stephen's Speech—Acts VII.2-53', *NTS* 4 (1957), 26; R.J. Coggins, 'The Samaritans and Acts', *NTS* 28 (1982), 426; Via, 212; Scroggs, 188;
Robert Maddox, *The Purpose of Luke–Acts* (FRLANT 126; Göttingen: Vandenhoeck
& Ruprecht, 1982), 53; Haenchen, 285. Others doubt this hostility: P. Doble, 'The
Son of Man Saying in Stephen's Witnessing: Acts 6.8–8.2', *NTS* 31 (1985), 73, 79,
80; Nils A. Dahl, 'The Story of Abraham in Luke–Acts', in *Studies in Luke–Acts*
(ed. Keck and Martyn; Philadelphia: Fortress, 1980 [1966]), 145-46; Dupont, 160;
Boismard, 185; Dennis D. Sylva, 'The Meaning and Function of Acts 7.46-50', *JBL*
106 (1987), 261-75.

1. Compare Via, 211; Dahl, 144.
2. That is, unable to perceive the promise which was ratified by circumcision (Acts
7.8).

Holy Spirit (7.51). With a few brush strokes the consequence brings the accusation home to the present. Your fathers persecuted the prophets who announced the righteous one; you murdered the righteous one; you have never kept the law as delivered by angels. Such amplifications, which constitute a brief historical review in their own right, nevertheless belong in the consequence, for they draw out what is implicit in the historical review and tie the accusation (7.51) squarely to Stephen's hearers. The speech is a unity; the invective in the consequence follows directly from the historical review.

As the speech argues a clear coherent case, so it fits nicely in its context. The stoning of Stephen adds further point to the consequence, for Stephen's role as God's messenger in delivering this speech is more fully developed than for any other speech in Acts (6.5, 8, 10, 15). In stoning Stephen Israel has added one more to the line of prophets killed for announcing God's message. The preceding context requires a speech of defense. Though rarely understood as such, Stephen's is an excellent defense speech. One mode of defense recognized in antiquity was to turn the tables on your accuser: 'Not I but you are guilty of the charges you are leveling against me'.[1] Kennedy defines this as stasis of counteraccusation.[2] According to the charges, Stephen has spoken blasphemous words against Moses and God (Acts 6.11). He has spoken against the holy place and the law. He has said Jesus will destroy this place and change the customs Moses gave us (6.13-14). Stephen's reply levels these charges directly against his accusers and judges. Not I but you have spoken against Moses and God; not I but you have sinned against God's sanctuary and have changed the customs Moses gave. Each of these points is developed in the historical review[3] and applied to Stephen's accusers and judges in the consequence. Hence Stephen's accusatory sermon is a good defense speech; it answers the charges specifically and well.[4]

The final turning of the tables occurs in Stephen's vision of the Son of man. Not only does the vision confirm the pattern developed in the historical review—as the Jews of the past unremittingly rejected the one God appointed as savior and judge (Joseph, Moses), so Jews of the present had rejected Jesus who now had received rule as Son of man—it also sets the whole scene within a greater judicial context. The Son

---

1. Boismard, 188; Doble, 77.

2. G.A. Kennedy, 121.

3. They have sinned against the holy place (7.47-48). They have changed Moses' customs (7.39-48). They have spoken against God every time they resisted his deliverer or the fulfillment of his promise.

4. See Richard, *Acts 6.1–8.4*, 317; Jervell, 119; Sylva, 268-74.

of man in Daniel is judge and ruler over all (Dan. 7.13-14).[1] Before his court his prophet Stephen has brought home the accusation against the rebellious people of God. Stephen's final utterance fits well this wider judicial context. Israel was fulfilling the pattern over again in the stoning of Stephen, and Stephen, though to their faces he accuses them, like a good prophet (like Moses), asks for forgiveness before the heavenly court.

It is significant that the message proclaimed by Stephen, the latest murdered prophet, is a revelation concerning the past. The accurate perception of the past revealed to the prophet shows the true state of affairs. Stephen, not his accusers, is righteous; the accusers, not Stephen, have transgressed and are transgressing. Within the argument of Luke–Acts the historical revelation in Stephen's speech is likewise significant. Hitherto most of the speeches have developed the positive aspects of God's plan: God has remembered his people (Lk. 1–2) and fulfilled his promises even though his people killed the righteous one (missions speeches). God calls Jews through repentance to enter these promises and has even opened the doors to the Gentiles (deliberative and missions speeches). This positive line of thinking develops themes revealed by the resurrected Jesus to his disciples in Luke 24. But there is also a negative line of thinking developed in the rejection of Jesus traced in the Gospel, in the judicial historical sermon Jesus directs against Jerusalem (Lk. 13.34-35), in the trial scenes and defense speeches of Peter and reaching a climax in Stephen's speech.[2] Those who reject the witnesses reject God. The apostates are not those kicked out of the synagogues or tried by the councils, but the councils and synagogues. Stephen's speech shows how a pattern of rejecting the fulfillment of God's promises has characterized Israel's history to the present day. Those who are trying Stephen, who have rejected the righteous one, stand in the long line of Israelites who have resisted God by rejecting the fulfillment of his promises. Though the inevitable sentence has yet to fall (perhaps hinted in the reference to Babylon in 7.43), in Stephen's speech the accusation has been made and the supporting evidence made plain. With this rejection by the Jews in

1. Acts (10.42; 17.31) mentions Jesus as judge.
2. Kilgallen, 111; Dahl, 147; Earl Richard, 'The Polemical Character of the Joseph Episode in Acts 7', *JBL* 98 (1979), 265. Maddox, *The Purpose of Luke–Acts*, 52-53. Of course Stephen's plea for forgiveness shows a door still open for Stephen's hearers.

Judea the mission now takes the portentous step from Judea to Samaria as it follows God's plan to the end of the earth (Acts 1.8).[1]

In a number of speeches Luke elaborates his thrust concerning the inclusion of the Gentiles. Chief among these are the hortative sermons at the Jerusalem council though Paul's forensic speeches also contribute to this theme.

Though they are hortative historical sermons, the speeches of Peter and James before the Jerusalem council are not missions speeches but determine what course of action the early church should take. In them Luke wished to make two points concerning the Gentile question: he wished to recall God's initiation of the Gentile mission and to show the fulfillment of scripture in it. As both historical and scriptural points fit nicely in Peter's first speech (Acts 1.16-22) so both could easily have been handled in one speech to the Jerusalem council, had Luke not wished to have James as well as Peter participate. In the resulting division of two ideas usually inseparable in Lucan writings, Peter tells the relevant history without expounding its fulfillment of scripture while James only mentions the history before interpreting it by the scripture. The customary unity of history and fulfillment, barely maintained in James' speech, is wholly neglected in Peter's.

Peter's speech

Historical Review	And after there had been much debate, Peter rose and said to them, 'Brethren, you know that in the early days God made choice among you, that by my mouth the Gentiles should hear the word of the gospel and believe. And God who knows the heart bore witness to them, giving them the Holy Spirit just as he did to us; and he made no distinction between us and them but cleansed their hearts by faith' (Acts 15.7-9).
Consequence	'Now therefore why do you make trial of God by putting a yoke upon the neck of the disciples which neither our fathers nor we have been able to bear? But we believe that we shall be saved through the grace of the Lord Jesus, just as they will' (Acts 15.10-11).

---

1. Possibly this movement toward the Gentiles is an acted sentence. Acts 28.25-29 contains a fitting consequence (a sentence) to Stephen's historical review, one which would convert it to a judicial historical sermon. Of course by the end of Acts, not only Joseph, Moses, Tabernacle, prophets, Jesus, and Stephen, but also Peter and Paul, have been rejected by the Jews.

James' speech

Historical Review James replied, 'Brethren, listen to me. Simeon has related how
God first visited the Gentiles, to take out of them a people for
his name. And with this the words of the prophets agree, as it
is written, "After this I will return,and I will rebuild the
dwelling of David, which has fallen; I will rebuild its ruins,
and I will set it up, that the rest of men may seek the Lord, and
all the Gentiles who are called by my name, says the Lord,
who has made these things known from of old"' (Acts
15.13b-18).

Consequence ' Therefore my judgment is that we should not trouble those of
the Gentiles who turn to God, but
should write to them to abstain from the pollutions of idols and
from unchastity and from what is strangled and from blood.
For from early generations Moses has had in every city those
who preach him, for he is read every sabbath in the synagogues' (Acts 15.19-21).

The logical connection in Peter's speech between the historical
review and the consequence is clear. God has already accepted the
Gentiles; we must fit in with what God has done. The interpretation of
scripture so dominates James' speech that at first glance it hardly seems
a historical sermon at all. However, the relevant history is summarized
in v. 14 and then interpreted by scripture in vv. 15-19. Past events can
best be understood when interpreted by divine insight into scripture.
The brevity of the historical summary results from proximity to
Peter's speech. Hence Luke considers an inspired view of the past
which can fit recent events into the plan of God from scripture the best
basis for decision making in the church. Luke, who so rigorously
portrays the church as guided by the Spirit,[1] portrays this guidance as
occurring through inspired history. More importantly in the present
context, Luke uses speeches by Christians filled with the Spirit (Acts
15.28) to prove that inclusion of the Gentiles belonged squarely in the
plan of God.

One of the three apologetic historical sermons advances this theme.
Peter's speech before the elders of the Jerusalem church is straight-
forward in form.

1. For the immediate context see 15.28.

Historical Review   Peter recounts his vision of unclean animals, his subsequent
                     journey to see Cornelius and the coming of the Holy Spirit on
                     the household of Cornelius. The whole is confirmed by a word
                     of the Lord: John baptized with water, but you shall be bap-
                     tized with the Holy Spirit (Acts 11.5-16).
Consequence   'If then God gave the same gift to them as he gave to us when
                     we believed in the Lord Jesus Christ, who was I that I could
                     withstand God?' (Acts 11.17)

The train of events he recounts exonerates Peter. Obviously Peter
can eat with and preach to anyone on whom God wills to bestow his
Spirit. The quotation from the Lord proves that these have been baptized into God's people by the Spirit. Blessings have come upon the
Gentiles according to God's plan.

Paul's defense speeches (22.1-21; 24.10-21; 26.2-23) are not historical sermons, but two of them (22.1-21; 26.2-23) deal significantly with
the past. Paul's speech before Agrippa (24.10-21; 26.2-23) can be
analysed loosely as a classical speech.[1] Before Agrippa Paul begins
with a graceful proem (26.2-3) then moves to a narration (26.4-18).
Interrupting the narration is a brief statement of what Paul hopes the
speech will show: I am on trial for hope in the promise (26.6-8; cf.
26.19-23). Paul's speech before the crowd begins well enough as a
classical speech with a proem (22.1) followed by a narration (22.3-
21), but the rowdiness of the crowd breaks off the speech before Paul
can get to a proof, if there was to be one. From the point of view of
the rhetorical handbooks, the most surprising feature of these speeches
is the inordinate space given to the narration. Ordinarily narrations
are preparatory to the proof. They tell events from the speaker's point
of view so that the judge will not be distracted by the facts when listening to the arguments. Paul's narrations do just that, but the proofs,
normally focal points of a judicial speech, are so short (or missing) as
to seem comparatively insignificant. The surprising length of these
narrations indicates Luke's interest in Paul's interpretive statement of
what has happened. By this time, Paul is well established as a witness-
prophet. Much of these narrations concerns the revelation he received
at his call. Hence these speeches are relevant to revealed history.

The repeated telling of Paul's call narrative justifies his behavior by
showing how Paul obeys God in all he does. These speeches thus do
defend Paul against the charges and suspicions of the Jews, but they

---

1. Jerome Neyrey, 'The Forensic Defense Speech and Paul's Trial Speeches in
Acts 22–26: Form and Function', *Luke–Acts: New Perspectives from the Society of
Biblical Literature Seminar* (New York: Crossroad, 1984), 210-24; Kennedy, 136-
38.

also play an important role in Luke–Acts. By reminding the readers that God, who called Paul like a prophet, sent him to the Gentiles (22.21; 26.17-18), in accord with the revelation from the resurrected Jesus (Lk. 24), Luke shows again how God's plan in Christ includes proclamation to the Gentiles. Like other parts of God's plan this one also is rejected by the Jews. As Stephen was persecuted so was Paul. Though sent to the Gentiles Paul joins the line of prophets and witnesses killed by Jews for fulfilling God's plan. The inclusion of the Gentiles is as important as any other part of God's plan for Luke. It also is part of the gospel. The final speech of Paul carries the lawsuit against Israel one step further. As the prophet Stephen indicted the Jews so the prophet Paul sentences them: they will not hear; hence God turns to the Gentiles (28.26-28).

Peter's first speech, a hortative historical sermon urging the choice of a replacement for Judas, does not fit neatly the revealed historical scheme in Luke–Acts:[1]

Historical Review   'Brethren, the scripture had to be fulfilled, which the Holy
                         Spirit spoke beforehand by the mouth of David, concerning
                         Judas who was guide to those who arrested Jesus. For he
                         was numbered among us, and was allotted his share in this
                         ministry. (Now this man bought a field with the reward of
                         his wickedness; and falling headlong he burst open in the
                         middle and all his bowels
                         gushed out. And it became known to all the inhabitants of
                         Jerusalem, so that the field was called in their language
                         Akeldama, that is Field of Blood.) For it is written in the
                         book of Psalms, "Let his habitation become desolate, and let
                         there be no one to live in it"' (Acts 1.16-20a).

1. The same might be said of Paul's farewell speech to the Ephesian elders (Acts 20.17-35). In terms of classical rhetoric it would have to be classified an epideictic speech of farewell but fits the form poorly. See Kennedy, 132-33. The references to past actions of the speaker and the lessons to be learned from them as well as predictions for the future suggest that the speech is a testament. See Schneider, *Apostelgeschichte*, 2.293 and the literature cited there. As with testaments generally the claims to inspiration are directed toward the future (20.23). Since the references to the past do not conform to what a witness in Luke–Acts usually proclaims and since explicit claims to inspiration are directed toward the future, this speech has tenuous relation to revealed history. The speech is important for Luke. It asserts Paul's innocence before the trial scenes: Paul has done exactly what God wanted. It reveals that Paul's imprisonment soon to come is God's will. It shows that Paul has completed, or nearly completed, his mission to the Gentiles. Luke thus uses it to put the events he will record in proper perspective.

Consequence

'And "His office let another take". So one of the men who have accompanied us during all the time that the Lord Jesus went in and out among us, beginning from the baptism of John until the day when he was taken up from us—one of these men must become with us a witness to his resurrection' (Acts 1.20b-22).

The key to understanding this speech as a historical sermon lies in grasping its mode of inspiration. Since Peter delivers it before the gift of the Spirit, this speech occupies a unique position in Acts. Of course the Spirit is not the only locus of inspiration in Luke–Acts. In the resurrection narratives Luke describes a special charismatic gift of understanding the scriptures which was given by the resurrected Jesus to the disciples: 'He opened their minds to understand the scriptures' (Lk. 24.45). In the context of the gifts of inspired interpretation known from Qumran, Josephus, and some apocalypses, this gift would certainly have been understood as a kind of inspiration. Peter, utilizing this gift of inspired interpretation, understands how the fall and death of Judas fits in God's plan. Such an inspired understanding of the history of Judas based upon scripture requires that a successor be appointed and Peter draws this consequence from his inspired view of history. The consequence dovetails well with Jesus' word from Luke that the apostles should rule on twelve thrones over the tribes of Israel.

The speech seems directed toward answering a difficult question concerning the proper understanding of Jesus' deeds. Jesus himself had chosen twelve apostles and had emphasized the necessity of twelve apostles ruling the tribes of Israel. This understanding of what would happen in history was threatened on two counts. As Luke had to explain why the apostles were ruling mostly Gentiles instead of Israel, so he had to explain why one of the twelve had himself rejected Jesus. Had Jesus chosen wrongly? He counters such doubts by revealing God's plan. As God ordained the inclusion of the Gentiles and rejection by the Jews so he planned the fall of Judas. A revealed understanding of history can explain the loss of an apostle and justify restoring the apostolic college to its proper number. Though it contributes to the correct understanding of Jesus' words and deeds, mentions a particular case of Jewish rejection and legitimates the college of witnesses in Acts, it contributes less to the revealed historical scheme of Luke–Acts as defined above than other speeches. Luke could use revealed history to support any of his special interests, whether central to the scheme of fulfillment of scripture, proper understanding of Jesus' words and deeds, rejection by Jews and inclusion of Gentiles, or ancillary to it. In this case he uses revealed history to guarantee the purity of the apostolate, to establish the witnesses emphasized in the prologue, the resurrection narratives and the missions speeches, and to exonerate Jesus in his choice of Judas.

Luke and Revealed History

Luke produces an array of 'eyewitnesses and ministers of the word', not to mention angels, prophets, and Jesus himself who reveal the past. With the exception of the words of Jesus in Luke, which were relatively fixed by long usage, the large majority of speeches in Luke and Acts reveal the past. Such revelations utilize a variety of forms and techniques of revelation: songs and prophecies inspired by the Spirit, angelic announcements, interpretations of scripture by Jesus during the ministry (Lk. 4) or after the resurrection (Lk. 24), judicial, accusatory, apologetic, or hortatory historical sermons, and apologetic speeches based on classical rhetoric. In discovering the true perspective on momentous recent events Luke recounts revelations concerning events past to the speakers in the narrative as well as those concerning events future to his characters but past to himself. Luke's familiarity with and reliance on revealed history is obvious; he never misses an opportunity to use it.

With few exceptions[1] inspired history in Luke–Acts has one object: the plan of God worked out in Jesus. God sends Jesus to fulfill his promise in the scriptures. This promise includes the rejection and death of Jesus, the rejection of the plan by many Jews, and the inclusion of many Gentiles. The plan, first stated in its entirety in Simeon's speech, then restated in Jesus' speech at the synagogue at Nazareth, in the speeches of the resurrected Jesus, and in the missions speeches in Acts, is revealed with greater and greater specificity as events unfold. Other speeches concentrate on particular aspects of this plan: the fulfillment of the promise (the canticles and angelic announcements in Lk. 1–2), rejection of the plan by the Jews (Stephen's speech, the defense speeches of Peter before the Jewish council), or the inclusion of the Gentiles (Peter's defense before the church in Jerusalem, speeches at the Jerusalem council, Paul's forensic speeches). The inspired historical speeches in Luke–Acts present a single consistent view of the events from the past recorded in the work. It follows that this interpretation of the events is the author's own.

The entire two-volume work is patterned on this same plan of God. It shows how God sent Jesus to fulfill his promise in the scriptures and

---

1. For instance, the judicial historical sermon concerning Ananias and Sapphira.

how the birth, ministry, death, and resurrection of Jesus, as well as the rejection of the Jews and inclusion of the gentiles belong to the plan of God. Luke–Acts has special affinity with the missions speeches. Like them Luke–Acts connects God's present activity with his past acts of redemption for his people and tells the story of Jesus, carefully fitting the death and resurrection of Jesus into God's plan. Like them he shows how rejection by the Jews and consequent inclusion of the Gentiles is orchestrated by God. Like the missions speeches, Luke–Acts embraces the argumentative form of a historical sermon. The final speech of Paul, which lacks its own historical review, offers a fitting consequence to the historical review in the work as a whole:

> The Holy Spirit was right in saying to your fathers through Isaiah the prophet: 'Go to this people, and say, You shall indeed hear but never understand, and you shall indeed see but never perceive. For this people's heart has grown dull, and their ears are heavy of hearing, and their eyes they have closed; lest they should perceive with their eyes, and hear with their ears, and understand with their heart, and turn for me to heal them.' Let it be known to you then that this salvation of God has been sent to the Gentiles; they will listen (Acts 28.25b-29).

The historical review (Luke and Acts 1.1–28.25a) supports the consequent sentence: the Spirit's word through Isaiah has been fulfilled; the Jews have heard but not understood; the salvation of God has moved from disobedient Jews to Gentiles who will listen. Such a reading of Acts would support Maddox's contention that the work was written in conflict over separation of church and synagogue to show how God's plan on the one hand could fulfill the expectation promised to God's people and on the other be rejected by the people he had chosen.[1] By showing how history called forth the sentence of the heavenly court, Luke–Acts explains the continual rejection of Jesus, the message about him, and his messengers and explains how the gospel is still from God even though believed by Gentiles but disavowed by those in synagogues. Facing ejection from synagogues, the author of Acts took a bold step in ratifying the status quo and thereby offered assurance (ἀσφάλεια, Lk. 1.4) to his readers.[2]

But to tie it too closely to conflict with the synagogue does not do justice to Luke's intention. In patterning Luke–Acts after a missions speech Luke himself has taken up that message delivered by Jesus to

---

1. Maddox, *The Purpose of Luke–Acts, passim.*
2. Moessner correctly points out that this speech does not cut Israel off from repentance; judicial sermons pressuppose the possibility of repentance. See David P. Moessner, 'Paul in Acts: Preacher of Eschatological Repentance to Israel', *NTS* 34 (1988), 96-104.

the apostles (Lk. 24) ordained as witnesses. Like his predecessors, Luke proclaims the gospel in Luke–Acts. Like them he is a witness of what he has seen and heard. Like them he writes empowered by the Spirit. Luke not only elaborates a message based on revelation but speaks as one inspired. Luke–Acts is inspired history.

Like the apocalyptic histories Luke–Acts explains puzzling recent events. Revelation explains the enigma of a messiah killed by his own people and—even more currently to the point—a salvation rejected by those it was meant to save but accepted by others. Every element of Luke's interpretation is called into question by such enigmas. How could Jesus fulfill the promises to Israel if he was rejected by Israel and followed by Gentiles? Luke incorporates each of these incompatible propositions into the plan of God revealed on so many different occasions by so many different prophets. From beginning to end prophets and witnesses declare that God fulfilled his promises by sending Jesus to be rejected and killed by his own for a blessing to Gentiles and a cause of fall and rising for many in Israel.

Even more closely than the apocalyptic histories, Luke–Acts parallels the work of Josephus. As Josephus interprets history in the *Jewish War* by the revelation he had received at Jotapata, so Luke interprets history by the pattern revealed to the many 'eyewitnesses and ministers of the word' in Luke–Acts. For Luke as for Josephus the reception of revelation lies prior to the writing of the work. Each looks back to revelation once received, then organizes the events using the revealed insight into God's plan as a key to meaning in history. For Josephus the revelation remains squarely in the past; his history is not inspired but is his best attempt at obedience to the call heard at Jotapata. The same cannot quite be said of Luke. True, he also relies on revelation received in the past, in his case revelation given to others, but he always portrays the proclamation of that revealed message as empowered by the Spirit. Though he would not consider himself the equal of Peter or Paul, he would consider himself as much a witness as they, and like them, like all Christians, he was filled with the Spirit. Luke–Acts is prophetic history. On the continuum between the *Jewish War*, which is based on revelation but not revelation itself, and *Jubilees*, which throughout is dictated by an angel, Luke–Acts lies just closer to *Jubilees* than Josephus does. For Luke the real locus of revelation is in the past yet the writing of the book partakes of that witness empowered by the Spirit.

Josephus names two qualifications essential to the best historians: they are prophets and they recorded the events of their own times (*Ag.*

Ap. 1.Proem.7 §§37-40).[1] The prophet interpreted events he or she was in the best situation to assess. Luke's emphasis on eyewitnesses behind his narrative does not indicate a concern for modern historical accuracy, but taken together with his emphasis on revelation of the past, it does indicate his concern with an ancient standard for historical accuracy. Luke claims for his work a carefully maintained connection with the events which he himself has certified and the revelation necessary to interpret the events correctly. In doing so he ranks his work with the best historians according to the standard attested by Josephus. Luke–Acts is an interpretative prophetic history. We now turn to another interpretative prophetic history, the Gospel of John.

---

1. See the discussion introducing Josephus above.

Chapter 13

THE GOSPEL OF JOHN

Although the relationship between the Gospel of John and early Christian prophecy is sometimes virtually ignored,[1] it is rarely if ever rejected. In this limited sense it seems proper to claim a consensus that prophetic elements in the Johannine tradition, composition, or community contributed to the peculiar character of the Fourth Gospel.[2] Yet between asserting that the Gospel of John has been influenced by early Christian prophecy and claiming that the Gospel is a product of early Christian prophecy lies a gap that has only more rarely been bridged.

Westcott first advances the thesis of a 'prophetic' origin for John to explain how someone who had known Jesus after the flesh could

1. Major commentators, Barrett, Brown, Bultmann, occasionally mention but do not develop prophetic features of the Gospel. Schnackenburg treats them with reserve. Perhaps their reticence reflects their rejection of the surprising theses the prophetic associations of John have been made to support: Cullmann's view of New Testament theology, Sasse's identification of the Paraclete with the author of the Gospel, or Kragerud's equation of the beloved disciple with the Johannine Community. For their brief allusions to a prophetic origin of the Fourth Gospel see C.K. Barrett, 'History', *Essays on John* (Philadelphia: Westminster, 1982), 117; *The Gospel According to St. John: An Introduction with Commentary and Notes on the Greek Text* (Philadelphia: Westminster, 1978), 143; 'The Holy Spirit in the Fourth Gospel', *JTS* ns1 (1950), 4; Raymond E. Brown, 'The Paraclete in the Fourth Gospel', *NTS* 13 (1966-67), 129; *The Community of the Beloved Disciple* (New York: Paulist, 1979), 28-29; Rudolf Bultmann, *The Gospel of John: A Commentary* (Philadelphia: Westminster, 1971), 625; *New Testament Theology* 2 (New York: Scribners, 1951/1955), 89; Rudolf Schnackenburg, 'Die johanneische Gemeinde und ihre Geisterfahrung', *Die Kirche des Anfangs. Festschrift für Heinz Schürmann zum 65. Geburtstag* (Erfurter Theologische Studien 38; Freiburg: Herder, 1977), 289; *The Gospel of St. John* (3 vols.; New York: Crossroad, 1982), 1.23; 3.150-51. See also Oscar Cullmann, *Salvation in History* (New York: Harper & Row, 1967); Hermann Sasse, 'Der Paraklet im Johannesevangelium', *ZNW* 24 (1925), 260-77; Alv Kragerud, *Der Lieblingsjünger im Johannesevangelium* (Oslo: Osloer Universitätsverlag, 1959).

2. Works supporting this consensus appear on this and subsequent pages.

acquire such an exalted christology.[1] Windisch, in articulating his hypothesis that John was written to displace the synoptics, strongly emphasizes the role of the Spirit in the composition of John.[2] Although the author incorporated traditional kerygma, church teaching expressed in the third person, and first-person words of Christ formed by analogy with synoptic, apocalyptic-prophetic, Old Testament and non-Christian prototypes, he also utilized new creations traceable to prophetic experience. The evangelist perceives his entire message about Jesus as revelation, either as inspired interpretation of the witness of the historical Jesus or as new thoughts and formulations received directly from the exalted Christ through the Spirit. 'Der Wille und die Überzeugung, ein normatives, fast kann man sagen, ein kanonisches Buch zu schreiben, ist seinem Evgl. unverkennbar aufgeprägt.'[3] According to Mußner, John attributes to the apostolic eyewitnesses inspired insight into the life of Jesus which enables them to recognize who Jesus is.[4] The Fourth Gospel sees itself as a particular instance of this apostolic witness to Jesus. Its witness is grounded in that of the beloved disciple who, as an eyewitness and charismatic interpreter of the history of Christ, surpasses Peter in importance to the church.[5] Since the tradition about Christ already derives from the work of the Spirit, the evangelist does no travesty to the tradition when interpreting the mystery of Jesus and the tradition about him by the inspiration of the Spirit.[6] Müller adduces data from Jewish farewell discourses to show that the Fourth Gospel regards itself as an expression of the Paraclete's work.[7] As the departing celebrity in Jewish farewell discourse records his knowledge and exhortation for the continuing community, so the understanding brought by the Paraclete to the revelation given in Jesus receives concrete expression in the Fourth Gospel. The Spirit guarantees the witness of the evangelist to the words of Jesus. 'Sein Evangelium ist das geistgewirkte Zeugnis

---

1. Brooke Foss Westcott, *The Gospel According to St. John: The Greek Text with Introduction and Notes* (2 vols.; London: Murray, 1908), 1.lxxxv, cx, cxii-cxiii, cxxix.

2. Hans Windisch, *Johannes und die Synoptiker* (Leipzig: Hinrichs, 1926), 135-50.

3. Windisch, *Johannes und die Synoptiker*, 149.

4. Franz Mußner, *The Historical Jesus in the Gospel of St. John* (New York: Herder & Herder, 1967); 'Die johanneischen Parakletsprüche und die apostolische Tradition', *BZ* n.F. 5 (1961), 56-70.

5. Mußner, *Historical Jesus*, 57.

6. Mußner, *Historical Jesus*, 58, 76.

7. U.B. Müller, 'Die Parakletenvorstellung im Johannesevangelium', *ZTK* 71 (1974), 31-77.

über Jesus, es erinnert wie der Geist an die Worte und Taten Jesu. Es ist damit die legitimierte Form der Offenbarung über Jesus.'[1] Westcott, Windisch, Mußner and Müller, though they do not use the term, already view the Gospel of John as an expression of revealed history. If they are right John as well as Luke–Acts is prophetic history since it clearly seeks to chronicle the past. Does John use revealed history? How does John fit into the general picture of revealed history developed so far?

Historical Revelation in John

Alone of the canonical Gospels, John has a putative author, the beloved disciple.[2] 'This is the witness who witnesses concerning these things and writes these things, and we know that his witness is true' (Jn 21.4; cf. 19.35). Though the trustworthiness of this eyewitness is impeccable, though he occupies a privileged position among Jesus' disciples, though he mediates between Jesus and Peter to obtain the true meaning of what Jesus said, and though following the resurrection he alone believes without seeing Jesus (20.8; contrast 20.25, compare 20.29), the Gospel does not explicitly claim inspiration for this shadowy figure. Instead John emphasizes his preeminence among the disciples, his closeness to Jesus, his qualifications as an eyewitness who believed. The beloved disciple, at least at first glance, provides the Gospel with a link to eyewitness testimony rather than a claim to inspiration.[3] The Fourth Gospel's claim to inspiration is more subtle than many of the

---

1. Müller, 50.

2. For present purposes it is unnecessary to decide in what sense (if any) the beloved disciple is the author of the Fourth Gospel; it is sufficient that the final edition of the Gospel claims him as its author. See R. Alan Culpepper, *Anatomy of the Fourth Gospel* (Hermeneia: Foundations and Facets; Philadelphia: Fortress, 1983), 47.

3. Though the Gospel makes no such claim, many students of John, probably correctly, attribute inspiration to the beloved disciple. Kragerud, 86-87; Culpepper, *Anatomy*, 47; Brown, 'Paraclete', 54; Walter Grundmann, *Zeugnis und Gestalt des Johannes-Evangeliums. Eine Studie zur denkerischen und gestalterischen Leistung des vierten Evangelisten* (Arbeiten zur Theologie 7; Stuttgart: Calwer, 1960), 19; George Johnston, *The Spirit-Paraclete in the Gospel of John* (SNTSMS 12; Cambridge: Cambridge University Press, 1970), 124. In *The Johannine School* Culpepper suggests that Johannine Christians understood the activity of the Paraclete on the basis of what the beloved disciple did among them (R. Alan Culpepper, *The Johannine School: An Evaluation of the Johannine School Hypothesis Based on an Investigation of the Nature of Ancient Schools* [SBLDS 26; Missoula, MT: Scholars Press, 1975], 266-70).

works studied so far.[1] The Johannine understanding of prophetic experience comes to clearest expression in the Gospel's portrait of Jesus. Jesus is the prophet *par excellence* who speaks what he hears from the Father.[2] Yet the promises in the farewell discourses invest the members of the Johannine community with a derivative prophetic experience. Investigation of these promises provides the best starting point for a study of revealed history in John.[3] Among these, three of the Paraclete promises have preeminence for the present study (14.25-26; 15.26-27; 16.12-15).

The Paraclete promises in 14.25-26 and 16.12-15 are closely related. With good reason those who find in the farewell discourses successive elaborations of an initial testamentary speech see one of these promises as a development of the other.[4] Each begins with Jesus speaking (14.25; 16.12), then moves to what the Spirit (τὸ πνεῦμα τὸ ἅγιον,[5] 14.26; τὸ πνεῦμα τῆς ἀληθείας, 16.13) will speak. Each promises the disciples further understanding from the Spirit.

The allusions to Jesus speaking in these two promises (14.25; 16.12) are particular instances of a wider pattern; the farewell discourses establish similar sayings as a refrain.[6] Each saying has two members: Jesus refers to what he has said or will say,[7] then to a purpose or cir-

---

1. Yet much more frequently asserted. In addition to Windisch, Westcott, Mußner, Müller, and those mentioned above see, for example, Cullmann, *Salvation in History*, 272; B.H. Streeter, *The Four Gospels: A Study of Origins* (New York: Macmillan, 1956 [1924]), 363-92; Günther Bornkamm in two essays from *Geschichte und Glaube*, I, (Gesammelte Aufsätze 3; Beiträge zur evangelischen Theologie; München: Kaiser, 1968): 'Der Paraklet im Johannes-Evangelium', (68-89); 'Zur Interpretation des Johannes-Evangeliums. Eine Auseinandersetzung mit Ernst Käsemanns Schrift "Jesu letzter Wille nach Johannes 17"' (104-21).

2. J. Ramsey Michaels, 'The Johannine Words of Jesus and Christian Prophecy', *SBLSP* 2 (1975), 240.

3. Boring can move directly from prophesying in the Gospel of John to a conclusion relevant to inspired history: 'It should be noted that the only occurrence of προφητεύω in the fourth gospel (11.51) reveals the form that prophecy takes for John, namely the divinely-given interpretation of the meaning of the life and death of Jesus, and not merely prediction' (M. Eugene Boring, *Sayings of the Risen Jesus: Christian Prophecy in the Synoptic Tradition* [SNTSMS 46; Cambridge: Cambridge University Press, 1982], 107).

4. Sasse, 276; Müller, 37, 74; C.K. Barrett, *St. John*, 454-55; John Painter, 'The Farewell Discourses and the History of Johannine Christianity', *NTS* 27 (1981), 526, 539-40.

5. I accept τὸ ἅγιον as original.

6. Jn 4.25, 29, 30; 15.11, 17; 16.1, 4a, 4b, 12, 15b, 25, 33.

7. None of these uses the present tense, though the form, ἀμὴν, ἀμὴν λέγω ὑμῖν, approximates it.

cumstance which qualifies his speaking.[1] These sayings occur at turning points in the discourse[2] but may follow (14.29 , 30-31; 15.11, 17; 16.4a, 15b, 33)[3] or precede (14.25; 16.1, 4b, 12, 25) the paragraphs of the discourse to which they belong. In every case they characterize the material they conclude or introduce, giving a general rubric which interprets the section. Like the similar ἀμὴν, ἀμὴν λέγω ὑμῖν formula, they emphasize the importance of what Jesus has just said or will say.[4] In both Paraclete promises (14.25-26; 16.12-15) a refrain saying introduces and concludes what Jesus proceeds to say. As the pattern suggests, these transitional statements set the tone for the material they bound.

The first of these two promises (14.25-26) falls within a section bounded by instances of the refrain (14.25, 29).[5] Although the first occurrence of the refrain may be more closely tied to the earlier parts of the section (vv. 26-27) and the second more closely tied to the later parts (v. 28), the entire section is determined by both sayings. The promises of the Paraclete and of peace and of his coming after his going are all said that the disciples should believe when it happens (14.29); they are all said while Jesus remains with them (14.25). In both refrains, the accent falls on what Jesus has said.[6] Even the reference to the future (And now I have spoken to you *before it happens that when it happens you should believe*, 14.29) contains a retrospective glance back at what Jesus has just said. When the disciples do remember Jesus' words and believe (14.29) they will surely do so because the Holy Spirit has reminded them of what Jesus said (14.26).

1. Purpose is introduced by ἵνα (15.11, 17; 16.1, 4a, 33) but the second member can be a ὅτι clause (16.4b,15b), a participial phrase (14.25), or coordinate clause (16.12,25).
2. Cf. Raymond E. Brown, *The Gospel According to John* (AB 29, 29A; Garden City, NY: Doubleday, 1966/1970), 29a.650.
3. 14.29-31 contains a double instance of the refrain. The first instance concludes the section beginning at 14.25, the second concludes the original discourse of ch. 14 (Painter, Woll; against Sasse, Bultmann). The entire present discourse also ends with the refrain (16.33).
4. Siegfried Schulz (*Das Evangelium nach Johannes* [NTD 4; Göttingen: Vandenhoeck & Ruprecht, 1972], 91-92) stresses the prophetic origin of the ἀμήν sayings. This refrain of the discourse may also be prophetic. ταῦτα λελάληκα ὑμῖν (14.25, 15.11; 16.1, 4b, 33) is not so far from the τάδε λέγει which introduces the letters of the Apocalypse (Rev. 2.1, 8, 12, 18; 3.1, 7, 14). For τάδε λέγει as a prophetic formula see David E. Aune, *Prophecy in Early Christianity and the Ancient Mediterranean World* (Grand Rapids: Eerdmans, 1983), 275-76. Brown (*John*, 29a.650) notes a parallel with the Old Testament prophetic 'I the Lord have spoken'.
5. Cf. similar pattern in 16.1-4a.
6. Notice the perfects λελάληκα (14.29), εἴρηκα (14.25, 29).

Hence the entire Paraclete promise (14.26) probably stands under this preoccupation with what Jesus has said in the past. The Spirit which will be sent in Jesus' name[1] will teach the disciples concerning Jesus' words as well as bring to remembrance what Jesus said. The context encourages taking ἅ εἶπον ὑμῖν ἐγώ[2] with both occurrences of πάντα in 14.26:[3] the Spirit shall teach you all things which I have said to you and bring them all to your remembrance.[4] Ταῦτα λελάληκα (14.25) is equivalent to the πάντα in the clause ἐκεῖνος ὑμᾶς διδάξει πάντα (14.26) and to the πάντα in the clause ὑπομνήσει ὑμᾶς πάντα as well as to ἅ in ἅ εἶπον ὑμῖν ἐγώ.[5] In this promise the Paraclete brings to remembrance and expounds what Jesus spoke during his ministry.

The reworking of this promise,[6] if such it be, stresses other aspects of the revelation brought by the Spirit (16.12-15). As with its counterpart in ch. 14, refrain sayings (16.12, 15b) frame a promise of revelation from the Spirit (16.13-15a). This time the introductory refrain saying (16.12) refers to words Jesus has yet to say instead of

1. Brown (*John*, 29a.653) notes that 'in Jesus' name' denotes union with Jesus.
2. Emphatic ἐγώ is missing in some witnesses.
3. So Ignace de la Potterie, 'The Paraclete', *The Christian Lives by the Spirit* (Staten Island, NY: Alba House, 1971), 63; against Mußner, 'Parakletsprüche', 60.
4. Interpreters differ concerning whether 'reminding' and 'teaching' refer to the same or different functions. I think the two are to be held together, as by Bultmann, *John*, 626 n. 6; Painter, 533; Brown, *John*, 29a.650; Edwyn Clement Hoskyns, *The Fourth Gospel*, ed. Francis Noel Davey (London: Faber & Faber, 1947), 461; D. Bruce Woll, *Johannine Christianity in Conflict* (SBLDS 60; Chico, CA: Scholars, 1981), 100. Others distinguish between the two. Hans Windisch, *The Spirit-Paraclete in the Fourth Gospel* (trans. James W. Cox, Biblical Series 20; Philadelphia: Fortress, 1968), 7; Mußner, 'Parakletsprüche', 60; B.F. Westcott, 2.182-83; W. Nicol, *The Semeia in the Fourth Gospel: Tradition and Redaction* (Supp. Nov. T. 32; Leiden: Brill, 1972), 126. Haacker, probably rightly, holds teaching and memory together but denies that the passage precludes revelation of new information. Klaus Haacker, *Die Stiftung des Heils. Untersuchungen zur Struktur der johanneischen Theologie* (Arbeiten zur Theologie 1.47; Stuttgart: Calwer, 1972), 154. Jn 14.26 assumes that the locus of revelation is in Jesus but assumes that the revelation in Jesus is so full that things presently unknown may be revealed by the teaching and reminding work of the Paraclete.
5. This equation is called into question by Haacker (154); Nicol (125); and Mußner (*Historical Jesus*, 60; 'Parakletsprüche', 60). Brown (*John*, 29a.650) maintains the equivalence of ταῦτα and πάντα by noting that the contrast between them does not necessarily concern quantity. The Paraclete will enable the disciples to comprehend the full meaning of Jesus' words.
6. Schnackenburg, *St. John*, 3.144; Painter, 526, 539-40; Ernst Bammel, 'Jesus und der Paraklet in Johannes 16', *Christ and Spirit in the New Testament: Studies in Honor of C.F.D. Moule*, 1 (Cambridge: Cambridge University Press, 1973), 207-208. Bammel thinks the 'reworking' goes the other way.

those he has already said (ἔτι πολλὰ ἔχω ὑμῖν λέγειν); its second member explains why he has not yet said them (ἀλλ' οὐ δύνασθε βαστάζειν ἄρτι). Since the refrain sayings characterize the sections to which they belong, the revelation brought by the Spirit should concern not what Jesus has already said, but what Jesus has yet to say.[1] At first the concluding saying seems to challenge this expectation, because its first member uses a past tense (διὰ τοῦτο εἶπον). But διὰ τοῦτο refers only to πάντα ὅσα ἔχει ὁ πατὴρ ἐμά ἐστιν (16.15a). Since it has such a specific reference it does not compete with the stress on future words of Jesus in the introductory refrain. The concluding saying contributes its own element to the characterization of the section; by resuming the last clause of the preceding verse (16.14) it stresses that whatever the Spirit shall speak will belong to Jesus (16.15c). The refrain sayings together define our expectations of what the Spirit of truth will speak. He will say what Jesus currently has to say but cannot because of the disciples' frailty and he will announce what belongs to Jesus. The two refrain sayings agree well with each other.

Underlying this promise of further revelation is the conception that Jesus, while he is speaking the discourse as well as before and since, has the sum of all possible revelation at his immediate disposal. 'Everything the Father has is mine' (16.14-15). He dispenses this revelation as he sees fit, some prior to the last discourse, some during it, some in the future through the Spirit (hence the partitive ἐκ τοῦ ἐμοῦ,[2] 16.14-15). Since Jesus has all revelation from the Father and since the Spirit makes known the truth that belongs to Jesus, the Spirit leads into all the truth. As Jesus has been speaking of things to come in this part of his testamentary speech (15.18–16.33) so the Spirit will complete this announcement of what is to come (τὰ ἐρχόμενα, 16.13). As the Father glorifies Jesus (8.54; 13.31) so does the Spirit for the Spirit announces the things which belong to Jesus (16.14). Hence, although many have sought to limit the revelation given in this passage to what Jesus has already said by analogy with Jn 14.25-26,[3] the accent here falls on revelations of what will happen to the community and revelations of Jesus' glory which Jesus presently knows but cannot now

---

1. Müller, 72, 74.

2. Barrett, *St. John*, 490-91; against Brown, *John*, 29a.708.

3. Brown, *John*, 29a.714-15; Bultmann, *Theology*, 2.89; Joseph Blank, *Krisis. Untersuchungen zur johanneischen Christologie und Eschatologie* (Freiburg im Breisgau: Lambertus, 1964), 330; Schnackenburg, *St. John*, 3.142-43.

speak.[1] Nothing hinders the Spirit from glorifying Jesus by revealing his present and future glory as in the Apocalypse[2] or by revealing his past glory as in the prologue to John. The passage has in view whatever Jesus has to say which he has not yet said and which if he did say the disciples could not yet receive.

A fascinating contradiction arises between 'I have yet many things to say to you but you cannot bear them now' (16.12), and 'I have called you friends because all things which I have heard from my Father I have made known to you' (15.15).[3] Why does the Gospel assert such conflicting propositions? Without prejudice to the many theories of subsequent editions of the farewell discourses, it would seem useful to see what sparks fly when these two statements are held together as they are in the Fourth Gospel.

Both horns of the dilemma are firm. Announcements of revelation to be given in the future so abound in Jewish and Christian, not to mention pagan, literature of the time[4] that it is difficult to see how an author could have written 16.12-15 without meaning that Jesus had other things to say which he could not now speak but which the community would receive from him later through the Spirit. If he had meant anything else, it is doubtful that a reader could have understood it. On the other hand 15.15 cannot be explained away as an isolated idea; the whole Gospel teaches that revelation is complete in Jesus.[5] 'The words which you have given to me I have given to them' (17.8). 'I have given them your word' (17.14). To Philip's correct statement 'Show us the Father and it is enough for us', Jesus says 'The one who has seen me has seen the Father' (14.8-9). Jesus has come to give life; life is the knowledge of God and of Jesus (17.3). Jesus has glorified[6] God on earth; hence his work is complete (17.4). Side by side with such statements others indicate that yet more is to be revealed. 'I have

---

1. Müller, 37, 72-74; D. Moody Smith, 'John 16.1-15 (Expository Article)', *Interpretation* 33 (1979), 61; Painter, 540; Sasse, 273; Windisch, *Johannes und die Synoptiker*, 147; *Spirit-Paraclete* 11-12; James D.G. Dunn, *Jesus and the Spirit* (Philadelphia: Westminster, 1975), 352; Bammel, 205-207; M.E. Boring, 'The Influence of Christian Prophecy on the Johannine Portrayal of the Paraclete and Jesus', *NTS* 25 (1978), 118.

2. Windisch, *Spirit-Paraclete*, 12. To claim that τὰ ἐρχόμενα refers to apocalyptic disclosures such as that in Revelation as Hill and Sasse (274) do goes beyond the evidence. See David Hill, *New Testament Prophecy* (Atlanta: John Knox, 1979), 151.

3. Cf. Bammel, 207; Brown, *John*, 29a.714; de la Potterie, 65.

4. *Herm.* Vis. 2.4.2; *4 Ezra* 9.23-25; 10.59; 12.39; 13.56; *2 Bar.* 20.5-6.

5. See Westcott, 1.lxxx.

6. In John 'glorify' can mean 'reveal the glory of'.

made known your name and shall make it known' (17.26). Jesus has glorified God on the earth; the Father has yet to glorify Jesus, that is to make known his glory which he had before the world was (17.4). In John the 'hour' (crucifixion, resurrection, ascension) reveals the glory of Jesus, but Jesus would have to say a great deal more before anyone would see there the glory he had before the world was.[1]

Probably, therefore, even the recognition that Jesus has more to say to the disciples that they cannot bear contains within it the presupposition that revelation directed toward the past is necessary.[2] Jesus in his earthly ministry 'has' all revelation; he has already perfectly declared it but it could not be perfectly perceived.[3] Therefore Jesus will continue to reveal what was revealed in him. From the perspective of the disciples it is new; they will hear messages they have never heard and see Jesus' glory as they had never seen it before he breathed the Spirit on them (20.22). Yet everything the Spirit will reveal is contained *in nuce* in the words and deeds of Jesus.[4] Jesus' ministry is a storehouse of revelation waiting to be unpacked by the Spirit of truth. Like all other works of revelation concerning the past, John also believes in continuing revelation. Yet John gives special significance to the past revelation. 'I have made known your name and I will make it known' (17.26). Both poles of this statement are important. Not everything the Spirit says need formally to interpret something Jesus actually said or did—he can say new things—but everything declared by the Spirit develops or elaborates the revelation brought by Jesus from the Father.[5] Whether the Spirit interprets Jesus' words or deeds

---

1. 17.4 and 17.24 show the period before the world was created to be a proper subject for revelation. The hymn in the prologue (1.1-4), like those in the *Odes of Solomon*, probably is to be viewed as an inspired song. It reveals just that glory of Jesus before the world was which Jesus expects to be revealed to his own.

2. De la Potterie (67) amasses evidence to show that ἀναγγέλλειν in Jn 16.13-15 means 'to explain a previous revelation'. Perhaps his evidence may stand as an added indication that 16.12-15 implies revelation directed toward the past, but it should not be made to limit the promised activity of the Paraclete to the past as de la Potterie does.

3. Westcott, 2.182: 'The revelation of Christ in his person and word was absolute and complete, but without the gradual illumination of the Spirit it is partly unintelligible and partly unobserved'.

4. Perhaps this is hinted at even in the passage promising further revelation when the Spirit of truth comes (16.12-15), for Jesus proceeds directly to speak about things to come which show his own glory (16.17, 28; cf. 16.13-14) and the disciples cannot bear them (6.17, 31-32).

5. Others have articulated a similar balance between these two poles. Mußner, 'Parakletsprüche', 59, 61-62; Haacker, 154, 158; Dunn, 351-52; D. Moody Smith, *John* (Proclamation Commentaries; Philadelphia: Fortress, 1976), 84.

(14.25-26) or speaks what Jesus had to say but could not because of the disciples' frailty (16.12-15), he only writes footnotes to the revelation brought by Jesus from the Father and perfectly declared by him.

In such a climate of thought historical revelation is inevitable. For the Johannine community the deeds and words of Jesus abound in revelation awaiting discovery. As the scriptures for the Qumran community contain secrets revealed by the inspired Teacher of Righteousness or the heavens for the apocalyptist hold mysteries to be revealed by a heavenly guide and interpreter so the words and deeds of Jesus contain everything the Johannine Christian needs to know and the Paraclete comes as heavenly guide and interpreter.[1] Therefore Jesus can say, 'I have spoken all these things to you in dark sayings (ἐν παροιμίαις); the hour comes when I will no longer speak to you in dark sayings but I will openly announce to you concerning the Father'. Though hidden, revelation inheres in the words and deeds of Jesus. Jesus later, by the Paraclete, will make it plain.[2] The Johannine localization of revelation in Jesus requires the device of revelation directed toward the past.

Each of these two promises of revelation from the Spirit contains concepts of importance to the rest of the Gospel. The promise that the Spirit shall glorify Jesus (16.14) picks up the continual stress on glorifying Jesus which pervades the Gospel. The promise that the Spirit would announce the things to come (16.13) picks up a theme of the last discourses. That the Spirit would teach and remind concerning what Jesus said (14.26) also echoes ideas developed elsewhere in the Gospel. Since these clues may show how the promised future revelatory activity of the Spirit pertains to the Gospel, each will be examined in turn.

In addition to the reminding work of the Paraclete (14.26), the Fourth Gospel mentions remembrance of the words and deeds of Jesus five times (μιμνήσκομαι, 2.17, 22; 12.16; μνημονεύω, 15.20; 16.4). The Johannine pericope, 'the cleansing of the Temple' (2.13-22), contains two elements: judgment against the Temple merchants (2.13-17) and a dialogue with the Jews in which Jesus prophesies the destruction of the Temple (2.18-22). Each section concludes by pointing out how the memory of the disciples supplied the missing interpretation to the

---

1. David E. Aune, *The Cultic Setting of Realized Eschatology in Early Christianity* (Leiden: Brill, 1972), 70-72; cf. Schnackenburg, *St. John*, 3.83.

2. In connection with this verse (Jn 16.25) Brown (*John*, 29a.734) mentions the 'inevitable mystery presented by one from above when he speaks to those who are on the earth'. This is the mystery the Paraclete enlightens (735). See Barrett, *St. John*, 495.

scene (2.17, 22). The latter reference, which specifies that this memory occurred after the resurrection, should interpret the former. After the resurrection the disciples remembered and for the first time understood what Jesus had said. Similarly into the account of the triumphal entry, interpreted by Ps. 118.25-26 and Zech. 9.9, the author interjects, 'These things the disciples did not understand (ἔγνωσαν) at first, but when Jesus was glorified then they remembered (ἐμνήσθησαν) that these things were written concerning him and that they did these things to him' (12.16). Such memory, which pulls together scripture and fulfillment to understand Jesus' words and deeds,[1] well exemplifies the promise that the Paraclete who would come after Jesus' departure would teach and remind the disciples concerning the things Jesus said (14.26).[2] Specifying that this memory occurs after the resurrection or after Jesus was glorified locates it squarely in the period of the Paraclete's activity.[3]

At least one of the occurrences of μνημονεύω shares this retrospective character. 'But these things I have spoken to you that when their hour comes you should remember them that I spoke them to you' (16.4). Jesus, who has been warning them of persecutions probably accomplished shortly before the completion of the Gospel, expects the disciples to remember the interpretation he had given their suffering when their hour came on them as his was shortly to come on him. This memory also fits the description and the time frame of the reminding of the Paraclete.

Once in the farewell discourses Jesus reminds the disciples of his own word and reinterprets it (15.20-21). Jesus takes up a word which he had spoken earlier, 'A slave is not greater than his master' (Jn 13.16). It had first enjoined humility, but Jesus reinterprets it to show how his disciples will be persecuted or obeyed just as he was.[4] Since

---

1. Cf. Lk. 24.6-8, 25-27, 44-46 for inspired memory of Jesus' deeds interpreted by scripture. The connection in John between Paraclete-inspired memory of Jesus' words and memory of scripture which interprets these words is frequently stressed: Barrett, 'Holy Spirit', 14; Mußner, *Historical Jesus*, 42; Cullmann, *Salvation in History*, 273; Rodney A. Whitacre, *Johannine Polemic: The Role of Tradition and Theology* (SBLDS; Chico, CA: Scholars Press, 1982), 101-102. Blank, 268; Woll, 98-100. Painter (533) connects this with Johannine reinterpretation of christological titles to express a high christology.
2. It is interesting that mnemonic interpretation after the resurrection opens and closes the public ministry of Jesus (2.22; 12.16).
3. Müller, 46.
4. Matthew also has this saying in the context of persecutions (Mt. 10.24); Luke uses a similar saying to show the necessity of sound teachers (Lk. 6.40). Apparently

the Paraclete reproduces the revelatory activity of Jesus,[1] Jesus' interpretive reminding of his own word illustrates the promise of the Spirit's reminding work. As Jesus called to memory what he had said, then filled it with new meaning applicable to the community situation of persecution so the teaching and reminding of the Spirit will recall Jesus' words and deeds and invest them with new meaning.

The passages in which the Gospel of John employs the concept of memory show the evangelist's awareness of the reference of the Spirit back toward the tradition of Jesus. Furthermore they show that the Gospel trusts such memory to interpret the words and deeds of Jesus. Paraclete-inspired memory which both recalls and interprets the deeds and words of Jesus is not an isolated idea, but informs the whole Gospel. Such interpretive memory is one constituent of the portrait of Jesus drawn in the Fourth Gospel.[2]

Although the Fourth Gospel does not necessarily limit revelation from the Spirit of truth to interpreting what Jesus has said and done, even the passage which permits the widest possible field for the Spirit's work (16.12-15) seems to have revelation concerning the past in view, at least in part. As the Spirit will reveal the things to come (16.13) and glorify Jesus by announcing the things that belong to him so the Fourth Gospel presents its own view of the glory of Jesus and the things to come.

The use of δοξάζω in the Fourth Gospel is complex. When Jesus says, 'Now glorify me, Father, with your own glory which I had with you before the world was', δοξάζω seems to mean 'invest with glory' (17.5). In the previous verse it means 'to manifest the glory of' for Jesus says 'I have glorified you on the earth' (17.4). Since in John Jesus never lays aside his glory but masks it (1.14; 2.11) and since glory almost implies its own manifestation, these two meanings approach one another. When Jesus asks God to glorify him with the glory he had before the world was, he asks God to manifest fully once again that

the saying was handed down independently. Thus 15.20-21 may show the Johannine method of augmenting and interpreting a traditional saying.

1. Haacker, 153. D.M. Smith (*John*, 49) remarks, 'It is by no means unreasonable to surmise that the specific function of the Spirit-Paraclete as described in the fourth gospel is actually represented in the figure and work of the Johannine Jesus.'

2. This conclusion has been frequently drawn. Nils A. Dahl, 'Anamnesis; Memory and Commemoration in Early Christianity', *Jesus in the Memory of the Early Church* (Minneapolis: Augsburg, 1976), 28; Painter, 533, 535; Heinrich Schlier, 'Zum Begriff des Geistes nach dem Johannesevangelium', *Besinnung auf das Neue Testament. Exegetische Aufsätze und Vorträge* 2 (Freiburg: Herder, 1964), 267; Oscar Cullmann, *Early Christian Worship* (SBT 10; Chicago: Regnery, 1953), 49; Woll, 169 n. 3.

glory which had constantly flashed through the ministry of Jesus (1.14; 2.11; 11.4).[1] For the Gospel of John the activity of Jesus is a repository of hidden glory.[2] The signs which Jesus does and the words which Jesus speaks both glorify God and glorify Jesus. Jesus glorifies God by doing signs which manifest God's glory (11.4, 40); God glorifies Jesus by giving him signs to do (11.4). Hence Jesus, who always seeks the glory of the one who sent him (7.18; 8.50), is always glorified by the Father (8.54). Hence Jesus can say, 'Glorify the Son that the Son may glorify you' (17.1), and when the hour has come for Jesus to be glorified (12.23) he can say, 'Father glorify your name' (12.28). The glory of God and the glory of Jesus are two sides of the same coin. As Jesus glorifies God throughout the ministry, so God glorifies Jesus throughout the ministry as it is recorded in the 'Book of Signs'.

Brown calls the last portion of the Gospel the 'Book of Glory' (13-20)[3] with good reason. This portion of the Gospel focusses on 'the hour' which contains the greatest manifestation of the glory of Jesus known to the Gospel; 'the hour', which includes the death, resurrection, and ascension of Jesus, is characterized as the glorification of Jesus (12.16, 23, 28; 13.31-32).[4] Hence for the Fourth Gospel, the prime manifestation of the glory of Jesus has occurred in the past.

The Gospel offers several hints that another prime locus for Jesus' glory lies even further in the past. Jesus' glory is that he had received because the Father loved him before the foundation of the world (17.24); it is the glory he had with God before the world was (17.5). In Johannine thought it is hard to see how the Spirit of truth can glorify Jesus by announcing the things which belong to Jesus without announcing the glory which Jesus had before the foundation of the world, during his ministry, and especially during 'the hour' in which the Son of man was glorified. Declaring this glory of Jesus, as the Gospel of John does,[5] requires revelation concerning the past.[6]

1. Westcott, xcviii; Nicol, 123.
2. 'Er, der Geist, enthüllt ja die in Jesu Wort und Tat und Weg verborgene und doch wirksame *Doxa*' (Heinrich Schlier, 'Der Heilige Geist als Interpret nach dem Johannesevangelium', *Der Geist und die Kirche. Exegetische Aufsätze und Vorträge* 4 [Freiburg: Herder, 1980], 173. Cf. Mußner, 'Parakletsprüche', 63).
3. Brown, *John*, 29.cxxxviii.
4. Blank, 267; Bornkamm, 'Paraklet', 86; Nicol, 129.
5. Windisch, *Spirit-Paraclete*, 12; Mußner, *Historical Jesus*, 64; Sasse, 274; Hoskyns, 66.
6. But declaring Jesus' glory also includes other kinds of revelation. In the two passages in which the Gospel uses δοξάζω first in the aorist then in the future, the future verb may refer to a manifestation of Jesus' glory subsequent to 'the hour' (Brown, *John*, 29a.606). Jesus requests that his disciples would be where he is to

The Spirit of truth will also announce the things to come (16.13).[1] In the context of this promise, Jesus has so thoroughly announced the things to come that it is hard to resist the conclusion that the Fourth Gospel contains everything about the future which the author thinks the community needs to know.[2] At least it is hard to see how the Spirit of truth could adequately announce the things to come without including the warnings of persecution and the promises of Jesus' coming and help which the Gospel records. The argument is not that the Spirit must only reinterpret the words of Jesus when announcing the things to come or the things belonging to Jesus, but only that in Johannine thought the Spirit must reinterpret the words and deeds of Jesus to announce adequately the things to come or to glorify Jesus.

The Gospel then is conscious of the fulfillment of the interpretive, reminding work of the Paraclete. Like the Paraclete, the Fourth Gospel serves to remind its readers of the words and deeds of Jesus and to interpret them properly. Furthermore, the Gospel announces things to come and glorifies Jesus by announcing the things belonging to Jesus. Since the Gospel performs precisely those functions it attributes to the backward glance of the Spirit, in all likelihood it is a manifestation of the retrospective work of the Spirit. The Gospel of John is a work of inspired history.

This section began by noticing the relationship between the gospel and the beloved disciple; the beloved disciple guarantees the contents of the Gospel by his own eyewitness testimony (21.24; cf. 19.35). It continued by noticing the presupposition of revelation by the Paraclete-Spirit concerning the deeds of Jesus and by showing how this also serves as a guarantee of the gospel. One of the Paraclete promises holds together the eyewitness and revelational basis for belief about Jesus:

---

see his glory (17.24). Whether this experience occurs after the disciples' death or before as I suspect, it is apparently an experience of the glory of Jesus *after* the hour.

1. Interpreters who equate apocalyptic thought with apocalyptic eschatology worry about this promise of revelation concerning the future in John where 'apocalyptic' categories have present reference. See Bultmann, *John*, 575; Brown, *John*, 29a.715, 716; Mußner, *Historical Jesus*, 65. When interpreted of the kinds of future things the gospel does announce (persecutions, help from the Paraclete, some eschatological concepts) the phrase creates no problem. Revelation in John has the same scope (past, present, future) as it has in virtually all other apocalyptic, prophetic, or mantic circles of the day.

2. Barrett (*St. John*, 490) also looks to the context to define the future things but concludes that both events of the passion and of eschatology are meant.

1. ὅταν ἔλθῃ ὁ παράκλητος
2. ὃν ἐγὼ πέμψω ὑμῖν παρὰ τοῦ πατρός
3. τὸ πνεῦμα τῆς ἀληθείας ὃ παρὰ τοῦ πατρὸς ἐκπορεύεται
4. ἐκεῖνος μαρτυρήσει περὶ ἐμοῦ
5. καὶ ὑμεῖς δὲ μαρτυρεῖτε
6. ὅτι ἀπ' ἀρχῆς μετ' ἐμοῦ ἐστε (15.26-27).

Lines 1 and 4 promise the Paraclete's witness; lines 5 and 6 describe the disciples' witness. Since the context assumes witness in the face of a hostile world (15.18-25; 16.1-4) and since the world cannot perceive the Spirit (14.17), the witness of the Spirit must occur in the witness of the disciples.[1] The Spirit speaking through the disciples to their enemies harmonizes well with synoptic tradition and with the Johannine conception of the Spirit revealing Jesus to the disciples (14.25-26; 16.12-15). One component necessary for true witnessing concerning Jesus is inspiration. When the disciples witness they speak as prophets and through them the Paraclete convicts the world of sin, righteousness, and judgment (Jn 16.5-11).[2] Another component of the disciples' witness concerns their being with Jesus from the beginning. The present tense of both verbs (lines 5 and 6 above) is significant. The disciples are continually with Jesus witnessing to him. Jesus who has been with the disciples from the beginning, will come to them after the brief space of the 'hour'. The present tense (μετ' ἐμοῦ ἐστε) includes in the disciples' witness their present experience of Jesus;[3] ἀπ' ἀρχῆς anchors their present experience securely to the past. The disciples' experience of Jesus from the beginning and the testimony of the Paraclete which interprets their experience of Jesus together make up the disciples' witness. The object of this witness, as shown by περὶ ἐμοῦ, is Jesus and, as shown by ἀπ' ἀρχῆς, includes the past. The disciples' witness therefore unites their experience of Jesus, which for John is itself revelation, with the witness of the Spirit of truth about Jesus: it contains inspired speech about the past.

The Fourth Gospel maintains a link between revelation and witness throughout.[4] John the Baptist witnesses to Jesus when God reveals to him who Jesus is (Jn 1.31-34). The Father testifies to Jesus as do the works the Father gives to Jesus (5.31-38). The Scriptures testify to

---

1. Mußner, 'Parakletsprüche', 60; *Historical Jesus*, 38, 61; Blank, 332; Brown, *John*, 29a.15. Windisch (*Spirit-Paraclete*, 9) makes the Spirit stand independently beside the disciples as a witness.
2. Blank (215) and Brown (*John*, 29a.690) point out the similarities to the Lucan concept of witness (Acts 1.8; Lk. 24.27).
3. Blank, 215; Brown, *John*, 29a.690; Nicol, 125-26.
4. Painter (10-11) well summarizes the 'complex network of witness' in John.

Jesus (5.39). Jesus witnesses concerning himself (8.14). True witness in John relies on revelation. Therefore, when the editors attribute the Gospel to the beloved disciple and describe his act of writing as μαρτυρῶν περὶ τούτων and as ἀληθὴς μαρτυρία (Jn 21.24; cf. 19.35), they not only claim for the Gospel the superiority of his experience of Jesus which goes back to a privileged closeness in the ministry of Jesus but also presuppose the inspiration which any true witness has.[1] The Gospel of John is revealed history.

Although not as clearly as those in the Fourth Gospel, a number of passages in the first letter of John seem to assume a doctrine of revelation directed toward the past. The letter presupposes two opposing groups, each claiming to know God and to have life in him. Life and death hinge on discerning which of these two groups remains in God. 1 John lists a variety of characteristics of divine life in the believer which can assure its readers that they belong to God and which serve to distinguish the 'true' life of God as experienced in the author's group from the 'counterfeit' life claimed by the group he opposes. Not surprisingly several of these assurances pertain to the believer's experience of revelation from God.

The author speaks of an 'anointing' (χρῖσμα) which teaches his readers concerning everything (περὶ πάντων), and he urges them to trust it (1 Jn 2.20, 21, 27). The context contrasts those who deceive (τῶν πλανώντων, 2.26; ἀντίχριστοι, 2.18, cf. 22; ὁ ψεύστης, 2.22) with this anointing. The issue concerns proper recognition of who Jesus is (2.22-24). Discerning accurately that Jesus is the Christ (2.22) demands remaining in what the readers heard from the beginning and trusting the anointing which teaches them (compare the witness from the beginning and from the Paraclete in Jn 15.26-27). In this passage from 1 John, the necessity of discerning who Jesus is by revelation is clear even if the reference to the past is fuzzy—possible but not explicit. True Christians are distinguished by an anointing which teaches them that Jesus is the Christ.

In a related passage the author distinguishes between the spirit of truth and the spirit of deceit (1 Jn 4.6). Since he speaks of false prophets, of testing spirits to see whether they are from God (4.2), and of true and false speech connected with the Spirit (4.2, 5-6), the author is concerned with speech inspired by one spirit or another, that is, with

---

1. Culpepper (*Johannine School*, 269) binds the Paraclete and the beloved disciple yet more closely together: the community interpreted the Paraclete promises by what the beloved disciple did.

true and false prophecy.[1] Faced with two people claiming to speak by the Spirit of truth, the Johannine Christian can distinguish the true from the false by what the Spirit reveals about who Christ was. A spirit is from God if it reveals Jesus Christ come in the flesh; if it does not confess Jesus (or if it annuls Jesus) it is not from God. Clearly the letters presuppose controversy over christology. This passage raises the possibility that rival Paraclete-prophets have perceived the glory of Jesus differently (Jn 16.14) and that Paraclete-memory produced rival interpretations of what Jesus said and did.[2] The author of the first letter of John does not deny the reality of inspiration directed toward the past. Both groups are inspired, but one has listened to the wrong spirit.[3] The author defines the true Spirit in terms of what it inspires concerning what has happened in Jesus.

A similar set of ideas surfaces again later in the same chapter (1 Jn 4.13-15). These verses describe two ways to discern who remains in God. 'By this we know that we remain in him and he in us, that he has given us from (partitive ἐκ) his Spirit' (4.13). 'Whosoever confesses that Jesus is the Son of God; God remains in him and he in God' (4.15). The passages already analysed and the inclusion formed by 13a and 15b argue that these are two different ways of saying the same thing. The gift of the Spirit of God (cf. 4.2) proves that its possessor remains in God and God in him; the proper confession (4.15a) proves that he or she has received the right spirit. Since the surrounding verses speak of the Spirit and his effects, probably v. 14 does also, and indeed 'We have beheld and we witness that the Father sent the Son as

---

1. Because every Johannine Christian makes the confession, Brown (*The Epistles of John* [AB 30; Garden City, NY: Doubleday, 1982], 489-90, 503-506) downplays the connection with prophecy, but in the Johannine community every believer is able to speak for God and hence is a prophet. See D. Moody Smith, 'Johannine Christianity: Some Reflections on its Character and Delineation', *NTS* 21 (1975), 233; *John*, 83. Stephen S. Smalley (*1, 2, 3 John* [WBC 51; Waco, Texas: Word, 1984], 218) likewise makes the connection with prophecy.

2. Painter (541) concludes that the thrust toward tradition in 1 John has crowded out the role of Spirit. Smith (*John*, 86), however, though admitting the obvious importance of tradition in 1 John, points out how meager is the body of tradition the author can bring to bear against his opponents. 1 John does not retreat from Spirit-inspired utterance, but like the Gospel of John, stresses the unity of the Spirit's witness with what was heard from the beginning. See Whitacre, 145, 167. Dunn, 352-53: 'We should simply note that in 1 John a similar balance between present inspiration and the original Kerygma is consistently and firmly maintained.'

3. Though unprovable, it is attractive to suppose that the opponents had another inspired view of what happened in Jesus—that in the *Ascension of Isaiah* or the *Odes of Solomon*?

savior of the world' (4.14) reads like a result of the gift of the Spirit (cf. Jn 15.26-27). The argument presupposes revelation about the past. Those who belong to God know what God has done in Jesus because he has shown them by his Spirit. Therefore they witness that God has sent (notice the aorist) his Son as savior of the world; they confess that Jesus is the Son of God.

A final passage from 1 John builds on similar concepts but contains many difficulties (1 Jn 5.6-12). In 1 John the witness of the Spirit probably refers to the witness the Spirit bears to Jesus, for the author has already connected the Spirit with witness (1 Jn 4.14; cf. Jn 15.26-27). If the water and blood allude to the issue from Jesus' side (Jn 19.34),[1] the three witnesses form the same unity between historical event and interpretation by the Spirit which the fourth gospel exhibits.[2] No indication from the context dissociates the witness of God (1 Jn 5.9) from the witness of the three;[3] if the witness of the three denotes the unity of revelatory event and revelatory interpretation (1 Jn 4.7-8), then it may logically be called the witness of God[4] who worked both. The witness is further defined in 1 Jn 5.11, 'And this is the witness: God has given to us eternal life, and this life is in his Son.'[5] The Spirit, water, and blood, a unity of revelatory event and interpretation, testify to the life which God gave in his Son.[6]

Hence 1 John presupposes just the concern for revelation of the past already seen in the Gospel. The Johannine school so values revelation of the past that it alludes to it repeatedly even in a document not directed to the past. Stemming from such a climate of thought, the Gospel of John must reflect the school's (or one portion of the school's) perception of inspired history. As the Spirit of truth recalls the words of Jesus and teaches concerning them, as he glorifies Jesus and reveals the things to come, as he witnesses to Jesus, so the Fourth Gospel reminds, teaches, witnesses and glorifies. The Spirit-Paraclete

1. An important idea to the Johannine school whatever it means. Note the emphasis in the following verse (19.35).

2. Is this same unity hinted in the tenses in 1 Jn 4.14? τεθεάμεθα (perfect) μαρτυροῦμεν (present).

3. With Smalley, 274, 283; against Brown, *Epistles*, 586-87.

4. 1 John has identified Spirit of God (4.2, cf. 13) with the Spirit of truth (4.6). Witness of God in the Gospel refers to the deeds he gave Jesus to do and perhaps also the words he gave Jesus to speak. That God should witness through events in Jesus' ministry and through the Spirit who like Jesus speaks what he hears makes good Johannine sense.

5. The witness may extend to v. 12 (cf. Brown, *Epistles*, 591).

6. This works whether the imagery behind water and blood be sacramental or sacrificial.

and the gospel do the same things. The Gospel is an expression of what the Paraclete reveals in the Johannine community; it is the school's prophetic history of Jesus.

The Goal of Historical Revelation: Grasping the Revelation in Jesus

To what purpose does the Gospel of John use revealed history? Answering this question should not only confirm the presence of revealed history in John but also contribute to a better understanding of the Fourth Gospel and of revealed history. An answer must consider the following cluster of ideas.

1. Jesus brings revelation from heaven as God's representative and antitype. To perceive this revelation is life.
2. Though Jesus brings all revelation only those who receive divine insight can perceive that revelation.
3. Unlocking who Jesus is begins during the ministry of Jesus but continues into the author's present and future.
4. The Gospel is written to present all the keys—past, present, and in the Paraclete, even future—that readers may believe Jesus is the Son of God and have life.

Unpacking each of these ideas should cast light on the purpose of revealed history in John.

The perfect revelation in Jesus has several aspects. As prophet *par excellence* Jesus speaks precisely what God gives him to say. As God's antitype Jesus acts as God's agent or representative. Jesus' descent and ascent draws upon the revelatory repertoire of apocalypticism. Investigation of these aspects will contribute to understanding the revelatory significance to the Fourth Gospel of what Jesus did and said.

Although the Gospel of John finds the title 'prophet' inadequate for Jesus,[1] it stresses the prophetic origin of Jesus' speech.[2] Jesus speaks precisely what God gives him to say.[3] As one who speaks the words of

---

1. John accepts the title as an initial recognition that Jesus speaks from God (4.19; 6.14; 7.40, 52; 9.17). Cf. Wayne A. Meeks, *The Prophet King: Moses Traditions and the Johannine Christology* (Supp. Nov. T. 14; Leiden: Brill, 1967), 34-35. See also Michaels, 235-41; Brown, *John*, 29a.632.

2. Even the signs Jesus does in John have prophetic affinities. 'They are the counterpart of the symbolic acts of the Old Testament prophets' (Boring, 'The Influence of Christian Prophecy', 121).

3. See for example Jn 3.31; 5.36; 7.16; 8.26-27, 28, 38; 12.49; 14.24; 15.15.

God, Jesus surpasses every other prophetic or apocalyptic seer.[1] John specifically shows how Jesus and his message surpass Moses and his message (1.17, 21; 9.28-29; 5.45-46).[2] Since Abraham and Jacob also were important revelatory figures by the first century,[3] the passages in John which show Jesus of greater importance than these patriarchs (Abraham, 8.33-40, 53-57; Jacob, 4.5, 6, 12; cf. 1.51) may make a similar point: the words of Jesus surpass in importance those of Moses, Abraham, and Jacob. Jesus underscores the importance of his word by flatly contradicting many prophetic or apocalyptic claims. No one has ascended to heaven but the one who has descended (3.13); no one has seen God at any time but Jesus has made him known (Jn 1.18; 5.37; 6.46; cf. 1 Jn 4.12).[4] Such statements stress the supreme importance of Jesus' words. They are the words of eternal life (Jn 5.24; 6.63, 68; 12.49-50). Paraphrasing Moses in Deuteronomy the Johannine Jesus might say, 'The word is not in heaven but I have brought it. Choose life and keep my command' (Deut. 30.11-15; cf. Rom. 10.6-8).[5] The Johannine Jesus, as the perfect prophet, has brought the perfect revelation. As Moses brought Torah which speaks of Jesus, so Jesus brings the words of life. As Moses delivered Torah to the people so Jesus delivers his word to his disciples.[6] 'Everything which I have heard from the Father I have made known to you' (Jn 15.15). 'The words which you [the Father] gave to me, I have given to them' (17.8). In John, Jesus' words are the words of God. Everything hinges on hearing, keeping and receiving them. In bringing revelation from heaven Jesus brings God's words as prophet *par excellence*.

In John Jesus is God's agent[7] and more than his agent, the bearer of his name (Jn 5.43; 10.25; 17.6, 26) and of his glory (Jn 17.5, 22, 24).[8]

---

1. The distinction between prophetic and apocalyptic thought is modern. The first century interpreted the prophets in apocalyptic categories.

2. Meeks, *passim*, shows how the superiority of Jesus over Moses extends throughout the Gospel.

3. See *Apocalypse of Abraham, Jubilees, Testaments of the Twelve Patriarchs*.

4. Meeks, 299. In the Gospel such statements are probably made against Jewish, non-Christian claims to revelation (Brown, *John*, 29.145), in 1 John perhaps against Christian.

5. Meeks, 300.

6. Meeks, 287-91.

7. Peder Borgen, 'God's Agent in the Fourth Gospel', *Religions in Antiquity: Essays in Memory of E.R. Goodenough* (ed. J. Neusner; Leiden: Brill, 1968), 137-47.

8. Judaism already knew such heavenly vice-regents of God. Jaoel in *Ap. Ab.* 10, who bears the ineffable name and rules the throne of Glory, Metatron, the lesser YHWH (*3 En.* 12.5; 48C.7; 48D.1 [90]) who also tends the throne, and that Son of

To see Jesus is to see the Father (12.45; 14.9; cf. 1.18). Jesus exercises the authority and power of God, acting in his stead. Jesus does God's works (5.17, 19, 36; 10.25, 32, 37-38; 13.31; 14.10). Like the Father, Jesus raises the dead (5.21; 6.40), judges (5.22), has life (1.4; 5.26) and gives it (10.28). Jesus creates (1.3). What belongs to God belongs to Jesus (3.35; 5.20; 10.29; 13.3; 16.15). To honor the Son is to honor the Father (5.23). Jesus and God are in some sense identified (1.1; 5.18; 10.30, 38; 14.10, 11, 20; 17.21) though the Father is greater than Jesus (14.28). Most importantly, to know Jesus is to know God (1.18; 8.19; 12.45; 14.6-9). To know God and Jesus is to have life (6.40; 17.3). It is of utmost importance then to grasp Jesus' revelation of the Father to which Jesus' works as well as his words contribute.

The Fourth Gospel views Jesus' descent and ascent as an apocalyptic disclosure.[1] As in Daniel, *4 Ezra* 7.1, *2 Baruch* 55, *Jubilees* 1.27-29, and Revelation 1–3, so in John a heavenly emissary descends from God to bring revelation (1.9; 3.13; 3.31; 6.38; 13.3; etc.). As seers falsely claim to *ascend* to heaven to see God (*Ap. Ab.* 15; Rev. 4; *Ascen. Isa.* 6–11)[2] so Jesus *descends* to make God known. This contrast is explicitly drawn: no one has ever seen God at any time, Jesus has made him known (1.18; cf. 6.46). 'No one has ascended to heaven except the one who has descended from heaven, the Son of man' (3.13). In a difficult verse (1.51) Jesus promises that Nathanael will see the heavens opened and angels ascending and descending on the Son of man. The Fourth Gospel applies a description appropriate to a heavenly trip to what Nathanael will soon witness in Jesus' ministry.[3] As those who claim to see the heavens opened describe angels ascending and

man in the *Similitudes of Enoch. 3 Enoch*, though admittedly late, continues many early traditions. I accept the early date for the *Similitudes*; cf. M.A. Knibb, 'The Date of the Parables of Enoch: A Critical Review', *NTS* 25 (1979), 345-59; J.H. Charlesworth, 'The SNTS Pseudepigrapha Seminars at Tübingen and Paris on the Books of Enoch', *NTS* 25 (1979), 315-23.

1. Cf. 'The apocalypticism of Revelation and the Gnostic-like conceptuality of the Gospel and Epistles of John may not stem from entirely different worlds' (Smith, 'Johannine Christianity', 234-35). See also Otto Böcher, 'Johanneisches in der Apokalypse des Johannes', *NTS* 27 (1981), 310-21, especially 318-19.

2. Michaels (253) finds in John polemic against prophets who claim to ascend to heaven. While the Gospel *may* not rule out heavenly trips by Christians, I see little to support Aune's conjecture that new birth is a qualification for heavenly trips. See Aune, *Realized Eschatology*, 100.

3. Jesus promises Nathanael will see greater things (1.50). Jacob's dream at Bethel (cf. Jn 1.51) was often considered a revelation of things to come. Cf. Hugo Odeberg, *The Fourth Gospel* (Uppsala: Almquist & Wiksells, 1929), 33-35. In *Jub.* 27.25 Jacob says of Bethel, 'this is the gate of heaven'.

descending in service to the heavenly throne, so Nathanael will see angels ascending and descending in service to Jesus; he will see Jesus' glory (2.11) and the glory of God (11.40).[1] The Fourth Gospel views the activity of Jesus as an inverted heavenly trip replete with revelation. Rather than the community ascending to heaven to see the Father, the Son has descended to make him known.

Hence the Fourth Gospel views the ministry of Jesus as heavy with revelation. Jesus delivered a perfectly complete message more important than that of any prophet. His actions, which were those of God, revealed God. From start to finish his ministry and everything that happened in it surpassed in revelatory import apocalyptic vision whether brought by a heavenly being or acquired on a heavenly trip. To glimpse this revelation, to grasp it and receive it in its various aspects, is life.

As apocalyptic visions frequently reveal little without further revelation to interpret them, so the perfect disclosure in Jesus requires further revelation. The truth in Jesus cannot be perceived except by divine insight.[2] Jesus is incognito. The world does not know him (1.10; 8.43); it cannot understand what he says (8.27; 10.6). Apart from revelation, even John the Baptist does not know him (1.31, 33). Unless begotten from above one cannot perceive the Kingdom of God (3.3). To receive Jesus one must be taught by God (6.45), be drawn by the Father (6.44), be given by God to Jesus (6.37, 65; 10.29), or be one of his sheep who alone hear his voice and follow him (10.4-5, 14, 26-28). Hence, apart from the activity of God no-one could perceive the revelation abundantly given in Jesus.

The Gospel grants various levels of understanding to those who receive or believe in Jesus. Those who reject him are blind (9.39-41); they know neither Jesus nor the Father (8.19; 16.3). Others believe that Jesus is from God but are untrustworthy (2.23–3.2) or do not remain in Christ's word (8.31).[3] Those who persist become disciples and know the truth (8.31-32). They perceive that he has the words of eternal life (6.68); they believe that he was sent from God (17.8). The beloved disciple may have a special status; he lies in the bosom of Jesus

---

1. Cf. John Painter, *John: Witness and Theologian* (London: SPCK, 1975), 56. Brown (*John*, 29.132-33) interprets the perfect tense (ἀναβέβηκεν) in Jn 3.13 to imply that Jesus throughout the ministry 'remains close to the Father when he is on earth (i 18)'.

2. The dialogue of Jesus with Nicodemus is a 'parody of a revelation discourse. What is revealed is that Jesus is incomprehensible'. (Wayne A. Meeks, 'The Man from Heaven in Johannine Sectarianism', *JBL* 91 [1972], 57).

3. See the movement of believers away from Jesus in chs. 6 and 8.

to make him known as Jesus lies in the bosom of the Father to make
him known (1.18; cf. 13.23). He is first to recognize Jesus and point
him out to the disciples (21.7); he alone believes without seeing.

Yet the evangelist specifically points out how much even the most
privileged disciples do not perceive. Right after the beloved disciple
believes without seeing (20.8) he underlines the ignorance of all the
disciples including the one Jesus loved: οὐδέπω γὰρ ᾔδεισαν τὴν
γραφὴν ὅτι δεῖ αὐτὸν ἐκ νεκρῶν ἀναστῆναι (20.9).[1] Emphasis on
Peter's denial is excruciating. Though exposed to strong testimony,
Thomas cannot believe without seeing (20.24-28). Mary Magdalene
cannot recognize Jesus when he is revealed to her (20.15).[2] In the last
discourse, the misunderstanding questions, which all along have underscored the failure of the world to perceive who Jesus is, for the first
time come from disciples.[3] Peter questions Jesus' desire to wash his
feet (13.8). Thomas denies that he knows the way where Jesus goes and
asks for it (14.4). Philip asks Jesus to show him the Father; he had not
known Jesus (14.8, 9). Judas asks how Jesus can manifest himself to
them and not to the world (14.22). All the disciples wish to ask Jesus
concerning the saying about the 'little while' but are afraid to do so
(16.17). When finally they think they understand (16.29-30) Jesus
dashes their confidence: their belief is woefully defective; they will all
forsake Jesus (16.31-33).

Hence, though the disciples have perceived darkly, though they have
believed that Jesus has the words of life, that God sent him, though
Jesus has given them the full message from the Father,[4] they have
grasped neither the significance of what they have seen nor the import
of what they have believed. Before the gift of the Spirit the disciples
have perceived only a modicum of that revelation brought by Jesus;
even what they have perceived comes from the teaching of God.
Though Jesus brings perfect revelation, it is closed to all unless further

1. This verse echoes Lucan wording; cf. Lk. 24.26 and especially Acts 17.3, τὸν
χριστὸν ἔδει παθεῖν καὶ ἀναστῆναι ἐκ νεκρῶν.
2. Peter, Thomas, and Mary Magdalene were held in high honor in some quarters
of the early church. Does John purposely put them down? Perhaps, but even the
beloved disciple did not fully know until afterwards.
3. Leroy concludes that the misunderstanding motif shows that all is ignorance
unless the revealer sends knowledge (Herbert Leroy, *Rätsel und Missverständnis. Ein
Beitrag zur Formgeschichte des Johannesevangeliums* [BBB 30; Bonn: Hanstein,
1968], 180).
4. Woll (101) argues, 'The obscurity and misunderstanding encountered by Jesus'
teaching is a sign, not of its inferior, earthly character, but of its heavenly,
otherworldly origin.'

revelation enables eyewitnesses to grasp what they have seen.[1] It is not enough to have been with Jesus. The acts of Jesus are like a vision which must be interpreted before the secrets it contains are known. The revelation Jesus brought requires insight from God to be perceived.

The evangelist has carefully shown his readers sources of insight into the acts and words of Jesus. These sources divide into two groups. Those which precede the gift of the Spirit provide the foundation for the partial understanding of the disciples before and during the hour. Those which follow the gift of the Spirit ground the fuller understanding promised by Jesus.

The evangelist portrays several sources of insight occurring in the ministry of Jesus. John the Baptist first announces the presence of the coming one. 'In your midst stands one whom you do not know' (1.26). Of course the Pharisees whom John addresses have not perceived Jesus, but neither has John himself. In his speech pointing out Jesus as the lamb of God (1.29-34), John twice expresses his former ignorance. This speech makes absolutely plain the necessity of revelation to perceive the revelation Jesus brings. John recognized Jesus only because God had given him a test (the one on whom you see the Spirit descend is the one who is coming) and a vision which fulfilled it (I saw the Spirit descending on Jesus, 1.33-34). To this revelation designating Jesus as the one who is coming John adds others disclosing who Jesus is: the lamb of God (1.29), the Son of God (1.34), the one preeminent over John (1.27, 30), the one for whose sake John came baptizing (1.31), the one who baptizes in the Spirit (1.33), the one on whom the Spirit remains (1.33). A second announcement of who Jesus is (1.36) motivates the first two disciples to seek Jesus (1.37). A prophecy imparting divine insight into the revelation in Jesus inaugurates both the belief of the first disciples and the revelation of Jesus in the Gospel.

Not only does John reveal who Jesus is, but Jesus reveals himself.[2] Hence, in the Fourth Gospel, he spends much time talking about himself. On the one hand such words of Jesus are part of the enigma to be interpreted as shown by how little even the disciples understand. On the other hand they do reveal clues of who Jesus is as shown by the partial comprehension of the disciples. When the man born blind believes and worships Jesus (9.38) or when the disciples meet Jesus and

---

1. See Painter, *John*, 9, 64; Culpepper, *Anatomy*, 49; Ernst Haenchen, *John 2: A Commentary on the Gospel of John Chapters 7–21* (ed. R.W. Funk, Ulrich Buss, Hermeneia; Philadelphia: Fortress, 1984), 139.

2. Windisch (*Spirit-Paraclete*, 18) speaks of three witnesses: John, Jesus, Paraclete.

announce his various titles (1.41, 45, 49), Jesus' self-revelation has reached its mark.

Even during the ministry God directly reveals who Jesus is. Again his activity is part both of the enigma and of its resolution. God gives Jesus signs and words which occasionally strike home. Although these frequently produce misunderstanding, for those who see and hear them fail to continue in Jesus' words, yet they accurately, if incompletely during the ministry, show who Jesus is. The Samaritan woman believing through Jesus' word or the disciples seeing his glory after the initial sign in Cana prove at least the limited effectiveness of these revelations. Of course, that anyone believes derives from God's revelatory activity in the believer (6.45).

Finally, the disciples reveal Jesus when they proclaim the revelation they have received whether from John the Baptist, from Jesus, or from God. The first chapter establishes a chain of such revelations. John the Baptist announces who Jesus is; Andrew listens to his message and seeks Jesus. When proclaiming Jesus to Simon, Andrew adds to the message of John his own grasp of what he has seen—Jesus is the messiah (1.41). A similar pattern inspires the portrayal of the chain of witness from Philip to Nathanael (1.41-51) and from the Samaritan woman to those in her village. These villagers well express this revelatory progression: 'They said to the woman, "No longer do we believe through your speech, for we ourselves have heard and we know that this one is truly the savior of the world"' (4.42).

Hence disciples receive divine insight into the revelation Jesus brings during the ministry of Jesus, but stress on their lack of comprehension shows how impoverished an account of Jesus would result if limited to what the disciples perceived before Jesus gave the Spirit. Hence the evangelist does not limit himself to what the disciples knew then, but avails himself of later insight from the Spirit of truth. The evangelist repeatedly acknowledges his retrospective insight into the events he relates. He describes the act of inspired remembrance which gave the disciples understanding after Jesus was glorified (2.17, 22; 12.16). The narrator interprets events by knowledge later acquired:[1] the Spirit was not yet because Jesus was not yet glorified (7.39). As mentioned previously, Jesus frequently looks forward to a time when the disciples will understand. The Paraclete promises (14.25-26; 15.26-27; 16.12-15), the promise of future plain speech (16.25), the promise that the disciples will not need to question Jesus (16.23), the things said to be remembered later (16.1, 4), and the acknowledgments that though the

---

1. Culpepper, *Anatomy*, 28.

disciples do not now understand, they will later (13.7),[1] all imply that revelation given once in Jesus is later unlocked by the Spirit. On its own premises, if the Fourth Gospel wants to give an accurate picture of what happened in Jesus, it must incorporate retrospective revelatory insight into the revelation brought by Jesus.

Both kinds of divine insight into the revelation brought by Jesus, that before and after the gift of the Spirit, are significant in the Gospel of John. Disciples in the evangelist's day need the insights granted the disciples in Jesus' day as well as those given later by the Spirit. If this were not so, why would the evangelist have written a Gospel? Yet if the evangelist and the school behind him took seriously the promises of the Paraclete, then both the tradition behind the Fourth Gospel[2] and the Gospel itself must take advantage of the insight into the past given by the Paraclete. The evangelist takes no interest in distinguishing insights into the revelation Jesus brought during his ministry from those given later. Hence, to use a metaphor drawn from an apocalyptic form, the evangelist has not recorded first vision (the ministry of Jesus as remembered by the disciples apart from the insight given later) then its interpretation (including the understanding which came later from the Paraclete)[3] but has intermingled the two. Or better, since apocalyptic interpretations customarily include a restatement of the vision as well as its revealed meaning, the Gospel of John is the 'interpretation' alone.

To what purpose does the Gospel of John use inspired history? The book tells us its own purpose, 'These things have been written that you should believe that Jesus is the Christ, the Son of God, and that believing you should have life in his name' (20.31).[4] Since perfect revelation which brings life has been given in Jesus but cannot be comprehended apart from divine insight and since such insight was given only incipiently during the ministry of Jesus but much more fully through the Spirit of truth which was given afterwards, the Gospel incorporates divine insights from the past right alongside

---

1. It seems unlikely that this is fulfilled in 13.12.

2. Many students of the Fourth Gospel very plausibly connect the reminding work of the Paraclete with the speeches of Jesus in John and the tradition behind them. See Windisch, *Johannes und die Synoptiker*, 135-50; Karl Kundsin, *Charakter und Ursprung der johanneischen Reden* (Acta Universitatis Latviensis, Theologijas Fakultates Serija 1.4; Riga: Latvijas Universitates Raksti, 1939), *passim*; Smith, 'Johannine Christianity', 232-33.

3. Windisch (*Spirit-Paraclete*, 18) and Schnackenburg (*St. John*, 3.146) compare the Paraclete with interpreting angels of the apocalypses.

4. Müller (50-51) and Mußner, 'Parakletsprüche' (68) connect 20.31 with the activity of the Paraclete.

insights from the present in retelling what Jesus did. The book employs inspired history to present the fullest possible understanding of what Jesus did and said. The Johannine school responsible for the Gospel may expect even fuller revelation of what Jesus said and did in the years to come. Perhaps the various editions of the Gospel posited by modern students derive from the school's continual reworking of the tradition to bring it in line with the latest perceptions from the Paraclete. Perhaps the Johannine letters reflect opposition between proponents of conflicting Paraclete-inspired insights into the work of Jesus.[1] Be that as it may, the Johannine school employs inspired history to unlock the secrets of revelation hidden in the words, deeds, and events surrounding Jesus of Nazareth. As the Teacher of Righteousness interpreted scripture or the apocalyptist interpreted visions by further revelation, so the evangelist interprets the supreme revelation in Jesus by revelation directed toward the past. He then tells what happened in Jesus replete with the fullest possible revelation of the glory in these past events so that his readers should believe that Jesus is the Christ, the Son of God, and that believing they should have life in his name.

The evangelist chose prophetic history—an inspired chronicle of the past—as the vehicle for his ideas. As noted when studying Luke, Josephus names two qualifications essential to the best historians: they are prophets and they experienced the events of their own times (*Ag. Ap.* 1.Proem.7 §§37-40).[2] The Gospel of John explicitly claims descent from an eyewitness, the beloved disciple. It presupposes inspiration from the Paraclete throughout. Perhaps when protesting its derivation from an eyewitness, the Fourth Gospel does not seek to justify itself as an objective account, but seeks to show that the author has both qualifications necessary to write a prophetic history: not only is he inspired by the Paraclete, but he is also an eyewitness.

This coincidence between Josephus' definition of good history and the evangelist's practice is striking. As an inspired eyewitness account, the Gospel of John may conform to an ideal of Jewish history writing characteristic of the first century. By claiming both eyewitness experience and prophetic inspiration the Gospel may claim to continue that succession of prophetic historians which Josephus thought had failed in the time of Artaxerxes (*Ag. Ap.* 1.Proem.8 §§39-40). Such a claim implies authority. The Gospel of John places itself on a footing equal to the 'Former Prophets'. Indeed it surpasses the Former Prophets for

---

1. Woll (128) finds such a conflict already in the Gospel. See Smith, 'Johannine Christianity', 236.
2. Cf. the discussion introducing Josephus above.

its subject is preeminent over theirs. The Gospel of John presupposes its own canonicity.[1]

Like Josephus' *Jewish War* and Luke–Acts, John fits perfectly the definition of interpretive prophetic history: the author relates events of his own time and interprets them by revelation. If Luke comes closer to presupposing the Spirit's work in his actual writing than Josephus does, John comes closer still. The Johannine evangelist seeks not merely to uncover the real meaning of past events but also to lay bare the perfect revelation concealed in all that Jesus did and said. For him that highly significant segment of the past in which Jesus had lived was replete with revelations of the highest conceivable kind. His was the great task of unlocking that revelation by the Paraclete and making it known that his readers might have life.

---

1. Windisch, *Johannes und die Synoptiker*, 149.

Chapter 14

EARLY CHRISTIAN USE OF REVEALED HISTORY:
FORMS AND IMPLICATIONS

Christian inspired histories show a marked degree of conformity to
their Jewish models. This deep-seated unity attains clearest expression
in the realm of form. Christian writers adopted all of the major genera
of inspired history from their Jewish matrix.

Surviving Christian works represent both species of prophetic history: interpretive and inspired. Luke–Acts and John have joined
Josephus' *Jewish War*. All three are interpretive prophetic histories:
they interpret by revelation past events known on other grounds.
Evidence from these three works taken together increases the
likelihood that Josephus in *Against Apion* reproduced well-known
arguments to support the excellence of Hebrew history. In preferring
Hebrew historians who record contemporary events on the basis of
their prophetic endowment to Greek historians who relied on hearsay
alone, he drew on a commonplace. The *Jewish War*, John and Luke–
Acts each take seriously both revelation of the past and connection
with eyewitnesses of past events. They attest the Hebrew view, perhaps
formed in competition with Greek historiography, that good history
must have both. On their own terms they can claim to compete favorably with the Greek historians from whom Josephus and the author of
Luke–Acts especially have borrowed much. Their accounts are not
only grounded on human observation of the facts but also upon their
true, heavenly interpretation. In the case of John and Luke–Acts the
unity of revelational and eyewitness accounts has further ramifications
as well. As works produced under the aegis of the prophetic Spirit,
John and Luke–Acts may lay claim to legitimate succession from the
former prophets. As prophets of old had recorded the history of Israel
so their successors recorded the history of Jesus. John and Luke–Acts
conform to the first-century thought on how Israel's authoritative
history books were produced and, in doing so, naively assume their
own authoritative status. The desire to succeed the former prophets
might explain Luke's Septuagintal style.

The study has also isolated two works of inspired prophetic history: *Jubilees* and the Vision in the *Ascension of Isaiah*. Both reveal events as well as their interpretations. Each grounds the doctrines normative for its group. The *Ascension of Isaiah*, in revealing the descent and ascent of the Beloved, makes it the cornerstone of right belief. By revealing how the law has been worked into the warp and woof of history, *Jubilees* discloses its excellence and underscores the necessity of keeping it. John comes close to bridging the gap between interpretive and inspired prophetic history. Though clearly claiming that unity of human observation and revelation of the past which characterizes interpretive prophetic history, it grants a larger role to inspiration. Like *Jubilees* it seeks from disclosures of the past revelations necessary for present life; John would say for eternal life.

Luke–Acts adds to the repertoire of inspired historical sermons two new kinds: apologetic and accusatory. The author of Luke–Acts chooses this form for speeches proclaiming the gospel, defending his witnesses before hostile courts, and guiding the church. All of these are prophetic occasions for Luke: they require revelation from God. Witnesses in the missions speeches proclaim that message entrusted to them by the resurrected Christ, in the defense speeches rely on the gift of words from the Spirit, and in the deliberative speeches carry out that guidance from the Spirit portrayed tirelessly in Acts. Luke portrays the historical sermon as a major form of early Christian prophecy adaptable to a variety of settings. For Luke, revelation of the past plays a major role in the early church.

The works considered have yielded no Christian apocalyptic world histories but do evidence limited apocalyptic history. The *Ascension of Isaiah* contains two limited apocalyptic histories, one reinterpreted by the other. Both follow closely their Jewish models, explaining difficult circumstances in the present by revelations of what has happened in baffling past events and continuing by revealing the end of the age soon to come. The *Shepherd of Hermas* uses this form but nearly empties it of historical interest.

Christian literature has produced one new form of revealed history: the author of the *Odes of Solomon* has produced a number of inspired songs with strong interest in disclosing the hidden meaning in the past events surrounding Christ. Since the christological hymns of Philippians 2, Colossians 1 and John 1 find their closest analog in the *Odes of Solomon*[1] circumstantial evidence favors identifying them also as

---

1. This is the conclusion of Jack T. Sanders, *New Testament Christological Hymns: Their Historical Religious Background* (SNTSMS 15; Cambridge: Cambridge University Press, 1971).

inspired historical odes (see Paul's 'Spiritual odes'). No indicators confirm a claim to inspiration for Philippians 2 or Colossians 2, but for the hymn of the Word in John 1 it is otherwise. Jesus specifically requests that his followers should be with him to see the glory the Father gave him before the foundation of the world (Jn 17.24; cf. 17.5). This well describes the kind of inspiration claimed by the odist in *Odes of Solomon* for he regularly identifies with Christ in cruciform prayer and joins him on the way to heaven. Like this odist's songs, the 'Hymn of the Word' may be an inspired historical ode.

Jewish works left the strong impression of diversity. As a persuasive technique, inspired history could take a number of forms too diverse to classify. *Shepherd of Hermas* and Luke–Acts especially use inspired history as flexibly as the Jewish works do. Paul's forensic speeches in Acts, the participial speeches concerning the pre-history of the church in *Hermas* and the parable and interpretation also in *Hermas*, though logical developments from inspired history, have too few analogs in surviving literature to qualify as genera of inspired history in their own right.

Though Christian works can use inspired history flexibly, the general impression they leave is one of greater unity than that of their Jewish counterparts. This impression of unity derives not from the genera of revealed history employed but from an overwhelming agreement on subject. By far the majority of these works seek to know about Jesus.

John, the *Odes of Solomon*, and the *Ascension of Isaiah* are bent on discovering who Jesus is and revealing his glory. For these works, salvation is tied up with correctly apprehending who Jesus is and what his words and deeds really meant. The *Ascension of Isaiah* distinguishes real Christians from false ones by belief in the descent and ascent of the Beloved. 1 John seeks to establish other criteria also based on past revelation. Though expressed variously the author clearly thinks all should 'confess Jesus Christ come in the flesh'. John views the ministry of Jesus as the locus of revelation *par excellence*. To know Jesus and the Father is eternal life. Jesus came revealing the Father. Understanding of this revelation comes from the Paraclete. John is written to illuminate this revelation so that his readers might believe and have life. The *Odes of Solomon* seems to work within similar categories. The ministry of Jesus is filled with hidden meaning. The inspired odist discloses new meaning in the birth and baptism of the messiah and in his walking on water. He also reveals deeds of the messiah otherwise imperceptible: *descensus ad inferos*, creation by the Word. All four of these works resemble one another in basing right

belief on the apprehension of Jesus gained by revelation. 1 John and
Ascension of Isaiah, and perhaps *Odes of Solomon* and John, counter
opposing prophetic groups by reaffirming their revealed versions of
who Christ is. It is too much to claim that these works are on a single
line of development. In many ways they do not seem to agree with
each other. But they attack similar problems with similar techniques.
Together they point to an embattled segment of the church for which
revelation of the past was central to faith and chief among weapons
used.

Shepherd of Hermas does not base right belief on revelation of the
past but understands by revelation the greatness of Christ: his authority
as the servant and his adoption as Son. Characteristically the revelation
supports exhortation: the shepherd urges imitation of Christ, 'refrain
from defiling the Spirit that you also may receive the reward'.

Though concerned with a revealed apprehension of who Christ is
Luke–Acts also has a wider interest. As *2 Baruch*, *4 Ezra*, *Apocalypse
of Abraham*, and Josephus' *Jewish War* must explain the inexplicable
destruction of the second Temple or as Daniel and the Animal Apocalypse must explain oppression by the Gentiles, so Luke must explain a
messiah rejected by the Jews he was to save. Luke–Acts reveals the full
plan of God. Jesus came fulfilling scripture in his death and resurrection as well as in his birth. Rejection by Jews and blessing on Gentiles
derives from God himself. By revelation Luke incorporates recent
events into salvation history.

Recognition of historical revelation in the matrix of early Christianity may help explain some well known puzzles. It may facilitate a new
understanding of early Christian prophecy and its object. An important
element in early Christian prophecy, whether directed to the past, present, or future, may have been the desire to understand Christ, who he
was, what he brought, what he does and will do, who he will be.
Christology may have been a special province of prophecy. The desire
to understand Christ and the salvation he brought by revelation unites
Paul and the Apocalypse with the works of revealed history studied
here. If so, modern students have a broader basis for understanding
early Christian prophecy than often thought. An intriguing corollary
follows: John and the Apocalypse, despite their acknowledged differences, have at least this in common: both by revelation want to
understand the glory of Christ and the present effects of his work.[1]
They differ in their decision to direct revelation primarily toward the
past earthly or primarily toward the present and future heavenly work

---

1. Hans Windisch, *Johannes und die Synoptiker* (Leipzig: Hinrichs, 1926), 148.

of the messiah. When the adjective 'apocalyptic' is recognized to mean something more than 'eschatological', John (and Luke) may well be the most 'apocalyptic' of the Gospels.

Historical revelation may provide a new ingredient in the movement from Jesus to the early church, the movement from the proclaimer to the proclaimed. One component in the shift from the message of a Jesus to that of a Paul may be apprehension of what happened in Jesus in all its cosmic and eschatological ramifications—an apprehension of Jesus based on revealed history.

Recognition of historical revelation in early Christianity may also provide a missing link between the 'historical Jesus' and the Gospels. Perhaps we must reckon not only with prophetic sayings of the resurrected Lord creeping into tradition about Jesus, but also with consciously inspired historical interpretations of the words and deeds of Jesus. If the evidence warrants positing a significant body of early Christians who sought by revelation to understand what Jesus did and meant it is not hard to imagine their interpretations shaping the tradition about Jesus. This also has an interesting corollary: some early Christians may have engaged in their own quest for the historical Jesus. Like their modern counterparts, they sought *was eigentlich gewesen ist*, but their understanding of historical explanation and methodology differed radically from the modern. The ancient and modern quests work at cross-purposes. The modern questers, intensely aware that they do not have eyewitness accounts of what the earthly Jesus said and did, seek to establish what an impartial modern observer would have seen. The ancient questers, intensely aware of the inadequacies of eyewitness accounts, sought by revelation to situate what Jesus said and did in the heavenly and earthly acts of God which gave them meaning. It is hoped that the present study will spawn not only a new understanding of some of the dynamics which shaped the tradition about Jesus, hence yielding the modern quest a new tool, but also a new appreciation of what early Christians wanted to do with their tradition about Jesus. Since they wanted to understand more about Jesus than a human perceiver would see, many of them inquired into the past by revelation.

Chapter 15

CONCLUSION

This study began with several questions: How widespread is revelation directed toward the past in the milieu shared by the Fourth Gospel and ancient Jewish apocalypses? In what ways was it used? What forms does it take? How does taking it seriously help in understanding the works in which it appears? It is fitting to conclude by summarizing answers to these questions.

What forms does revealed history take? While revealed history is much more than the sum of certain forms, it does divide neatly into genera and species. Prophetic histories base a chronicle of past events on revelation. Like *Jewish War*, Luke–Acts, or John, prophetic histories may be interpretive or, like *Jubilees* and the Vision of Isaiah, they may be inspired. Inspired prophetic histories receive both the knowledge of the events and their interpretations by revelation; interpretive prophetic histories base knowledge of events on direct or indirect experience but receive by revelation an interpretation of these events. The chief goal of prophetic histories is always to recount and understand past events. For this reason interpretive prophetic histories can approximate Greek history writing.

Inspired historical sermons probably develop from an oral prophetic form. They have two major parts: the historical resume in which a divine being or prophet recounts past events and the consequence which draws a conclusion from the historical summary in the résumé. Historical sermons occur throughout *Liber Antiquitatum Biblicarum* and Luke–Acts and also in Judith, the *Jewish War*, *4 Ezra*, and Daniel. The form enters our period already fixed. It occurs not only in Ezekiel but also in other prophets and in Judges. Between 200 BCE and 130 CE the form has considerable flexibility and power. Five different species of historical prophecy can be isolated and defined depending on the type of consequence drawn. The consequence can be a sentence (judicial historical sermons), a general principle (inductive historical sermons), an exhortation (hortative historical sermons), a defense (apologetic historical sermons), or an accusation (accusatory historical sermons). Judicial and hortative historical sermons predominate in the works studied.

Apocalyptic histories are vision reports, visions and interpretations, or heavenly travelogues which begin by recounting events in the apocalyptists' past before considering the present and future. Apocalyptic histories which review world history from creation to consummation, such as *1 Enoch* 83–90, *2 Baruch* 53–74, and *Apocalypse of Abraham* 21–32, are apocalyptic world histories. Apocalypses, such as those in Daniel, *Ascension of Isaiah* and *Shepherd of Hermas*, which review a segment of world history are limited apocalyptic histories. Apocalyptic histories of either type, whether Christian or Jewish, seek to explain some perplexing period of world history in which God's activity is puzzling and appears unjust.

Of course many revelations of the past resist classification according to form. Authors modified and invented forms at need. Certain works show great flexibility in the use of revealed history. Foremost among these are *4 Ezra*, *Jubilees*, and Luke–Acts. On the basis of the sample studied such a list should also include *Sibylline Oracles* and *Shepherd of Hermas*, though I suspect these works have borrowed forms current in their hellenistic-Roman environment.

How widespread was revealed history in the milieu shared by the Fourth Gospel and the ancient Jewish apocalypses? Revealed history was not only widespread but pervasive. It was used by writings on continua from the most to the least literary pretension, from the most vehemently Hebrew (*Jubilees*) to the most complacently Greek (*Sibylline Oracles*), from serious history writing to mere illustration.

It is pervasive as to time. Revealed history enters the period studied in fully-fledged form in such works as the Animal Apocalypse, *Jubilees*, and Daniel and exits thriving in the spate of works immediately before the Bar Kochba revolt (*Apocalypse of Abraham*, *Ascension of Isaiah*). It concentrates at certain periods of stress in which enigmatic periods of history require special explanation. Jewish works cluster around the Antiochan period (*Jubilees*, Daniel, Animal Apocalypse) and the destruction of Jerusalem in 70 CE (*2 Baruch*, *Apocalypse of Abraham*, *4 Ezra*, Josephus, *Sibylline Oracle* 4). Christian works, because of their interest in understanding Jesus, cluster less clearly around such difficult periods, but the necessity to explain the separation of Christians from the Synagogue (John, Luke–Acts) or the present sorry plight of the Church and rejection of the community (*Ascension of Isaiah*) show the principle operating still.

Individual genera of revealed history concentrate in certain periods. The last quarter of the first century CE saw a remarkable flowering of prophetic history; Luke–Acts, John, the *Jewish War*—all the interpretive prophetic histories of which I am aware—were written in this period. In *Against Apion* Josephus expressed the theory then current for the composition of the historical books in the Hebrew scriptures: in them prophets were inspired to understand and write events of their own times. Luke–Acts and John stem from communities experiencing a recent, powerful upsurge in prophecy. Current Hebrew historical theory required the best historians to be prophets, the best histories to be prophetic histories. Being prophets themselves and knowing many applicable prophetic oracles form other prophets, the authors of Luke–Acts and John set out to write prophetic histories. They naturally supposed that the current theory of how the ancient historical books were written described how a prophet should write history. Both take pains to show that the necessary elements underlie their work: Luke–Acts and John emphasize connection with the events by underscoring their connection with eyewitnesses; both lay claim to inspiration by showing the inspiration of these witnesses and by adopting their messages. John even lays claim to be written by an eyewitness. Probably Luke and almost certainly the author of John assume the working of the Spirit through them in the composition of their works. They undertake different tasks. Luke–Acts seeks to reveal the plan of God in history; hence Luke writes Acts as well as Luke. John seeks to reveal Jesus and the revelation in him. Perhaps neither would have been surprised at the canonical status their works achieved. After all, in an era of the Spirit's renewed outpouring they had consciously set out to imitate books already acknowledged to be authoritative. Without the advantage of a recent outpouring of the Spirit, Josephus imitates the ancient prophets with more reserve. Throughout his work the locus for revelation remains the cave at Jotapata and the call he received there. His work does not presuppose the working of the Spirit in its composition. Yet he too deliberately claims to be writing the best kind of history, prophetic history. At the end of the first century the right juxtaposition of ideas brought about these three interpretive prophetic histories.

Apocalyptic histories contribute to the clusters of revealed history around the Antiochan persecution and the fall of the second temple. Surviving extensive apocalyptic histories explain the confusing period culminating with Antiochus or the confusing period beginning with the Jewish War and continuing in its aftermath. This concentration discloses something essential to apocalyptic history: it thrives on uncomfortable periods in which history makes no sense according to normal Hebrew presuppositions and where deliverance is sorely needed.

Historical sermons are widely scattered in the period; yet the two works that utilize them most—*LAB* and Luke–Acts—were written within fifty years of each other. No good explanation for this suggests itself, but it may reflect a general trend.

Although revelation of the past occurs throughout the period studied, surviving works indicate a rising interest in revealed history in the second half of the first century CE. Luke–Acts, John, Josephus, *2 Baruch*, *4 Ezra*, *Odes of Solomon*, *Ascension of Isaiah*, *Shepherd of Hermas*, *Apocalypse of Abraham*, and *Sibylline Oracles* 4 were all written in the last quarter of the first century CE or the first quarter of the second. It is possible to trace this remarkable conjunction of works in part to the difficulties of the period, but another factor is also necessary. This period acknowledged the presuppositions of revealed history and recognized the value of arguments based upon them. Only because revealed history was widely respected at this period could so many authors have chosen it as their weapon against the difficulties of the day.

Jewish and Christian revealed history is also widespread geographically. Works considered here stem from everywhere on the eastern Mediterranean between Egypt and Rome. Again, however, interesting clusters appear. Sibylline literature has a special but not exclusive affinity for Egypt. *Jubilees*, Daniel, and the Animal Apocalypse stem from Palestine in the mid-second century BCE. *2 Baruch*, *4 Ezra* and *Apocalypse of Abraham* are also Palestinian and roughly contemporary (late first, early second century CE). Interesting correlations appear within some of these groups. Frequently there are connections of thought or even literary relationships between works from a given place and time. These clusters probably reflect more or less loosely related communities for whom revealed history was highly important. Groups of the wise resisting Antiochus, accommodators to Greek culture in Egypt, and apocalyptic teachers after the temple's fall especially valued revealed history and wrote works based upon it.

Perhaps the most noteworthy geographical concentration occurs in the Christian groups studied. Luke–Acts, John, the *Odes of Solomon*, and the *Ascension of Isaiah* have all, with good reason, been thought to originate from Syria or northern Palestine. Such a collocation of ancient works is probably significant, especially when it includes an overwhelming majority of a sample. Of those Christian works which qualified for this study only one, *Shepherd of Hermas*, does not fit this geographical pattern. All four of these Syrian works employ revealed history primarily to understand who Jesus was and what God did in him. Though these works echo one another in other respects, they do not stem from the same school of thought. They may actually oppose one another. This evidence suggests that many Syrian Christians of this period agreed as to the question requiring solution: Who was Jesus? They agreed as to presuppositions and method of inquiry: revealed history. They disagreed only in the question's answer. It is tempting to see Syrian Christianity of this period divided into several rival prophetic groups with one of the chief causes of tension being differing revealed pictures of Jesus and what he came to do. This picture fits especially well the *Ascension of Isaiah* and the Johannine literature. *Odes of Solomon* also knows of false prophets. Luke–Acts alone does not imply rival prophetic schools, unless the resolute picture of early Christian unity in Acts despite evident divisions reflects this kind of strife and no other. Of course Luke–Acts antedates the other writings as well.

However, revealed history was never so pervasive that all Jews or Christians who wrote history were constrained to use it. Matthew finds it unnecessary. Mark, despite its congeniality with his own presuppositions, does not use it explicitly. Josephus, who employs revealed history in the *Jewish War* and defines it in *Against Apion* writes *Antiquities* without it. Recognition of revealed history probably will help explain some Jewish and Christian works which do not meet the criteria for inclusion in this study, but it should not be sought everywhere. Jews and Christians were not limited to this way of looking at the past.

In what ways was revealed history used? There are as many ways as there are texts, yet certain generalizations hold true. Revealed history presupposes a world view: events, whether past, present, or future, have heavenly as well as earthly components. This world view requires a corresponding view of what counts as historical explanation: an adequate explanation of the past must consider heavenly events and plans imperceptible to human beings as well as those earthly events which human beings can perceive. This world view thus requires revealed history: only as God grants insight to the prophets can *was eigentlich gewesen ist* be understood.

This epistemology governs the ways in which revealed history was used. Theoretically it was applicable in any glance at the past, but in practice it thrived when the past and present were especially puzzling, when the generally accepted principles of heavenly action did not hold true. Jewish works used it especially when God was not blessing the righteous. During the Antiochan period the righteous were suffering despite the newly awakened movement to return to God (the children in *Jubilees*, the wise in Daniel, the white lambs with open eyes in the

Animal Apocalypse). Jerusalem fell despite the fact that Israel was seeking to be righteous and trusting in God (*2 Baruch, 4 Ezra, Jewish War, Apocalypse of Abraham, Sibylline Oracles* 4). Christian works also explained difficult events: the shocking reality of a messiah rejected by his people (Luke–Acts, John) or by the church (*Ascension of Isaiah*). Christians had a different kind of puzzle which called forth the major thrust of Christian inspired history: they had to explain what God was doing in Jesus of Nazareth. They were convinced that something momentous had occurred in the heavenly and earthly realm surrounding him, but Jesus did not fit any expected categories of heavenly action and subsequent events added to the enigma. There is little wonder that Christians who were convinced that they were filled with the Spirit turned to revelation to understand what God had done and was doing in Christ.

Revealed history was not only an epistemological technique but also a rhetorical one; it was used by Jews and Christians quite flexibly as a tool for persuasion. Time after time apocalyptists, prophets, historians, and witnesses used revelations about the past to comfort, exhort, or admonish their hearers. Because the past could only be understood by revelation, revelation of the past was a powerful tool in the hand of those who wielded it. It gave them an ethos so powerful and an argument so unassailable that, could they but pull it off, their point was gained. The survival of the works studied here proves that a number of authors were successful. Their view of history proved useful and convincing to their contemporaries and to subsequent generations.

How does taking revealed history seriously help in understanding the works in which it appears? Probably the greatest gains of this study lie in the fresh interpretations given each work as revealed history was taken seriously. The purposes of the authors and the arguments by which they make their case are clearer than before. Unfortunately these gains are hardly susceptible to summary. Josephus, in the *Jewish War*, reveals the destinies of Roman kings and that, at this juncture, God is on the Roman side. *Jubilees* reveals the combinations of ancient institution and heavenly ordination which undergird the law and the emptiness of the flashy Greek wisdom. The Animal Apocalypse discloses the sinful administration of the seventy heavenly shepherds. As heavenly sin was judged in the time of Noah so it shall shortly be again. *2 Baruch* reveals the greater Deuteronomic pattern which enclosed the lesser ones; the present is inexplicable without recognizing that the age has changed. The *Apocalypse of Abraham* reveals the reign of Azazel and the deliverance God is working through those apostate Jews who worship the man he supports. Daniel reveals a series of patterns within the four-kingdom scheme which explains the inexplicable delay in the blessings for Israel. By a plethora of revelations of the past, *4 Ezra* asserts the inevitability of damnation for the many and assures knowledge adequate for the salvation of the wise. The *Sibylline Oracles* show the proper way to appreciate Greek culture or the necessity of repentance for Gentiles. The *Shepherd of Hermas* reveals the adoption of Jesus and the salvation of ancient worthies by belief and baptism in Christ. The *Ascension of Isaiah* reveals the descent and ascent of the Beloved and the degeneracy of the church. The *Odes of Solomon* inquire into the meaning of tradition about Jesus to reveal the Word's activity in creation or the *descensus ad inferos* and delights in what is discovered. Luke–Acts reveals the plan of God worked out in Christ: fulfillment of scripture, proper understanding of Jesus in life and death, rejection by many Jews, blessing on many Gentiles. John bestows insight into Jesus, the perfect revelation, as an apocalyptic interpretation bestows insight into the vision it explains. Each author uses revealed history distinctively; each uses it with greater complexity and subtlety than a short statement can capture.

This study began by analysing Jewish works and isolating forms of revealed history in them; it concluded by analysing and applying forms of revealed history to Christian works. Ample material remains for other studies. Revealed history was a favored tool of many Gnostic sects in the late second and early third centuries. The vast array of Greco-Roman, Babylonian, Egyptian or ancient Hebrew instances of revealed history is still virtually untouched. Some Jewish and Christian works are relevant to revealed history but have too indistinct a claim to inspiration or too fuzzy a reference to the past for inclusion here. Paul, the *Testament of Levi*, or the *Testament of Moses* are prime examples. Each of these fields deserves a study of its own, but the present study is complete. It has gained a clearer perspective on Jewish and Christian revealed history as a method of interpreting the past.

Appendix

SOURCES BEHIND 2 BARUCH 53–74

The Cloud Vision of *2 Baruch* and its interpretation diverge at several points. The concluding words of the interpretation occur in 71.2-3, before the bright lightning or the twelve rivers in the vision have been explained.[1] The verses following this conclusion explain the deliverance wrought by the messiah not as an interpretation of the lightning and the twelve rivers but as an interpretation of a final bright waters not mentioned in the vision. The best explanation for this tension between interpretation and vision assumes the author's use of a source.[2] Probably the author of *2 Baruch* or a predecessor excised an objectional version of the appearance of the messiah as lightning and replaced it with a messiah and image better fitting his own purpose and standpoint. Although *2 Baruch* was almost certainly written after the Jewish War and the fall of Jerusalem, the vision and its interpretation mention the glory of the Second Temple but not its destruction. The apocalyptist's source may antedate the fall of Jerusalem. A higher degree of precision in dating is difficult to attain, for the source treats the Second Temple period sketchily (*2 Bar.* 68)[3] and the following woes are vague and stereotypical (*2 Bar.* 70). Only one thing is certain, the source was written

---

1. This frequently noted anomaly has been variously explained. Violet regards *2 Bar.* 71.2 as the close of the interpretation and notes that what follows can stand on its own. He conjectures that *2 Bar.* 72–74 is a Jewish apocalypse perhaps appended by the author of 2 *Baruch*. Charles thinks the passage is dislocated. Bogaert thinks it introduces and emphasizes what follows. See Bruno Violet, *Die Apokalypsen des Esra und des Baruch in deutscher Gestalt* (Die griechen christlichen Schriftsteller der ersten drei Jahrhunderte; Leipzig: Hinrichs, 1924), 309-13; R.H. Charles, *The Apocalypse of Baruch Translated from the Syriac. Edited with Introduction, Notes and Indices* (London: A. & C. Black, 1896), 114; Pierre Bogaert, *Apocalypse de Baruch: traduction du syriaque et commentaire* (Sources Chrétiennes 144-45; Paris: Les Editions du Cerf, 1969), 2.126.
2. Wolfgang Harnisch, *Verhängnis und Verheißung der Geschichte. Untersuchungen zum Zeit- und Geschichtsverständnis im 4. Buch Esra und in der syr. Baruchapokalypse* (FRLANT 97; Göttingen: Vandenhoeck & Ruprecht, 1969), 261-62. Bogaert (1.7) minimizes the difference, assuming that the connection between the bright lightning and the messiah or the twelve rivers and the bright waters would have been more obvious to the apocalypse's first readers than to us. Charles (*Baruch*, 114), without manuscript authority, emends *my' nhyr'* (bright waters) to *bdq' nhyr'* (bright lightning) but does not explain the missing interpretation of the twelve rivers.
3. Charles (*Baruch*, lviii) on tenuous grounds dates it between 50 and 70 CE.

in a time sufficiently dark to make the Second Temple period seem good, for all its faults.[1]

If the author altered the depiction of the messiah in his source he may have adapted his source at other points as well. Frequent agreements between the Cloud Vision and interpretation on the one hand and the rest of *2 Baruch* on the other increase the likelihood that the author has freely changed the source to suit the argument. Hence it is safer to base a study of revealed history on the final version of the material than on a tentative reconstruction of the source behind it. It is sufficient to point out that the source also can be classed as an apocalyptic world history.

---

1. The preceding paragraph owes much to discussions with Orval S. Wintermute. The expectation that the land should protect its own (*2 Bar*. 71.1) and many of the features of ch. 70 would fit well a situation in the course of the Jewish War, but they would also fit other periods and are typical of *2 Baruch*; see 29.2; 48.32-37.

BIBLIOGRAPHY

Abramowski, Louise, 'Sprache und Abfassungszeit der Oden Salomos', *Or Chr* 68 (1984), 80-90.

Abramowski, R., 'Der Christus der Salomooden', *ZNW* 35 (1936), 44-69.

Andersen, F.I., '2 (Slavonic Apocalypse of) Enoch', in *OTP*, 1.91-221.

Aune, David E., *The Cultic Setting of Realized Eschatology in Early Christianity* (Leiden: Brill, 1972).

—'The Odes of Solomon and Early Christian Prophecy', *NTS* 28 (1982), 435-60.

—*Prophecy in Early Christianity and the Ancient Mediterranean World* (Grand Rapids: Eerdmans, 1983).

—'The Use of ΠΡΟΦΗΤΗΣ in Josephus', *JBL* 101 (1982), 419-21.

Bammel, Ernst, 'Jesus und der Paraklet in Johannes 16', in *Christ and Spirit in the New Testament: Studies in Honor of C.F.D. Moule* (Cambridge: Cambridge University Press, 1973), 199-217.

Barrett, C.K., *The Gospel According to St. John: An Introduction with Commentary and Notes on the Greek Text* (Philadelphia: Westminster, 1978).

—'History', in *Essays on John* (Philadelphia: Westminster, 1982), 116-32.

—'The Holy Spirit in the Fourth Gospel', *JTS* ns 1 (1950), 1-15.

Bauckham, Richard, 'The Worship of Jesus in Apocalyptic Christianity', *NTS* 27 (1981), 322-41.

Bauer, W., 'The Odes of Solomon', in *NTA*, 2.808-10.

Beasley-Murray, G.R., 'The Interpretation of Daniel 7', *CBQ* 45 (1983), 44-58.

Beckwith, I.T., *The Apocalypse of John: Studies in Introduction with a Critical and Exegetical Commentary* (Grand Rapids: Baker, 1979 [1919]).

Berger, Klaus, *Das Buch der Jubiläen* (JSHRZ 2.3; Gütersloh: Gütersloher Verlagshaus Gerd Mohn, 1981).

Bernard, J.H., *The Odes of Solomon Edited with Introduction and Notes*, (Texts and Studies 7.3; Cambridge: Cambridge University Press, 1912).

Betz, Otto, 'Die Vision des Paulus im Tempel von Jerusalem. Apg 22, 17-21 als Beitrag zur Deutung des Damaskus Erlebnisses', in *Verborum Veritas, Festschrift für Gustav Stählin zum 70. Geburtstag* (ed. Otto Bücher und Klaus Haacker; Wuppertal: Brockhaus, 1970), 113-23.

—*Offenbarung und Schriftforschung in der Qumransekte* (WUNT 6; Tübingen: Mohr-Siebeck, 1960).

Bidawid, R.J., *The Old Testament in Syriac According to the Peshitta Version* (Part 4, Fascicle 3; Leiden: Brill, 1973).

Blank, Joseph, *Krisis. Untersuchungen zur johanneischen Christologie und Eschatologie* (Freiburg im Breisgau: Lambertus, 1964).

Blenkinsopp, J., 'Prophecy and Priesthood in Josephus', *JJS* 25 (1974), 239-62.

Böcher, Otto, 'Johanneisches in der Apokalypse des Johannes', *NTS* 27 (1981), 310-21.

Bogaert, Pierre, *Apocalypse de Baruch, traduction du syriaque et commentaire*, 2 vols. (SC 144-45; Paris: Les Editions du Cerf, 1969).

—'La Datation', in *Pseudo Philon: Les Antiquit és Bibliques* II, by D.J. Harrington, J. Cazeaux, C. Perrot, and P.-M. Bogaert (2 vols. SC 230; Paris: Les Editions du Cerf, 1976).

Boismard, M.-E., 'Le martyre d'Etienne. Acts 6:8–8:2', *RSR* 69 (1981), 181-94.

Borgen, Peder, 'God's Agent in the Fourth Gospel', in *Religions in Antiquity: Essays in Memory of E.R. Goodenough* (ed. J. Neusner; Leiden: Brill, 1968), 137-47.

Boring, M. Eugene, 'The Influence of Christian Prophecy on the Johannine Portrayal of the Paraclete and Jesus', *NTS* 25 (1978), 113-23.

—*Sayings of the Risen Jesus: Christian Prophecy in the Synoptic Tradition* (SNTSMS 46; Cambridge: Cambridge University Press, 1982).

Bornkamm, Günther, 'Der Paraklet im Johannes-Evangelium', in *Geschichte und Glaube* (Gesammelte Aufsätze 3; Beiträge zur evangelischen Theologie, München: Chr Kaiser Verlag, 1968), 1.68-89.

—'Zur Interpretation des Johannes-Evangeliums. Eine Auseinandersetzung mit Ernst Käsemanns Schrift "Jesu letzter Wille nach Johannes 17"', in *Geschichte und Glaube* (Gesammelte Aufsätze 3; Beiträge zur evangelischen Theologie; München: Kaiser, 1968), 1.104-21.

Bowker, J.W., 'Speeches in Acts: A Study in Proem and Yelammedenu Form', *NTS* 14 (1967-68), 96-111.

Box, G.H., '4 Ezra', in *APOT*, 2.542-624.

—Introduction to *The Ascension of Isaiah*, by R.H. Charles (London: SPCK, 1919).

Box, G.H. and J.I. Landsman, *The Apocalypse of Abraham* (New York: Macmillan, 1919).

Braun, F.-M., 'L'énigme des Odes de Salomon', *RevThom* 57 (1957), 597-625.

Breech, Earl, 'These Fragments I Have Shored Against My Ruins: The Form and Function of 4 Ezra', *JBL* 92 (1973), 267-74.

Brown, Raymond E., *The Birth of the Messiah: A Commentary on the Infancy Narratives of Matthew and Luke* (Garden City, NY: Doubleday, 1977).

—*The Gospel According to John* (AB 29, 29A, Garden City, NY: Doubleday, 1982).

—*The Community of the Beloved Disciple* (New York: Paulist, 1979).

—*The Epistles of John* (AB 30; Garden City, NY: Doubleday, 1982).

—'The Paraclete in the Fourth Gospel', *NTS* 13 (1966-67), 113-32.

Bruce, F.F., 'Josephus and Daniel', in *Annual of the Swedish Theological Institute* 4 (1965), 148-62.

Bultmann, Rudolf, *The Gospel of John: A Commentary* (Philadelphia: Westminster, 1971).

—'History and Eschatology in the New Testament', *NTS* 1 (1954), 5-16.

—*New Testament Theology* (2 vols.; New York: Scribners, 1951/1955).

Buss, Matthäus Franz-Joseph. *Die Missionspredigten des Apostels Paulus im Pisidischen Antiochien* (Forschung zur Bibel 38; Stuttgart: Katholisches Bibelwerk, 1980).

Carmignac, Jean, 'Un Qumranien converti au Christianisme: l'auteur des Odes de Salomon', in *Qumran Probleme* (ed. H. Bardtke, Deutsche Akademie der Wissenschaften zu Berlin, Schriften der Sektion für Altertumswissenschaft 42; Berlin: Akademie Verlag, 1963) 75-108.

Chadwick, Henry, 'Some Reflections on the Character and Theology of the Odes of Solomon', in *Kyriakon: Festschrift Johannes Quasten* (2 vols., ed. P. Granfield and J.A. Jungmann; Münster: Aschendorff, 1970), 1.226-70.

Charles, R.H., *The Apocalypse of Baruch Translated from the Syriac. Edited with Introduction, Notes and Indices* (London: A. & C. Black, 1896).

—*The Ascension of Isaiah Translated from the Ethiopic Version, which, together with the New Greek Fragment, the Latin Versions and the Latin Translation of the Slavonic, is here Published in full* (London: A. & C. Black, 1900).

—'Book of Enoch', in *APOT*, 2.163-277.

—*The Book of Enoch* (Oxford: Clarendon, 1912).

—*The Book of Jubilees or the Little Genesis*, London: A. & C. Black, 1902.
—*A Critical and Exegetical Commentary on the Book of Daniel* (Oxford: Clarendon, 1929).
—*The Ethiopic Version of the Book of Jubilees* (Oxford: Clarendon, 1895).
Charles, R.H. and J.M.T. Barton, 'The Ascension of Isaiah', in *AOT*, 775-812.
Charlesworth, James H., 'Les Odes de Salomon et les Manuscrits de la Mer Morte', *RB* 77 (1970), 522-49.
—'Odes of Solomon', in *OTP*, 2.725-72.
—'The Odes of Solomon—Not Gnostic', *CBQ* 31 (1969), 357-69.
—*The Odes of Solomon: The Syriac Texts* (Society of Biblical Literature Texts and Translations 13, Pseudepigrapha Series 7; Missoula, MT: Scholars Press, 1977).
—'Qumran, John, and the Odes of Solomon', in *John and Qumran* (ed. J.H. Charlesworth; London: Chapman, 1972), 107-36.
—'The SNTS Pseudepigrapha Seminars at Tübingen and Paris on the Books of Enoch', *NTS* 25 (1979), 315-23.
Charlesworth, James H. and R.A. Culpepper, 'The Odes of Solomon and the Gospel of John', *CBQ* 35 (1973), 298-322.
Coggins, R.J., 'The Samaritans and Acts', *NTS* 28 (1982), 423-34.
Collins, John J., *The Apocalyptic Imagination: An Introduction to the Jewish Matrix of Christianity* (New York: Crossroad, 1984).
—*The Apocalyptic Vision of the Book of Daniel* (Harvard Semitic Monographs 16; Missoula, MT: Scholars Press, 1977).
—'The Court-Tales in Daniel and the Development of Apocalyptic', *JBL* 94 (1975), 218-34.
—'The Place of the Fourth Sibyl in the Development of the Jewish Sibyllina', *JJS* 25 (1974), 365-80.
—'The Sibylline Oracles', in *Jewish Writings of the Second Temple Period* (ed. Michael E. Stone; Philadelphia: Fortress Press, 1984), 357-81.
—'The Sibylline Oracles', in *OTP*, 1.317-472.
—*The Sibylline Oracles of Egyptian Judaism* (SBLDS 13; Missoula, MT: Scholars Press, 1974).
—ed. *Apocalypse: The Morphology of a Genre* (Semeia 14; Missoula, MT: Scholars Press, 1979).
Conzelmann, Hans, *The Theology of St. Luke* (New York: Harper & Row, 1960).
Cullmann, Oscar, *Early Christian Worship* (SBT 10; Chicago: Henry Regnery, 1953).
—*The Johannine Circle* (trans J. Bowden; Philadelphia: Westminster, 1976).
—*Salvation in History* (New York: Harper & Row, 1967).
Culpepper, R. Alan, *Anatomy of the Fourth Gospel* (Hermeneia: Foundations and Facets; Philadelphia: Fortress, 1983).
—*The Johannine School: An Evaluation of the Johannine School Hypothesis Based on an Investigation of the Nature of Ancient Schools* (SBLDS 26; Missoula, MT: Scholars Press, 1975).
Dahl, Nils A., 'Anamnesis: Memory and Commemoration in Early Christianity', in *Jesus in the Memory of the Early Church* (Minneapolis: Augsburg, 1976), 11-29.
—'The Story of Abraham in Luke–Acts', in *Studies in Luke–Acts* (ed. Leander E. Keck and J. Louis Martyn; Philadelphia: Fortress, 1980 [1966]), 139-58.
Daube, David, 'Typology in Josephus', *JJS* 31 (1980), 18-36.
Davenport, Gene L., *The Eschatology of the Book of Jubilees* (Leiden: Brill, 1971).
Davies, G.I., 'Apocalyptic and Historiography', *JSOT* 5 (1978), 15-28.
DeVilliers, Pieter G.R., 'Understanding the Way of God: Form, Function and Message of the Historical Review in IV Ezra 3:4-27', *SBLSP* (1981), 357-78.
Dibelius, Martin, 'The Speeches in Acts and Ancient Historiography', in *Studies in the Acts of the Apostles* (New York: Scribners, 1956), 138-85.

—*Der Hirt des Hermas*, Handbuch zum Neuen Testament (Die Apostolischen Väter 4; Tübingen: Mohr/Siebeck, 1923).

Dillon, Richard J., *From Eye-Witnesses to Ministers of the Word: Tradition and Composition in Luke 24* (Analecta Biblica 82; Rome: Pontifical Biblical Institute, 1978).

—'The Prophecy of Christ and His Witnesses according to the Discourses of Acts', *NTS* 32 (1986), 544-56.

Doble, P., 'The Son of Man Saying in Stephen's Witnessing: Acts 6:8–8:2', *NTS* 31 (1985), 68-84.

Doran, R., 'Cleodemus Malchus', in *OTP*, 2.883-87.

Downing, F. Gerald, 'Ethical Pagan Theism and the Speeches in Acts', *NTS* 27 (1981), 544-63.

Drijvers, H.J.W., 'Facts and Problems in Early Syriac-Speaking Christianity', *Second Century* 2 (1982), 157-75.

—'Kerygma und Logos in den Oden Salomos dargestellt am Beispiel der 23. Ode', in *Kerygma und Logos. Beiträge zu den geistesgeschichtlichen Beziehungen zwischen Antike und Christentum. Festschrift für Carl Andresen zum 70. Geburtstag* (Göttingen: Vandenhoeck & Ruprecht, 1979), 153-72.

—'The 19th Ode of Solomon: Its Interpretation and Place in Syrian Christianity', *JTS* 31 (1980), 337-55.

—'Die Oden Salomos und die Polemik mit den Markioniten im Syrischen Christentum', in *Symposium Syriacum 1976* (Orientalia Christiana Analecta 205; Rome: Pontifical Biblical Institute, 1978), 39-55.

—'The Odes of Solomon and Psalms of Man: Christians and Manichaens in Third-Century Syria', in *Studies in Gnosticism and Hellenistic Religions Presented to Gilles Quispel on the Occasion of his 65th Birthday* (ed. R. van den Broek and M.J. Vermeren; Leiden: Brill, 1981), 117-30.

Dunn, James D.G., *Jesus and the Spirit* (Philadelphia: Westminster, 1975).

Dupont, Jacques, 'La structure oratoire du discours d'Etienne (Acts 7)', *Biblica* 66 (1985), 153-67.

Eissfeldt, Otto, *The Old Testament: An Introduction* (trans. Peter R. Ackroyd; New York: Harper & Row, 1965).

Ellis, E.E., 'Midrashic Features in the Speeches of Acts', in *Mélanges Bibliques en hommage au R.P. Béda Rigaux* (ed. A. Descamps and R.P. André de Halleux; Gembloux: Duculot, 1970), 303-12.

—'The Role of the Christian Prophet in Acts', in *Prophecy and Hermeneutic in Early Christianity: New Testament Essays* (Grand Rapids: Eerdmans, 1978), 129-44.

Emerton, J.A., 'Notes on Some Passages in the Odes of Solomon', *JTS* ns 28 (1977), 507-19.

Endres, J.C., *Biblical Interpretation in the Book of Jubilees* (CBQMS 18; Washington: Catholic Biblical Association, 1987).

Feldman, Louis H. 'Prophets and Prophecy in Josephus', *SBLSP* (1988), 431-33.

Fitzmyer, Joseph A., *The Gospel According to Luke* (AB 28, 28A; Garden City, New York: Doubleday, 1981).

Flemming, J., Hugo Duensing, and David Hill, 'The Ascension of Isaiah', *NTA* 2.642-63.

Flusser, David, 'The Four Empires in the Fourth Sibyl and in the Book of Daniel', *Israel Oriental Studies* 2 (1972), 148-75.

Furnish, Victor Paul, *II Corinthians* (AB 32A; Garden City, NY: Doubleday, 1984).

Geffcken, Johannes, *Die Oracula Sibyllina* (Leipzig: Hinrichs, 1902).

—*Komposition und Entstehungszeit der Oracula Sibyllina* (Leipzig: Hinrichs, 1902).

Giet, Stanislas, *Hermas et les pasteurs* (Paris: Presses Universitaires de France, 1963).

Ginsberg, L., 'Abraham, Apocalypse of', in *The Jewish Encyclopedia* (New York: Funk & Wagnall, 1901), 91-92.

Grayson, A.K. and W.G. Lambert, 'Akkadian Prophecies', *Journal of Cuneiform Studies* 18 (1964), 7-30.

Grundmann, Walter, *Zeugnis und Gestalt des Johannes-Evangeliums. Eine Studie zur denkerischen und gestalterischen Leistung des vierten Evangelisten* (Arbeiten zur Theologie 7; Stuttgart: Calwer Verlag, 1960).

Gry, L., *Les Dires prophétiques d'Esdras (IV Esdras)* (2 vols.; Paris: Geuthner, 1938).

Gunkel, Hermann, 'Die Oden Salomos', *ZNW* 11 (1910), 291-328.

Haacker, Klaus, *Die Stiftung des Heils. Untersuchungen zur Struktur der johanneischen Theologie* (Arbeiten zur Theologie 1.47; Stuttgart: Calwer Verlag, 1972).

Haag, Ernst, *Studien zum Buch Judith. Seine theologische Bedeutung und literarische Eigenart* (Trierer Theologische Studien 16; Trier: Paulinus, 1963).

Haenchen, Ernst, *The Acts of the Apostles: A Commentary* (Oxford: Basil Blackwell, 1971).

—*John: A Commentary on the Gospel of John* (2 vols., ed. R.W. Funk and Ulrich Buss, Hermeneia; Philadelphia: Fortress, 1984).

Hall, Robert G., 'The Ascension of Isaiah: Community Situation, Date, and Place in Early Christianity', *JBL* 109 (1990), 289-306.

—'The "Christian Interpolation" in the Apocalypse of Abraham', *JBL* 107 (1988), 107-10.

—'The Installation of the Archangel Michael', *Coptic Church Review* 5 (1984), 108-11.

Harnisch, Wolfgang, 'Die Ironie der Offenbarung: Exegetische Erwägungen zur Zionvision im 4.Buch Esra', *SBLSP* (1981), 79-104.

—*Verhängnis und Verheißung der Geschichte. Untersuchungen zum Zeit-und Geschichtsverständnis im 4. Buch Esra und in der syr. Baruchapokalypse* (FRLANT 97; Göttingen: Vandenhoeck & Ruprecht, 1969).

Harrelson, Walter, 'Ezra among the Wicked in 2 Esdras 3–10', in *The Divine Helmsman: Studies on God's Control of Human Events, Presented to Lou H. Silberman* (ed. J.L. Crenshaw and S. Sandmel; New York: Ktav, 1980), 21-39.

Harrington, D.J., 'Pseudo-Philo', in *OTP*, 2.297-377.

Harris, Rendel and Mingana, Alfonse, *The Odes and Psalms of Solomon* (2 vols.; Manchester: Manchester University Press, 1920).

Hartman, Louis F., and DiLella, Alexander A., *The Book of Daniel* (AB 23; Garden City, NY: Doubleday, 1978).

Hayman, A.P., 'The Problem of Pseudonymity in the Ezra Apocalypse', *JSJ* 6 (1975), 47-56.

Hengel, Martin, *Judaism and Hellenism* (2 vols.; Philadelphia: Fortress, 1983).

Hill, David, *New Testament Prophecy* (Atlanta: John Knox, 1979).

Homer. *The Iliad* (trans. A.T. Murray, LCL; New York: G.P. Putnam's Sons, 1924).

—*The Iliad of Homer* (trans. Richmond Lattimore; Chicago: University of Chicago Press, 1951).

Hoskyns, Edwyn Clement, *The Fourth Gospel* (ed. Francis Noel Davey; London: Faber & Faber, 1947).

Isaac, Ephraim, '1 (Ethiopic Apocalypse of) Enoch', in *OTP*, 1.5-89.

James, M.R., 'Notes on Apocrypha', *JTS* 16 (1915), 405.

Jervell, Jacob, 'Sons of the Prophets: The Holy Spirit in the Acts of the Apostles', in *The Unknown Paul* (Minneapolis: Augsburg, 1984).

Johnson, Gary Lance, 'Josephus: Heir Apparent to the Prophetic Tradition?', *SBL Seminar Papers* 22 (1983), 337-46.

Johnston, George, *The Spirit-Paraclete in the Gospel of John* (SNTSMS 12; Cambridge: Cambridge University Press, 1970).

Jonge, Marinus de, 'Josephus und die Zukunftserwartungen seines Volkes', in *Josephus-Studien. Untersuchungen zu Josephus, dem antiken Judentum und dem Neuen Testament. Otto Michel zum 70. Geburtstag* (ed. Otto Betz, Klaus Haacker, and Martin Hengel; Göttingen: Vandenhoeck & Ruprecht, 1974), 205-19.

Josephus, *Against Apion* (trans. H.St.J. Thackeray, LCL; New York: G.P. Putnam's Sons, 1926).

Juel, Donald, 'Social Dimensions of Exegesis: The Use of Psalm 16 in Acts 2', *CBQ* 43 (1981), 543-56.

Kee, Howard Clark, *Community of the New Age: Studies in Mark's Gospel* (Philadelphia: Westminster, 1977).

Kennedy, George A., *New Testament Interpretation through Rhetorical Criticism* (Chapel Hill: University of North Carolina Press, 1984).

Kilgallen, John, *The Stephen Speech: A Literary and Redactional Study of Acts 7:2-53* (Analecta Biblica 67; Rome: Pontifical Biblical Institute, 1976).

Kliesch, Klaus, *Das heilsgeschichtliche Credo in den Reden der Apostelgeschichte* (BBB 44; Köln-Bonn: Peter Hanstein, 1975).

Klijn, A.F.J., 'The Sources and Redaction of the Syriac Apocalypse of Baruch', *JSJ* 1 (1970), 65-76.

—'Stephen's Speech—Acts VII.2-53', *NTS* 4 (1957), 25-31.

Knibb, Michael A., 'The Date of the Parables of Enoch: A Critical Review', *NTS* 25 (1979), 345-59.

—'Martyrdom and Ascension of Isaiah', in *OTP*, 2.143-76.

Knibb, Michael A. and Eduard Ullendorf, *The Ethiopic Book of Enoch* (2 vols.; Oxford: Clarendon, 1978).

Koch, Klaus, 'Esras erste Vision. Weltzeiten und Weg des Höchsten', *BZ* 22 (1978), 46-75.

—'Spätisraelitisches Geschichtsdenken am Beispiel des Buches Daniel', *HZ* 193 (1961), 1-32.

Koenen, L., 'Prophezeihungen des "Töpfers"', *ZPE* 2 (1968), 195-209.

Koester, Helmut, *Introduction to the New Testament*, Vol. 2: *History and Literature of Early Christianity* (Hermeneia: Foundations and Facets; Philadelphia: Fortress, 1982).

Kolenkow, Anitra Bingham, 'The Fall of the Temple and the Coming of the End: The Spectrum and Process of Apocalyptic Argument in 2 Baruch and Other Authors', *SBLSP* (1982), 243-50.

Kragerud, Alv, *Der Lieblingsjünger im Johannesevangelium* (Oslo: Osloer Universitätsverlag, 1959).

Kundsin, Karl, *Charakter und Ursprung der johanneischen Reden* (Acta Universitatis Latviensis, Theologijas Fakultates Serija 1.4; Riga: Latvijas Universitates Raksti, 1939).

Kurfess, Alons, 'Die Oracula Sibyllina XI–XIV nicht christlich, sondern jüdisch', *ZRGG* 7 (1955), 270-72.

—*Sibyllinische Weissagungen* (Berlin: Tusculum, 1951).

Kurz, William S., 'Hellenistic Rhetoric in the Christological Proof of Luke-Acts', *CBQ* 42 (1980), 171-95.

Lacocque, André, *The Book of Daniel* (Atlanta: John Knox, 1979).

Lanchester, H.C.O., 'The Sibylline Oracles', in *APOT*, 2.368-406.

Lattke, Michael, 'The Apocryphal Odes of Solomon and the New Testament Writings', *ZNW* 73 (1983), 294-301.

—*Die Oden Salomos in ihrer Bedeutung für Neues Testament und Gnosis* (2 vols.; Göttingen: Vandenhoeck & Ruprecht, 1979).

Leroy, Herbert, *Rätsel und Missverständnis. Ein Beitrag zur Formgeschichte des Johannesevangeliums* (BBB 30; Bonn: Hanstein, 1968).

Lindars, Barnabas, 'A Bull, a Lamb, and a Word: 1 Enoch XC.38', *NTS* 22 (1976), 483-86.

Lindner, Helgo, *Die Geschichtsauffassung des Flavius Josephus im Bellum Judaicum* (AGAJU 12; Leiden: Brill, 1972).

Lohse, Eduard, *Die Texte aus Qumran* (München: Kösel, 1964).

Luck, Ulrich, 'Kerygma, Tradition und Geschichte Jesu bei Lukas', *ZTK* 57 (1960), 51-66.

McNeil, Brian, 'The Odes of Solomon and the Scriptures', *OrChr* 67 (1983), 104-22.

Maddox, Robert, *The Purpose of Luke–Acts* (FRLANT 126; Göttingen: Vandenhoeck & Ruprecht, 1982).

Marcus, Joel, 'Mark 4:10-12 and Marcan Epistemology', *JBL* 103 (1984), 557-74.

Marshall, I. Howard, *The Gospel of Luke: A Commentary on the Greek Text* (New International Greek Testament Commentary; Grand Rapids: Eerdmans, 1978).

Martin, François, *Le Livre d' Henoch* (Paris: Letouzey et Ané, 1906).

Mayer, Reinhold and Christa Möller, 'Josephus—Politiker und Prophet', in *Josephus-Studien. Untersuchungen zu Josephus, dem antiken Judentum und dem Neuen Testament. Otto Michel zum 70. Geburtstag* (ed. Otto Betz, Klaus Haacker, and Martin Hengel; Göttingen: Vandenhoeck & Ruprecht, 1974), 271-84.

Meeks, Wayne A., 'The Man from Heaven in Johannine Sectarianism', *JBL* 91 (1972), 44-72.

—*The Prophet King: Moses Traditions and the Johannine Christology* (Supp. Nov. T. 14; Leiden: Brill, 1967).

Mendels, D. ' "Creative History" in the Hellenistic Near East in the Third and Second Centuries BCE: The Jewish Case', *JSP* 2 (1988), 13-20.

Michaels, J. Ramsey, 'The Johannine Words of Jesus and Christian Prophecy', *SBLSP* 2 (1975), 233-64.

Milik, Josef T. and Matthew Black, *The Books of Enoch: Aramaic Fragments of Qumrân Cave 4* (Oxford: Clarendon, 1976).

Minear, Paul S., 'Luke's Use of the Birth Stories', in *Studies in Luke–Acts* (ed. Leander E. Keck and J. Louis Martyn; Philadelphia: Fortress, 1966 [reprinted in 1980]), 111-30.

—*To Heal and to Reveal: The Prophetic Vocation According to Luke* (New York: Seabury, 1976).

Moessner, David P., 'Paul in Acts: Preacher of Eschatological Repentance to Israel', *NTS* 34 (1988), 96-104.

Montgomery, James A., *A Critical and Exegetical Commentary on the Book of Daniel* (ICC; Edinburgh: T & T Clark, 1927).

Mueller, James R., 'The Apocalypse of Abraham and the Destruction of the Second Jewish Temple', *SBLSP* (1982), 341-50.

Müller, Ulrich B., 'Die Parakletenvorstellung im Johannesevangelium', *ZTK* 71 (1974), 31-77.

Murphy, F.J., *The Structure and Meaning of 2 Baruch* (SBLDS 78; Atlanta: Scholars Press, 1985).

Mußner, Franz, *The Historical Jesus in the Gospel of St. John* (New York: Herder & Herder, 1967).

—'Die johanneischen Parakletsprüche und die apostolische Tradition', *BZ* 5 n.F. (1961), 56-70.

Myers, Jacob M., *I and II Esdras* (AB 42; Garden City, NY: Doubleday, 1974).

Neusner, Jacob, 'Beyond Myth, After Apocalypse: The Mishnaic Conception of History', *Response* 14 (1984), 17-35.

Newsom, Carol A., 'Historical Résumé as Biblical Exegesis', summarized in *Enoch and the Growth of an Apocalyptic Tradition*, by James C. VanderKam (CBQMS 16; Washington, DC: Catholic Biblical Association, 1984), 165 -67.

—'The Past as Revelation: History in Apocalyptic Literature', *Quarterly Review* 4 (Nashville, 1984), 40-53.

Neyrey, Jerome, 'The Forensic Defense Speech and Paul's Trial Speeches in Acts 22-26: Form and Function', in *Luke–Acts: New Perspectives from the Society of Biblical Literature Seminar* (New York: Crossroad, 1984), 210-24.

Nickelsburg, G.W.E., *Jewish Literature between the Bible and the Mishnah* (Philadelphia: Fortress, 1981).

Nicol, W., *The Semeia in the Fourth Gospel: Tradition and Redaction* (Supp. Nov. T. 32; Leiden: Brill, 1972).

Nikiprowetzky, Valentin, *La Troisième Sibylle* (Etudes Juives 9; Paris: Mouton, 1970).

Noth, Martin, 'The Understanding of History in Old Testament Apocalyptic', in *The Laws in the Pentateuch and Other Studies* (Edinburgh: Oliver & Boyd, 1966), 194-214.

Odeberg, Hugo, *The Fourth Gospel* (Uppsala: Almquist & Wiksells, 1929).

Oesterley, W.O.E., *II Esdras (The Ezra Apocalypse) with Introduction and Notes* (Westminster Commentaries; London: Methuen, 1933).

O'Reilly, Leo, *Word and Sign in the Acts of the Apostles: A Study in Lucan Theology* (Analecta Gregoriana 243; Rome: Pontifica Universita Gregoriana, 1987).

Osiek, Carolyn, *Rich and Poor in the Shepherd of Hermas: An Exegetical-Social Investigation* (CBQMS 15; Washington, DC: CBA, 1983).

Painter, John, 'The Farewell Discourses and the History of Johannine Christianity', *NTS* 27 (1981), 525-43.

—*John: Witness and Theologian* (London: SPCK, 1975).

Pennington, A, 'The Apocalypse of Abraham', in *AOT*, 363-91.

Pernveden, Lage, *The Concept of the Church in the Shepherd of Hermas* (Studia Theologica Lundensia 27; Lund: Gleerup, 1966).

Peterson, Erik, 'Die Begegnung mit dem Ungeheuer', in *Frühkirche, Judentum und Gnosis. Studien und Untersuchungen* (Freiburg: Herder, 1959), 285-309.

—'Kritische Analyse der fünften Vision des Hermes', in *Frühkirche, Judentum und Gnosis. Studien und Untersuchungen* (Freiburg: Herder, 1959), 271-84.

Philonenko, Marc, 'Le Martyre d'Esaïe et l'histoire de la secte de Qoumrân', in *Pseudepigraphes de l'Ancien Testament et Manuscrits de la Mer Morte* (ed. M. Philonenko; Paris: Presses Universitaires de France, 1967), 1.1-10.

Philonenko-Sayar, Belkis and Marc Philonenko, *Die Apokalypse Abrahams* (JSHRZ 5.5; Gütersloh: Gütersloher Verlagshaus Gerd Mohn, 1982).

Plummer, Alfred, *Gospel According to S. Luke* (5th edn, ICC; Edinburgh: T & T Clark, 1922).

Potterie, Ignace de la, 'The Paraclete', in *The Christian Lives by the Spirit* (Staten Island, NY: Alba House, 1971).

Rahlfs, Alfred, ed., *Septuaginta* (Stuttgart: Deutsche Bibelstiftung, 1935).

Rajak, Tessa, *Josephus: The Historian and His Society* (Philadelphia: Fortress, 1983).

Reid, Stephen Breck, *Enoch and Daniel: A Form Critical and Sociological Study of Historical Apocalypses* (Bibal Monograph Series 2; Berkley, CA: Bibal, 1989).

—'1 Enoch: The Rising Elite of the Apocalyptic Movement', *SBLSP* 22 (1983), 147-56.

Reiling, J., *Hermas and Christian Prophecy: A Study of the Eleventh Mandate* (Leiden: Brill, 1973).

—'The Use of ψευδοπροφήτης in the Septuagint, Philo, and Josephus', *Nov.T.* 13 (1971), 147-56.

Rhoads, David M, *Israel in Revolution, 6–74 C.E.* (Philadelphia: Fortress, 1976).

Richard, Earl, *Acts 6:1–8:4, The Author's Method of Composition* (SBLDS 41; Missoula, MT: Scholars Press, 1978).

—'The Polemical Character of the Joseph Episode in Acts 7', *JBL* 98 (1979), 255-67.

Rössler, Dietrich, *Gesetz und Geschichte. Untersuchungen zur Theologie der jüdischen Apokalyptik und der pharisäischen Orthodoxie* (WMANT 3; Neukirchen: Neukirchener Verlag, 1960).

Rowland, Christopher, *The Open Heaven: A Study of Apocalyptic in Judaism and Early Christianity* (New York: Crossroad, 1982).

Rubinkiewicz, Ryszard, 'La vision de l'histoire dans l'Apocalypse d'Abraham', in *Aufstieg und Niedergang der Römischen Welt* II.19.1 (Berlin, New York: Walter de Gruyter, 1979), 137-51

Rubinkiewicz, R., and H.G. Lunt, 'The Apocalypse of Abraham', in *OTP*, 1.681-705.

Rubinstein, A., 'A Problematic Passage in the Apocalypse of Abraham', *JJS* 8 (1957), 45-50.

Rudolph, Kurt, 'War der Verfasser der Oden Salomos ein "Qumran-Christ"? Ein Beitrag zur Diskussion um die Anfänge der Gnosis', *RevQ* 4 (1964), 523-55.

Sanders, Jack T., *The New Testament Christological Hymns: Their Historical Religious Background* (SNTSMS 15; Cambridge: Cambridge University Press, 1971).

Sasse, Hermann, 'Der Paraklet im Johannesevangelium', *ZNW* 24 (1925), 260-77.

Sayler, Gwendolyn B., *Have the Promises Failed? A Literary Analysis of 2 Baruch* (SBLDS 72; Chico, CA: Scholars Press, 1984).

Scherrer, Steven J., 'Signs and Wonders in the Imperial Cult', *JBL* 103 (1984), 599-610.

Schlier, Heinrich, 'Der Heilige Geist als Interpret nach dem Johannesevangelium', *Der Geist und die Kirche. Exegetische Aufsätze und Vorträge* 4 (Freiburg: Herder, 1980), 165-78.

—'Zum Begriff des Geistes nach dem Johannesevangelium', in *Besinnung auf das Neue Testament. Exegetische Aufsätze und Vorträge* 2 (Freiburg: Herder, 1964), 264-71.

Schnackenburg, Rudolf, *The Gospel of St. John* (3 vols.; New York: Crossroad, 1982).

—'Die johanneische Gemeinde und ihre Geisterfahrung', in *Die Kirche des Anfangs. Festschrift für Heinz Schürmann zum 65. Geburtstag* (Erfurter Theologische Studien 38; Freiburg: Herder, 1977), 277-306.

Schneider, Gerhard, *Die Apostelgeschichte* I (Herders Theologischer Kommentar zum Neuen Testament 5; Freiburg: Herder), 1980.

Schubert, Paul, 'The Final Cycle of Speeches in the Book of Acts', *JBL* 87 (1968), 1-16.

—'The Place of the Areopagus Speech in the Composition of Acts', in *Transitions in Biblical Scholarship* (ed. J.C. Rylaarsdam; Chicago: Chicago University Press, 1968), 235-61.

—'The Structure and Significance of Luke 24', in *Neutestamentliche Studien für Rudolf Bultmann zu seinem siebzigsten Geburtstag am 20. August 1954* (Beihefte zur Zeitschrift für die neutestamentliche Wissenschaft und die Kunde der Älteren Kirche 21; Berlin: Töpelmann, 1954), 165-86.

Schulz, Siegfried, *Das Evangelium nach Johannes* (NTD 4; Göttingen: Vandenhoeck & Ruprecht, 1972).

Schwarz, Eberhard, *Identität durch Abgrenzung* (Europäische Hochschulschriften 29.23.162; Frankfurt am Main: Peter Lang, 1982).

Schweizer, Eduard, 'Concerning the Speeches in Acts', in *Studies in Luke–Acts* (ed. Leander E. Keck and J. Louis Martyn; Philadelphia: Fortress, 1980 [1966]), 208-16.

Scroggs, Robin, 'The Earliest Hellenistic Christianity', in *Religions in Antiquity: Essays in Memory of Erwin Ramsdell Goodenough* (ed. J. Neusner; Leiden: Brill, 1968).

Smalley, Stephen S., *1, 2, 3 John* (WBC 51; Waco, Texas: Word Books, 1984).

Smallwood, E. Mary, *The Jews under Roman Rule From Pompey to Diocletian* (Leiden: Brill, 1981).

Smith, D. Moody, 'Johannine Christianity: Some Reflections on its Character and Delineation', *NTS* 21 (1975), 222-48.

—*John*, Proclamation Commentaries (Philadelphia: Fortress, 1976).

—'John 16:1-15 (Expository Article)', *Interpretation* 33 (1979), 58-62.

Snyder, Graden F., *The Shepherd of Hermas; The Apostolic Fathers: A New Translation and Commentary*, vol. VI (Camden, NJ: Nelson, 1968).

Sophocles, *Oedipus Rex* (ed. R.D. Dawe; Cambridge: Cambridge University Press, 1982).

—'Oedipus the King', trans. David Grene, in *Greek Tragedies* (ed. David Grene and Richmond Lattimore; Chicago: University of Chicago, 1960).

Stone, Michael E., 'Apocalyptic Literature', in *Jewish Writings of the Second Temple Period* (ed. Michael E. Stone, Compendia Rerum Judaicarum ad Novum Testamentum 2.2; Philadelphia: Fortress, 1984, 383-441).

—'Coherence and Inconsistency in the Apocalypses: The Case of the End in 4 Ezra', *JBL* 102 (1983), 229-43.

—'Lists of Revealed Things in the Apocalyptic Literature', in *Magnalia Dei: The Mighty Acts of God* (ed. F.M. Cross, W.E. Lemke, P.D. Miller, Jr.; Garden City, NY: Doubleday, 1976), 414-52.

—'Reactions to the Destruction of the Second Temple', *JSJ* 12 (1981), 195-204.

—'The Concept of the Messiah in 4 Ezra', in *Religions in Antiquity: Essays in Memory of Erwin Ramsdell Goodenough* (ed. Jacob Neusner, Studies in the History of Religions 14; Leiden: Brill, 1968), 295-312.

Streeter, B.H., *The Four Gospels: A Study of Origins* (New York: Macmillan, 1956 [1924]).

Strugnell, John, Review of *L'Apocalypse Syriaque de Baruch: Introduction, traduction du syriaque et commentaire*, by Pierre Bogaert, *JBL* 89 (1970), 484-85.

Sylva, Dennis D., 'The Meaning and Function of Acts 7.46-50', *JBL* 106 (1987), 261-75.

Tannehill, R.C., *The Narrative Unity of Luke–Acts, Vol. 1: The Gospel according to Luke* (Philadelphia: Fortress, 1986).

Testuz, Michael, *Les Idées Religieuses du Livre des Jubilés* (Genève: E. Droz, 1960).

Thompson, Alden Lloyd, *Responsibility for Evil in the Theodicy of IV Ezra* (SBLDS 29; Missoula, MT: Scholars Press, 1977).

Thyen, Helmut, *Der Stil der jüdischhellenistischen Homilie* (FRLANT 47; Göttingen: Vandenhoeck & Ruprecht, 1955).

Tiede, David L., *Prophecy and History in Luke-Acts* (Philadelphia: Fortress, 1980).

Tisserant, Eugène, *Ascension d'Isaïe. Traduction de la version ethiopienne avec les principales variantes des versions greque, latines et slave. Introduction et notes* (Paris: Letouzey et Ané, 1909).

Unnik, Willem Comelis van, *Flavius Josephus als historischer Schriftsteller* (Franz Delitzsch Vorlesung, Neue Folge; Heidelberg: Lambert Schneider, 1978).

VanderKam, James C., *Enoch and the Growth of an Apocalyptic Tradition* (CBQMS 16; Washington, DC: Catholic Biblical Association, 1984).

—'The Putative Author of the Book of Jubilees', *Journal of Semitic Studies* 26 (1981), 209-17.

—*Textual and Historical Studies in the Book of Jubilees* (Harvard Semitic Monographs 14; Missoula, MT: Scholars Press, 1977).

Van Koningsveld, P.J., 'An Arabic Manuscript of the Apocalypse of Baruch', *JSJ* 6 (1975), 205-207.

Via, E. Jane, 'An Interpretation of Acts 7:35-37 from the perspective of Major Themes in Luke–Acts', *SBLSP* 14.2 (1978), 209-22.

Violet, Bruno, *Die Apokalypsen des Esra und des Baruch in deutscher Gestalt* (Die griechischen christlichen Schriftsteller der ersten drei Jahrhunderte; Leipzig: Hinrichs, 1924).

Virgil, *The Aeneid* (trans. Robert Fitzgerald; New York: Vintage/Random House, 1984).

Walker, Alexander, *Apocryphal Gospels, Acts, and Revelations* (Ante-Nicene Christian Library 16; Edinburgh: T & T Clark, 1870).

Westcott, Brooke Foss, *The Gospel According to St. John: The Greek Text with Introduction and Notes* (2 vols.; London: John Murray, 1908).

Whitacre, Rodney A., *Johannine Polemic: The Role of Tradition and Theology* (SBLDS; Chico, CA: Scholars Press, 1982).

Whittaker, Molly, *Der Hirt des Hermas* (Die griechischen christlichen Schriftsteller 48; Berlin: Akademie Verlag, 1956).

Wiesenberg, Ernest, 'The Jubilee of Jubilees', *Revue de Qumran* 3 (1961), 3-40.

Wilckens, Ulrich, *Die Missionsreden der Apostelgeschichte. Form- und traditionsgeschichtliche Untersuchungen* (WMANT 5; Neukirchen: Neukirchener Verlag, 1961).

Windisch, Hans, *Johannes und die Synoptiker* (Leipzig: Hinrichs, 1926).

—*The Spirit-Paraclete in the Fourth Gospel* (trans. J.W. Cox, Biblical Series 20; Philadelphia: Fortress, 1968).

Wintermute, Orval S., 'Jubilees', in *OTP*, 2.35-142.

Woll, D. Bruce, *Johannine Christianity in Conflict* (SBLDS 60; Chico, CA: Scholars Press, 1981).

Wrede, William, *The Messianic Secret* (trans. J.C.G. Greig; Greenwood, SC: Attic Press, 1971).

Zeitlin, Solomon, *The Book of Jubilees, its Character and Significance*, (Philadelphia: Dropsie, 1939).

Zenger, Erich, *Das Buch Judith* (JSHRZ 1.6; Gütersloh: Gerd Mohn, 1981).

INDEXES

INDEX OF BIBLICAL REFERENCES

OLD TESTAMENT

Genesis					
1	161	19.2	158	20.3-4	49
		22	166	20.5-29	49f.
Numbers		104	160n3,	20.30-43	50f.
31.16	57n1		161	20.44	51
		118.25-26	219	23	48, 49ff.
Leviticus				23.2-21	49
25.6	38	*Proverbs*		23.22-34	50f.
25.8-55	37	8.22	155	23.35	51
27.14-24	37			23.36-44	51
		Isaiah		23.45-49	51
Deuteronomy		61	191		
30.11-15	228	66	112	*Daniel*	
				2–6	85n1
Judges		*Jeremiah*		2	82, 83,
17	54	7.16	98		84n3,
		11.14	98		92, 94
2 Samuel		15.1	98	2.27-45	82
7	112	25	65, 66,	2.27-30	94n1
			91, 92	2.28	94
1 Kings		25.4-7	66	2.31-45	83
8.27	196n1	25.9-11	91	5	95
22	56	25.11-12	66	5.17-28	48n1,
26–28	57	25.15-38	66		82, 92f,
		25.17-26	91		94
2 Kings		25.30-38	91	5.17	92
6.17	176n2	27	177n2	5.18-23	93
22	85	29.10-11	91	7	82, 83ff,
					94, 95,
2 Chronicles		*Ezekiel*			119
6.18	196n1	16	48, 49ff.	7.2-9	86
		16.2	49	7.4	84
Job		16.3-34	49	7.5	84
1–3	85	16.35-42	50f.	7.6	84
		16.43-52	51	7.7	85
Psalms		16.43	51	7.7-8	85
18.31	56n2	16.53-63	51	7.9	153
		20	48, 49ff.	7.11b-12	85

7.13-14	85, 153, 199		95, 117, 177n2	11.5-6	89
7.13	85, 86	9.2	92	11.7-13	89
7.14	86, 175n4	9.13-14	175n4	11.14	89
		9.12	91	11.15-19	89
7.19-27	86	9.24-27	91	11.20	89
8	82, 86ff, 94, 95	9.25	91	11.24	89
		9.26	92	11.25	89
8.3-8	88	9.27	92	11.27	89
8.3-4	87	10–12	82, 89ff, 94, 119	11.30-35	89
8.5-8	87			11.31	90
8.9-11a	87	10–11	95	11.33-34	90
8.11-12	88	10.2–11.1	90	11.33	95
8.13-14	88	10.2-9	91	11.36-39	89
8.24-25	88	10.7-9	91	11.40-44	89
8.25	87n1, 88	10.13-14	90	11.45	89
9	65, 82, 90n1, 91f, 94,	10.15-19	91	12.5-13	90
		11.1	90	12.5-8	91
		11.2	89		
		11.3-4	89	*Zechariah*	
				9.9	219

NEW TESTAMENT

Matthew		2.27	182n6, 190	18.31-34	176, 178
10.24	219n4	2.29	190	18.34	173, 179
25.34-39	52n1	2.31-32	190	21.14-15	183
		2.32	190	24	176n4, 177n1,
Mark		2.34-35	190		180,
4.11	125	2.36-38	192		181,
8.22-26	125	3.3	191n2		183,
10.46-52	125	4	205		199,
		4.14-15	190		203,
Luke		4.18-21	190		205, 207
1–2	199, 205	4.18-19	190	24.1-9	172
1	192	4.18	191n2	24.5-7	174
1.4	171, 206	4.21	190	24.6-8	219n1
1.14-17	192	4.23-24	190	24.6	174
1.32-37	192	4.24	190	24.10-11	172
1.36	192	4.25-27	190, 191	24.12	172
1.41-55	192	4.28-29	190	24.16	173n5,
1.41-45	192	4.29	190		176
1.41	182n6	4.30	190	24.17	172
1.67-79	192	6.40	219n4	24.19-24	172
1.67	182n6	7.18-23	190	24.19-21	175
1.77	191n2	9.26	175n4	24.19	175n2
2	192	9.44-45	176	24.18-24	180
2.10-14	192	9.44	173n2	24.21	173
2.10-12	192	9.45	173, 179	24.23-25	175
2.25-35	192	12.11-12	183	24.25-27	219
2.25	190	13.34-35	193n1, 199	24.25	172
2.26	190			24.26	175, 231

24.27	175, 176, 223n2	1.36	232	6.46	228, 229
		1.37	232	6.63	228
24.30-32	174	1.41-51	233	6.65	230
24.31	176	1.41	233	6.68	228, 230
24.32	173, 175, 176	1.45	233	7.16	227n3
		1.49	233	7.18	221
24.36-49	189	1.50	229n3	7.37-38	160n2
24.36-43	173, 178	1.51	228, 229	7.39	233
24.41	173	2.11	220, 221, 230	7.40	227n1
24.44-46	219n1			7.52	227n1
24.47	191n2	2.13-22	218	8.14	224
24.44-49	176n4, 178	2.17	218, 219, 233	8.19	229, 230
24.44-47	179	2.22	218, 219, 233	8.26-27	227n3
24.44	174, 178, 179	2.23–3.2	230	8.27	230
		3.3	230	8.28	227n3
24.45-49	174	3.13	228, 229	8.31-32	230
24.45	173, 179, 188, 204	3.31	227n3, 229	8.33-40	228
		3.35	229	8.38	227n3
24.46-49	178	4.5-6	228	8.43	230
24.46-47	180, 188	4.12	228	8.50	221
24.46	179	4.19	227n1	8.53-57	228
24.47	179	4.25	212n6	8.54	215, 221
24.48	179, 188	4.29	212n6	9.17	227n1
24.49	179	4.30	212n6	9.28-29	228
24.50-51	175	4.42	233	9.38	232
24.52	172	5.17	229	9.39-41	230
		5.18	229	10.4-5	230
John		5.19	229	10.6	230
1	238, 239	5.20	229	10.14	230
1.1-4	217n1	5.21	229	10.25	228, 229
1.1	229	5.22	229	10.26-28	230
1.3	229	5.23	229	10.28	229
1.4	229	5.24	228	10.29	229
1.9	229	5.26	229	10.29	230
1.10	230	5.31-38	223	10.30	229
1.14	220, 221	5.36	227n3, 229	10.32	229
1.17	228	5.37	228	10.37-38	229
1.18	228, 229, 231	5.39	224	11.4	221
1.21	228	5.43	228	11.40	221, 230
1.26	232	5.45-46	228	12.16	218, 219, 221, 223
1.27	232	6.14	227n1	12.23	221
1.29-34	232	6.17	217n4	12.28	221
1.29	232	6.31-32	217n4	12.45	229
1.30	232	6.37	230	12.49-50	228
1.31-34	232	6.38	229	12.49	227n3
1.31	230	6.40	229	13–20	221ff.
1.33-34	232	6.44	230	13.3	229
1.33	230	6.45	230, 233	13.7	234
				13.8	231
				13.12	234n1

13.16	219	16.4	212n6, 213, 218, 219, 233	17.24	217n1, 221, 228, 239
13.23	231			17.26	217, 228
13.31-32	221	16.5-11	223	19.34	226
13.31	215, 229	16.12-15	212-14, 216, 217, 214, 218, 220, 223, 233	19.35	211, 222, 224, 226n1
14.4	231				
14.6-9	229				
14.8-9	216, 231				
14.9	229			20.8	211, 231
14.10	229			20.9	231
14.11	229			20.15	231
14.17	223			20.24-28	231
14.20	229			20.25	211
14.22	231	16.12	212, 213, 214, 216	20.22	217
14.24	227n3]			20.29	211
14.25-26	212, 213, 215, 218, 223, 233	16.13-14	217n4	20.31	234
		16.13	212, 215, 218, 222	21.4	211
				21.7	231
14.25	212-14	16.14-15	215	21.24	222, 224
14.26-27	213	16.14	215, 218, 225		
14.26	106, 174n5, 2112, 214, 218, 219	16.15	212n6, 213-15, 229	*Acts*	
				1.1–28.25	206
				1.6	173
		16.17	217n4, 231	1.8	200, 223n2
14.28	213, 229			1.9	175n4
14.29-31	213n3	16.23	233	1.16-22	200, 203f.
14.29	213	16.25	212n6, 213, 218n2, 233	1.16	182n6
14.30-31	213			1.21-22	180
15.11	212n6, 213			2	176n4, 183n6
15.15	216, 227n3, 228	16.28	217n4	2.4	181
		16.29-30	231	2.14-39	183n6
		16.31-33	231	2.14-36	181, 184
15.17	212n6, 213	16.33	212n6, 213	2.16-21	189
15.18–		17.1	221	2.17-21	182
16.33	215	17.3	216, 229	2.17-18	176n4
15.18-25	223	17.4	216, 217, 220	2.17	189
15.20-21	219			2.21	186, 189
15.20	218	17.5	220, 221, 228, 239	2.22-23	186
15.26-27	212, 223, 224, 226, 233			2.22	188
		17.6	228	2.23	177n1, 186, 189
		17.8	216, 228, 230	2.24-32	189
16.1-4	213n5, 223			2.29	176n4
		17.14	216	2.25-32	189
16.1	212n6, 213, 233	17.21	229	2.25-31	186
		17.22	228	2.32	189
16.3	230			2.33	186
				2.34-35	186

2.34	189	6.13-14	198	15	192
2.36	186, 188, 189	6.15	181, 198	15.7-11	200
		7	28, 183n1	15.13-21	201
2.38-40	184			15.15-21	182n5
2.38-39	181	7.2-53	193, 195ff.	15.28	182, 201
2.38	186, 189			17.2-3	176n3
2.39	189	7.2-8	195f.	17.3	175, 196n1, 231
2.41	186	7.8	197n2		
3	183n6	7.22	175n2		
3.12-26	183n6, 184	7.35	195n1	17.31	199n1
		7.43	199	20.17-35	203n1
3.13-14	188, 189	7.44-50	195n1	20.23	203n1
3.13	187	7.47-48	198n3	20.27	191
3.14-15	189	7.51	198	22.1-21	202
3.15	189	7.52	183	22.1	202
3.16	187	8.30-35	176n3	22.3-21	202
3.17	189	9.1-9	183	22.6-16	183
3.18	189	10	183n6	22.14	183n5
3.19	189	10.3-6	188	22.15	180, 183n4
3.21-26	189	10.33	182		
3.22-25	187	10.34-43	183n6, 184f.	22.21	203
3.25-26	187, 189			24.10-21	202
4	183n6	10.34	189	26.2-23	202
4.6	183n1	10.39	189	26.2-3	202
4.8-12	181, 193, 194	10.40-43	189	26.4-18	202
		10.40-42	189	26.6-8	202
4.8	181, 182n6, 183n1	10.41	189	26.16	180
		10.42	199n1	26.12-18	183
		10.43	189, 191n2	26.15-18	26n3
4.9-12	183n6			26.17-18	203
4.10	183n1	11.5-17	193, 202	26.18	191n2
4.13	182n6	11.16	174n5	26.19-23	202
4.19-20	181, 193-95	13	183n6	28.25-29	200n1, 206
		13.2	182		
5.3-5	193n3	13.4	182	28.26-28	203
5.9	193n2	13.9-10	182n6		
5.28	194	13.9	182	*Romans*	
5.29-32	193	13.15	182	9–11	125
5.30-32	183n6, 194	13.16-40	185	10.6-8	228
		13.16-38	183n6	11.25-26	125
5.31	191n2	13.18	188n1		
5.32	181, 182n6	13.23	189	*1 Corinthians*	
		13.27-29	189	2.6	124
6.5	181, 182n6, 198	13.27	189	2.7	124
		13.30-37	189	2.8	124
		13.31	189	2.9-10	124
6.8	198	13.32-41	189	2.10	124
6.10	28, 181, 182n6, 183n1, 198	13.38	189, 191n2	2.11	124n1
				2.12	124, 159n2
		13.40-41	189		
		13.46	189	7.40	125
6.11	198	13.47	189	10.1-5	125

2 Corinthians		1 John		Revelation	
3.7-18	125	2.18	224		139
3.12-18	176n4	2.20	224	1–3	229
		2.21	224	2.1	213n4
Galatians		2.22-24	224	2.8	213n4
1.11	26n3	2.22	224	2.12	213n4
1.12	125	2.26	224	2.18	213n4
1.15-22	125	2.27	224	3.1	213n4
1.15	26n3	4.2	224,	3.7	213n4
1.16	125		225,	3.14	213n4
3.7-13	125		226n4	4	229
4.4-5	125	4.5-6	224	4.1-2	144n2
		4.6	224,	5	85
Philippians			226n4	12	126,
2	238, 239	4.7-8	226		139n2
		4.12	226	12.5	126
Colossians		4.13-15	225	12.6	126
1	238	4.13	226n4	12.10-11	126
2	239	4.14	226	12.12	126
		5.6-12	226	12.14	126
1 Timothy				12.16	126
3.16	175n4			13	126
				17	126

PSEUDEPIGRAPHA

Judith		87	80	3.5-9	70
5–6	56	87–88	67	14	71n2
5.5-21	28, 56,	87.3	67	14.1-3	71
	57	88–90	81	14.1	72
6.2	28, 56	89.1-8	67	14.4-8	71
6.4	56	89.51-54	66	14.8-9	71
6.5-9	57	89.67	63	20.5-6	216n4
		89.9-58	66	20.6	72
Sirach		89.36	84n3	24.3-4	72
17.17	65n1	89.59–		27.15	75
		90.16	66, 81	28.4	75
1 Enoch		89.70	63	29.2	250n2
4.10-12	98	89.76	63	31.1–32.8	69
4.13-21	98	90.13-19	65n2	32.8–33.3	72
5.34-40	98	90.14-16	67, 81	44.1–46.7	69
83–90	61, 62ff,	90.17-27	66	46.1-3	72
	79-81,	90.17-26	67	46.4-7	75
	243	90.17-28		48.2-3	72
83.7-9	63	90.26-28	67	48.31-37	72
84.2-4	63	90.29-42	67, 81	48.32-37	250n2
84.4	63, 84n3	90.40-42	62	48.32	75
84.6	63	90.41	62	48.38	75
85–86	80	93.1-14	18	53–74	61, 68ff,
85	66				72, 79,
85.1-3	62	2 Baruch			80, 243,
86	66	1–77	69n4		249f.

55	229
56–66	80
56.2	72
56.3	73
64–65	73
66.1	73
66.5	73
67	80
67.7	68
68	81, 250
68.3-4	73
69–71	81
69	72
69.3-4	73
70–74	75
70	73, 250
70.3-5	72, 73
70.3-4	74
70.6	81
70.8	73n2
71.1	250n2
71.2-3	249
71.2	68n2
72–74	68n2, 249n1
72	81
73–74	81
77.1-17	69
77.13-16	72
77.15-18	75
78–87	69

3 Enoch
12.5	228n8
48C.7	228n8
48D.1	228n8

4 Ezra
3.1-27	99
3.1-3	99n2
3.28-36	98n1, 99
4.5-8	98n3
4.12	98n3
4.26-32	99
4.27	100
4.28	100
4.29	100
4.30	100
4.33	100n1
5.21-22	99n2
5.21-30	99
5.28-29	98n1

6.1-6	100
6.35-37	99n2
6.38-59	99
6.55-59	98n1
7.1	229
7.18	100
7.19-20	100
7.21-24	100
7.25	100
7.70	100
9.17-22	101
9.18-21	101
9.23-25	216n4
9.26-29	99n2
9.27	99n2
9.29-37	99
9.46–8.36	98n2
10.16-17	102
10.24	102
10.28	104
10.32	104
10.34-35	98, 104
10.59	216n4
11	177n2
12.39	216n4
13.39-48	103
13.56	216n4
14	106, 174n5
14.3-6	105
14.3-5	106
14.5	105
14.20-22	
14.21-22	106
14.21	105
14.28-35	106
14.47	104
14.23-35	48n1

Apocalypse of Abraham
6–8	78
10	228n8
15	229
21–32	61, 75ff, 79, 243
21–23	80
21–24.2	79
22.2	75
23.10-11	76
23.12	76
23.13	76
23.14	76

24–26	79
24–25	77
24	80
24.1	76
25–28	81
25–27	77
25.1-4	76
26.1	76
27–29.4a	79
27.3	76n3
27.6	76
27.7	76, 78
29	79
29.1-12	81
29.3-13	77
29.4-7	77
29.8	78
29.10	77n2
29.12-13	78
29.13	78, 81
29.14	78
29.14-16	81
29.17-21	78, 81
30–32	79
31.1-8	81
31.6-8	77

Ascension of Isaiah
1.1-13	139n3
1.2-4	145nn2,4
1.5	142, 145
2.7-11	139n3
2.9	143, 145
3	138
3.1-13	139n3
3.6-13	146
3.7-10	146
3.13–4.22	137-39, 141
3.13-31	137, 139
3.13-20	139
3.13	146
3.18	143, 145, 146
3.20-31	139
3.21-31	140
3.21	140, 146
3.26	140
3.28	140
3.30	140
4.1-22	138
4.1-16	137

4.2-3	138	1.27-29	229	24.28-33	41, 42
4.4-13	138	1.27	31n1	27.25	229n3
4.6-9	138	2.1	31n1	28.6	33
4.10	139	2.17-21	34	30.9	33
4.11	138	2.27	34	30.12	31n1
4.13	139n2	2.30	34, 37	30.19-20	31n1
4.16	139	2.32	34	30.21	31n1
5	145n2	3.10	33	31.32	31n1
5.15-16	142, 145n2	4.4-5	33	32.21-26	41, 106, 174n5
		4.11-12	41		
6–11	137, 140, 144, 229	4.17-18	35n1	33.18	31n1
		4.18	35n1	34.18	35
6.1–7.1	137	6.10	33	35.1–36.18	42
6	1348, 144n2, 145	6.17	34	36.9-11	41, 42
		6.18-19	34	39.6	41n2
		6.18	34	45.16	41
6.1-17	144	6.22	31n1	49	35
6.4-5	144	6.23-29	35	50.1-5	37
6.6	144	6.28-29	31n1, 35	50.1	38
6.8	144	6.29	35n1	50.2	38f.
6.9	144	6.37	37	50.3	38
6.17	145	7.20-60	42	50.4	36, 38
7–11	143	8.9	40	50.6	31n1
7.1	138n1	8.10-30	111n3	50.13	31n1
7.21-22	141	8.10-11	40		
7.25	162, 163	8.18-20	41	*LAB*	
8.5	141	9.1-13	40	15.5-6	52f.
8.26	145	9.1	40	18.5-6	55f.
9.13-18	142	9.10	40	18.7	56
9.26	143	9.14-15	111n3	18.13	57n1
9.27-42	162, 163	9.14	40	23.3-13	55
9.28	142, 163	10.10-14	41	32.1-11	55n1
9.30	163	10.29-33	111n3	32.12-17	55n1
9.42	163	10.30	40	44.5-10	54
10.1–11.35	137	11.16-17	41	44.6-15	53
10.7-15	141	12.20	42	53.8-10	53
10.12-15	142	12.25-26	41		
10.17– 11.35	141	12.27	41	*LAE*	
		13.25	33	12–17	18
11.2-15	142, 167	15.11	33		
11.23-24	142	15.26	33	*Odes of Solomon*	
11.36-40	137	15.27	33	4.9f.	155n3
		15.31-32	42, 65n1	6	157, 159-62, 166, 169
Jubilees		16.1-4	36		
1.5	31n1	16.9	31n1	6.1-8	160
1.6	44	18.19	35	6.1-7	157
1.7-25	43	20–21	42	6.1-2	148
1.7	31n1	21.10	41n2	6.3	159
1.22-25	43	23	44	6.4	159
1.23	44	23.11-32	43	6.5	159
1.26	31n1	23.26-27	43	6.5f.	155n3
		23.32	31n1		

Ref	Pages	Ref	Pages	Ref	Pages
6.6	159, 170	16.6-7	160	31.1-5	167
6.8-12	157, 159	16.8	152	31.3	167
6.8	159	16.10-19	160	31.8-13	167
6.9-19	160	16.19	152, 158	35	164
6.9	159, 160	16.20	160	35.5ff.	167
6.11	159	17	161, 165, 166, 169	35.7	163, 164
6.13-18	157			36	157, 161, 162
6.20-22	160	17.5	165	36.1-2	162, 163
6.35	159	17.6	155, 165	36.3-8	162, 163
7.16b-21	164n5	17.8	165	36.3	163
8	151, 154, 156, 168	17.13	165	36.4	163
		17.15	155n3	36.6	163
8.1-7	154	18.7	155n3	36.7	163
8.1	156	19	166, 168, 169	37.1-4	164n5
8.8	154			38	165
8.9	154	19.1	166	38.1-22	163
8.13	155	19.2-5	166f.	39	151, 152, 159, 167n3, 168, 169
8.14	154n1	19.2	154n1, 167		
8.20-22	154				
9.3	152	19.6-11	167		
10	157, 161, 162, 166, 169	19.6	167n2		
		22	161, 166, 169	39.1-4	151
				39.1	159n3
		23	151-54, 169	39.5-7	151
10.1-3	161			39.8	151
10.1	162	23.5	152	39.9-13	151
10.3	162	23.12	152, 153	41	151, 155, 156, 165, 169
10.4-6	161	23.13-14	153		
10.4	162	23.16	153		
11.4-9	159	23.18	153		
11.16	163	23.19	153	41.1	155
12	157, 158, 160-62, 166, 169	23.22	152	41.2-7	155n3
		24	167n3, 168, 169	41.7	155
				41.8-10	155, 156
		24.1	153, 168	41.8	155, 165
12.1-3	148, 157, 158	24.7	152, 168	41.9	155
		24.8	168	41.11-15	155
12.2-3	159	26.12	164n5	41.11	155n3
12.4-12	157, 158	27	163, 164	41.16	156
12.4	158	27.1-3	163, 164n5	42	153, 161, 165, 166, 169
12.8	158				
12.9-11	158	27.3	164		
12.12	158	28	161, 165, 166, 169		
12.13	157, 158			42.1-2	163, 164
14.2	154n1			42.2	164
14.7-8	164n5	28.1	165	42.3	164
16	157, 158, 160-62, 166, 169	28.17	166	42.6	150n1, 164, 170
		28.9	165	42.11	152, 165
		30	160	42.14	153
16.1-9	160	30.6	160	42.17-18	165
		31	167, 169		

42.21-24	155n3	3.401-88	108, 109f.	4.112-13	113
				4.115	113
Sibylline Oracles		3.401-18	109	4.130-36	113
3–5	107ff.	3.421ff.	110	4.152-61	113
3	97, 115	3.421	109	4.162-70	113f.
3.1-7	108n2	3.423, 424	109	4.171-78	113
3.97-161	108, 110f.	3.429-30	109	4.174-92	112
		3.431-32	109	5	97, 109, 115, 120
3.97-109	110	4	97, 108, 111ff., 115		
3.108-109	110			11	108, 115
3.110-55	110				
3.114-20	111n3	4.1-23	112	*Testament of Levi*	
3.154-58	111	4.18-21	112	14–18	17
3.295-97	108n2	4.18	108n2		
3.319	109	4.24-49	112	*Testament of Moses*	
3.350-488	109	4.49-101	111	1.14	17
		4.50-192	113	2–10	17

JOSEPHUS

Jewish War		5.9.4 §§376-419	28	1. Proem. 3 §15	22
	117-19	6 §§285-315	29n3	1. Proem 7	
1.3.5 §§78-80	24n4	6.2.1 §§91-111	28	§§30.36	22
2.7.3 §113	24n4	6.2.1 §§93-111	27	1. Proem 7 §§37-40	208, 235
2.8.12 §159	24n4, 26	7.218	78n3	1. Proem 7	
3.8.3 §§350-54	25			§37	22, 23, 30n1
3.8.3 §51	27, 174n5	*Antiquities of the Jews*		1. Proem 8	
3.8.3 §351	26	1.239-41	30n1	§§39-40	23, 235
3.8.3 §354	26, 27	4.6.6 §129	57n1	1. Proem 8	
3.8.5 §361	26	6.4.2 §56	25n3	§41	
3.8.9 §400	27	6.5.2 §76	25n3	1 Proem 8	
3.8.9 §407	27	10.10.2		§42	23
3.8.9 §§406-407	27	§189	25n4	1. Proem 9	
4.10.7 §623	27	10.10.2		§47	24
4.10.7 §626	27	§194	25n4	1.7.37	31n2
5.8.4 §§375-419	27, 57, 58ff.	*Against Apion*		1.8.40	31n2
		1. Proem			
5.8.4 §§391-93	27	1-10 §§1-156	22	*Life* 42 §209	25

ANCIENT AUTHORS

Homer, the Iliad		*Sophocles,*		*Virgil, The Aeneid*	
1.1-7	14n4	*Oedipus Rex*		6.78	108n2
2.484-93	14	362	15	6.82-95	108n4
		366-67	15	6.821-30	103n3
		556	15	6.970-1202	15n2

6.1151-54	15	Sim. 5.6.2-4a	134, 135	4-8	132	
		Sim. 5.6.2-3	135	Sim. 9.12.4	131	
Shepherd of Hermas		Sim. 5.6.2	135	Sim. 9.15.4-		
Sim. 5	131, 133ff.	Sim. 5.6.3	135	16.7	131, 132	
Sim. 5.1	133	Sim. 5.6.4b-7.4	134	Sim. 9.15.4	132	
Sim. 5.2	134	Sim. 5.6.4b-7	134	Sim. 9.16.6-7	133	
Sim. 5.3	134	Sim. 5.6.4b-8	134	Vis. 1.1.2	130	
Sim. 5.3.1-9	134	Sim. 5.7.1-4	134	Vis. 1.1.6	129, 130n1	
Sim. 5.3.1	134n1	Sim. 7	128	Vis. 1.3.4	128n1, 129f.	
Sim. 5.3.2-9	134n1	Sim. 8	128, 131, 136	Vis. 2.1.3-2.3.4	128n1	
Sim. 5.4	134	Sim. 9	128, 131ff., 136	Vis. 2.1.3-4	128n1	
Sim. 5.4.1-5.7.4	134			Vis. 2.2.4-8	131	
Sim. 5.4.1-5	134n1	Sim. 9.12.1-14	131	Vis. 2.4.1	129, 130	
Sim. 5.5.1-7.4	134n1	Sim. 9.12.1-3	132	Vis. 2.4.2-3	128n1	
5.5.1-6.4a	134	Sim. 9.12.3	131	Vis. 2.4.2	216n4	
Sim. 5.5.1-3	134	Sim. 9.12.		Vis. 3	128, 131, 136	
Sim. 5.5.2	135			Vis. 5.5-7	128n1	
Sim. 5.5.2-3	134					
Sim. 5.5.4-6.4b	134					

Abramowski, L. 149n6
Abramowski, R. 149n7, 150n2, 152n1, 163n3
Anderson, F.I. 17n1
Aune, D.E. 24n1, 25n2, 27n1, 28n2, 125n1, 148n1, 149nn6,9, 155n3, 156n2, 164nn3,4, 166n2, 169n1, 213n4, 218n1, 229n2

Bammel, E. 214n6, 216nn1,3
Barrett, C.K. 209n1, 212n4, 215n2, 218n2, 219n1, 222n2
Bauckham, R. 141n1, 142n1
Bauer, W. 149nn6,7
Beasley-Murray, G.R. 88n1
Beckwith, I.T. 126n1
Berger, K. 31n1, 32n2, 35n3, 39n1, 40n1
Bernard, J.H. 149n6, 158n3, 160n2, 168n1
Betz, O. 26nn1,3
Bidawid, R.J. 99n2
Blank, J. 215n3, 219n1, 221n4, 223nn2,3
Blenkinsopp, J. 24nn2,3,6, 26nn1,2
Böcher, O. 229n1
Bogaert, P. 52n2, 68n2, 69nn1,4, 73n2, 249nn1-2
Boismard, M.-E. 182n1, 195n1, 196n1, 198n1
Borgen, P. 228n7
Boring, M.E. 212n3, 216n1, 227n2
Bornkamm, G. 212n1, 221n4
Bowker, J.W. 186n1
Box, G.H. 100nn1-2, 102nn1,3, 103n4
Box, G.H. & Landsman, J.I. 76nn1,3
Braun, F.-M. 149nn5,6, 152n1, 153n2
Breech, E. 97n1, 104n3

Brown, R.E. 183n3, 209n1, 211n3, 213nn2,4, 214nn1,4,5, 215nn2-3, 216n3, 218n2, 221, 222n1, 223nn2-3, 225n1, 226nn3,5, 227n1, 228n4, 230n1
Bruce, F.F. 25n1, 26n1
Bultmann, R. 11n5, 12n2, 209n1, 213n3, 214n4, 215n3, 222n1
Buss, M.F-J. 187n2, 188n2

Carmignac, J. 148n4, 149n6, 156n1
Chadwick, H. 150n2, 167n4
Charles, R.H. 31n1, 34n2, 39n1, 40n1, 62nn1,2, 63nn2,3,4, 64n3, 65n2, 66n1, 68n2, 69nn1,3, 84n3, 93n1, 138n2, 139n1, 142n2, 144n3, 146n2, 249nn1-2, 250n1
Charles, R.H. & Barton, J.M.T. 144n1
Charlesworth, J.H. 148n4, 149nn4,6,8, 150n1, 151nn1,3, 153nn3,4, 154, 156n1, 158n1, 159nn1,3, 161-63, 164n1, 167n2, 228n8
Charlesworth, J.H. & Culpepper, R.A. 149nn2,6
Coggins, R.J. 196n1
Collins, J.J. 11n3, 39n1, 61n1, 83nn1,3,4, 84n3, 94n1, 98n3, 108nn1,3, 109nn1-3,5, 110nn2-3, 111n5, 112nn1-2, 113nn1-2, 114n1
Conzelmann, H. 174n2
Cullmann, O. 209n1, 212n1, 219n1, 220n2
Culpepper, R.A. 211nn2-3, 224n1, 232n1, 233n1

Dahl, N.A. 196n1, 197n1, 199n2, 220n2
Daube, D. 29n1
Davenport, G.L. 44
Davies, G.I. 11n4, 43n1, 61n1

DeVilliers, P.G.R. 99n1, 104nn1,4
Dibelius, M. 128nn1,3, 129n1, 130n1, 132n2, 133nn1-2, 135n1, 185n3, 195n1
Dillon, R.J. 172n1, 173nn1,4,5, 175n1, 179n3, 180n1, 182nn3,4, 191n2
Doble, P. 196n1, 198n1
Doran, R. 30n1
Downing, F.G. 189n3, 194n2
Drijvers, H.J.W. 149n6, 152n1, 153n5, 167n1
Dunn, J.D.G. 216n1, 217n5, 225n2
Dupont, J. 195n1, 196n1

Eissfeldt, O. 48n2
Ellis, E.E. 182n2, 186n1
Emerton, J.A. 159n3
Endres, J.C. 42n1

Feldman, L.H. 23n1, 24n2
Fitzmyer, J.A. 171n2, 172n2, 174n3, 175n3, 178, 183n2, 190n2, 191n1
Flemming, J. *et al.* 142n2, 144n3
Flusser, D. 83n2, 111n6
Furnish, V.P. 124n1

Geffcken, J. 108n1, 109nn3,4
Giet, S. 128n2, 132n1
Ginsberg, L. 76n1
Grayson, A.K. & Lambert, W.G. 14n2
Grundmann, W. 211n3
Gry, L. 103nn1,4
Gunkel, H. 161-63, 164nn1-2

Haacker, K. 214nn4,5, 217n5, 220n1
Haag, E. 56n2
Haenchen, E. 187n1, 195n1, 196n1, 232n1
Hall, R.G. 18n1, 77n2, 78nn1,5, 137nn1-2, 138n1, 139n3, 145n1
Harnisch, W. 69n2, 70n2, 71nn1-2, 72n1, 74n1, 97n1, 101n1, 102n4, 103n2, 104n2, 249n2
Harrelson, W. 103n5, 104n2
Harrington, D.J. 52n2, 53n1
Harris, R. & Mingana, A. 148n3, 149nn3,6, 151nn3-4, 152n1, 154, 155nn1-2, 156n1, 158n2, 159nn1,3, 160nn1-2, 161, 162, 164n1, 165n1, 166n1, 167n4, 168n1

Hartman, L.F. & DiLella, A.A. 90n1, 92n1, 93n1
Hayman, A.P. 104n3
Hengel, M. 65n2, 66n1
Hill, D. 216n2
Hoskyns, E.C. 214n4, 221n5

Isaac, E. 64n1

James, M.R. 69n1
Jervell, J. 176n4, 1182n6, 183n1, 198n4
Johnson, G.L. 24n2, 26n1
Johnston, G. 211n3
Jonge, M. de 25n4, 29n3
Juel, D. 176n4

Kee, H.C. 125
Kennedy, G.A. 194n1, 198n2, 202n1, 203n1
Kilgallen, J. 182n4, 196n1, 199n2
Kliesch, K. 48n2, 186n1
Klijn, A.F.J. 69nn1,3, 70n1, 196n1
Knibb, M.A. 140n2, 145n4, 228n8
Knibb, M.A. & Ullendorf, E. 62n3, 64n1
Koch, K. 83n3, 85n1, 104
Koenen, L. 14n1
Koester, H. 133n1
Kolenkow, A.B. 71n3, 74n2
Kragerud, A. 209n1, 211n3
Kundsin, K. 234n2
Kurfess, A. 108n1
Kurz, W.S. 173n1, 176n1

Lacocque, A. 84n3, 90n1, 93n1
Lanchester, H.C.O. 109n3
Lattke, M. 149n6, 157n1, 159n1
Leroy, H. 231n3
Lindars, B. 62n1
Lindner, H. 26nn1,4, 27
Lohse, E. 36n3
Luck, U. 171n1, 179nn2,3

McNeil, B. 149n6
Maddox, R. 196n1, 199n2, 206n1
Marcus, J. 125n3
Marshall, I.H. 172n2, 178nn1,3, 179n1, 190n2
Martin, F. 66n1
Mayer, R. & Möller, C. 27n4
Meeks, W. A. 227n1, 228nn2,4,6, 230n2
Mendels, D. 46n1
Michaels, J.R. 212n2, 227n1, 229n2

Milik, J.T. & Black, M. 62n2, 65n2
Minear, P.S. 171n3, 183n2
Moessner, D.P. 206n2
Montgomery, J.A. 84nn1,3, 87n1, 90n1, 92n1
Mueller, J.R. 76n1
Müller, U.B. 11n2, 210, 221n1, 212n4, 215n1, 216n1, 219n3, 234n4
Murphy, F.J. 69n4, 73n1
Mußner, F. 210, 214nn3,45, 217n5, 219n1, 221nn2,5, 222n1, 223n1, 234n4
Myers, J.M. 97n1, 99n2, 100nn1-2, 102n2, 103n1

Neusner, J. 22n1
Newsom, C.A. 11n4, 65n3, 86n2, 89n1, 91n1
Neyrey, J. 202n1
Nickelsburg, G.W.E. 31n3, 64n2, 65nn1,2
Nicol, W. 214nn4,5, 221n4, 223n3
Nikiprowetzky, V. 111nn1,2,4
Noth, M. 85n1

Odeberg, H. 229n3
Oesterley, W.O.E. 103nn1,4
O'Reilly, L. 182n2
Osiek, C. 128n2

Painter, J. 212n4,213n3, 214nn4,6, 216n1, 219n1, 220n2, 223n4, 225n1, 230n1, 232n1
Pennington, A. 76n3
Pernveden, L. 128n2, 129n2
Peterson, E. 129n1
Philonenko-Sayar, B. & Philonenko, M. 77n1
Plummer, A. 178n3
Potterie, I. de la 214n3, 216n3, 217n2

Rahlfs, A. 175n4
Rajak, T. 25n1
Reid, S.B. 11n5, 64n3, 68n1
Reiling, J. 24n3, 128n2
Rhoads, D.M. 29n2
Richard, E. 187n1, 198n4, 199n2
Rössler, D. 11n5, 83n3
Rowland, C. 11n4, 32n1, 61nn1,2
Rubinkiewicz, R. 77n1
Rubinkiewicz, R. & Lunt, H.G. 76n1, 77n3

Rubinstein, A. 76n2
Rudolph, K. 149n5,7, 150n2
Sanders, J.T. 148n2, 149n1, 150n2, 238n1
Sasse, H. 209n1, 212n4, 213n3, 216nn1-2, 221n5
Sayler, G.B. 69nn1,4, 70nn1-2
Scherrer, S.J. 139n1
Schlier, H. 220n2, 221n2
Schnackenburg, R. 209n1, 214n6, 215n3, 218n1, 234n3
Schneider, G. 183n6, 203n1
Schubert, P. 177n1, 178n4, 183nn5-6, 186n2, 192n1
Schulz, S. 213n4
Schwarz, E. 31n3
Schweizer, E. 185n3
Scroggs, R. 195n1, 196n1
Smalley, S.S. 225n1, 226n3
Smallwood, E.M. 78n4
Smith, D.M. 216n1, 217n5, 220n1, 225nn1,2, 229n1, 234n2, 235n1
Snyder, G.F. 128n2, 1291, 131n1
Stone, M.E. 77n1, 98n3, 104nn2-3, 105n1
Streeter, B.H. 212n1
Strugnell, J. 69n1
Sylva, D.D. 196n1, 198n4

Tannehill, R.C. 177n1
Testuz, M. 31n1, 33n2, 34n1, 37, 44
Thompson, A.L. 97n1, 103n5
Thyen, H. 48n2, 186n1
Tiede, D.L. 173n1
Tisserant, E. 144n3

Unnik, W.C. van, 24n5, 25n1,3

VanderKam, J.C. 31n1,3, 36nn2,3, 41, 62n1, 63nn1,2, 65nn2,3, 66n2, 91n1
Van Koningsveld, P.J. 69n4
Via, E.J. 187n1, 196n1, 197n1
Violet, B. 68n2, 69nn1,4, 100nn1-2, 249n1

Walker, A. 18n2
Westcott, B.F. 210n1, 214n4, 216n5, 217n3, 221n1
Whitacre, R.A. 219n1, 225n2
Whittaker, M. 129n4
Wiesenberg, E. 36n4, 37nn1,2

Wilckens, U. 183n6, 185n3, 188n3
Windisch, H. 11n1, 210, 214n4,
   216nn1,2, 221n5, 232n2, 234nn2-
   3, 236n1, 240n1
Wintermute, O.S. 31n1, 33n1, 34n2,
   37n4, 39, 40n1, 42n2, 43n2, 45,
   250n2

Woll, D.B. 213n3, 214n4, 219n1, 220n2,
   231n4, 235n1
Wrede, W. 173n4, 174nn1-2, 190n1

Zeitlin, S. 34n1, 35n3
Zenger, E. 56n1

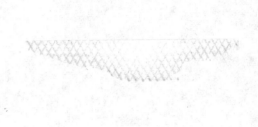